Across the Secular Abyss

Across the Secular Abyss

From Faith to Wisdom

William Sims Bainbridge

LEXINGTON BOOKS

A division of
ROWMAN & LITTLEFIELD PUBLISHERS, INC.
Lanham • Boulder • New York • Toronto • Plymouth, UK

LEXINGTON BOOKS

A division of Rowman & Littlefield Publishers, Inc.
A wholly owned subsidiary of The Rowman & Littlefield Publishing Group, Inc.
4501 Forbes Boulevard, Suite 200
Lanham, MD 20706

Estover Road
Plymouth PL6 7PY
United Kingdom

British Library Cataloguing in Publication Information Available

Library of Congress Cataloging-in-Publication Data

Bainbridge, William Sims.
  Across the secular abyss : from faith to wisdom / William Sims Bainbridge.
    p. cm.
  Includes bibliographical references and index.
  ISBN-13: 978-0-7391-1678-4 (cloth : alk. paper)
  ISBN-10: 0-7391-1678-9 (cloth : alk. paper)
  1. Secularism. 2. Secularization. I. Title.
  BL2747.8.B28 2007
  200.9'05—dc22   2007019753

Printed in the United States of America

⊖™ The paper used in this publication meets the minimum requirements of American
National Standard for Information Sciences—Permanence of Paper for Printed Library
Materials, ANSI/NISO Z39.48–1992.

To Constance May Bainbridge,
who values both knowledge and imagination.

Contents

Figures

1
Introduction

God is dead.
—*Thus Spake Zarathustra*,[1]
Friedrich Nietzsche

In 1891, the philosopher Friedrich Nietzsche famously reported the death of God, and religious scholars ever since have argued the vitality of faith. Nietzsche is often scorned for the poetic rather than rigorous nature of his writings, and stigmatized for appealing chiefly to adolescents and radicals. Yet he understood the crisis of morals that could result from the demise of religion, and he was a precursor of the twentieth-century Existentialist movement that explored the implications if humanity were alone in the universe. This book takes advantage of the rise of rigorous social science, that has occurred since Nietzsche wrote, to examine his questions afresh. Each chapter will begin with a quotation from his work, and each will be inspired by his dedication to honest answers for tough questions.

The Shape of Faith

Is God in fact dying? What would the consequences be? Social scientists and policy makers have debated the apparent erosion of religious faith and wondered whether western civilization was turning its back on religion. Today, the issue has reached a crisis point. In most advanced industrial nations, with the possible exception of the United States, the influence of religion in public affairs has declined rapidly, and fewer citizens participate actively in the sacraments of faith. In the United States, a new battle between faith and science has erupted within educational institutions, as political polarization progressively divides the country along religious lines.[2]

Twenty years ago, Rodney Stark and I argued that secularization tends to be a self-limiting process.[3] As some denominations lose their faith and fervor, others arise to take their place, through processes of schism and innovation. Thus, it should not be taken for granted that religion really is fading. The resolute secularism of many European nations gives the impression that Christianity is weakening, whereas Islam remains strong. Occasionally, across the broad sweep of human history, a religious tradition does die, so it is possible that this is happening today to Christianity. Throughout this book we will see evidence on this point. But our theme is the meaning and consequences of secularization, if it does in fact occur. The focus will be on western civilization, which means essentially Christendom, and this is the civilization that has created modern science and technology. If it is true that science erodes faith, can it also replace religion?

This process of secularization may be connected to a number of other trends, notably the catastrophic collapse of fertility in most advanced societies, especially visible in nations like Germany where the death rate is already greater than the birth rate. After a century-long truce in which religion and science implicitly agreed to leave each other alone, science is again invading the territory of religion, most obviously in cognitive science that is debunking religious notions of the human soul, and in the broad convergence of many branches of science into one that leaves few gaps where supernatural beliefs could survive. Religion, for its part, is resisting a range of emerging technologies that could transform human nature, namely human reproductive cloning and the kinds of transformative technologies advocated by the Transhumanist movement. This book will draw upon the best and latest social-scientific evidence to understand the scope and consequences of the profound religious changes occurring in advanced societies today.

Religion is a complex phenomenon, so religious change is a complicated process. About forty years ago, sociologists Charles Glock and Rodney Stark suggested that religion had five dimensions: belief, practice, knowledge, experience, and consequences.[4] A given person may be strong on one dimension but weak on another, for example someone who professes personal faith but never prays or attends a house of worship. Another person may believe deeply and frequently practice religious rituals, yet be ignorant of some of the fundamental facts in his or her denomination's holy book. A third person may know the Bible backward and forward, attend church, and hold strong beliefs, but never experience transcendental feelings. Finally, many devout people may lack the strong moral compass they hope their faith would give them, in consequence behaving badly in relations with other people. Secularization could manifest itself in one dimension, but not others, for example if church attendance declines while private professions of faith remain constant.

Perhaps a sixth dimension should be added to the five proposed by Glock and Stark. Call it *establishment*, and define it as the degree to which a religious institution is connected to other institutions of the society. In its establishment clause, the Constitution of the United States proclaims, "Congress shall make no law respecting an establishment of religion." Establishment of a religious denomination would mean that the government recognized it as the official religion of the nation, giving it a unique status with economic and political benefits. The separation of church and state entails the disestablishment of former state churches. The proverbially longest legitimate word in the English language, *antidisestablishmentarianism*, means being against the separation of church and state. Here we can use the term *establishment* more broadly, referring to special relations with a variety of secular institutions, not the government alone. Clearly, secularization has been progressing for centuries along this sixth dimension of religion, as state churches become disestablished, and religious pluralism confuses the role of faith in public education or in other cultural institutions.

This book will emphasize the relation between religion and science, not only the role of science in driving secularization, but also the increasing ability of science to understand religion. In the first instance, science erodes belief. Without belief, practice becomes meaningless. Science also transforms knowledge about religion, thereby disrupting old assumptions and adding potentially burdensome new facts. Science tends to be abstract, thus unrelated to experience, but through technologies it can transform important aspects of human life, indirectly affecting this dimension as well. Social science can evaluate ancient hopes about the consequences of religion, and it may find that some of them have always been—or have recently become—false. By forging its own relations with the state and other societal institutions, science competes with religion for influence.

Cultural Background of the Research

A reviewer of the original manuscript of this book noted that it combines topics usually treated separately, addresses challenging questions, and could benefit from an introduction that places the issues in context. Specifically, this reviewer suggested I add a brief autobiography to the preface. *Of course, the reader is free to skip this section*, but upon reflection I think my background does help explain the scientific approach of the research and theory reported here. I suppose it is unusual for a well-established sociologist of religion to be running grant programs in the computer science directorate of the National Science Foundation while playing a central role in the movement to unify the physical sciences. But it seems quite natural to me because my family heritage stresses scholarship in a cosmopolitan context where natural science, social science, and the humanities converge.

About a dozen members of my family have published non-fiction, and several have written about religion and society. The earliest extant example is an essay published in 1856 by my clergyman great-great-grandfather, Samuel McMath Bainbridge (1816–1865). Called "The Last Great Shaking," it offers an intellectual analysis arguing that the religious millenarianism of the period was converging with revolutionary developments in the socio-political sphere.[5] Samuel drew its text from the twelfth chapter of Paul's epistle to the Hebrews, where the Lord said, "Yet once more I shake not the earth only, but also heaven."

His son, William Folwell Bainbridge (1843–1915), was a clergyman, scholar, and linguist who undertook a great project to develop what he called "a science of missions" based on observations carried out in an 1879–1880 tour of American Protestant missions in Japan, China, Burma, India, and the Middle East.[6] While in China, he exchanged ideas and information with his cousin, John Nevius, a prominent missionary responsible in great measure for the success of the Presbyterian effort in Korea.[7] My great-grandfather was very interested in unusual religions, for example studying the Yazidis in Iraq during 1880, and I believe their discussions led immediately to Nevius's questionnaire survey study of spirit possession in China.[8] Near the end of his life, William Folwell Bainbridge became aware of developments in physics like Einstein's theory of relativity. He wrote to his son: "Don't be too dead sure in scientific work. Perhaps you do not need such caution, as you are naturally conservative, but all along the line we have reached the period of uncertainty. Dogmatism must go to the scrap heap, in all the sciences as well as in theology. Do not be ashamed of reasonable agnosticism. A world of knowledge is yet to be approached by: 'I don't know.'"[9]

William Folwell Bainbridge was accompanied on his world research tour by his wife, Lucy Seaman Bainbridge (1842–1928) and their young son, William Seaman Bainbridge (1870–1947). From 1891 through 1906, Lucy directed the Woman's Branch of the New York City Mission Society, whose 50 nurses and social workers assisted poor immigrants in Lower Manhattan. Co-editor of the Society's monthly magazine, she published extensively, both about her observations of exotic realms and religions, and about the social problems of the poor.[10]

William Seaman Bainbridge was an internationally-prominent surgeon and medical scientist, the author of eleven books and about 100 journal articles.[11] His most influential work, *The Problem of Cancer*—which was translated into Italian, Spanish, French, Polish, and Arabic—is a comprehensive treatise, including the epidemiology of the disease that incorporates social variables.[12] Another influential work was his *Report on Medical and Surgical Developments of the War*, a study of how treatment of wounded soldiers was organized, on both sides of the western front, based on extensive observations and interviews, presented as a medical volume written for the U. S. Navy, but arguably a work of social science.[13] I inherited many scientific artifacts from my grandfather, including his microscope, his collection of gas masks showing their technological development during the First World War, and his travel diaries that were like an anthropologist's notebooks and collected information for his books about medical practices across the length and breadth of civilization.

One of my grandfather's first cousins, Louis Livingston Seaman, documented Japanese medical practices during the Russo-Japanese War of 1904–1905.[14] His brother-in-law, Consuelo Andrew Seoane, served as cartographer during the Philippine Insurrection and in 1909–1911 was a spy for the United States Army, traveling under a pseudonym throughout the Japanese Empire with Joseph "Snake" Thompson, pretending to be a herpetologist studying coastal reptiles and amphibians, but actually charting invasion routes.[15] Snake Thompson, incidentally, was the person who taught L. Ron Hubbard about psychoanalysis and thus prepared Hubbard to found the psychoanalysis-like Church of Scientology.

Succeeding generations worked in or at the borders of social science, always in a multidisciplinary context, and often with some connection to religion. One of my uncles, John Seaman Bainbridge (1915–2006), was a law school dean who had invested ten years setting up and staffing law schools in sub-Saharan Africa, writing a book about the efforts.[16] Another uncle, Angus McIntosh (1914–2005), was a professor of historical linguistics.[17] His son, Christopher McIntosh, has published extensively about esoteric religious and spiritual groups.[18] I earned my doctorate in sociology from Harvard in 1975 with a dissertation on the technological social movement that created spaceflight.[19]

After publishing my first book, on the space program, and my second book about the Process cult, I began collaborating with Rodney Stark at the University of Washington in a major program of work reflected in three books. Published in 1985, *The Future of Religion* offered a series of empirical studies about secularization, revival, and religious innovation, employing a great diversity of data organized by key theoretical concepts.[20] Two years later, *A Theory of Religion* developed a formal theory of religious cognition and behavior. Both of these books won awards, and they provided a major impetus to what some call the *rational choice* approach to religion, although I see it as *exchange theory*, a convergence between social science and cognitive science.[21] A decade later, we published *Religion, Deviance and Social Control*, beginning to explore the role of religion in shaping public morality, a topic taken further in this volume.[22] While in Seattle, I carried out the research for my second book-length study of the culture of advanced technology, *Dimensions of Science Fiction*, published by Harvard University Press.[23]

Returing to Harvard, I began programming computer simulations and data analysis programs, in order to develop means for strengthening the formal rigor of the theory of religion. But I also experimented with such things as working out how to connect a Scientology e-meter to my computer, so that I could study the actual behavior of this electronic device used in Scientology's spiritual practices. One day, I demonstrated my software and hardware system on a visiting editor from Wadsworth, a textbook publisher. The result was a series of four book and software packages, incorporating software simulations and analysis tools I had programmed: *Experiments in Psychology, Sociology Laboratory, Survey Research*, and *Social Research Methods and Statistics*.[24]

After my visiting term at Harvard, I became a full professor at Illinois State University, then chaired a multidisciplinary department at Towson University that combined sociology, cultural anthropology, archaeology, and criminal justice studies. I also published my third major study of technological culture, *Goals in Space*.[25] In August, 1992, I joined the National Science Foundation to run the Sociology Program. Very quickly, I organized workshops on the potential of artificial intelligence techniques in sociology, and on the role of religion in processes of democratization and transition to market economies. The Directorate for Social, Behavioral and Economic Sciences appointed me its representative on technology initiatives: High Performance Computing and Communications, Digital Libraries, Knowledge and Distributed Intelligence, Information Technology Research, and Nanotechnology. In 2000, I moved to the Directorate for Computer and Information Science and Engineering, to run the Artificial Intelligence and Human-Computer Interaction programs. I represented computer science on the Human and Social Dynamics initiative, and on Nanotechnology.

Starting in 1999, I collaborated with Mihail Roco, the visionary leader of the National Nanotechnology Initiative, in a series of conferences and books exploring the future of technology.[26] Hundreds of leading scientists and engineers helped us understand that the chief significance of nanotechnology would be its role in unifying other fields in what we called Converging Technologies. The unification of science as a comprehensive understanding of nature will radically transform human culture, especially through the "NBIC" union of Nanotechnology, Biotechnology, Information technology, and new as-yet unnamed technologies emerging from rapid progress in Cognitive science. I also edited a two-volume encyclopedia of human-computer interaction, in which a hundred authors explored the convergence of information technology and cognitive science.[27]

At NSF, I continued to do research and wrote the textbook, *The Sociology of Religious Movements*.[28] While running the NSF Sociology Program, I managed funding for the General Social Survey, and used this experience in a questionnaire study of 1,025 members of the Children of God ("The Family"), comparing their responses to 235 GSS questions with those of a random sample of Americans.[29] Most recently, I published *God from the Machine*, an exploration of the theory of religion based on a multi-agent simulation of a community consisting of 44,100 artificial intelligences.[30]

For me, and for a number of people in my background and current environment, it is quite natural to practice multiple sciences simultaneously, and to be interested in the collisions between religion and science. In particular, I am my family have constantly been drawn back to issues about the role of religion in society, the opportunities for radical religious innovation, and the possibility that science or some kind of cultural movement derived from it might just possibly replace religion.

In *The Future of Religion*, Rodney Stark and I explored the thesis that religion would permanently be a central part of human experience. Two key ideas informed the argument: First, religion seemed almost infinitely capable of innovation, and secularization was therefore a self-limiting process that would restore religion whenever it began to weaken.

Second, religion offered humans hope when all secular sources of aid failed, including science. However, we did not seriously entertain the possibility that science could develop to the point that it could answer all meaningful questions and support technologies capable of meeting all human needs. Nor did we examine critically all the claims that religion served valuable functions for humans. Here, I will explore that dangerous but fascinating intellectual territory.

Plan of the Book

Just as one may doubt ancient religious beliefs, every aspect of the secularization thesis is open to question. Will religious revival and innovation defeat the secularizing forces of science, technology, and bureaucratic rationalism? Can a secular society be viable in the long run, or is secularization a rapid descent into an abyss of immorality, chaos, and profound pessimism? Will entirely new faiths arise that combine the truths discovered by science with a beneficial morale and a humanly meaningful understanding of life? Can science and technology actually solve the problems for which religion was a pseudo-solution? Will humanity evolve beyond the point at which it needs illusions?

The ten chapters that follow will explore many aspects of these questions, beginning with an introduction that provides theoretical raw materials, followed by three chapters about the consequences of religion, looking for evidence about secularization in the possible weakening of faith's benefits. Chapter 2 outlines four competing theories of religion and draws upon a major online questionnaire study to survey the many competing perspective that ordinary people hold about the future of religion.

Chapter 3 considers how religion can be beneficial for individuals. Other things being equal, religious people tend to live longer, to avoid various "vices" such as drug abuse, and to experience less stress. They may be less susceptible to the profound depression or helplessness that leads to suicide. The decline of religion could, therefore, be harmful for individual human beings, but improved public health and secular movements promoting healthy lifestyles may more than compensate for religion's lost functionality.

Chapter 4 documents the collapse of fertility that threatens the very existence of the human species. Most advanced industrial societies now have birth rates too low to sustain the population in the long run, whereas traditional societies where religion is more powerfully integrated into family life continue to have high birth rates. The United States is an important test case, because the birth rate is almost high enough to offset the death rate, and America is the most religious large advanced nation. In modern society, children are costly rather than making economic contributions to the family as in traditional societies. Other factors reducing fertility in modern societies are the wide availability of effective birth control techniques, legalization of abortion, alternative sexual practices, women's equal participation in the economy and workforce, and the fragmentation of the family. It is not clear that mild religion will be able to offset all these factors, and it may be that only fundamentalist societies will be able to sustain high enough fertility rates over the long term.

Crime and deviant behavior are the theme of Chapter 5. People have always hoped and believed that religion enforced morality, and the great religious traditions explicitly teach moral principles like the Ten Commandments. Evidence from modern societies supports the idea that religion can indeed deter some forms of crime, such as petty theft, but may not be able to deter major crimes, such as murder. In addition, religion may deter controversial behaviors, what sociologists call deviant behavior, that are not currently illegal but do violate the norms that prevailed decades ago. The aim of this chapter will be to survey the kinds of criminal or deviant behavior that religion could traditionally deter, to predict which such behaviors are likely to increase if religion weakens further.

The next three chapters explore the kinds of parareligion, religion, and irreligion that may replace traditional faiths, beginning with Chapter 6 about the so-called "New Age" movement. An abundance of evidence shows that weakening of religious authority permits deviant religions and quasi-religious superstitions to arise. For example, religious cults are more common in parts of the United States and Europe where relatively few people attend conventional churches.[31] This is also one explanation for the emergence of New Age spiritual practices such as astrology, tarot reading, and communication with spirits. New Age beliefs are most common among people who are somewhat religious, rather than extremely religious or non-religious, and thus represent the boundary of secularizing religion, where supernatural beliefs persist but are no longer well organized.

Chapter 7 concerns present and future scientistic religions. During the twentieth century, a number of new religions claimed a scientific basis for their beliefs. Christian Science, arising before the beginning of the century, really had no connection to science. In later decades, however,

Scientology, Transcendental Meditation, and others made more aggressive scientistic claims. This chapter examines the prospects for more popular pseudoscientific religions over the coming century, asking if they might sustain a viable society indefinitely.

Chapter 8 examines Atheism, the dead end of religion. Atheism is not merely a passive lack of faith, but active disbelief in the supernatural. It is more common among men and among better educated people, but until recently we lacked data to probe its sources further. We shall see that Atheists are much more likely to be people who lack deep social obligations to others. This suggests a demographic vicious circle: Reduced fertility means fewer children, fewer children means less social obligation, this in turn increases Atheism, reduces religious support for fertility, and produces fewer children. Can Atheists develop moral and social philosophies to replace the lost guidance of religion?

The three concluding chapters consider the possibility that science and technology have entered a new phase, in which they not only oppose religion aggressively, but offer a viable alternative. Chapter 9 is about cognitive science, and thus draws heavily upon the cognitive theory of religion. Yale cognitive psychologist Paul Bloom has predicted that science and religion will battle to define the human mind in the twenty-first century. Already, many cognitive scientists have sought to explain religion as the natural result of human biological evolution, and in so doing to explain it away. Bloom himself argues we falsely believe we possess souls, because we are not conscious of the way our brains operate.[32] Computer scientists have achieved slow but steady progress creating artificial intelligence, and success in this endeavor could further erode faith in souls and gods. Cognitive science thus may have the power to dispel myths, and it may also give us new conceptions of ourselves at odds with those taught by religion.

Technological transcendence is the topic of Chapter 10. The prospect of vastly increased human power to control nature promises to render faith unnecessary. If this is true, exchange theory would predict dire consequences for religion. Cognitive theory is already eroding the plausibility of religious beliefs, and it can contribute to the development of technologies that address human emotional needs better than religion does. Religion can be expected to defend itself, and the best defense is a good offense. Thus, religion may seek to block scientific and technological progress.

The final chapter describes our era as an age of transition. The evidence presented in the earlier chapters indicates that the status of religion in western civilization is unstable, although the transition to new stability -may require a century or more. Will the future world be divided into fundamentalist blocs, such as Christianity in the western hemisphere and Islam in the eastern, gaining fertility and morality while losing scientific and technological progress? Or, will an as-yet unimagined science-oriented culture offer a viable alternative to religion?

Despite the gradual nature of change, crucial policy decisions to be made today will imply one or the other future. Among such issues are radical biotechnologies, the role of faith in education, laws concerning abortion and sexual behavior, faith-based responses to crime and poverty, and the appropriate ideology with which the West can compete against Islam. All individuals alive today will face decisions concerning the role of religion in their own lives, balancing doubt against well-being. Those who are aware of the facts and ideas offered in this book may face the dilemma of how to have faith in a beneficial religion that they cannot really believe.

2
Secularization

> Ye are not eagles:
> thus have ye never experienced
> the happiness of
> the alarm of the spirit.
> And he who is not a bird
> should not camp
> above abysses.
> —*Thus Spake Zarathustra,*[1]
> Friedrich Nietzsche

Nietzsche's eagle is a metaphor for an intellectually autonomous individual who has been liberated from the superstitions of the tribe. Eagles see the world clearly, as it really is, but they must rely upon their own powers to survive as they soar above their former community. Superstitions can be useful, guiding the individual safely along a well-worn path through life, avoiding dangers that would attract the curiosity of an unbeliever. It is widely conjectured that religion is good for people, both individually and collectively. Its beliefs can be "true" in the sense of "loyal," forcing people to sacrifice for sake of the group, and encouraging the group to support each person. From the perspective of an eagle, blind religious faith is bad faith. Belief prevents the human mind from seeking the truth. However well-adapted a particular faith may be to the conditions of the past, it may be dysfunctional for the future. If we wish to fly like eagles, we must examine religion carefully from different perspectives, to see if it truly is a liberating or an enslaving force.

13

Explaining Religion

From the vast literature on religion, it is possible to draw four general perspectives, four rational theories of what religion is and how it operates. Arranged chronologically from the most ancient to most recent, they can be named the supernatural, societal, exchange, and cognitive theories. In the *supernatural theory*, divine beings actually exist, and religion is the direct result of their action upon the souls of human beings. For the *societal theory*, religion is a reflection of society, functioning to sustain societal institutions, community unity, and shared values. The *exchange theory* says humans interact with each other to get rewards and avoid costs, based on socially-constructed beliefs, and when a valuable reward cannot readily be obtained, they will encourage each other to believe in divine exchange partners. The *cognitive theory* asserts that the human brain evolved to facilitate social interaction and to deal with predators or prey, so it naturally assumes that complex phenomena result from the actions of aware beings, incidentally favoring belief in gods.

The *supernatural theory* is of course the most ancient one, being an abstract statement of religious faith itself. In the Old Testament, God talks directly to Abraham, tells Noah to build a boat, and dictates commandments to Moses. Thus, God himself created Judaism. For Christians, the ministry of Jesus is the direct involvement of an aspect of God in the world of humans, not only speaking to us but sharing our suffering. Mohammad's role in Islam is that of principal messenger of Allah, and all the world's religions have been created through messiahs and prophets who mediated between ordinary mortals and transcendent consciousness. But this theory does not merely say that members of a religion believe it is divinely ordained; it says that faith is based on true contact with the divine.

The problem, of course, is that there are many religions on the face of the Earth, and they differ greatly. The task becomes identifying the one true religion, which was divinely created, and explaining why all the others disagree with it. This would not be a problem for polytheistic Paganism, which fundamentally believes in a vast number of different supernatural beings of varying characteristics and degrees of significance, most of whom dwell in specific local areas. But it is a serious problem for monotheism and the great world religions, because they claim universality for their deity or spiritual principles. Monotheism logically implies only one faith in one God. This was especially important for established religions having a close partnership with the state, notably traditional agricultural kingdoms for which a king in heaven justified one on earth. But it is also important for a supernatural theory of religion, because the source of truth is the supernatural itself.

A classical solution to the problem is to argue that many religious denominations actually share the same fundamental beliefs or values, differing only in superficial details. Will Herberg's influential book, *Protestant, Catholic, Jew*, suggested that these three traditions had become equally valid reflections of a single, American religion.[2] Today, one would have to argue that Islam should be added, as another reflection, and Mormonism as well. The fact that these traditions differ in both authority structure and in which books they consider holy presents some difficulties in jointly deciding which words came directly from God, but at least there is some common ground. However, it is doubtful that much commonality exists for the whole range of major world religions. Back in 1893, organizers of the World's Parliament of Religions in Chicago hoped to find that common ground, but it proved difficult to bridge between such different perspectives as Evangelical Protestantism and Zen Buddhism.[3]

An ecumenical supernatural theory of religion is forced to limit those aspects that must be explained supernaturally to whatever common ground it recognizes between the participating faiths. Other religious phenomena are open to secular explanation using other theories. Many social scientists of religion are themselves religious, and many are primarily employed by religious organizations. A well-known example is Andrew Greeley, who is simultaneously a leading sociologist and a Roman Catholic Priest. Human beings may have many facets, and as proof of this point Greeley is also the author of many mystery novels. In a sense, religious social science distinguishes peripheral mysteries that should be solved scientifically, from central mysteries that must be approached reverently. That inhibits but does not prevent social science research.

The *societal theory* of religion is fully secular, but many social scientists have found it compatible with religious faith. The classical proponent, Emile Durkheim, was a secular Jew working in a secularizing Catholic country, namely France a century ago. He dedicated his career to establishing sociology as an autonomous discipline. In order to assert the autonomy of sociology, and prevent social facts from being reduced to individual psychology, Durkheim conceptualized society as a distinct entity, existing in and for itself.[4] Thus, society was sacred, and religion was its collective expression. When people worshipped God, they were really adoring society. Heaven was not a myth but a metaphor, because deceased people lived on through their contributions to society.[5] Among nations with a deep tradition of individual rights, France is famous for emphasizing the power of the centralized state, and Durkheim's reification of society thus harmonized with cultural assumptions of the nation in which he wrote.[6]

As originally formulated, the societal theory failed to explain how individuals were motivated to play their assigned roles in society, and why they would consider society sacred. American sociologists in the two decades after the Second World War attempted to fill these gaps, establishing the societal theory as the dominant sociological perspective, often calling it *structural-functionalism* or simply *functionalism*.[7] For example, Kingsley Davis and Wilbert Moore argued that society rewarded most highly those kinds of work most essential to its own survival, thus creating the stratification system of social classes.[8] Their teacher, Talcott Parsons, explained that religion was one of four primary evolutionary universals—along with language, families, and technology—that were necessary for the survival of any society.[9]

Understanding religion in terms of the functions it performs for society naturally emphasizes the consequences dimension. These would include providing a sense of shared identity, political unity, and stable morality. In the 1960s, functionalism came under severe criticism, because it seemed to justify unjust social arrangements (such as social class inequality) through the claim that they served functions for society.[10] Many branches of sociology rejected functionalism, not only on political grounds but also because its sweeping claims have proven difficult to test empirically. The societal theory remained very popular within the sociology of religion, and in adjacent fields of social science interested in the topic. Today, the theory probably has much to contribute, most often in combination with one or both of the two more recent theories.

The *exchange theory* was based on longstanding ideas from a number of sources, but coalesced in the early 1980s as the first really modern theory that sought to understand the mechanisms that create, sustain, and change religion.[11] Humans are complex, social animals that have evolved powerful brains capable of processing information in many ways, and communicating it through language. Like other animals, humans seek rewards (such as food) and want to avoid costs (such as danger). In pursuit of rewards, humans use their complex brains and language to frame plans, what was originally called *explanations* in the exchange theory of religion, but I now prefer to call *algorithms*. In computer science jargon, an algorithm is a set of instructions for achieving a goal.

Each individual learns his or her own distinctive set of algorithms for solving problems, big and small, but we often encounter problems that are difficult to solve. Through language, humans share algorithms designed to achieve goals that otherwise might be hard to reach. Algorithms to gain remote or non-existent goals are hard to evaluate, so they spread like rumors through the human population. A principle underlying many effective algorithms is that rewards which individuals cannot find for themselves can often be obtained from other humans. Indeed, much human interaction consists of the exchange of rewards between exchange partners. Religion is the attempt to exchange with supernatural beings, who are believed to have the power to provide otherwise unobtainable rewards.

Although this theory is widely known and reasonably well respected in the sociology of religion, few sociologists actually use or test it. Perhaps the reason is that religious studies tend to be favorably disposed toward faith, whereas exchange theory tends to debunk belief in the supernatural. It calls supernatural beliefs *compensators*, because they compensate a personal psychologically for the lack of a desired reward. The implication is that compensators are false beliefs, although exchange theory publications often note that compensators are like IOUs that might possibly be redeemed for the actual rewards under conceivable future circumstances. The theory in fact is rather ambivalent toward religion. One the one hand, it argues that religious faith is a natural result of human needs, mental capabilities, and social interaction. On the other hand, it debunks religion as a structure of illusions and deceptions.

The *cognitive theory* of religion emerged in the 1990s at the intersection of psychology and anthropology in the recently-developed field called cognitive science. Among the early benchmarks in the field of "Cog-Sci" were the founding of the scientific journal, *Cognitive Science*, in 1977, and the Cognitive Science Society in 1979. To a certain extent, it represents a dissatisfaction with professional psychology, which some rigorous scientists feel is dominated by pedestrian test administrators and quack psychotherapists. Perhaps more importantly, cognitive science is a multidisciplinary field, uniting cognitive psychology, portions of linguistics and cultural anthropology, cognitive neuroscience, epistemology in philosophy, and artificial intelligence work in computer science.[12] Notably absent from this list are sociology and political science, which study relevant phenomena such as ideology and persuasion, and economics which is based on a cognitive theory of decision-making. A key principle invoked by theorists is that the human brain developed through a process of biological evolution that caused it to become adapted to the environment in service of human survival and reproduction.

The environment to which humans are adapted is not today's world, however, but the world of thousands of years ago. Our ancestors needed to be able to escape dangerous predators, and to be able to hunt prey successfully. They also had to be able to cooperate and communicate with each other. To do these things, humans needed the mental ability to think about situations from the standpoints of other beings: predators, prey, and partners. Apparently, evolution crafted a module in the mind, perhaps located in a specific brain structure, that modeled other minds. Evolution made us vigilant for other minds, so we could quickly detect another person's or animal's presence and intentions. This predisposed us to imagine that a conscious being was responsible for complex natural events and processes, which is the first step toward believing in supernatural beings. Cognitive analyses of religion also place considerable stress on the ease with which different beliefs can be communicated and remembered, especially ideas about the characteristics of supernatural beings and religious narratives.[13]

Cognitive theory does not necessarily take a position about the truth or falsity of religious beliefs. It is possible to argue, as Talcott Parsons did, that religion itself is an adaptive human trait. However, many variants of the cognitive theory imply that religious experiences and beliefs are the erroneous result of hyperactive brain modules. Belief in gods may result from false overgeneralizations by cognitive modules that evolved to serve practical functions. The current cognitive theories seem better adapted to explaining religion and magic in pre-industrial, even pre-agricultural societies, which believed in a variety of small spirits analogous to the many different animals in the environment, and which lack the elaborate organizations and professional roles of modern religions.

The exchange and cognitive theories would seem to have much to offer each other, and as scientific explanations they would be far more powerful in combination than separately. I have shown the strong cognitive aspects of exchange theory in my recent book, *God From the Machine: Artificial Intelligence Models of Religious Cognition.*[14] Both theories concern the exchange of information between individuals, and both theories discuss how the human mind conceptualizes problems. Unfortunately, the social and cognitive sciences have tended to be quite separate in recent years, and the chasm between them probably caused many scientific opportunities to be missed. This book will give some consideration to all four of the theories, but it will especially highlight the most recent pair and seek to understand religion in terms of both exchange and cognition.

Science and Secularization

It would be nice if contemporary social science could give us a simple, definitive measure of religious change, but we have already seen that religion is complex and may not change equally along all dimensions. Furthermore, secularization is a slow process. We do not all wake up one Sunday morning and suddenly decide not to go to church. Rather, individual life experiences such as higher education may gradually undermine religious commitment over a period of years, and each generation may on average be slightly more secular than the one before. Unfortunately, we lack high quality data that measure the same facet of religion over a period of many years. Thus, the first ambiguity about the relation between religion and science is that social science is not well prepared to document secularization.

In research that compared 35 countries, using data from the World Values Survey, Ronald Inglehart and Wayne E. Baker noted that attendance at religious services was rising in some formerly Communist societies, but declining in many other societies that could be described either as advanced industrial democracies or developing low-income countries.[15] Among twenty of the advanced societies they listed, two were actually just the politically divided counties of Ireland which had high rates of attendance. In Northern Ireland, 69 percent of adults attended religious services at least once a month, in the most recent data reported, compared with fully 88 percent in the Irish nation. The comparable figure for the United States was 55 percent. The average of rates for the other seventeen countries reported (Australia, Belgium, Canada, East Germany, Finland, France, Great Britain, Iceland, Italy, Japan, Netherlands, Norway, South Korea, Spain, Sweden, Switzerland, and West Germany) was just 23 percent.

In contrast, the average attending religious services at least once a month in eight developing countries (Argentina, Brazil, Chile, India, Mexico, Nigeria, South Africa, and Turkey) was 57 percent. Although religious participation tended to be rising in seven ex-Communist nations (Belarus, Bulgaria, Hungary, Latvia, Poland, Russia, and Slovenia) that had recent been officially Atheistic, the average had reached just 28 percent. Poland was most religious, having a rate of 74 percent, and the average for the other six ex-Communist nations was only 20 percent.

Clearly, the data show religious weakness in many advanced post-industrial nations, compared with developing countries. It is interesting to see that Ireland, Poland and the United States buck the trend of secularization. The United States is exceptional in many ways, and yet its prominence and wealth of sociological data make it the prime candidate for research. The General Social Survey (GSS) is a questionnaire study of a random sample of American adults, administered ever since 1972, that contains many religion questions, some of which have been asked repeatedly.

From 1988 to 2000, the GSS shows no net change in belief in God, but possibly slight evidence of polarization. Over these dozen years, those saying "I know God really exists and I have no doubts about it" increased from 63.5 percent to 65.8 percent. Those giving either atheistic or agnostic responses also increased, from 5.3 percent to 7.0 percent. A question asking how frequently the respondent prays gives a similar result. From 1983 to 2004, the percent who pray several times a day increased from 24.6 to 30.1, while the percent who never pray increased from 3.9 to 10.6. From 1972 to 2004, those attending religious services more than once a week increased from 6.3 percent to 8.5 percent, and those never attending rose from 9.4 percent to 15.6 percent. However, the numbers hop around from year to year, and the trends are weak, so our confidence in the trends is doubly weak. Nonetheless, the idea that America may be slowly splitting into two societies, one religious and one secular, matches the American political rhetoric of the early twenty-first century, and it may actually be the case.[16]

From 1972 to 2004, the GSS data indicate that the percent of American adults who say they have no religion increased substantially, from 5.2 percent to 14.3 percent.[17] It is worth noting that Americans without religion tend to be politically more liberal than the average. A standard GSS question asked people to place themselves on a 7-point scale from liberal to conservative. Liberals constituted 45.6 percent of those lacking religion, compared with 25.4 percent of people having some kind of religious affiliation. Among non-religious respondents, only 21.5 percent considered themselves politically conservative, compared with 35.4 percent of others. The remainder in each group were neither liberal nor conservative.

We will have much more to say later about non-religious people, especially in Chapter 8 about Atheism. We will also see many other kinds of information that help us understand how real and significant secularization may be, especially in chapters 3 through 5 that directly concern consequences for society.

Secularization is not simply the result of scientific discovery and modern education. Rather, there have always been pressures within society working against the established religious tradition, and these often lead to religious innovation as well as to the development of an elite, anti-religious culture. Today, other societal factors eroding religion include bureaucratization, government social services, and cosmopolitanism facilitated by global communication. A very important factor for the future is the consolidation of scientific progress through the convergence of the separate sciences into a single explanation of the world based on concepts like evolution, complex physical systems, and quantum cosmology that work against traditional notions of God.

For over a century, historians and social scientists have debated whether science and religion are necessarily antagonistic to each other.[18] If science is anathema to religion, then professional scientists would be non-religious. However, data from one survey of college professors indicated very substantial levels of religiosity among scientists, comparable to levels in the population at large.[19] In a different 1998 study, Edward Larson and Larry Witham replicated surveys done by James H. Leuba in 1914 and 1933, finding that belief in God among was lower among leading scientists than run-of-the-mill scientists, and was declining in this elite group.[20] In the 1990s, 60.7 percent of all scientists expressed disbelief our doubt about God's existence, compared with 93.0 percent of leading scientists. Put the other way around, just 7.0 percent of leading scientists confidently believe in God, compared with 27.7 percent back in 1914.

Historians have actually argued that the modern emergence of science was facilitated by religion of a particular kind, either Protestantism specifically or monotheism more generally.[21] The belief that the universe was created by a single God embodying his unified laws provides a religious basis for the scientific assumption that there are natural truths capable of being discovered through research. On the other hand, it is widely believed that science and religion concern two quite separate realities, and thus are irrelevant to each other.

There has not been very much serious social-scientific research on these theories, and the results have tended to be inconclusive. Thus, logically, we can imagine three quite different futures for religion, with respect to science. First, religion remains a strong and independent force in the world, but it changes according to its own dynamic principles. Second, religion and science merge to some extent, such that scientific discoveries are incorporated into core doctrines of religious movements and entirely new denominations arise based on spiritual technologies. Third, religion fades as the rise of science continues, both discrediting traditional doctrines and reducing the social-psychological factors that sustain faith in the supernatural.

The following sections will consider ideas related to all three of these possibilities, organized by the simple rubric: religion without science, religion with science, and science without religion. The discussion is based on qualitative data from a massive Internet-based questionnaire, *Survey2000*, which was supported by the National Geographic Society.[22] About half of the 46,000 adult respondents wrote sentences or paragraphs in response to the following open-ended item I included in the questionnaire: "Imagine the future and try to predict how the world will change over the next century. Think about everyday life as well as major changes in society, culture, and technology." Following methods developed in earlier computer-assisted work, content analysis of the resulting vast corpus of text identified 2,000 distinct ideas about the future, approximately 100 of which concerned religion.[23]

Religion without Science

Whether or not scientific progress continues, it may not be especially relevant for the future of religion. However, religions do evolve, partly in response to social change (which may be stimulated indirectly by science-derived technology) and partly according to their own internal socio-cultural dynamics. Thus it is wise to begin by considering some purely religious transformations, and we will do so through six scenarios based on the ideas expressed by *Survey2000* respondents distilled directly from their verbatim responses. These scenarios are a form of brainstorming, developing ideas uncritically, to develop a wide range of possibilities.

Scenario 1: Revival of Conventional Faith.

One might think that the surprise-free scenario for the future of religion extrapolates current conditions without change, but religion is always
changing so stasis is hardly conceivable. A more realistic surprise-free
view of the future predicts that world-wide revival will occur in established religious traditions, allowing many of them to survive. Several
Survey2000 respondents felt there will be a great awakening in the mainstream churches, and religion will play a large part in many peoples'
lives a century from now. Denominations could be large in membership
but few in number. New religious sects would have burned themselves
out, leaving the more experienced denominations to sustain the faith.
There could be a great spiritual renewal as Christianity becomes increasingly missionary-focused. Formerly communist countries will experience
a resurgence of the Church, becoming unusually religious, and Christianity may even be strongest in Africa and China, extending even into the
countries in Indochina and the mountainous areas of Nepal and Tibet.
Religious services will be conducted on the Internet. Monastic activity
will bring the church back to harmony with nature. Belief in God and
spirituality will grow, overcoming increasingly difficult worldly challenges. In this scenario of conventional revival, people will turn to God
in their search for help, solace, and the happiness they could not achieve
through materialism. Many will be more interested in serving God and
humankind than in material possessions. Some *Survey2000* respondents
hoped that people in all walks of life will trust in the love of their divine
Creator and renew a commitment to good moral and ethical living.

Scenario 2: Proliferation of Religious Movements.

Several *Survey2000* respondents argued traditional denominations
will weaken, but new religious movements will thrive. For example, the
rapidly-growing Church of Jesus Christ of Later-Day Saints (Mormons)
may be the largest religious denomination in the year 2100. The Baha'i
Faith, which seeks to unify several religious traditions, could play a vital
role in the emerging world culture, one respondent asserted. The spiritual
deadness affecting prosperous societies could lead to a proliferation of
strange movements. Novel religions outside the traditional mainstream
will be embraced by the general public. Small, distinctive sects and cults

will proliferate. It will be common for people to build their own religions that address the particular needs they feel in complex modern society. It is possible that prophetic religions like Christianity and Islam will fade, and more nature-oriented religions will flourish. That would imply a resurgence of the old Earth-based creeds that worship a female deity. Already, there are feminist currents in the diffuse neo-pagan movement, notably the various Wiccan (witchcraft) groups and the Covenant of the Goddess.[24] A century is ample time for the large number of small groups that exist today to grow into a set of major religious denominations.

Scenario 3: The New Age.

Other respondents predict that the New Age Movement will grow stronger over the next century, saying that non-traditional spiritual exploration will be very important in the year 2100.[25] Eastern religions will make further inroads into the West, and non-Christian religions will be practiced by a large number of people in western societies. Many people around the world will adopt the Buddhist consciousness that all people and things are inextricably linked with one another. In this scenario, there will be rapid growth in meditation, yoga training, and other pseudo-spiritual activities. If traditional religion revives, then alternative new age philosophies will grow rapidly as a counter to rigid fundamentalism. Faith in non-linear forms of understanding will be valued more than science. For example, many people will trust in astrological horoscopes. Spiritualism will be a great source of comfort in an increasingly complex and confusing world. God will be a private, personal concept, and people will believe they have their own angels. Spirituality will be important, but formalized religion will be unimportant.[26] The influence of organized religion will wane, but personal spirituality will be a more common practice.

Scenario 4: Fanaticism.

Some *Survey2000* respondents were worried about the growth of religious movements they considered reactionary and dictatorial. They fear that fundamentalist religions will take over, everywhere in the world. This, they think, would threaten the very existence of democracy. The greatest threat to world stability could be religious fundamentalist thinking. Colonies of religious fanatics will spring up all around the world, creating havoc and potentially causing cause great destruction. There may be a major spiritual movement as significant as the Great Awakenings of the past two centuries, although not necessarily Christian. Perhaps a new world religion will emerge, based on Pentecostal or Evangelical principles.[27] Other new religions will emerge through combination of aspects of existing religions. At least one will rise to prominence, fed by the masses looking for something to combat the modern world. Optimistically, a new religion will take hold from the existing chaos and brutality, and in later centuries it will lead humanity to a more happy world.

Scenario 5: Religious Conflict.

In this scenario, the division between Christians and non-Christians could intensify. To end divisive arguments, religious leaders in some countries will seize political power and establish a theocratic government. Around the globe, there could be a movement away from Christianity toward Islamic culture, and Islam will become an extremely powerful political force. First, an Islamic renaissance will lead to political unification in the Middle East. Then, all the Islamic people of the world will unite. Expansion of Islamic society in Africa will be a great source of conflict. There will be world-wide religious conflict between Christians and Muslims. Christianity may lose members as Islam grows, until Islam will be the dominant religion of the world. A major nuclear world war could occur between the West and Islamic states, and conflict between Muslim and Christian societies could be the final downfall of mankind. If humanity survives, the world could be dominated by a unification of the nations of the Islamic faith, and the Judeo-Christian minority will be driven underground. Judaism will be even more threatened than in the past, in this conflictual scenario.

Scenario 6: The Millennium.

For some believers, revival of religion will be accomplished by direct divine activity in the world. Some anticipate that Jesus Christ will return to Earth. Those who do not accept Jesus as their savior will perish in a time of terrible tribulation. After God destroys all the wicked during the battle of Armageddon, people will live in an Earth-wide paradise. Then God will bring an end to war, famine, and disease. He will rule over the Earth, destroy wickedness, and bring perfection to mankind. He will wipe every tear from the eyes of believers, and they will see death no more. All good people who have died in the past 6,000 years will be resurrected and live forever on God's clean and beautiful Earth. Government will be by divine intervention, since human government has not achieved good for all mankind, and only God can do that. God will be the most important force, and angels will influence people's lives.

These six scenarios, with the exception of the last one, are quite compatible with current thinking in the sociology of religion. The sixth scenario, predicting the literal Millennium, is based on supernatural rather than social-scientific assumptions. Yet of all the "futurologies" that one may find in bookstores or the visual mass media, none has a richer heritage or has greater influence over people's daily lives than the one rooted in the Bible.

Some religious denominations are growing, rather than contracting, and these tend to be doctrinally conservative.[28] Roger Finke and Rodney Stark estimated that the percent of the American population who formally belonged to religious organizations doubled from 17 percent in 1776 to 34 percent in 1850 and nearly doubled again to 62 percent in 1980.[29] Since then, the rate of church membership has held constant. Secularization does occur within the most liberal religious denominations, as highly educated clergy adopt the intellectual values of secular academics. In so doing, they tend to lose touch with the spiritual needs of the laity in their own churches, and membership declines.[30]

As highly secularized denominations lose membership, more fervent sects grow. In time, the sects themselves become more worldly and stall in their growth, but at this point schisms generate new sects. Thus, secularization and revival tend to balance off as individual denominations weaken but religion in general remains strong. This is a cycle of secularization and revival in which the wheel of faith turns but does not move either forward or back.[31]

At certain historical periods, such as the early Roman Empire and possibly the present day, a revolution in faith does take place.[32] An increased rate of secularization, accelerated by contact with alien cultures and by secular intellectual developments, so weakens the prevailing religious tradition that many religious innovations occur. A few of these establish fresh religious traditions.

Science with Religion

More than a century ago, religious movements began to arise calling themselves sciences. Both Christian Science and Divine Science were already well established by the dawn of the twentieth century. Religious Science was established in the 1920s, and Scientology in the 1950s. Transcendental Meditation claims to be based on "The Science of Creative Intelligence." The Raelian Movement offers a high-tech human cloning service. Many future religious groups could likewise employ scientific metaphors to communicate their novel spiritual visions. Chapter 7 will focus on this possibility, so here we will merely recognize it.

Some new religions may be inspired by scientific ideas that challenge every-day notions of reality. For example, it has been many years since the development of relativistic physics, quantum theory, and fundamental discoveries about inconsistency and undecidability in mathematics. Yet the wider culture appears oblivious to them. Scientists and mathematicians have recently explored alternatives to religious myths of the origin of life in the universe, based on chaos and complexity, self-organizing systems, and random models of biological evolution.[33] Together, these ideas describe an indeterminate and chaotic universe very different from the God-centered cosmos envisioned by the Judeo-Christian-Islamic tradition. Perhaps such radical concepts could have a powerful impact on the general public if they were repackaged in theologies that gave them readily-understandable but transcendent meaning.

Scenario 7: Scientism.

Many *Survey2000* respondents thought that science and religion will support each other over the coming century. Perhaps religions will modernize and become more science oriented rather than biblical. At the extreme, science will become the official state religion, with scientists as high priests. Conversely, science may come to the conclusion that God must exist, or that mysticism is a physical, psychological, and spiritual reality. Perhaps people will seek God once again as science comes full circle and decides that Darwin was wrong about evolution. The mystical will come to hold an increasingly important place in daily life, while the scientific will become less obtrusive. The pendulum could swing back from a totally scientific society to a totally faith-based society once again. New science-oriented religions are likely to emerge. Some will be oriented toward the social or cognitive sciences, as people seek mastery of their own minds, tapping into the greater consciousness. Awareness of the mind-body connection will develop greatly in science, medicine, and spirituality. People will be able to tune in to the emotional fields of others, sharing their feelings in perfect sympathy. Consciousness expansion through psychedelic drugs could be regarded as true science, some *Survey2000* respondents said.

Science without Religion

Although Parsons argued that religion was a fundamental feature of society, required for the evolution of complex societal institutions, many intellectuals have long imagined that it was steadily losing strength, in the complex but inexorable process called *secularization*.[34] In this view, science, rationality and secular institutions are destined to overwhelm religious faith. The exchange theory of religion suggests that science will need to provide many of the actual rewards for which religion offers only compensators, if it is to conquer faith. The cognitive theory would suggest that a wide range of scientific ideas would have to become influential in everyday life, in order to give people ways of thinking that are free from the ancient habits that support religion.

Scenario 8: Secularization.

A number of *Survey2000* respondents believe that churches will progressively feel threatened by science and technology. Discoveries achieved in space exploration could challenge religion, or scientific findings in other areas will erode dependence upon religious beliefs. By 2100, science might have discovered conclusively that the underlying order to the universe is not God. Religion will start to die a slow death, as people become more informed and start thinking for themselves. The Christian Church will become increasingly irrelevant. Christian beliefs will no longer prevail in decisions that affect mankind, and Judeo-Christian influence will fade from the political agenda. Younger people who have grown up in every major religion will question their beliefs and abandon their basic systems. Universities will have expunged religious ethics, which they consider antiquated. People will come to realize that morality does not need religious justification, and it will be established on a secular basis. Church attendance will be replaced by secular community activities and community events. The Roman Catholic Church will have liberalized into a weak corporation with a dwindling customer base, and it will gradually disintegrate.

In this scenario, only the devout will belong to religions, while most others will become secular, and Atheism will gradually increase in popularity. Religious groups will become further separated from mainstream society, trying to live according to their particular doctrines. From a Christian perspective, society as a whole will be depraved and distant from God. Believers will feel they are submerged in an increasingly immoral world, and there will be extreme polarization between practicing Christians and secular society. Religion will be weaker in technology-rich nations than in poorer nations. In time, religion will disappear, except from underdeveloped countries, and will be regarded as a mere curiosity. The world will be less dependent on God and more dependent on self, as technology has given humans a god-like image. People will be intolerant of those who profess a Judeo-Christian-Islamic religion. Eventually, religion will be viewed as a harmful nuisance and will be outlawed from society, according to some *Survey2000* respondents.

Conclusion

The thousands of people who contributed their images of the future to *Survey2000* saw a tremendous range of discordant possibilities. Perhaps the future really will incorporate elements of all these ideas, in an incoherent tangle of conflicting tendencies, with the ever-present possibility of total disaster. However, it could be a mistake to think that this represents a complete change from the past. The notion that communities of the past were stable, supportive social units held together by shared religious faith may be a nostalgic illusion. If societal leaders in earlier centuries stressed faith, stable families, and community wellbeing, they may have done so chiefly because these conditions did not exist, or existed only precariously, and religion expressed hope for stability rather than being a supporter of it.

When Ferdinand Tönnies published *Gemeinschaft und Gesellschaft* in 1887, he was merely giving formal names to concepts that social scientists had debated throughout the nineteenth century.[35] *Gemeinschaft*, or *community*, referred to the supposed traditional form of human society, marked by close, enduring social relationships, as they had perhaps been known in agricultural villages where individual interests were submerged in group interests. *Gesellschaft*, or *society*, is based on complex division of labor that encourages individualism and is more compatible with modern technical and economic conditions.[36] Tönnies was far from the only theoretician to propose such ideas, and we can perhaps trace them all the way back to the Garden of Eden and similar myths of an idyllic early period in human history, which anthropologists find in cultures around the world.[37]

Unfortunately, European social theory was largely detached from the kind of empirical, skeptical, often quantitative research that was performed by many social scientists in both Europe and America during the nineteenth century. Twentieth-century American sociology was heavily influenced by thinkers like Tönnies and tragically ignored much of the best empirical work. For example, American psychiatrist and sociologist Edward Jarvis (1803-1884) is entirely unknown to sociologists, despite the fact that he extensively published theory-based quantitative social research on many topics, helped to found and presided over a national social science association, and was the leading consultant for the United States Census.[38] Jarvis began publishing quantitative studies in 1842, exploring the possibility that increasing individualism in society was causing an increase in mental illness.[39] His 1855 statistical study of all the mentally ill of Massachusetts established the important connection between mental illness and low social class, but a century later the most influential work on the topic did not even cite his study.[40]

By the middle of the twentieth century, however, researchers were finding that simple notions of an historical shift from *Gemeinschaft* to *Gesellschaft* were untenable. In *Family and Kinship in East London*, Michael Young and Peter Willmott found both alienated suburbs and cohesive urban communities in a modern metropolitan area.[41] They noted that marriages in earlier generations faced similar levels of instability to modern marriages, if more often caused by death than by divorce. From the publication of Peter Laslett's 1965 book, *The World We have Lost*, historical demographers have documented extensive social instability in past centuries.[42] Sociologists found *Gemeinschaft* and *Gesellschaft* within walking distance of each other in modern Boston, and anthropologists documented considerable instability in some contemporary "primitive" societies.[43]

Thus, without a careful examination of empirical evidence, we can only conjecture about the changing role of religion in society. Perhaps, as the societal theory argues, religion served to strengthen traditional society and thus improve individual wellbeing. It is also possible that religion was an inescapable but inefficient solution to problems experienced by people in earlier centuries, expressing their needs and hopes rather than satisfying them. If religion really was helpful in the past, it may have lost this function with the improvement in socio-economic and health conditions that has taken place in many societies. It may be that religion could be helpful today, were it not for the skepticism that comes with secular education and cosmopolitan mass culture. Beginning with the next chapter, we will do our best to address such issues, but the fundamental point is that social science could answer many questions about the role of religion in society, if concerted research efforts were supported, but with the risk that aggressive research could kill the research subject.

3
Well-Being

Christianity finds sickness necessary,
just as the Greek spirit had need
of a superabundance of health—
the actual ulterior purpose of the whole system
of salvation of the church is to make people ill.
—*The Antichrist,*[1]
Friedrich Nietzsche

Both science and religion claim they contribute to human well-being. If true, it would be folly to dispense with either one of them. Yet science can ask the question of whether religion really contributes to human well-being, or merely exploits misery to its own profit. The answer will not be an easy one to find or to digest, and the related questions are among the most painful to human beings. Where shall we find meaning? Who can cure our bodies and our souls? Would the net benefit be greater if we sought salvation through faith or from faith? Is faith the only source of confidence and calm, in a world of danger and disorder? Overshadowing the scientific approach to answers is a great paradox: The benefits of religion may vanish the moment we understand them.

Co-Existence

Many people believe that science and religion can co-exist in the modern world, if they respect each other and agree to avoid invading each other's legitimate domains. Science should deal with the ages of rocks, and religion should deal with the rock of ages, they say.

Scientist Stephen Jay Gould was perhaps the most eloquent proponent of this view in the 1999 book, *Rocks of Ages*. Gould was a popularizer of science, as well as a scientist, who had battled against religion when it attacked evolutionary principles of his own realm, paleontology. Perhaps more importantly, Gould was a serious person, who recognized that religion was the main way that most people dealt with some of the harshest facts of human existence, notably death. His own life was lived in the shadow of death, since 1982 when he learned he had a highly fatal form of cancer.[2] The fact that he survived for twenty years, and apparently died of a different cancer, did not detract from the fact that he had solemnly faced his own mortality.

Gould did not embrace religion, and he remained on the other side of the religion–science divide. But in *Rocks of Ages* he enunciated a principle he called NOMA, Non-Overlapping Magisteria. He urged mutual respect for:

1. our drive to understand the factual character of nature (the magisterium of science)
2. our need to define meaning in our lives and a moral basis for our actions (the magisterium of religion)[3]

Thus, Gould assigns two functions to religion, *meaning* and *morality*, and this book will consider them in separate chapters. The present chapter will consider meaning as part of the broader issue of individual human well-being. The fifth chapter will consider morality and its opposite, crime and deviant behavior. For sake of symmetry with religion, Gould should have said that science has two functions as well: *understanding* and *technology*. All four are major themes of this book.

The Meaning of Religion

It is not a foregone conclusion that religion actually provides meaning, or that humans need it, so I must immediately violate Gould's NOMA principle by suggesting that science can evaluate the extent to which religion serves this function. Philosopher Daniel C. Dennett has strenuously argued that we must not take the benefits of religion on faith, but must evaluate them scientifically.[4] Depending upon what science discovers when it investigates this sensitive issue, science will either give us reason for respecting religion's magisterium, or will conquer part of it. A first step is to consider what *meaning* means.

The standard way of seeking the meaning of a word has a somewhat frustrating result. The primary dictionary definitions of *meaning* concern language itself:

    1a: the thing one intends to convey especially by language; purport
    1b: the thing that is conveyed especially by language; import
    2: something meant or intended; aim
    3: significant quality; especially implication of a hidden or special sig-
        nificance
    4a: the logical connotation of a word or phrase
    4b: the logical denotation or extension of a word or phrase[5]

These definitions can be read in different ways. From the standpoint of modern information science, they refer to the transmission and translation of information, from one person or system to another. What does the German word *Bedeutung* mean in Spanish? Significado. Both translate into English as *meaning*. However, the English-cognate German word *Meinung* means opinion in English. Meaning, first of all, is about words and the human intention to communicate ideas. The third definition hints that meaning can be hidden, and religions commonly refer to "hidden truths" that are not obvious to observers and may be known only through the practices or instructions of the religion itself.

Like all subtle parts of language, these terms are drenched in metaphors. We imagine we have a thought, and then we put it into words. In a sense, this may often be the case. We have a memory of going to church, that in our mind's eye (is that more than just another metaphor?) is a visual experience of walking into the building, taking a place in the pews, and kneeling in prayer. Then, with "that picture in mind," we describe it in words like those I have just used. The other person, upon hearing them, may attempt to reconstruct a visual image from the words, but it is unlikely to be identical to our own. One can also argue that we often do not have a thought in mind until we frame the words.

Consider three words in the definitions: *import*, *significant*, and *significance*. *Import* can refer to something imported, literally the information received in a communication. *Significant* and *significance* can refer to what a symbol signifies, and to the signification of a string of words. Symbols have power, and *in hoc signo vinces* ("in this sign you shall conquer") refers to the political power of the cross. But all three words can also refer to the value, consequence, or influence of a thing. Winning a million dollars, or being in a car wreck, are both important events, because they have big consequences for the person involved. If people seek in religion the meaning of their lives, then they seek a symbolic connection between their lives and something else. They want their lives to matter. As Charles Glock and Rodney Stark argued, "at the core of all religions is a set of beliefs about the nature, meaning, and purpose of reality."[6]

In his book, *Man's Search for Meaning*, Viktor Frankel says a person is "a being whose main concern consists in fulfilling a meaning and in actualizing values, rather than in the mere gratification and satisfaction of drives and instincts."[7] Like Gould, Frankel had faced death and sought a serious response to his dire experience. In a concentration camp in the Second World War, he survived while his parents, wife, and brother died. People seek purpose in their lives, but ultimately a purpose that is oriented outside themselves. For some people, a meaningful life is one that matters to God. For others, a life of service to other people or to an abstract principle can be meaningful. In his actual work as a psychotherapist, Frankel assisted his patients in the construction of a life story that was coherent and ennobled by a sense of transcendent value, rather than a religious life. In this context, *construction* can be the noun form either of *construct* (build) or *construe* (interpret), and the social construction of reality was a favorite topic for sociologists of the 1960s when Frankel published his influential book.[8]

As Frankel's own work illustrates, religion is by no means the only source of transcendence in human life. Philosophy, art, family love, national loyalty, and a warrior's code of courage are among the many other candidates. Even sports can provide a sense of pride, identity, and purpose, to fans as well as players. Can science provide meaning? The answer will emerge gradually throughout this book. Does religion provide meaning effectively? We will examine that issue shortly, in the broader sense of looking at the well-being that logically would be connected to meaning. First, we must consider where religious meanings come from.

Religious Innovation

In exploring the origin of religious meanings, it is practically impossible to separate meaning from a related possible benefit, namely hope. The key factor is the way that religion promises something more than ordinary secular institutions and the natural environment can offer. About seventy-nine generations of humans separate us from the crucifixion of Jesus, and even more generations stand between us and Buddha, Confucius or Abraham. Thus it is hard to study the origins of their movements. Yet astronomers analyze the distant stars in terms of chemical and nuclear processes they observe in their own laboratories, so it is scientifically valid to examine modern innovative religions and extrapolate from them to the origins of the world's great faiths.

The religious explanation of the source of religious beliefs is simple: They are true and their revelation to humans was the work of God. One problem with this explanation, is that most religious revelations are manifestly false, from the perspective of any one religion.

In a very real sense, polytheism is a workable solution to this problem. In modern Hinduism, as in the religions of ancient Rome, the standard view is that many of the competing revelations are simultaneously true, because they reflect different supernatural beings. The devotions of any single person can be dedicated to this or that god, or this or that shrine, on the basis of locality or the aspect of life that is important at the moment. More philosophically minded people can seek a divine unity underlying the many deities, and talk about them all as avatars of one hidden god. The emergence of thorough-going monotheism, however, establishes a religious orthodoxy that excludes the possibility of the vast majority of religious revelations, in favor of a small set, such as those in the Bible associated with Abraham, Moses, and Jesus.

Therefore, from the perspective of modern monotheism, as well as from secularism, most revelations are false. How, then, do people come to have any faith in them at all? From the perspective of social science, the answers may apply to all religious revelations, whatever someone might think about their truth or falsity. Importantly, the societal theory of religion would seek answers that explain not only how faith is generated but also how it comes to serve functions for the society.

To address these questions, I will return to three compatible models of religious innovation that Rodney Stark and I sketched only one generation ago rather than seventy-nine like the Christian revelation, and bring them up to date.[9] The models were based not on abstract speculations, but on things I had actually observed inside a number of innovative religious movements, and had found in well-documented historical records. They concern very intimate and potentially shameful aspects of real people's private lives. This fact makes it difficult to talk about them, because compassion overrides the desire to offer graphic examples. Notice the sharp edges of pain in the first of the three, the *psychopathology model*:

1. Some mentally ill individuals interpret their delusions, hallucinations, and compulsions in religious terms.
2. If such a person retains some degree of mental coherence during a psychotic episode, the result may be a set of beliefs coherent enough to function as part of a religious faith.
3. After such psychotic episodes, some individuals regain a significant degree of mental equilibrium, while becoming confirmed in their idiosyncratic beliefs.
4. A formerly psychotic person can convince others to adopt the beliefs if: 1) the person possesses skills, status, or interpersonal attractiveness; 2) the new beliefs energize the individual by supporting self-esteem; 3) the person is part of a social network that has not rejected him; 4) others in the network lack personally satisfactory religious affiliation; and 5) specific beliefs or practices address people's unresolved life problems.
5. Key followers moderate the new religion by interpreting the original vision in spiritual rather than psychiatric terms, and managing any further psychopathology of the founder, as the new faith spreads through the social network.

Standard theories of shamanism, folk healing, and cult formation in cultural anthropology are versions of the psychopathology model. In terms of meaning, some people have a surplus of meanings, caused by mental illness, whereas ordinary people suffer a deficit of meaning and thus become potential consumers of the visions if they can be repackaged as sacred rather than insane.[10] Julian Silverman argued that a messiah or sorcerer goes through five stages: 1) serious personal problem typically involving low self-esteem, 2) preoccupation with the problem causes withdrawal from social life, 3) self-initiated sensory deprivation, 4) dream-like images and ideas flood the mind in an episode of acute schizophrenia, and 5) cognitive reorganization as the person tries to convert other people to his vision.[11]

Historical examples abound. John Humphrey Noyes, founder of the famous Oneida cult, suffered from alternating bouts of depression and elation, what today would be called bi-polar disorder.[12] Some cases may be mixed or marginal, based on mental problems that fall short of full psychosis. In his book *Mental Healers*, Stefan Zweig argued that Mary Baker Eddy, founder of Christian Science was a victim of hysteria.[13] Ellen White, the source of inspiration for Seventh Day Adventism, had periodic visions, but she was supported by a well-balanced husband who compensated for her sometimes extreme psychological states.[14] A variant of the model covers cases in which a person seeks or accidentally has a

psychotomimetic experience caused by drugs, high fever, or other unusual physiological states.

Nearly thirty years ago, I did a brief observational study of a group
called The Love Family, founded by a man who had changed his name
from Paul Erdman to Love Israel, after a revelation triggered by psychedelic drugs. The group renovated a group of houses on Seattle's Queen
Anne Hill, built a greenhouse-like building out of old windows scav-
enged from the streets, and was gradually transforming the location into
an aesthetic marvel. Many had taken new names, like Love and Understanding, that expressed the virtues of Christ. The group's new culture
included hieroglyphic writing, spiritual gardening, and the requirement
that new members have psychedelic experiences like that of the founder.
Love held great power over his followers' love lives, arranging relationships between them. I was very much impressed by his reconditioned
school bus, complete with a turret and archery equipment that I fancied
let him hunt like an ancient Babylonian monarch from his chariot. From
a peak membership of perhaps 350, the group declined through a schism
and defections, and in 2003 filed for bankruptcy protection.[15] A fragmentary website still asserts the altered-consciousness revelation that "We
are One:"

> Oh yes, individually we can be blessed with peak experiences that re-
> veal these fundamental truths to any one of us at any time—moments
> when the sun breaks through the clouds so intensely that when the
> clouds re-gather, we can't help but remember the truths of that sun that
> we saw; and it is important that we each aspire to these peak experi-
> ences because they are the foundation stones of our higher mind. But
> without each other's witness and confirmation of these peak experi-
> ences, our minds will continue to be a confusing mish-mash of concep-
> tions.[16]

Some messiahs, however, appear to be much cooler, even calculating
in the way they develop their novel beliefs and practices. A second theoretical approach, which I called the *entrepreneur model*, applies to cases
in which launching a new cult is like opening a new business, or designing a new product. An entrepreneurial messiah is more like a businessman or engineer than a madman.

1. Cults are businesses, which offer products and services to customers,
   in exchange for money, honor, and social power.

2. The job of designing and selling a new package of religious compensators requires skill and training, so successful cult entrepreneurs
   first must serve an apprenticeship in an earlier, somewhat successful cult.
3. The process of designing a novel package of religious compensators
   involves several methods; most typically the cult engineer: 1) starts
   with the culture of an already-existing successful cult; 2) discards
   some elements of the culture that seem non-essential; 3) adds elements of culture drawn from other cults and non-religious sources;
   4) renames or otherwise disguises key cultural elements to conceal
   their origins, and 5) emphasizes cultural elements the engineer personally finds attractive.
4. The entrepreneurial messiah goes through a formative period, experimenting with the first converts and adjusting the culture to increase its attractiveness for its audience.
5. At some point, whether under leadership of the founder or after others have taken over the business, a period of consolidation sets in
   during which the culture takes on its final form, and innovation
   practically ceases.

Examples of this model are easy to find. Charles Taze Russell was a
successful businessman, who drew upon Adventism to create Jehovah's
Witnesses, without any discernable evidence of psychopathology.[17] In
the decade around 1940, Arthur L. Bell became rich by founding a cult
he called Mankind United, claiming to be but the vanguard of a vast but
undoubtedly fictitious movement.[18] However, it would be wrong to claim
that all entrepreneurial religious movements are frauds. In the modern
age, all kinds of products and services are consciously engineered, and it
is reasonable for inventors and salesmen to get rich off good merchan-
dise, so why not religion? It cannot be denied, however, the cults fitting
both the psychopathological and entrepreneur models can sometimes be
harmful, especially in those remarkable cases when both models apply.
    Shoko Asahara is generally considered a madman, but he could also
be described as a religious entrepreneur who turned to desperate measures when members and outsiders denied the value of his business. He
was the fourth of seven sons of a Japanese mat maker so poor that for a
time the floor of their one-room home was simply mats placed on bare
ground. From birth, he suffered from glaucoma, and he eventually lost all
sight in the left eye and much of that in the right. He attended a public
boarding school for blind children, where he became a leader partly because he could see well enough to guide the other children around. He
ran in a school election and suspected fraud when he lost. A strong

young man, he studied Judo and was charged with assault soon after graduation. He was intelligent and had hoped to become a doctor, but his vision was not good enough, so he obtained a license as an acupuncturist. In 1982, Asahara was arrested for selling fake Chinese herbal medicines.

From 1982 to 1984 Asahara served an apprenticeship in a Buddhist religious group named Agonshu, led by Yasuo Kiriyama. Although firmly rooted in ancient religious traditions, Agonshu is strongly oriented toward the future and employs at least the image of modern science. In five locations, it operated meditation facilities called Japan Meditation Centers, with a special room where the floor, ceiling, and all four walls are electrified. Equipment beams microwaves around the meditators, and twenty to thirty man-made sapphires dot the ceiling. During sessions, the room is bathed in recorded natural sounds selected for the particular purpose of the meditation: waterfalls, streams, raging ocean waves, wild birds, and the voices of insects. Agonshu teaches that meditation is the source of religion, art, science, and education. In the late 1980s Kiriyama deemphasized supernatural power somewhat, but Asahara took it up as the foundation for a movement of his own.

Asahara and his wife left Agonshu to start their own movement, and in 1984 they opened a yoga center called Aum Shinsen no Kai or Aum Shinsen Association. Asahara claims that in 1986 he received a secret curriculum of advanced spiritual training in Tantra Vajrayana in the Himalayas and received the final revelation that confirmed his supernatural powers. The following year, he changed the name of his movement to Aum Shinrikyo or Aum Supreme Truth.[19]

Many of Asahara's recruits were talented young men, including science students and college graduates, and the elite corps of members tended to have extensive technical training. They were able to synthesize their own hallucinogenic drugs, and Asahara devised a number of very intense initiatory experiences, one mimicking death, in the expressed attempt to elevate members to a higher level of being. Like a financial corporation cooking its books when success fell short of expectations, Aum began inflating the value of its treatments, and trying progressively more extreme methods. On the night of June 27, 1994, an attack team used sarin nerve gas against judges who were deciding a law suit against Aum Shinrikyo, injuring one of them, sickening 400 people, and killing seven. Less than a year later, after problems with apostates and opponents had escalated, the group carried out its sarin attack on the Tokyo subway, killing eleven people.[20]

The third model, *subculture evolution*, is more gentle, because it conceptualizes the emergence of a new religion in a large number of small steps, guided by many people rather than by a single messiah.

1. Religious innovation takes place through intense interaction among several individuals who have committed themselves to achieving difficult or impossible goals.
2. The outcome is most likely to be new religious compensators if the group is already embedded in a religious culture, in a quasi-religious magical activity, or in one of the modern analogs for religion, such as psychotherapy.
3. As individuals interacting in pursuit of collective goals that they cannot readily achieve, their obligations to each other cause them to inflate to some degree their claims of progress, in a cycle that sustains morale but gradually assembles a set of compensators rather than real rewards.
4. Factors that encourage this escalation of hopes include: 1) a dense network of social relationships linking the individuals; 2) some degree of social separation from uninvolved outsiders; 3) success of the group in providing incidental emotional rewards to members, such as love, status, and mutual help, and 4) a resultant process of social implosion, increasing the connectedness and isolation of the network.
5. To consolidate the new religious beliefs and associated practices, the group must develop a new relationship to the surrounding society, for example through incorporation as a religious organization with a distinct name.

Members of the group may play various roles, some acting as organizational leaders managing its activities, others innovating and experimenting, and others primarily following but offering respect in return for the hope provided by leaders and innovators. Because the process of religious evolution takes place in many small steps, there may be many mistakes and steps backward, but none is so significant as to discredit the group to most members. At times, individual leaders may act out minor versions of the psychopathology and entrepreneur models, but only as part of a larger social process and not as autonomous messiahs. In our theoretical treatise, Rodney Stark and I observed:

This model describes how people can progressively commit each other to a set of compensators they simultaneously construct. Thus it sketches *mutual conversion* that assembles a compensator system while accomplishing a *social implosion* that results in a cohesive, closed group broken away from the rest of society.[21]

There are many examples, and all religious groups may go through periods of group innovation that approximate this model. One could argue that all folk religions, Judaism among them, are products of subculture evolution, as a people struggle through an historical series of challenges, to which they respond by developing compensatory religious beliefs. We cannot at this great distance guess whether the experiences of communication with God reported by Abraham and Moses were psychotic episodes or conscious inventions, but they were parts of a much larger socially-based emergence of a religious tradition.

My favorite example, because I studied it closely through observation and interview, was the subculture evolution of The Process, Church of the Final Judgement, which we will also consider in Chapter 7.[22] Robert and Mary Anne de Grimston, the couple who founded the group, became acquainted in the London, England, branch of Scientology. Ambitious to develop their own psychological methods, they left Scientology and established Compulsions Analysis, based on a combination of methods they had learned in Scientology with principles from Alfred Adler's version of Psychoanalysis. Adding group sessions to individual treatment of people who were already members of their extended social network, they established the conditions for a social implosion. About two dozen people became fully involved, interacting intensely with each other and withdrawing from the surrounding social world. After setting up a highly visible center in London, they embarked on a spiritual quest that took them to a ruined coconut plantation in the Yucatán region of Mexico, then throughout North American and Western Europe.

Each person in the group made some kind of contribution to the development of an increasingly novel and increasingly religious culture. Formal incorporation as the Process church followed. The female founder was especially able to develop the social network by stimulating and controlling emotions. The male founder took responsibility for developing scripture, in interaction with his closest associates, and served as the public figurehead of the group. Other members designed symbols, clothing, and rituals. Although there was a clear leadership structure, input from all of the original members guided the emergence of the Process.

Notice that all three of the compatible models of religious innovation depend upon unmet human needs. Without unfulfilled desires, faith would not arise, in the exchange theory of religion. Faith provides meaning, placing human suffering in a symbolic context, but it does more than that. It compensates people emotionally for the lack of rewards they strongly desire. Each of the models explains how the religious vision adjusts to the needs of followers, at least to some extent. Cults that better satisfy members' needs will tend to survive and even grow, as unsatisfactory cults die out. This raises the difficult question of how well religion really satisfies human desires. The following sections explore the capacity of faith to provide general well-being, health benefits, and deterrence of suicide.

General Well-Being

Political scientists Pippa Norris at Harvard and Ronald Inglehart at the University of Michigan have argued that religion is largely a comfort for people who suffer objectively acute insecurity in their lives. Although chronic suffering may be found anywhere, it is especially common in poor underdeveloped nations:

> The inhabitants of poor nations remain highly susceptible to premature death—above all from hunger and hunger-related diseases. They also face sudden disasters from drought or flood, or weather-related emergencies. Poor nations have limited access to the basic conditions of survival, including the provision of uncontaminated water and adequate food, access to effective public services offering basic healthcare, literacy, and schooling, and an adequate income. These countries also often face endemic problems of pollution from environmental degradation, conditions of widespread gender inequality, and a legacy of deep-rooted ethnic conflict. Lack of capacity to overcome these difficulties arises from corruption in government, an ineffective public sector, and political instability. Poor nations often have weak defenses against external invasion, threats of internal coup d'etat, and, in extreme cases, state failure.[23]

Norris and Inglehart thus explain that underdeveloped nations should be much more religious than developed nations. Using data from the massive World Values Surveys, questionnaires administered in 74 societies, they indeed found this to be the case. On average, 44 percent of people in poor agrarian countries attend religious services at least weekly, compared with 25 percent in industrial developing nations and 20 percent in postindustrial societies. In agrarian societies, 52 percent pray every day, compared with 34 percent in industrial societies and 26 percent in postindustrial ones. The percentages saying religion is very important to them vary in a similar but stronger way: 64, 34, and 20. Compared with postindustrial societies, a greater percentage of people in agrarian societies believe in life after death, the soul, heaven, hell, and God.[24]

The exceptional society, in the World Values data as well as many other measures, is the United States. Norris and Inglehart offer two partial explanations, but admit the religiousness of the United States remains something of a mystery. First, societies may differ by religious culture somewhat, from the level of religiousness caused by their degree of insecurity. Second, among advanced postindustrial societies the United States is unusual for its high degree of socio-economic inequality, which means that a large fraction of the population suffers from insecurity.

The religious culture of the United States has deep roots in the nation's tradition of religious freedom, dating from the colonial period and enshrined in the Constitution. The historical development of democratic institutions in other Christian countries often took place in a context in which religion supported conservative movements and aristocratic interests, while anti-clerical left wing parties pressed for change. The period is largely over in which state churches discredited religion by resisting genuine democratic movements, so in their 2000 book, *Acts of Faith*, Rodney Stark and Roger Finke have predicted that religious freedom will unleash a revival of faith throughout Christendom.[25] In the brief period since Stark and Finke wrote, however, the United States appears to have become even more exceptional, not only in its foreign policy but also in political polarization along religious lines.

Gregory S. Paul argues that the United States is exceptional in another way, its relatively low level of health and well-being given the nation's wealth. Paul used data from the International Social Survey Program, similar in many respects to the World Values Surveys, to explore the connections between religiousness and well-being in 18 prosperous democracies. Religiousness of a nation correlated with reduced lifespan, increased teen pregnancies, abortions, and infant mortality. The United States was an extreme case, high in religion and low in well-being, but these tendencies showed up across the other nations, as well.[26] Another cross-national study, reported in the *Journal of the American Medical Association*, found much poorer health at all economic levels in the United States compared with the United Kingdom, attributing the difference to the worse diet and higher stress levels in America.[27]

The World Values Surveys can be used to compare individual people within nations, as well as nations within the world. The library of the University of Michigan has helpfully put much of the data on the web, so we can try a simple analysis here.[28] One question inquired about respondents' general level of happiness. The English language version was: "Taking all things together, would you say you are: very happy, quite happy, not very happy, not at all happy?" Figure 3.1 reports the percent of respondents who said they were very happy in ten predominately Christian nations, divided into Catholics, Protestants, and those who belong to no denomination. The nations selected all had at least 300 respondents from each group. For example, 640 unaffiliated people in the United States responded to the question, 261 of them said they were very happy, and this is 40.8 percent.

In three of these ten nations (Latvia, Netherlands, and the United States), those with no religion are more likely to be very happy than Protestants or Catholics. People lacking religious affiliation are worst off in four (East Germany, Finland, South Africa, South Korea). In the remaining three, the unaffiliated are either in the middle (Canada, West Germany), or tied with the Catholics (Australia).

Table 3.1, in the appendix of this book, shows more scattered data from eighteen other nations, lacking either sufficient Protestants, Catholics, or both. Ten Catholic nations (Argentina, Belgium, Brazil, Dominican Republic, France, Mexico, Portugal, Slovenia, Spain, and Uruguay) have enough respondents professing no religious affiliation for analysis. On average, counting nations equally, 24.0 percent of Catholics are very happy, compared with 20.5 percent of those with no affiliation. In one Protestant nation (Great Britain), Protestants seem much happier than those without religion. In Russia, 5.9 percent of both the Catholic and unaffiliated groups are very happy, versus 5.3 percent of Orthodox members. Three smaller Slavic nations show three different patterns. In Belarus, irreligious people are happier than the Orthodox. In Ukraine, they are equal, and in Bulgaria the Orthodox are happier. In two parts of the former Yugoslavia (Macedonia and Bosnia-Herzegovina), the unaffiliated are more likely to be very happy than Muslims, who are more likely than the Orthodox. In Japan, 21.2 percent of Buddhists are very happy, compared with 32.4 percent of those who have no denomination. In South Korea, which is included in Figure 3.1, just 10.4 percent of Buddhists are very happy.

What do these numbers show? Frankly, the picture is not very clear. There are hints that lacking a religious affiliation may work against happiness, but the differences between nations are much greater than those between religious groups. The relatively high level of happiness among South African Protestants may merely reflect the country's heritage of racism, if the Protestants are disproportionately of English and Dutch descent. In predominantly Catholic countries, without a substantial Protestant community, having no affiliation may be socially disadvantageous or reflect serious alienation.

Figure 3.1: Percent Very Happy, Different Religions

Nations	No Denomination	Catholics	Protestants
Australia	38.6%	38.6%	41.2%
Canada	32.3%	37.2%	24.5%
Finland	18.0%	18.5%	20.8%
Germany, East	12.9%	19.6%	14.7%
Germany, West	15.1%	14.1%	15.8%
Latvia	3.8%	3.6%	2.7%
Netherlands	45.0%	41.8%	40.5%
South Africa	20.9%	21.3%	32.0%
South Korea	8.8%	13.3%	12.8%
United States	40.8%	38.0%	39.1%

Source: World Values Surveys

When a simple analysis is not decisive, social scientists not only turn to more complex methods, but also rely upon a vigorous scientific debate to dig out the truth. Shortly, we will offer careful summaries of two such lines of research, concerning the capacity of religion to guard physical health and deter suicide. But the results of the World Values Surveys warrant brief discussion.

It seems clear from the work of Norris and Inglehart that religion is largely a response to human misery, being stronger in nations where many people's lives are insecure. However, involvement with religion does not apparently cause much greater happiness than non-involvement. One possibility is that religion is a failure, unable to overcome much suffering but attractive to sufferers when there are no other alternatives. Another very different possibility is that religion succeeds in overcoming much suffering, but this success is hidden by the fact that faith is most attractive to those most in need. That is, desperate people turn to religion, gaining much but not enough to surpass in happiness the people who were never desperate. This reminds us that secularization is not a random process, and the most secular people may tend to have better educations and thus enjoy better economic situations than traditionally religious people have.

Probably, the influence of religion is complex and contradictory. A good example, using World Value Surveys data, is a 2003 study that Robert Barro and Rachel McCleary published in the prestigious *American Sociological Review*.[29] On the basis of a sophisticated statistical analysis, Barro and McCleary argued that religion both promotes and retards economic growth, because different aspects of religion have different effects. Religious beliefs may encourage people to work harder, therefore building the economy. Church attendance is costly, because money invested in churches and clergy could otherwise build the economy by being invested in industry or commerce. The net effect of religion, then, depends on the balance between belief and attendance. The ambivalent economic impact of religion is only one of many contradictions we shall encounter.

Health Benefits

A very large number of statistical studies of health include information about religion, but only a very few of these studies have the right focus or are rigorous enough to evaluate the possible benefits of faith or church attendance. When Richard Sloan and Emilia Bagiella did a systematic search of articles published in 2000 that were indexed in Medline, they found hardly any high-quality studies on the topic.[30] My own informal summary of some of the literature suggests to me that religion can indeed promote health, although it interacts with other factors and is certainly not indispensable for good health.

The study that most strongly influences my thinking was published in the leading population journal *Demography* in 1999, by a team of four highly competent experts, including both experienced senior researchers and brilliant young scientists: Robert Hummer, Richard Rogers, Charles Nam, and Christopher Ellison.[31] The team used an excellent set of data that built on the work of many other researchers. In 1987, a huge questionnaire study of heath risk factors was administered to a national sample of Americans, then data about whether the respondents were still alive in 1995 was added. Of the 21,204 people in the dataset, 2,016 had indeed died after the passage of these eight years. The measure of religiousness was how often a person attended church or other religious services, and the measure of health was whether the person was still alive in 1995. Using sophisticated statistical and demographic methods, the team offered a particularly lucid measure of the benefit of religion: a person's life expectancy at age 20 in years. For the entire sample of respondents, a person age 20 could on average expect to live an additional 59.1 years, therefore dying at age 79 plus a few weeks. This is both a demographically valid way of expressing the complex statistical results, and a way that is immediately meaningful to non-technical readers.

The study reported that a 20-year-old person who never attended church could expect to live another 55.3 years. The average person of age 20 attending church occasionally, but less than once per week, might live 59.7 years. Those attending once a week had a life expectancy of 61.9 years, and attending more than once a week gave a life expectancy of 62.9 years. Any involvement at all in religion seems to give a person 59.7 - 55.3 = 4.4 years. That's a lot! Increasing religious participation to the maximum adds 62.9 - 59.7 = 3.2 more years, for a total of 62.9 - 55.3 = 7.6 years. Clearly, if the added life was actually caused by religion, this would be a vast benefit.

As everybody can imagine, people who are very sick have trouble attending church. One of the functions of radio and TV ministries is to serve shut-ins, but watching a TV program does not count as church attendance. That is, part of the connection between church attendance and longevity reflects the fact that sick and feeble people are less likely to attend and more likely to die. Much of the research team's analysis involved correcting for the people's health conditions at the start of the study, a very difficult job. The research produced a number of different mortality models, so we cannot say exactly how many years religion really gives a person. But at the end it was clear that the benefit was significant and operated in at least two ways: 1) The social relationships provided by church attendance were beneficial, and 2) Religion beneficially discouraged some kind of behaviors that endangered health such as tobacco and alcohol use.

There are many ways in which religion might promote health. In the same year as the above study, team member Christopher Ellison co-authored with Darren Sherkat a review essay on the hot topics in the sociology of religion.[32] In the sociological literature, they found five main explanations of health benefits:

1. health behaviors and individual lifestyles
2. social integration and support
3. psychological resources
4. coping behaviors and resources
5. various positive emotions and healthy beliefs

This list misses what might be the most popular explanation, the idea that God himself favors people who are religious, intervening directly to give them longer and healthier lives. It is hard to imagine the methodology we would need for a definitive study of this question, but some studies of something remotely similar have been published. In 1988, Randolph C. Byrd carried out a study of 393 hospital patients with heart problems, to explore the benefit of *intercessory prayer*.[33] At random, half of the patients were prayed for, and the other half were not. Although the patients had consented to be part of a study of prayer, they did not know whether they were in the prayer group or the control group. Some health benefit did apparent result from prayer, but of course one cannot have great confidence in a small, early study.

In 2006, the *American Heart Journal* published results of a study involving 1,802 heart bypass patients, divided at random into three groups.[34] Two of the groups were told about the study but not told whether they would be prayed for. Complications arose in 52 percent of these cases that were prayed for, which is actually slightly worse than the 51 percent complication in the cases in which the patient was not prayed for. A third group was told it would be the beneficiaries of intercessory prayer, and this group did worst of all, 59 percent suffering complications from their heart bypass.

This highly-publicized study was not good news for those who believe in the objective power of prayer. However, I must hasten to point out the theological problem with this study. Why would God follow the wishes of the strangers doing the intercessory prayer? It is said that God always answers prayers, but the answer often is "No." Sophisticated members of traditional religious denominations do not believe they can force God to do anything. Opinions differ about whether prayer can really encourage God to do something, or is rather a time of communication with the deity in which people place themselves in the hand of the

Lord. The funder of this costly study of intercessory prayer was the Templeton Foundation, a private philanthropy that some observers associate with the New Age movement. As we shall consider in Chapter 6, the New Age imagines that humans have spiritual power, and thus might conceptualize the topic of this study as spiritual healing rather than intercessory prayer.

The health impact of religion may vary across different groups in the population, some receiving greater benefit than others, and different religious factors operating more or less strongly. Elderly people face many health problems plus the knowledge that death approaches, and many may look back on the course of their lives and wonder whether it was all meaningful.[35] Religion may be especially valuable to many of them. One study suggests that religion may encourage elderly people to help others in need, to the benefit of their own health.[36] A number of studies have explored possible differences in the value of religion for different ethnic groups, perhaps reflecting their different average levels of well-being and a tendency of deprived people to turn to religion for comfort.[37]

Christopher Ellison has often suggested that religion is of greater value for the health and subjective well-being of poorly educated people, implying it may not be much good for the highly educated.[38] This idea has several possible implications. Optimistically analyzed, it may mean that highly educated people have a greater range of alternative sources of emotional support, better coping skills, and the resources to get high quality medical attention. If all of society becomes educated and prosperous, the need for religion may decline in parallel with the decline of faith itself. On the other hand, Ellison's observation may mean that educated people are less able to gain hope and guidance from religion, perhaps precisely because they have been taught to be skeptical.

One recent but admittedly modest study found no benefit of organized religion for geriatric patients, but significant benefit of personal spirituality.[39] Socio-cultural changes over time may provide alternatives to the health benefit of traditional religion, offsetting corrosive effects of secularization. Many studies find that benefits of religion are intertwined with the benefits of stable families, and of moderate lifestyles.[40] That is, much religion may primarily be the ideological and organizational reflection of traditional communities, which are threatened by social change.

Suicide Deterrence

The classic topic of sociological research, connected to religion and social change, is suicide. Surely if religion can deter suicide, it must provide potent meaning, hope, or social support to people in distress.

Over a century and a half ago, after governments had been systematically collecting death statistics for a few years, it became apparent that suicide rates differed greatly from one society to another. In 1864, German economist Adolph Wagner reported that suicide rates were higher in Protestant than Catholic communities.[41] Fifteen years later the Italian Enrico Morselli expanded the empirical basis for this observation, calling "the influences of religion" among "the strongest motive powers which act on the will of man."[42] In 1881, Thomas Masaryk, future president of Czechoslovakia, argued that increasing suicide rates were the result of weakening religious faith.[43] Indeed, he said that Protestantism was a secularized form of Catholicism, so the Protestant superiority with respect to suicide merely represented a covert kind of secularization in which religion weakened from within. In 1897, French sociologist Emile Durkheim drew upon these earlier studies to offer a distinctly sociological theory that has remained influential but hotly debated to the present day.[44]

Durkheim argued that suicide was powerfully shaped by social forces, reflecting the condition of society even more than the despair of an individual. Using terms that were already in wide use by intellectuals,[45] Durkheim identified four different kinds of suicide:

1. Fatalistic, resulting from a realistic lack of hope
2. Altruistic, resulting from excessively strong social demands
3. Egoistic, resulting from excessively weak social bonds
4. Anomic, resulting from a lack of norms or meaning

Fatalistic suicide was discussed only in a footnote in Durkheim's book, and the book also dismissed the idea that profound mental illness was a major cause of suicide. Durkheim was most interested in Egoistic and Anomic suicide, which represented different ways in which a society could be too weak to protect its members from self-murder, if they encountered a stressful period in their lives.

The exact boundaries of altruistic suicide are difficult to judge. If Jesus knew he would be crucified, and intentionally sacrificed himself to redeem the sinners of the world, then his death was a religiously-inspired altruistic suicide. This speculations aside, at least one suicide was directly connected to the crucifixion, as Matthew 27: 3-5 reports: "Then Judas, which had betrayed him, when he saw that he was condemned, repented himself, and brought again the thirty pieces of silver to the chief priests and elders, saying, I have sinned in that I have betrayed the innocent blood. And they said, What is that to us? see thou to that. And he cast down the pieces of silver in the temple, and departed, and went and hanged himself." The Donatists of the fourth and fifth centuries were apparently prone to religious suicide, and in recent years we have seen mass suicides of the People's Temple, Solar Temple, and Heaven's Gate. Hypothetically, belief in an afterlife could erode commitment to this life, but altruistic suicide is primarily caused by excessive dominance of the individual by the society.

Egoistic suicide, Durkheim said, was caused by weakness or instability of social relations. He attributed the higher suicide rates reported for Protestant European countries to fragmentation of the community that eroded the moral support that Catholics could provide each other within their more unified religious tradition. Oddly, he did not connect anomic suicide to weakness of religion, ignoring the widespread view that religion provides morality and meaning. Instead, Durkheim chiefly illustrated anomic suicide by connecting it to changes in the economic situation. He claimed that the suicide rate increased not only during unusually bad economic times, but also in unusually good economic times, so uncertainty of norms must be the cause of suicide. Unfortunately for Durkheim's analysis, in 1954 Andrew Henry and James Short showed that suicide rates do not go up in unusually good economic times, so the original support for Durkheim's concept of anomic suicide evaporated.[46] More recent research indicates that the apparent propensity of Protestants to suicide was an illusion, based on overly aggressive interpretation of rates from a few parts of Europe.[47]

In the wreckage of Durkheim's very influential theory, the key ideas of egoistic and anomic suicide still have some relevance. Religion can provide a supportive community in which social relationships might prevent the depression that motivates suicide and deter individuals from violating the norm against self-murder. At the same time, religion can provide hope and meaning. Many secular institutions can provide social bonds, so we should concentrate on what religion can distinctively offer a desperate person. Steven Stack nicely summarized the exchange theory of religion and suicide:

As Stark and Bainbridge (1980) pointed out, religion assuages all manner of human disappointments—death, unemployment, poor health, divorce, and so on. Suffering can be more readily endured if eternal salvation and heavenly glory are offered as a future relief to those who suffer. Indeed, earthly adversity can be viewed as short-lived, a mere moment in time compared to eternity; as such, it can be endured with less pain. In addition, religions often promote a belief that God is watching and cares about the suffering of people. One's earthly problems may be more endurable if one believes that God knows about them and cares.[48]

In the early twentieth century, Durkheim's student Maurice Halbwachs continued to work on suicide, and in 1952 Austin Porterfield published an article analyzing American data from 1936.[49] In the 1970s, Whitney Pope raised serious questions about Durkheim's methodology and theories.[50] At the beginning of the 1980s, Rodney Stark carried out a pioneering study, with the help of graduate students Daniel Doyle and Jesse Rushing.[51] Statistics on suicide and various demographic variables came from government publications, including the 1970 census. The Glenmary Research Center had published geographically detailed 1971 statistics on membership in 53 denominations, and Stark developed procedures for turning them into reasonable estimates of total church membership.[52] The dataset covered 214 metropolitan areas, and for some parts of the analysis Stark and his students examined just the 60 largest where the large numbers are less susceptible to random variations. Results showed clear patterns. The suicide rate was not affected by the balance of Protestants versus Catholics among church members. High rates of church membership were associated with low rates of suicide.

Appropriately, Stark's team applied statistical controls for stability of social relationships. Some cities in America have much more stable populations than others, in the sense that people are not frequently moving from one home to another, or in and out of the city. Durkheim had used religion as a measure of social cohesion, but social cohesion may also be a cause of religion. When people move to a modern city that has many religious denominations, they may not quickly join a church, being more concerned with getting a home and a job. At both locations, they will make friends with people of different religious denominations, and this diversity will slow their movement toward affiliation with any particular church. If the residential turnover is very high, churches will be weak and even a majority may not belong to any.

The statistical controls that Stark applied did not eradicate the association between high church membership and low suicide rates, but it did reduce it. This was a pioneering study, so we cannot be sure it used the best methods either for calculating church member rates, or for constructing control variables.

Shortly afterward, I performed a similar analysis of data from the marvelous censuses of "religious bodies" (i.e. congregations) carried out by the U.S. Census Bureau in 1906, 1916, and 1926.[53] In each of these three years from the early twentieth century, suicide statistics existed from a sufficient number of cites, and the results were the same as for 1971. Differences between Protestant and Catholic areas were insignificant, church membership was connected to low suicide rates, and reasonable statistical controls did not change the picture. The data from 1926 are undoubtedly the best. Reporting of death rates was well established by then, and the 1926 survey of church membership was probably the most thorough of all time. The Census Bureau had gotten completed questionnaires from fully 232,154 individual churches representing 212 denominations.

Figure 3.2 shows a sample analysis of these excellent 1926 data, suicide rates and church membership in the 79 largest cities, those having populations over 100,000. The names of the cities with suicide rates above 25 per 100,000 are shown, and most are "wild west" towns where life was more chaotic than in some of the more settled parts of the nation. I have drawn a trend line through the dots, showing the general tendency of church membership to deter suicide. No city in 1926 had a church membership rate above 90 percent or below 20 percent, and the range was actually from 25 percent to 85 percent. The trend line suggests that church membership reduced the suicide rate over this range from about 25 per 100,000 to 10 per 100,000, a substantial savings of life.

Shortly after I completed the study of data from early in the twentieth century, data from 1980 became available, so I tried the analysis again. A new survey of denominations carried out in 1980, supplemented with data from a Jewish yearbook, gave me the raw material for estimating membership figures, and the 1980 census offered good demographic variables, some of which I needed for controls. To my surprise, the power of religion to deter suicide seemed *much weaker* in 1980 than in 1926. Figure 3.3 compares 1926 cities with 1980 metropolitan areas visually.

Figure 3.2: Suicide and Religion, American Cities in 1926

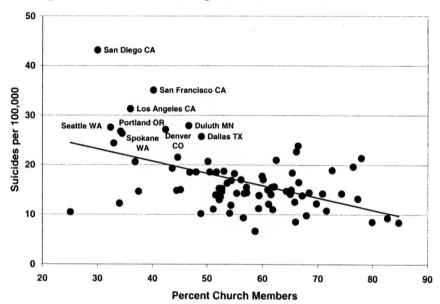

As we have already mentioned, correlations like these strengthen the larger the cities become, which would give 1980 an unfair advantage over 1926, because the nation had grown. In 1926, there were 165 cites over 50,000 in population. In 1980, there were 289 metropolitan areas (outside New England where church member rates could not be calculated), and the smallest one had a population of 62,820. It is possible that big cities show higher correlations not only because size reduces randomness but also because religion might be more effective in big cities. Or, to put the point the other way around, small towns may be more supportive of individuals, whether or not they are religious. Socially isolated individuals may find religion a good way of getting socially connected in big cities, but not need it in smaller communities. Whichever explanation is more correct, the graph shows the apparent deterrence power of religion in cities of different sizes.[54] Each point on the graph represents 75 cities, located in terms of the average population of the cities, and the percent of the variance in suicide across the cities that can be attributed to religious differences. That is, the explained variance was calculated for the 75 cities with the smallest populations, to get one data point. Then, the smallest city was dropped; city number 76 was added, and the explained variance was calculated again to get the second data point. This process of dropping and adding cities continued, until the set consisted of the 75 largest cities, and the explained variance for them became the last data point for one of the lines.

Figure 3.3: Religion's Declining Power to Deter Suicide, 1926–1980

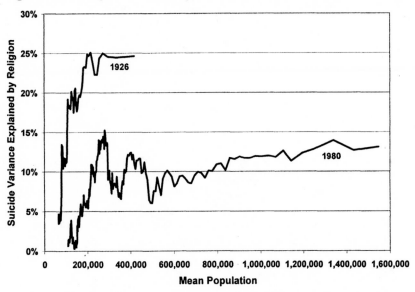

The religion effect in 1980 was also *less robust*, meaning that it essentially vanished when I used my best statistical controls. Modern U.S. censuses include a question about whether people have moved to a different home in the past five years, and this is an excellent measure of social instability, but less effective control variables, such as the percent of residents born outside the state also reduce the apparent power of religion in 1980 much more than in 1926.[55] Different corrections and controls give pretty much the same picture, especially when you account for the increased city size from 1926 to 1980. The power of religion to deter suicide is much greater for the earlier year. Religion seems to have lost much of its ability to deter suicide through the hope offered by religious faith, outside of social support. It may still have some power through the social relationships it builds in congregations, because the statistical controls may have discounted religion as an intermediary between social stability and suicide.[56]

Robert Baller and Kelly Richardson analyzed the relation between religion and suicide in the United States in 1990, finding that residential stability was much more important than church membership.[57] Recently,

Roger Finke and Christopher Scheitle published good membership rates for American states in the year 2000, so I analyzed the connection to suicide rates for 2002.[58] Yes, suicide had a negative correlation with church membership, but its negative correlation was much stronger with residential stability, measured by living in the same house for the past five years.[59] Controlling statistically for residential stability essentially erased the apparent ability of religion to deter suicide.[60] Thus, religion probably is losing a life-saving ability.

Conclusion

We have seen some evidence that religion really does contribute to human well-being, notably to physical health and to resistance against suicide. Although our three models of religious innovation were not at all flattering to faith, they did suggest how religion might come to serve human needs. These findings also suggest how two theories of religion might fit together: classical societal theory (or functionalism) and modern exchange theory. In order to satisfy their own needs through exchange with their followers, religious leaders must help the followers live more successful lives.

However, this chapter has suggested that the connections between religion and well-being might be complex and changeable. In particular, we saw evidence that religion's apparent power to deter suicide was weakening. This is consistent with Masaryk's 1881 theory that suicide rates were increasing because secularization was eroding religion. In a 1996 book, Stark and I compared suicide rates for 14 European nations in 1870 and 1980, finding that on average their rates more than doubled over this span of 110 years.[61] Suicide rates in many countries have continued to rise until the present day, although it is difficult to know how much of this increase represents additional suicides versus a greater tendency of suicides to be recognized and counted.[62] To summarize our current state of knowledge about religion's ability to deter suicide in modern nations, the truth is probably some combination of the following three principles:

1. Religion has lost some of its former power to deter suicide.
2. Part of the apparent power to deter suicide in the past was an illusion, resulting from reluctance in religious communities to count a death as a suicide.[63]

3. The remaining weak power of religion to deter suicide comes from the ability of some denominations to encourage supportive social relations among members.[64]

We saw evidence of other variabilities as well. Nations in which the populace feels secure are less religious than nations where people experience great insecurity. When we examined one very simple measure of subjective well-being, respondents' willingness to say they were "very happy," we saw much greater differences across nations than between religious and unaffiliated individuals within one nation. Clearly, religion is only one of many factors that affect well-being, and it may have complex relationships with the others.

In social-scientific research it is often difficult to distinguish cause from effect. The experimental method can do this, because in laboratory experiments a scientist can manipulate the supposed cause to see what happens. Experimenting with people's religion to see what would happen to their health would be both impractical and unethical. Thus, scientists must make do with elaborate statistical methods using large numbers of control variables, and the results are often uncertain. On both logical and empirical grounds, it seems that part of the connection between religion and well-being is spurious. While church attendance may support good health, people who are chronically sick may not be able to attend. But some significant number of people seem to benefit from religion, at least under some common conditions.

Given the multiplicity of other factors, religion is probably not essential to individual well-being. Educated people may be more ready to find alternative sources of help, as may modern people who live in smaller and thus better-connected communities. One study estimated religion added around 3 years to the lives of coronary patients, which was significant but comparable to the benefit from statin-type drugs and about half the benefit of regular exercise.[65] This chapter has suggested that the death of God would diminish human well-being, but we could survive without him and might find adequate substitutes in the future.

4
Fertility

Most advanced industrial societies now have birth rates too low to sustain the population in the long run, whereas some traditional societies where religion is more powerfully integrated into family life continue to have high birth rates. The United States is an important test case, because the birth rate is almost high enough to offset the death rate, and America is among the most religious advanced nations. In their landmark study of secularization, Pippa Norris and Ronald Inglehart say, "One of the most central injunctions of virtually all traditional religions is to strengthen the family, to encourage people to have children, to encourage women to stay home and raise children, and to forbid abortion, divorce, or anything that interferes with high rates of reproduction."[2] They argue that the ironic result is that secularization makes the world more religious, because irreligious adults have few children, while religious ones continue to reproduce.

Population Trends

Each year in Germany, on average for every 1,000 people, 8.33 are born and 10.55 die. The population is only just beginning to shrink, because the age distribution has not fully adjusted to the low birth rate, as it will do over time. The average age of a female German is more than 43, so nearly half are already incapable of bearing children. Another factor holding the population steady is the net immigration rate of 2.18 per 1,000. However, if German infertility is just a manifestation of post-industrial civilization, then all the nations that are currently sending immigrants to Germany will eventually see their own fertility collapse, as they modernize. In Austria, the birth rate is 8.81 per 1,000, compared with a death rate of 9.70. Indeed, the birth rate for the European Union as a whole is slightly lower than the death rate, 10.00 compared with 10.10 in 2005.[3] The problem is not limited to Europe, and Japan has announced that its death rate exceeded its birth rate for the first time in 2005.[4]

A good source of data with which to compare the demographics of the nations of the world is the CIA's *World Factbook*, conveniently offered to friends and foes alike on the World Wide Web.[5] Figure 4.1 shows 2005 data for the thirty most populous nations, all those with at least 40,000,000 population. To be sure, all the numbers are estimates, even the apparently precise population numbers, and they were collected from a very wide range of sources having different but unknown degrees of quality. We see higher death rates than birth rates in Russia, Germany, Italy, Ukraine, and South Africa. The net migration rates are either positive (more people move in than move out) or negative (more people move out than move in).

It would seem to be a simple matter to use birth, death, and migration rates to project future trends of the total population size, but these rates are very sensitive to the age structure. As we all know, unfortunately old people tend to die, so as the population ages the death rate may go up. Children tend to be produced by young adults, so if a society has an unusually large number of children already, there will be a high birth rate as they mature through the child-bearing years. And, as a large segment of the population ages out of young adulthood, the birth rate will tend to drop.

Perhaps the easiest single statistic to use in understanding population trends is the "total fertility rate," an estimate of how many children the average woman will bear during the entirety of her child-bearing years. In order to replace herself and her husband, a woman needs to produce 2 children. However, some children die before reaching the child-bearing years of adulthood, and a slight excess of boy babies (unbalanced sex ratio) must also be figured in. In a modern society with good nutrition, public health, and medical care, a total fertility rate of 2.1 is generally

Figure 4.1: Demographics of the 30 Most Populous Nations, 2005

Nation	People	Rates per 1000 Birth	Death	Migrate	Fertility
1. China	1,306,313,812	13.14	6.94	-0.40	1.72
2. India	1,080,264,388	22.32	8.28	-0.07	2.78
3. USA	295,734,134	14.14	8.25	3.31	2.08
4. Indonesia	241,973,879	20.71	6.25	0.00	2.44
5. Brazil	186,112,794	16.83	6.15	-0.03	1.93
6. Pakistan	162,419,946	30.42	8.45	-1.67	4.14
7. Bangladesh	144,319,628	30.01	8.40	-0.69	3.13
8. Russia	143,420,309	9.80	14.52	1.03	1.27
9. Nigeria	128,765,768	40.65	17.18	0.27	5.53
10. Japan	127,417,244	9.47	8.95	0.00	1.39
11. Mexico	106,202,903	21.01	4.73	-4.57	2.45
12. Philippines	87,857,473	25.31	5.47	-1.49	3.16
13. Vietnam	83,535,576	17.07	6.20	-0.43	1.94
14. Germany	82,431,390	8.33	10.55	2.18	1.39
15. Egypt	77,505,756	23.32	5.26	-0.22	2.88
16. Ethiopia	73,053,286	38.61	15.06	0.00	5.33
17. Turkey	69,660,559	16.83	5.96	0.00	1.94
18. Iran	68,017,860	16.83	5.55	-2.64	1.82
19. Thailand	64,185,502	15.70	7.02	0.00	1.88
20. Congo	60,764,490	44.38	14.43	-0.17	6.54
21. France	60,656,178	12.15	9.08	0.66	1.85
22. UK	60,441,457	10.78	10.18	2.18	1.66
23. Italy	58,103,033	8.89	10.30	2.07	1.28
24. S. Korea	48,640,671	10.08	6.26	0.00	1.26
25. Ukraine	46,996,765	10.49	16.42	-0.38	1.40
26. Burma	46,996,558	18.11	12.15	-1.80	2.01
27. S. Africa	44,344,136	18.48	21.32	-0.22	2.24
28. Colombia	42,954,279	20.82	5.59	-0.31	2.56
29. Spain	40,341,462	10.10	9.63	0.99	1.28
30. Sudan	40,187,486	35.17	9.16	-0.02	4.85

considered sufficient to maintain a population at a given level, assuming zero net migration and no distortions attributed to the age structure. The fertility rate in the European Union is only 1.47, far too low to sustain the population over the long term.

The large nations with total fertility rates above 3 are all very poor and possess traditional cultures that integrate religion into social life: Pakistan, Nigeria, Philippines, Ethiopia, the Democratic Republic of Congo, and Sudan. The United States is among the large nations with rates between 2 and 3, along with nations that must be described as *developing*: India, Indonesia, Mexico, Egypt, Burma, South Africa, and Columbia. All the large advanced industrial or post-industrial nations other than the United States have below-replacement fertility, as do some developing nations, notably China and Brazil. At the same time it was attempting to eradicate religion, the government of China instituted extreme efforts to limit fertility, but neither can be said for Brazil.[6] The natural conclusion is that modernization causes fertility collapse, with secularization assisting the process of fertility decline. The world was not well prepared for the impending demographic collapse, in large part because demographers and other social scientists had focused instead on the danger of population explosion.

Demographic Transition

The most influential single publication in the history of demography is the 1798 book, *An Essay on the Principle of Population*, by Thomas Malthus.[7] At the time he wrote, intellectuals were debating social reforms intended to improve the living conditions of humanity, and Malthus used a demographic argument to suggest that this laudable goal was unattainable. His key assertion was that human population would rise more rapidly than the human ability to exploit resources in the environment, for example more rapidly than the food supply. Any attempts to improve the conditions of the poor would only allow them to have more children, thereby overwhelming any social reform efforts. His often-repeated fundamental assumption was that human erotic nature would ensure that people always reproduced at a rate significantly greater than that required to sustain a constant population. The factors that regulated population, therefore, would be those that increased the mortality rate or otherwise set physical limits on fertility, notably war, sickness, and famine.

Malthus pointed out that population growth was far greater in the United States than in Western Europe, attributing this to the greater abundance of natural resources in the Americas. From 1800 until 2000, the U.S. population increased by a factor of more than 50, from about 5.3 million to 281.4 million, through a mixture of immigration and fertility.[8] Contrary to the predictions of Malthus, well-being improved over the two centuries, rather than holding constant or even worsening, as measured by increased average lifespan and per capita economic production.[9] The life expectancy at birth is slightly lower for Americans than for residents of the European Union, 77.7 years versus 78.3.[10] In contrast, gross domestic product per capita (purchasing power parity), is higher in the United States, $40,100 versus $26,900. Malthus may have been wrong to predict that humans would produce too many babies, but maybe they should. Perhaps humanity must reproduce up to the ceiling set by resources, and be limited painfully by war, sickness, and famine. Otherwise, the human population will decline to extinction.

In the middle of the twentieth century, a new perspective emerged, called *demographic transition theory*. It concerns the interplay of fertility and mortality rates as improved technology and related economic growth transform the material and social conditions of life. In his 1922 classic, *Social Change*, William F. Ogburn argued that the emergence of industrial society transformed the conditions of women's lives, reducing the need for them to dedicate themselves to child bearing and rearing, through reduced childhood mortality, the development of public schools, and industrial production of many products that women formerly produced at home.[11] But for a time the institutions of society did not adjust to these fundamental changes, creating a situation Ogburn called *cultural lag*. It was necessary for a feminist social movement to force change, securing greater opportunities outside the home. Ogburn's general model assumed that societies tend to achieve equilibrium, in which institutions work harmoniously together under given material conditions. Significant new technological innovations will upset the balance temporarily, and a period of cultural lag will ensue until the society can adjust its institutions to achieve a new equilibrium.

Many social scientists applied this model to demography, notably Kingsley Davis.[12] Traditional societies have high rates of fertility because they need high birth rates to offset the high mortality they experience because of their limited ability to produce food and to combat disease. The demographic transition begins when technological development reduces the death rate directly through improved nutrition and health, and indirectly through economic growth. Cultural lag keeps the birth rate high for a number of years, as the death rate declines. This causes the population explosion that has been such a concern for decades.[13] Eventually, social movements and other mediators of social change overcome cultural lag and bring fertility down until it is again in balance with mortality. When this demographic transition is complete, society will once more be in equilibrium, with low birth and death rates, and a stable population.

Note that this whole theory depends upon the assumption that societies get the fertility rates that they need. This is the *functionalist* assumption that was explicit in Ogburn's work and dominated sociology prior to the 1960s: The culture and institutions of a society tend to work together for the benefit of the society as a functioning social unit.[14] Although it is possible to justify this assumption on evolutionary grounds,[15] it was merely assumed by many sociologists, and the functionalist consensus collapsed in the 1960s when the focus shifted to social conflict, to the ways that institutions may be dominated by elites who exploit the rest of the people, and to the process in which society emerges from the interactions of individuals rather than being an autonomous entity in its own right.[16]

By the mid 1980s, demographers themselves began abandoning the final part of demographic transition theory and recognizing that they simply did not know what would happen to fertility after cultural lag was overcome. A few demographers distracted attention from this fact by arguing that that demographic transition theory may have misrepresented past fertility rates, for example suggesting that rates were somewhat low before the historical development of agriculture or in post-Renaissance Europe.[17] However, the challenge of falling fertility rates became a hot topic of discussion within both demography and government policy circles.[18] Now, it is widely recognized as a serious problem.[19]

Since the demographic warnings of the 1980s, the problem has become well-known to intellectuals associated with pro-family religious groups. A 1987 book, *The Birth Dearth*, by conservative Ben Wattenberg, undoubtedly played a role in fostering this awareness.[20] Especially notable today as a source of public information about the relations between religion and demography is the Howard Center for Family, Religion and Society in Rockford, Illinois. The Center's website explains that its "purpose is to provide research and understanding that demonstrate and affirm family and religion as the foundation of a virtuous and free society."[21] The group asserts "that the natural human family is estab-

lished by the Creator and essential to good society," and it decries social
problems that result from abandoning the natural family, including "below-replacement fertility."[22] The Center's website offers extensive and
constantly updated abstracts of social-science publications relevant to
their mission, including such standard social-science publications as
Population and Development Review, *Social Forces*, and *Population
Studies*. A constant complaint is that most secular intellectuals and social
scientists continue to advocate fertility-reducing feminism and to ignore
the birth dearth.

The Changing Role of Women

Fully ninety years ago, in the pages of the *American Journal of Sociology*, feminist Leta S. Hollingworth asserted three claims about women
and reproduction:

1. The bearing and rearing of children is necessary for tribal or national
   existence and aggrandizement.
2. The bearing and rearing of children is painful, dangerous to life, and
   involves long years of exacting labor and self-sacrifice.
3. There is no verifiable evidence to show that a maternal instinct exists
   in women of such all-encompassing strength and fervor as to impel
   them voluntarily to seek the pain, danger, and exacting labor involved in maintaining a high birth rate.[23]

She concluded that men, who have traditionally been in control of
society, have employed various strategies to compel women to have babies. These have included establishing a personal ideal for women that
caused them to value large families, public opinion that pushes them
back into line if they deviate from high fertility, legal provisions to discourage women from developing their individual interests, pro-natal religious beliefs, limited education aimed at giving girls a self conception as
wife and mother, art that glorifies the maternal role, the illusion that child
bearing is easy, and a whole host of minor assumptions that buttress
commitment to fertility. In the intervening decades, many of these methods of control by men over women have broken down, and it is doubtful
whether they could or should be reimposed.

Granting that women's liberation is otherwise a good thing, it has
been associated with reduced fertility in several ways. As Hollingworth
argued, traditional culture makes women want (or think they want) more

children. What determines how many children people want? Kingsley Davis speculated, "there is an incompatibility, or tension, between the family on the one hand and the industrial economy on the other."[24] Industrial economies reward people for achievement in the marketplace, whereas family status is ascribed by birth or marriage into a family, clan, or caste. In advanced industrial societies, everything becomes a matter of individual production and consumption, and family obligations are marginalized. Women enter the labor force outside the home, and their careers interfere with their fertility.[25]

Some governments try to promote pro-natal population policies through tax breaks or even direct payment. Buttner and Lutz have argued that East German fertility actually did increase after paid maternity leave benefits were introduced by the government in 1976.[26] In that case, however, the birth rate remained below the replacement level. The cost of children is so high—including the opportunity costs for the mother who is prevented by child rearing from engaging in other activities—that demographer Nathan Keyfitz concluded that voluntary economic incentives could not be influential enough to succeed.[27]

A key factor that can prevent people from having their desired number of children is delay; the longer a woman waits before having her first child, the sooner thereafter she will become infertile due to age. Kohler, Billari and Ortega recently commented, "The majority of the world's population is living in countries with near-replacement or below-replacement fertility."[28] They attributed this largely to delay in childbearing, and suggested that soon fertility in all societies may drop below the replacement level. Prominent among the causes of delay are the trend toward higher education. Governments could possibly increase the birth rate by establishing child-care programs at universities. It could pay for them by ending public support for higher education itself, which could also directly increase the birth rate by driving many women out of college, unless doing so had the paradoxical effect of keeping them in school longer as they struggled to combine studies with a paying job.

The Force of Faith

One of Hollingworth's modes of patriarchal control is religion, yet religious faith, taken by itself, can provide positive benefits and be experienced as either a natural characteristic of one's own self or as a voluntary choice. Many kinds of evidence support the proposition that traditional forms of religion tend to increase the birth rate, although there is some debate whether they do this by restricting women's autonomy.[29] Nations with high rates of religious participation tend to have high birth rates.[30]

In the 1990s, the World Values Surveys asked people in more than fifty nations how often they attended religious services, and I have graphed attendance and fertility of 53 of these nations in Figure 4.2. I have left out Nigeria, because it would be off the chart, with a total fertility rate of 5.53 babies per woman.[31] This high birth rate in part is required to offset a high death rate. According to the World Values Surveys, 89 percent of Nigerians attend religious services every week. The chart names the nations with total fertility rates over 2.00 and weekly church attendance over 40 percent. Although the dots are well spread out in the graph, there is a significant positive correlation between religious attendance and fertility.[32]

Figure 4.2: Fertility and Religious Attendance in 53 Nations

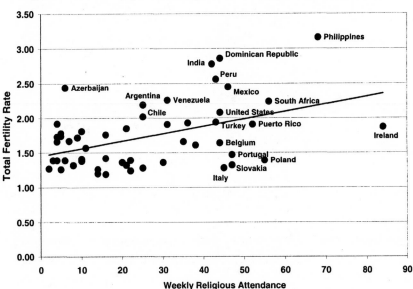

The positive correlation is visible in Figure 4.2, because as your eye scans to the right, the dots tend to rise. I have drawn a trend line, based on statistical analysis, showing the general tendency of fertility to rise as religious attendance rises. Or, one could say that the vertical spread increases and thus the average rises. The nations having religious attendance rates around 50 percent, the vertical band from the Dominican Republic down to Italy, suggest an interesting possibility. Perhaps strong religion *allows* high fertility but does not *cause* it. In comparison, the nations at the left side of the graph are closely grouped together in a band well below the replacement level of 2.1, with the exception of Azerbaijan, a Muslim developing nation whose religious institutions may not have recovered yet from years of Soviet domination.

Individuals within nations differ in a manner similar to nations within the world. A set of questions in the General Social Survey asked American adults, "In general, what do you feel about each of these family sizes?" One of the questions concerned, "a family with four children or more," and another concerned "a family with no children." Another question divided respondents into groups in terms of their beliefs about God. Only 16 Atheists ("I don't believe in God") answered all three questions, and just 6 percent of them felt four or more children were desirable, compared with 38 percent who felt no children were desirable. Agnostics ("I don't know whether there is a God and I don't believe there is any way to find out.") were more positive toward child bearing, 20 percent feeling four or more were desirable, compared with 21 percent who felt none were desirable. Tentative believers ("While I have doubts, I feel that I do believe in God.") were much more positive, 31 percent giving the pro-children answer, versus 17 percent giving the anti-children answer. Among firm believers ("I know God really exists and I have no doubts about it."), fully 43 percent were in favor of four or more children, and only 16 percent felt no children might be desirable.

One of the standard GSS questions asked people what their religious affiliation was, and those who had an affiliation were often asked how strong it was. For example, Protestants would be asked, "Would you call yourself a strong Protestant or a not very strong Protestant?" Some respondents would volunteer that they were between the two alternatives, somewhat strong but not very strong. We can compare members of all religious groups who said their affiliation was strong with those who had professed no religion at all. Among those who claimed strong religion, only 22 percent felt that a family with no children is desirable, compared with 59 percent of nonreligious respondents. In contrast, 50 percent of strongly religious people felt that a family with four children is desirable, compared with only 19 percent of those having no religion. Other GGS family questions tell similar stories. Among strongly religious people, 68 percent feel that having children is one of the most important values, but only 41 percent of nonreligious respondents agree.

A module of the 1996 General Social Survey focused on gender roles, and asked several relevant questions. For example, did the traditional family hurt women? Among American women who said they have no religion, 54 percent claimed that it did, compared with only 33 percent of strongly religious women. In contrast, 42 percent of non-religious women said that women benefited from the traditional family, compared with 52 percent among strongly religious women. Another question asked, "If the husband in a family wants children, but the wife decides that she does not want any children, is it all right for the wife to refuse to have children?" Among non-religious women, 85 percent said it was all right for the wife to refuse, compared with 61 percent of strongly religious women. The 1996 GSS also contained an item about whether it was all right for a husband to refuse to have children, if his wife wanted them, and 70 percent of non-religious men agreed, compared with 53 percent of strongly religious men.

We can look for religious differences on a variety of other fertility-related issues. For example in other versions of the GSS, 81 percent of strongly religious people say, "Sexual relations between two adults of the same sex is always wrong." This view is held by only 37 percent of persons having no religion. Among strongly religious people, 63 percent say, "Divorce in this country should be more difficult to obtain than it is now," compared with 31 percent of the nonreligious. Prior to the 1960s in the United States, divorce was difficult and homosexual behavior was often illegal. Birth control was officially discouraged until the widespread adoption of birth control pills in the 1960s, and there remain some differences of opinion about contraception even today. A large majority of strongly religious people, fully 87 percent, agree, "Birth control information should be available to anyone who wants it." However, agreement is even higher among nonreligious respondents, at 96 percent. Another GSS item concerned teenagers: "Methods of birth control should be available to teenagers between the ages of 14 and 16 if their parents do not approve." Whereas 46 percent of strongly religious respondents agreed, fully 78 percent of the nonreligious did so.

The GSS has included several items about abortion, including: "whether or not you think it should be possible for a pregnant woman to obtain a legal abortion if . . . the woman wants it for any reason?" Among strongly religious respondents, just 26 percent said "yes," compared with 67 percent of nonreligious people. The social-scientific literature examining the religious roots of opposition to abortion is quite vast, and the issue remains politically significant.[33] The controversy reminds us that religion can influence fertility not only through shaping the voluntary decisions of individuals, but also through setting the agenda for governments.

Here, to get clear contrasts, we have been looking just at people who gave extreme responses to a question about how religious they judged themselves to be, comparing those with "strong religion" against those claiming no religion. Given the powerful tendency for fertility rates to collapse in most advanced nations, perhaps only strong religion could do the job. The question then become how one could encourage increased religiousness in a society, without violating principles of separation of church and state. Perhaps the point is that the fertility problem cannot be solved within the standard value assumptions of contemporary secular culture.

In the previous chapter we looked at suicide rates for the 50 American states, finding a small negative correlation between suicide and church membership, which however sank into insignificance when we controlled for residential mobility. Normally, we would not place much credence in a study that merely looked at three variables across 50 cases, and I introduced that simple analyses merely to show that recent data gave results similar to the results of a very much more complex study using older data. I also checked the 50-state correlation between the church member rate and how many children were ever born per 1,000 women, using 2004 data from the Census Bureau.[34] It turns out that religion is only very weakly associated with higher fertility by this very approximate measure.[35] There is an interesting hint that religion deters births out of wedlock, but we cannot be confident that religious attitudes really translate into significant differences in fertility.

There are many possible explanations for the relatively high fertility rate in the United States. For the year 2004, the total fertility rate for non-hispanic white women was about 1.9, compared with 2.8 for hispanic women, so part of the answer may lie in higher fertility among Latin immigrants. Another factor is unplanned births, which are more common among the poor and in socially disorganized communities. In 2004, fully 35.7 percent of births were to unmarried mothers. For better or worse, American birth rates appear to be sustained to some extent by social instability and social problems, rather than by religious traditionalism. The religiousness of the nation is at least partly a response to these social pressures. Thus, if the United States were to become more culturally traditional, it is possible the fertility rate would ironically go down rather than up.[36]

Thinking about Complexity

Many factors combine in obscure ways to determine the fertility rate and the religious census of a society. Thirty years ago, there was great optimism among quantitative sociologists that multivariate statistical analysis could handle the complex interplay of many variables. Certainly much good work has been accomplished by these means, but the level of enthusiasm for the methods is today more realistic, which is to say, more modest. We seldom have rich enough data to measure all the variables accurately, and this is certainly the case for the problem of religion and fertility. Nonetheless, we need to be able to think clearly about complexity.

One way to get a sense of the dynamics of a complex system like society is through mathematical or computer simulations. They may be simpler than reality; they may rely upon too many assumptions, but at least they are dynamic. Even an extremely simple simulation can be instructive.

Imagine a society with exactly 1,000,000 people, divided equally into two groups, 500,000 religious people and 500,000 secular people. Imagine also that the fertility rates differed, with a higher rate among the religious. For the calculations that follow, we will assume the total fertility rate in the religious group is 2.50, and among the secular group it is 1.50. We will ignore infant mortality and assume an equal sex ratio, so the fertility rate required to sustain a population is 2.0 rather than a more realistic 2.1 that we actually find in advanced industrial societies. Our aim is to work with clear assumptions and simple calculations, rather than to construct the most precise possible model of a particular real society.

I am an experienced computer programmer, but these simulations were so simple they could be done with ordinary spreadsheet software. We will do several runs of the simulation, running forward 10 generations each time to see what happens to the total population. The simulations will differ only in terms of one variable: The net rate of conversion between the religious and secular groups. For sake of simplicity, we assume that this conversion takes place before the person starts raising children, and that each child starts out in the same religious group as his or her parent.

Suppose there is no net conversion: secular people become religious at the same rate as religious people become secular. The original population has 500,000 religious people and 500,000 secular people. To calculate how many children the religious people will have, you divide the total fertility rate by 2 (because the total fertility rate refers only to women and humans have two sexes), getting 1.25. Then multiply 1.25 times 500,000, getting 625,000. Similarly, for the secular people, you divide their 1.50 fertility rate by two, getting 0.75, multiply this by 500,000, getting 375,000. Add the results together: 625,000 + 375,000 = 1,000,000. So, this first generation of children is the same size as the generation of their parents, but 62.5 percent religious rather than 50 percent.

Population growth starts with the second generation of children. The 625,000 religious people have 781,250 children, and the 375,000 secular people have 281,250 children. This is a total of 1,062,500 members in this generation, 73.5 percent of whom are religious. As we grind this simulation forward, not only does the population grow, but the fraction religious grows, which has the effect of accelerating the rate of population growth. The tenth generation of children would consist of 4,684,770, of whom 99.4 percent are religious. Once secular people have been wrung out of the population, the 2.50 fertility rate of religious people will apply to the entire society, and it will grow at a constant rate.

The only chance for low-fertility secularism to survive, let alone triumph, is if it can recruit people from the religious group. So, now we will consider what happens if there is a net conversion from religiousness to secularism. That is, some religious people become secular, and some secular people become religious, but more of the converts are children of religious parents who become secular and raise their children in a secular environment.

The second simulation uses a net conversion rate of 10 percent to secularism. Again, at the very beginning 625,000 children are born to religious parents. But ten percent of them convert to secularism, meaning that only 562,500 of the first generation of children become religious parents, and 437,500 are secular parents. The population of the society will grow, and become more religious, but at a slower rate than in the first simulation. The tenth generation of children will consist of 1,623,661 religious people and 559,991 secular people, for a total population of 2,183,652, of whom 74.4 percent are religious.

Especially interesting is the third simulation, in which the net conversion rate to secularism is set at 20 percent. The population remains 1,000,000, generation after generation, with a constant 50-50 split between religious and secular groups. This is perfect stability, perfect sustainability.

If the net rate of conversion to secularism is raised to 30 percent, population decline sets in. Interestingly, the secular part of the population grows for a while, at the expense of the religious group. Both start at 500,000, but the third generation of offspring includes 583,008 secular people, compared with only 334,961 religious people. The tenth generation has a total of only 469,838 people, less than half the original 1,000,000, only 28.0 percent of them religious.

A 50 percent rate of conversion to secularism would be catastrophic for the society. At the end of the simulation, after ten new generations, the total population of the society would have collapsed to 150,751, less than 1/7 of the original size. Just 3.0 percent of the population would be religious.

We can also imagine that more people might be converted to religion than away from it. A net conversion rate of 10 percent in the direction of religion would result, after ten iterations, in a total population of 5,272,534, of whom 99.8 percent were religious. A simulation using a 50 percent net conversion rate to religion ends with 6,652,320 people, approximately 100.0 percent religious. Only 10 secular people would belong to the 10th generation of offspring, an infinitesimal minority lost in the rounding error.

To be sure, real society is far more complicated. There are many religious denominations, each perhaps having its own characteristic fertility rate, and different ways of being non-religious. Rates of conversion between groups undoubtedly fluctuate, as do the fertility rates of different groups, in ways we do not currently know how to predict. Secularization is only one of several factors driving lower fertility rates, although religion is implicated one way or another in the dynamics of the other factors. But it is important to think of society as a complex system, in which secularism and fertility interact in complex ways across different segments of the population.

Can Governments Desecularize?

When governments set out to support religion, does their effort have the effect of increasing fertility and population growth? By coding the descriptions of 196 nations in the 2003 International Religious Freedom Report, Brian Grim and Roger Finke have developed a set of three measures: government favoritism, government regulation, and social regulation.[37] I was able to analyze the connection between each of these measures and fertility for 193 of the nations, as shown in Table 4.1 in the appendix. How government policy affects citizens is partly determined by how competent the government is, quite apart from its intentions. As a very rough check on this distorting factor, I repeated the analysis for the 141 nations outside Africa. The results are a little clearer with the special problems faced by Africa out of the equation, but they are substantially the same either way.

Government favoritism means that tax money goes to support a particular denomination or set of denominations, that the government applies regulations unfairly to the advantage of one religion over others, and that the government invests in religious schools, spreading the message of one religion, and paying clergy salaries. Perhaps surprisingly, favoritism does not appear to increase fertility or population growth. This finding undercuts the idea that governments could sustain the populations of their nations by promoting a particular religion.

Both government regulation and social regulation are connected to higher fertility and population growth, although only moderately. As defined by Grim and Finke, government regulation means prohibiting missionary work, restricting preaching and conversion, interfering with the individual's right to worship, and providing no support for freedom of religion. Social regulation refers to the behavior of organizations outside the government and to the attitudes of individual citizens. In societies with strong social regulation, individuals have markedly negative attitudes toward other religions, conversion from one faith to another, and proselytizing. In such societies, established religions try to prevent others from invading, and there are social movements agitating against some religions. Both kinds of regulation strike me as attributes of traditional societies that take religion very seriously, and thus they may simply be measures of general religiousness, comparable to the measure from the World Values Surveys we used above.

Among the most difficult questions is how scientists might separate the effect of religion in traditional societies from other factors. A number of researchers who have made good attempts to do this argue that religion is at most a contributory factor rather than the fundamental cause of low women's autonomy and high fertility in traditional societies. For example, Shireen Jejeebhoy and Zeba Sathar have reported on a massive interview study carried out in Pakistan and India, comparing women in

Islamic versus Hindu families.[38] One might expect Islamic women to experience less freedom and to be under greater pressures to produce children than Hindu women. But the crucial factor turned out to be the total way of life of people living in different regions. In poor, rural areas, fertility was high, for both religious groups, but in more modern areas education and economic activity raise autonomy for women in both religions.

A good deal of irony can be found in studies of the conditions under which women in poor countries adopt modern birth control methods. Many studies find a connection between education and restriction of fertility, so we jump to the conclusion that educating a girl gives her more modern values and knowledge, encouraging her to take greater charge of reproduction in her own life. However, William Axinn and Jennifer Barber found that in Nepal what really matters was living near schools, not attending them.[39] This suggests that the key change is not so much in the minds of individuals as in the community and the local economy. The birth control practices of the women studied were influenced by their husband's education, their children's opportunities for education, and by the education of others in their neighborhood. Once birth control methods have become widely available, their use may spread through women's networks of friends and relations, quite apart from their own personal formal education.

Using Mozambique as a case study, Victor Agadjanian has shown that information about birth control methods, and receptivity toward using them, can spread through the friendship networks of women who belong to the same church.[40] Agadjanian notes it has long been known that innovations tend to spread from opinion leaders in a community, and that information travels rapidly through dispersed social networks composed of *weak ties*.[41] Thus, a growing religious movement, with many branches spread over a wide territory, provides a social network through which contraceptive practices may spread, from woman to woman, even if the clergy disapprove. Once birth control has become solidly established in the culture, religion may lose importance as a factor either encouraging or discouraging its use. A well-documented example concerns Catholics in the United States. In defiance of their church's opposition to artificial birth control, already by the 1970s American Catholics were using birth control as frequently as Protestants.[42]

Polygamous and Communal Religions

Could population collapse be halted by adopting the unconventional marital practices promoted by a few radical sects? One idea that would probably be attacked on both ethical and fertility-related grounds would be to permit polygamy. Certainly one could argue in the present cultural climate, when many people find gay marriage a reasonable idea, that collective marriage should also be allowed and given the same tax and other economic benefits as conventional, heterosexual monogamy. Polygamy has three forms: *polygyny* (a man having multiple wives, which is not uncommon in pre-industrial societies), *polyandry* (a woman having multiple husbands, which is rare but has existed), and unrestricted *polygamy* in which any combination of husbands and wives is permissible. A key ethical issue is that polygyny is associated with low status for women; for example, ending polygyny in Islamic societies is said to be one of the prerequisites for female equality.[43]

The fertility issue is that polygyny actually reduces the overall birth rate in society, even though it increases the number of offspring for the minority of men who have two or more wives.[44] Among the factors determining fertility in polygynous families is the age difference between the husband and his wives, whether all of them actually live together, and differences of seniority among the wives.[45]

It is possible that polygamy in some form might be a useful part of the fertility-enhancing mechanisms under some social conditions. For example, polygyny was practiced in the early days of Mormonism, and one explanation is that there were more women than men, and the only way all women could be members of families was to allow men to have more than one wife. According to Nels Anderson, increased fertility was an explicit goal of Mormon polygyny, in the context of imbalanced sex ratio.[46] Guttentag and Secord have argued that an excess of marriageable females—or deficit of males—can exacerbate social problems among modern populations, such as African-Americans.[47] Guttentag and Secord say that when there are "too many women" the men have little need to be faithful, because they can easily find another partner. Men with unstable family relations are more likely to commit crimes, and often their children will suffer.

The kind of Atheistic communism practiced by the Soviet bloc is not helpful. Post-Soviet societies have among the lowest fertility rates. Figure 4.1 showed a Russian rate of only 1.27, and 1.40 for Ukraine. The CIA World Factbook shows very low current rates for Belarus (1.39),

Bulgaria (1.38), Czech Republic (1.20), Estonia (1.39), Hungary (1.32), Latvia (1.26), Lithuania (1.19), and even Poland (1.39) where the Roman Catholic Church was so influential in promoting national liberation from Soviet dominance. It is interesting to note that prior to reunification, the communist and capitalist parts of Germany had almost identical fertility rates.[48]

Two centuries of voluntary communal experiments in the United States have explored a wide range of alternative family structures, and their almost universal failure might be attributed either to the fact that their deviant systems were not supported by the surrounding legal and economic system, or to defects in their social design. The communes that lasted longest were organized around radical religious beliefs, so one would think that religious communes could be a way of successfully institutionalizing the high fertility of sectarian religion.[49] However, fertility rates tended to be low in historical religious American "utopian communities," because some like the Shakers practiced celibacy, and because others delayed child bearing until they had become economically well-established.

Among the most famous nineteenth-century social experiments was the "perfectionist" commune at Oneida, New York. Founded by a Yale-educated intellectual named John Humphrey Noyes, Oneida sought to achieve spiritual perfection and publicized its radical philosophy aggressively through publications, including one of the classic books on communes, *History of American Socialisms*, by Noyes himself.[50] Oneida practiced a form of group marriage, in which all adults were in some sense married to each other. Exclusive love was forbidden, and if a man and woman became "too sticky," they were separated. The children were raised collectively, and urged to avoid very close emotional attachments to their own parents.

Noyes taught the men at Oneida a form of birth control based on controlling ejaculation, and he advocated *amative intercourse* designed to share love among the adults but without producing children. Believing that the most spiritually advanced members could engender children who were already on the way to perfection, Noyes arranged for an elite group of men, himself most prominent among them, to father many of the children. Under the guidance of senior members, adults were encouraged to engage in perpetual courtship, constantly changing partners for amative intercourse. This system collapsed after Noyes fled Oneida, weakened by his advancing age and threatened by outside critics. Oneida cannot provide a blueprint for twenty-first century group marriage experiments, but it provides a useful historical example to compare with newer ideas.

One contemporary communal religious movement with somewhat high fertility, called The Family or The Children of God, shows it is at least possible to imagine that "communist" alternatives to free markets could be one solution to fertility collapse. I studied this group in very close detail, by three methods: observing life in communes in three nations, interviewing members about their past histories, and administering a large questionnaire to 1,025 members.[51] I selected this group for study in part because it was the most radical American-born religious movement that was willing to cooperate in a study, providing questionnaire data to compare members with the general public. The general finding was that members do not differ very much from non-members, and they are certainly not innately strange, crazy, or pathological. Instead, The Family consists of normal people living within a distinctive culture.

The group began as the immediate family of David Brandt Berg, the son and grandson of Protestant evangelists, and recruited its first significant number of members at Huntington Beach, California, in the late 1960s. It would be perhaps too simplistic to say that The Family was a marriage of sectarian Protestantism with the Hippie Movement, but there is some truth to that description. At the time, the Hippies were part of a diverse *counterculture*, a term Milton Yinger defined as "a set of norms and values of a group that sharply contradict the dominant norms and values of the society of which the group is a part."[52] When the counterculture crashed around 1970, many participants turned to religion as a way of "getting saved from the sixties."[53] The Family rejected some aspects of the counterculture, such as drug use, but accepted others, such as sexual freedom.

By the mid-1970s, the group had begun to spread out across the world, and Berg had developed a new kind of ministry to non-members based on giving God's love in erotic form. Called "flirty-fishing" or "FF-ing," this ministry seems to have gained the group supporters but not a significant number of members, involving to at least a mild degree as many as a million non-members, over 200,000 of which may have reached sexual orgasm. This practice, ended in 1987 for strategic as well as hygienic reasons, contributed to the group's notoriety, and was a chief justification for episodes in which government authorities in several nations seized about 600 children from the group, before returning them traumatized by the ill-advised attempts to rescue them.

More relevant to our current discussion, in varying degrees over the years the Family has practiced sexual sharing among adults within the group, not directed by the leadership as at Oneida but decided by the rank and file members who were involved. Members live in communes distributed around the world, living primarily off donations rather than paid jobs, and schooling their children at home. Thus, they are a relatively closed social world, in which individuals, couples, and groups frequently move from one city or country to another. Often, adults who may or may not be married, find themselves in a commune without a partner, and others in the commune may take it upon themselves to satisfy the individual's erotic needs. According to the General Social Survey, 78.4 percent of Americans feel it is always wrong for a married person to have sexual relations with someone other than his or her wife or husband, but my questionnaire found that only 1.2 percent of Family members feel this way.[54]

When GSS respondents are asked what the ideal number of children for a couple might be, 54.7 percent say 2 children, 20.9 percent say 3 children, and the remaining quarter of respondents are split up among a large number of different answers. In contrast, among Family respondents to my questionnaire, only 2.4 percent say 2 children, 6.0 percent say 3 children, and fully 59.5 percent say "as many as you want." That is, they reject the very idea of calculating how many children to have.

I also looked at how many children adults age 30 and over actually have. For the general American public, the average is 2.1, while for the Family it is 5.4. In the Family, 10.7 percent of those age 30 or over have 6 children, and 40.3 percent have 7 or more.[55] Thus, the culture and social structure of this radical religious group do indeed support higher fertility. If a significant minority of people in society belonged to such groups, say one third, then the future of the population would be assured.

It is my impression that the unusual sexual norms and family structure in the group compensate to some extent for instability. It is not merely that members move geographically often, although that is very important. The group also seems to have a level of divorce and marital separation that rivals that of the surrounding society, and might even be higher. To at least some extent, the culture of the Family buffers people against this instability, and I have seen communes accept a mother with her children even without a husband. I cannot say how well the system functions, but at least in principle a religious community can offset the damage from marital instability.

As was the case with the nineteenth-century American communes, a crucial question concerns how stable the group as a whole is. I do not have exact figures, but it appears that the Family has lost a considerable number of second-generation members to the surrounding society, and membership growth halted years ago. Members are economically dependent upon the larger society, but not social integrated into it. Presumably, society itself would need to change significantly, before high-fertility communal movements would find it a conducive environment for long survival and even growth. It is at least conceivable that properly-designed laws permitting but regulating group marriage or polygamy might possibly strengthen marriage and fertility in modern societies. There is no way to know without trying.

Conclusion

Peter McDonald, head of the Demography and Sociology Program at Australian National University, is among the demographers who believe there is a secular solution to collapsing fertility rates.[56] He argues that attempts to return to a traditional family-oriented culture will fail, noting that fertility rates are actually higher among the most liberal advanced industrial societies than those like Italy that have more traditional sex roles. Further, he says that the current problem is not secularization but the new market economic system, which orients people toward short-term economic gain and stresses competition between individuals rather than family cooperation. McDonald believes that advanced nations could significantly increase fertility if they provided significant economic benefits to women who have children, gender equality, and a high level of economic security to all citizens. Admitting that his policies might face great political opposition, he advises action in three areas:

1. Financial incentives, such as regular cash-payments to parents, tax rebates, and housing subsidies.
2. Family-friendly work arrangements, like paid maternity and paternity leave, subsidized childcare, and flexible work hours.
3. Broad social change, including designing jobs about child raising, greater family responsibilities for men, and building social attitudes that encourage marriage and child birth.

The reader can judge whether it would be feasible to adopt such policies at all vigorously in his or her own political environment. We have already seen that it is not certain whether government attempts to strengthen religion would positively influence fertility. We have also considered the radical idea of encouraging communal religions that would experiment with alternative family structures. Perhaps governments could reasonably remove the current prohibitions against alternative family forms, and that plan might be politically feasible in advanced democratic societies.

Perhaps religion might restore fertility, not by returning to traditional ways of life, nor through government support, but through a mechanism many religious people find uncomfortable: evolution by natural selection. If there were a diversity of religions, including some that were novel and radical, a few would have high birth rates. If the children were strictly raised in their parents' faith, those fertile faiths would grow. A more complex version of our computer simulations could project the conditions under which the society would be demographically sustainable, through the constant emergence of new cults. However, this solution to the birth-dearth is dubious. For this approach to work, government would need to give the groups considerable freedom to set their own norms for behavior, which might often conflict with national laws. Thus, we must be alert to other possible solutions associated with secularization.

5
Crime and Deviance

> Are we not standing
> on the threshold of a period
> which we might at first designate
> negatively as beyond morality?
> —*Beyond Good and Evil,*[1]
> Friedrich Nietzsche

For many years, criminologists ignored religion. For example, only 4 of 28 criminology textbooks checked by Stack and Kanavy in 1983 mentioned religion in their indexes.[2] Social science has often been accused of Atheism, and it is true that many sociologists may have ignored religion either because they despised it or because they falsely imagined it was a thing of the past. Some criminologists may have ignored the role of religion in preventing crime because their aim was to provide a scientific basis for government policies, either in the area of law enforcement or in devising social programs for at-risk youth. With this goal in mind, religion may not have seemed a legitimate tool of government policy, in the modern age of strict separation between church and state. Since around 1980, however, a considerable amount of social science research has explored the power religion may have to deter crime, delinquency, and hedonistic deviance. It would be too much to claim that we know all the answers, now, but the topic can be discussed on a fairly solid empirical basis.

Criminology and the Sociology of Deviance

The social science of crime, delinquency and deviant behavior is exceedingly rich in theory, so we will begin with a theoretical overview. The theories in the field are so rich and numerous, however, that we will do just a brief reconnaissance of ideas that may be especially relevant for the broader debates covered in this book. Because the power of religion apparently varies across kinds of deviance, I have divided the discussion into three main sections where that power does appear to operate differently: petty crime such as larceny or theft, violent crime including homicide, and hedonistic deviance such as alcohol or drug use. A section will also be devoted to what I called the *Stark effect*, a phenomenon discovered by Rodney Stark that illuminates central issues concerning religion and deviant behavior.

Supernatural theories of religion argue that God directly helps believers live righteous lives. Different faiths understand differently the role of the individual's free will in the equation, but most hope that supernatural power can help a religious person avoid committing crimes or wallowing in vices. In the powerful imagery of the twenty-third psalm, God shepherds his followers along a moral path: "He restoreth my soul: he leadeth me in the paths of righteousness for his name's sake" (Psalm 23:2).

Fear of divine punishment may be a powerful motivator of good behavior for some people.[3] The Bible contains many divine threats, such as those in Leviticus 26:14–22:

> But if ye will not hearken unto me, and will not do all these commandments;
>
> And if ye shall despise my statutes, or if your soul abhor my judgments, so that ye will not do all my commandments, but that ye break my covenant:
>
> I also will do this unto you; I will even appoint over you terror, consumption, and the burning ague, that shall consume the eyes, and cause sorrow of heart: and ye shall sow your seed in vain, for your enemies shall eat it.
>
> And I will set my face against you, and ye shall be slain before your enemies: they that hate you shall reign over you; and ye shall flee when none pursueth you.
>
> And if ye will not yet for all this hearken unto me, then I will punish you seven times more for your sins.
>
> And I will break the pride of your power; and I will make your heaven as iron, and your earth as brass:
>
> And your strength shall be spent in vain: for your land shall not yield her increase, neither shall the trees of the land yield their fruits.
>
> And if ye walk contrary unto me, and will not hearken unto me; I will bring seven times more plagues upon you according to your sins.

I will also send wild beasts among you, which shall rob you of your
children, and destroy your cattle, and make you few in number;
and your high ways shall be desolate.

Such wrathful words may scare people into conformity, quite apart
from whether God actually exists. Other humans, including the police,
may mouth threats, but a clever thief may deceive them, or a swift killer
may avoid capture. God knows all, believers think, and sees all. Thus
divine surveillance may add strength to terrestrial law enforcement, all
the more important in societies and circumstances when ordinary detec-
tive work is unsuccessful.

Religion may also inculcate a sense of values, a feeling that certain
actions are fundamentally immoral. Sociologists of the functionalist
school, advocating the societal theory of religion, distinguish values from
divine surveillance. Supposedly, a person internalizes values, so that a
small set of overarching principles guides every aspect of his or her life.
A person does not conform because he fears God, but because he feels
that God's law is morally right. As Robert K. Merton argued, values give
a person the goals worth striving for in life, thus binding the individual's
fate to that of the surrounding society.[4]

On the other hand, exchange theory has long been skeptical of the
concept of values, and of the claim that people internalize abstract principles of behavior.[5] In A Theory of Religion, Rodney Stark and I argued
that people learn a large number of very specific things, including what
detailed actions are rewarding in daily life, and then gradually abstract
slightly more general principles from them.[6] First people gain specific
explanations about how to handle tiny details of life, and only with difficulty do they develop more general explanations. This led me to write an
article for a linguistics encyclopedia suggesting that values were mere
verbal principles, useful as texts for sermons but having little real power
over human behavior.[7] That is, values are compensators, expressing people's hopes that human behavior is governed by transcendent principles.
Thus, religion could be closely connected to values, but values could be
powerless.

I was thinking about these issues, not long ago, when it occurred to
me that cognitive science might have something new to say about the
reality of cultural values. I had a long discussion with my colleague,
Rodney Cocking, who was then managing the Human Cognition and
Perception Program of the National Science Foundation. He recast the
problem in terms of the transfer of learning from one kind of situation to

another. If we learn a principle in one area, can we easily apply it in another area? Cocking reported that cognitive research on education had found that transfer of learning was very difficult, and he pointed to a report he had co-authored for the National Academy of Sciences that surveyed the research as of 1999.[8] Clearly, we need research specifically designed to test theories of cultural values, but Cocking provided the basis for a preliminary judgment. Religion could possibly enable overarching values, but only with great difficultly and thus only when it had a high degree of influence over believers.

I believe this observation is objectively very important, but it is impressed upon me personally by a poignant fact. Soon after we talked, Rodney Cocking was murdered by an investment fraud artist he had unluckily become involved with. The killing of a scientist who still had much to contribute reminds us why we need to understand the factors that shape crime, and reinforces the transcendent value of every bit of knowledge science gains us.

Religious organizations typically enmesh communicants in a congregation or social network, and these relationships may deter deviant behavior through social influence. Almost any societal institution that provides strong social relationships thereby enforces conformity to the morality shared by most members, but religion may do this more effectively by asserting the importance of moral behavior in those relationships. However, one could also argue that secular schools do this, as does military service, and that membership on any effective work team in business or industry imposed a morality.

One of the standard explanations of crime and deviance, advocated by Travis Hirschi and a number of other criminologists and sociologists, is often called *control theory*. This perspective asserts that people who lack strong, stable, social bonds are relatively free to deviate.[9] People who do possess social bonds must take into account the wishes of their associates when contemplating violating a norm, and concern about possible loss of their valuable relationships weighs in their deliberations against deviance.

Quite apart from the effect of religion on individual behavior, it may serve to organize the community against crime. The commandments of a religion put on record the rules people are supposed to follow, drawing a clear line between normal and deviant behavior. Modern legal codes may also accomplish this, relying upon mass media such as murder mysteries and television crime news, to publicize the rules. Perhaps religious people are more likely to support collective action to block crime, such as increased funding for police and courts. One question regularly asked in the General Social Survey is, "are we spending too much, too little, or about the right amount on halting the rising crime rate." Combining all surveys up through the one done in 2002, 70.1 percent of 11,283 Protestants said that too little was being spent, indicating they wanted more effort to control crime. Among 4,590 Catholics, 70.6 percent felt this way, and 72.4 of 397 Jews. In contrast, just 60.0 percent of 1,317 nonreligious respondents felt too little was being spent to control crime. While this is a majority, it is much less than the majorities in the three religious groups.

There are also several ways in which religion can conceivably cause deviance rather than prevent it. Perhaps people who believe in an immortal soul feel that killing somebody is not so serious, because the victim will continue to live on in some supernatural context. Some religious groups oppose things that the state may require, such as military service, blood transfusions, or secular schooling. Other groups may practice something as a matter of faith that is banned by the state, such as psychedelic drug use, polygamy, or female genital mutilation. And other groups may feel so strongly that something permitted by the state is immoral that they violate laws of various degrees of severity in pressing their case to have it banned. In the modern context, abortion is the obvious example, and people may violate minor laws regulating public demonstrations even if one does not want to include the cases of violence against abortion clinics.

Probably the most serious examples in which religion causes or encourages crime are cases of inter-group conflict. I cannot confidently evaluate the current debate about the extent to which the "War on Terror" is a case of radical sects attacking civilization versus Islamic martyrs resisting a Christian crusade. The apparent complicity of European churches in the Nazi crimes of the Holocaust is a question beyond my capacity to answer. I see some reason to believe that the Nazis themselves were a religious cult, given that the leader claimed to be guided by spiritual experiences; top Nazis were attracted to a range of New Age fads, and the movement's Wagnerian symbolism gave the Third Reich a Nordic Pagan veneer.

Of enduring relevance are the numerous episodes in the Bible when the ancient Hebrews and their God commit acts against non-Hebrews that would be crimes if committed by a citizen of a modern society. I recognize that this is an inflammatory topic, but it must be addressed if we want to understand ways in which religion may encourage deviance.

Abraham forced his wife into prostitution in the Pharaoh's service (Genesis 12:14–20). Other acts that modern standards might call crimes were Jehovah's killing of the first born of Egypt, when he might simply have had a personal chat with Pharaoh about letting the Hebrews go (Exodus 11:5; Exodus 12:29), and the way the Hebrews borrowed valuable items from their Egyptian neighbors with no intent of returning them, which is a deceitful form of theft (Exodus 3:22; Exodus 11:2; Exodus 12:35).

Two points of some significance deserve mention here. First, the Bible can be read as an historical record of the gradual moral awakening of human beings, and thus modern morality should be different from that of ancient days. The particular crimes mentioned in the paragraph above took place before Moses had received commandments such as "Thou shalt not steal" (Exodus 20:15). For Christians, the moral awakening continued when Jesus added a commandment to the traditional ten: "For this, Thou shalt not commit adultery, Thou shalt not kill, Thou shalt not steal, Thou shalt not bear false witness, Thou shalt not covet; and if there be any other commandment, it is briefly comprehended in this saying, namely, Thou shalt love thy neighbour as thyself" (Romans 13:9).

Second, traditional religions promulgated moral codes intended for the particular tribe or other social group, and the modern attempt to cultivate universal morality that applies to all humans is a very difficult expansion of faith to include unbelievers. At one point, the Lord says, "Ask of me, and I shall give thee the heathen for thine inheritance, and the uttermost parts of the earth for thy possession. Thou shalt break them with a rod of iron; thou shalt dash them in pieces like a potter's vessel" (Psalm 2:8–9). In the ancient world, and indeed in any world where societies compete for scarce resources, religion may often serve one group to the disadvantage of others. To do this, it establishes a moral order within the group, but urges blatant expediency in dealing with outsiders. Edward B. Reeves has argued that, "One implication of the linkage between religion and morality is that moral compassion ends at the boundary of the religious community."[10]

Property Crime and Other Lesser Offenses

In 1935, William F. Ogburn examined the correlation between the crime rate and church membership as reflected in the 1926 census of churches we used back in Chapter 3, for 16 large, 24 medium, and 22 smaller cities.[11] In each case he found a negative correlation, implying that religion deterred crime. Remarkably for the period in which he wrote, Ogburn used statistical controls, but the small number of cities he was analyzing in each group left him uncertain whether the apparent effect of religion was robust. Criminologists have long known that different kinds of crime pattern differently, and thus should be analyzed separately, when possible. Ogburn had used a combined crime rate, lumping together homicide, rape, robbery, assault, burglary, and larceny. A later analysis concerning convictions for seven separate crimes uncovered strong correlations linking both burglary and larceny to low rates of church membership.[12] Unique among the datasets I have seen, forgery was also included, and it had the strongest negative correlations with church membership. The correlation between murder and church membership was negative, but too weak to give us any confidence.[13] Given the consistent differences we find between relatively mild crimes and serious ones, this chapter will consider serious crimes like homicide in a separate section.

Evidence that religion can deter lesser offenses abounds in studies comparing crime and church membership rates across cities. Working with two of his graduate students, Daniel Doyle and Lori Kent, Stark analyzed the data from 1971, parallel to the suicide research the group had done.[14] Again, there were strongly negative correlations between church membership and both burglary and larceny, and there was an almost identical negative correlation with the general category of property crimes.[15] I myself examined the 1980 data for 75 metropolitan areas.[16] As appendix Table 5.1 shows, church membership had a strongly negative correlation with both burglary and larceny. I tried a rather aggressive set of control variables, and both relationships survived, revealing the robustness of religion's power to deter these property crimes. However, religion appeared to have significantly more power to deter larceny, the mildest of property crimes counted by government agencies, than burglary which is more serious.[17]

Whenever possible, social scientists should apply more than one methodology to a problem, and for petty crimes it is also possible to employ questionnaire research. In the period 1973–1984, the General Social Survey asked random samples of Americans, "Have you ever received a ticket, or been charged by the police, for a traffic violation—other than for illegal parking?" Identical fractions of Protestants and Catholics had been ticketed, 44.4 percent of each, and 44.9 percent of Jews. But 60.8 percent of those with no religion had been ticketed. The GSS also asked, "Were you ever picked up, or charged, by the police, for any (other) reason whether or not you were guilty?" Only 5.1 percent of Jewish respondents replied "yes," compared with 9.8 percent of Protestants and 11.1 percent of Catholics. Fully 25.1 percent of those with no religion admitted being picked up by the police. Thus those with no religion were more likely than religious people to have these negative interactions with police by a difference of about 15 percentage points.

A great wealth of questionnaire data exists concerning adolescents, and we will explore its complexities in the following section. For example, in 2002, Christian Smith and Robert Faris reported findings on religion and delinquency from a survey of 2,478 American high school seniors.[18] Of those who said religion was very important to them, only 25.1 percent said they had ever "received a ticket (or been stopped and warned) for moving violations, such as speeding, running a stop light, or improper passing," compared with 39.2 percent of those for whom religion was not important. Religious students were consistently less likely to report they had been in trouble with police, stolen items, or vandalized property. Of course, it is possible that religious students are more concerned about making a good impression, so some religious delinquents may lie, claiming to be more virtuous than they truly are. That point brings us to one of the best sociological studies of the 1960s, that set the standard for high quality delinquency research.

The Stark Effect

When Rodney Stark was at the University of California, Berkeley, his colleague Travis Hirschi carried out a major questionnaire study of 4,077 adolescents, to test competing theories of juvenile delinquency.[19] *Control theory*, which Hirschi himself advocated, holds that delinquency results when the individual's bond to society is weak, for example when he or she lacks attachments to other people. *Strain theory* asserts that delinquency can be caused by frustrations, as when the individual finds that he or she cannot attain the values extolled by society through the use of legitimate means, and it predicts that children from disadvantaged households will be more likely to commit crimes.[20] *Subcultural deviance theory* argues that adolescents who belong to a deviant subculture, consisting of other adolescents who are already delinquent, will be influenced to commit delinquent acts.[21] In addition to comparing these competing theories empirically, Hirschi collaborated with Stark to explore the power of religion to deter delinquency.

This study had a number of strengths. For one thing, Hirschi obtained additional information to assess delinquency, including school records and police lists of which adolescents had gotten into trouble. Thus, the study was not entirely dependent upon what the adolescents claimed about their own behavior. By collaborating with Stark, who at the time was the chief collaborator with Charles Y. Glock, the preeminent survey researcher on religion, Hirschi assured that the religion items in his questionnaire would be good ones.[22] This excellent set of data revealed that religious adolescents were no less likely to be delinquent than their non-religious classmates.[23] That is, *religion seemed to have no power to deter delinquency.*

This was not the first study to get this result, because back in 1928 Hugh Hartshorne and Mark A. May had discovered that children who attended Sunday school were no less likely to become delinquent than children who avoided this experience of religious indoctrination.[24] However, the 1920s Hartshorne and May study was largely forgotten, and it was methodologically vastly inferior to the 1960s study. Hirschi and Stark had convincingly shown that adolescents who believed in the supernatural sanctions represented by the Devil and life after death were just as likely to commit delinquent acts as were nonbelievers. Furthermore, church attendance did not show the negative association with delinquency that the societal or functional theory of religion predicted, and that clergy long claimed. Widely cited and reprinted, this study was taken by many non-religious social scientists as proof that religion was moribund and irrelevant in the modern world.

Some subsequent studies appeared to confirm the Hirschi and Stark findings, notably research published by Steven R. Burkett and Mervin White five years later, who reported that religion failed to deter larceny among the young people who responded to their questionnaire.[25] I myself carried out a questionnaire study of 1,465 college students, finding no tendency of religion to deter larceny, vandalism, or burglary.[26] Criminologist Robert Crutchfield and I also used the same dataset to see if traditional sex role ideology, a different kind of belief that might be related to religion, had any effect. Hypothetically, culturally traditional girls might be less delinquent than feminist ones, and traditional boys might be more delinquent because of their macho values, but we found no differences on these property crimes.[27]

The Hirschi and Stark study had been done in northern California, and the research done by Burkett, White, Crutchfield, and myself were done in the Pacific northwest area of the United States. During the 1970s and 1980s, however, studies done outside the American far west found that religion did indeed seem to have some power to deter larceny and similar forms of delinquency.[28] At this point in this book, we should be alert to the possibility that religion's influence is highly variable, notably across geographic boundaries, but twenty years ago the conflicting results posed quite a puzzle.

Working with two graduate students, Lori Kent and Daniel P. Doyle, Stark attacked the problem.[29] Noticing that the negative results had come from the Pacific region of the United States, where our team's research had already shown that organized religion was especially weak, Stark set out to examine the geographic variation. Re-analyzing data collected by other researchers, he found that religion deterred delinquency in the highly religious community of Provo, Utah, but not in the highly secular city of Seattle, Washington. Re-analysis of a national dataset showed that religion's power to deter delinquency was strong in religious areas of the United States, and weak in secular areas. Here is how Stark himself expresses the principle in a later publication:

> Religious individuals will be less likely than those who are not religious to commit delinquent acts, but only in communities where the majority of people are actively religious.[30]

I would like to report the current scientific status of the Stark effect, now that more than two decades have passed since its discovery, but I am not sure that we really know much more now than we did then. A few social scientists interpreted the Stark effect merely to mean that the social context matters, but then they did empirical studies that defined context very differently from a religious community, and thus obtained results that are not really relevant.[31] Recent reviews of the literature related to "Hellfire and Delinquency" tend to dismiss disagreements between studies as a sign that studies failing to find a powerful religion effect must have been methodologically flawed.[32] One rather good review article described the Stark effect in some detail, examined high quality empirical studies, then concluded that religion almost certainly did deter delinquency, without ever really engaging the possibility that its power to do so might depend on the existence of a religious community.[33]

A research study published by Lisa Pearce and Dana Haynie in 2004 is very much influenced by the Stark effect, but takes its logic in a somewhat different direction.[34] Pearce and Haynie analyzed an excellent dataset, the National Longitudinal Study of Adolescent Health (Add

Health). A survey wave in 1995 obtained data about the religiousness of 10,444 children and their mothers, and a second wave in 1996 determined if the adolescents had committed any delinquent acts.

Especially interesting for purposes of this book, when both mother and child in the Add Health study were religious, the child was very unlikely to have committed delinquent acts. There was a high risk of delinquency, if the mother was religious but the child was not. Remarkably, there was also a high risk of delinquency if the child was religious but the mother was not. This is not exactly the Stark effect, but it documents a similar situation when the personal religiousness of an adolescent does not apparently restrain delinquency, without the support of a religious environment (in this case the home rather than the community). Finally, the situation where neither the child nor the mother is religious may suggest the common pattern for a highly secular society. Of the four situations, this turns out to be the one with the second-lowest level of delinquency, higher than if both are religious but lower than either of the situations in which mother and child disagree.

There is some possibility that the apparent power of religion to deter delinquency in religious communities is spurious. For example, perhaps religiousness is merely a marker for conformity. Adolescents who conform are religious. Adolescents who conform are non-delinquent. They follow all the rules. Adolescents who break the rules, for whatever reason, will abandon religion as they embrace delinquency. In secular communities, religiousness is not a marker for conformity, so many kids who are conformist lack religiousness, and this implies nothing about them being delinquent. But for present purposes, let us grant that religion deters delinquency in religious communities but not in secular ones. What does this imply?

First of all, as Stark himself noted, it means that the influence of religion operates socially, not individually. But take this a step further. *The Stark effect implies that religious beliefs are false.* The Stark effect implies that if God exists, he chooses not to help religious adolescents live better lives than their infidel peers. A distant, unhelpful god like that is not the concept of deity that most people hold.

Religion may help deter delinquency and petty adult crimes in religious communities. But it apparently does so through the social relationships of the community, rather than by divine intervention. That is, the societal or functionalist theory may be true, and the social exchange theory may be true, but the supernatural theory of religion is not, with respect to faith's deterrence of delinquency.

Serious Crime

Our consideration of the power of religion to deter homicide and other serious crimes will be brief. Precisely because these crimes are serious, they are rare and we cannot expect people to be candid about them. Therefore, questionnaire research can play only a very minor role. Marc Hauser and Peter Singer of Harvard University found no difference in how religious and non-religious research subjects responded to moral dilemmas that involved the possible death of a person.[35] There is a huge distance from mere attitudes about killing to actually taking a life.

In the 1926 data for 48 American states, that we examined earlier, and in the 1971 data on metropolitan areas, there are extremely small negative correlations between church membership and the murder rate.[36] I looked at homicide and church member rates for 78 large American cities in 1926, finding no tendency of religious cities to have less homicide.[37] My 1980 dataset showed absolutely no ability of religion to deter homicide, comparing across metropolitan areas, with an infinitesimal correlation that is actually on the plus side.[38] In Chapter 3, we found that suicide rates from the year 2002 for the 50 U.S. states showed only a weak negative correlation with the church membership rate. The 2002 homicide rate has a vanishingly small negative correlation with this measure of religion.[39]

The study by Gregory S. Paul that we mentioned in Chapter 3, comparing well-being across 18 prosperous democracies, did not find a connection between religiousness and homicide. Yes, the United States is religious and has a high murder rate, but the other 17 advanced nations showed no connection between faith and killing, either positive or negative.[40]

The fact that religion seems to have some ability to deter larceny, but none to deter homicide, suggests that the Ten Commandments have differing power. "Thou shalt not steal" has more power than "Thou shalt not kill." Perhaps the motives that cause murder are simply too powerful to be blocked by mere words, ideals, or values. On the other hand, one sees much killing in the Bible, and at times religion may encourage killing. Faith often is pressed into service to justify loyalty during war, when the national goal is killing. As Yaakov Ariel documents, many Christians deny that Christianity was complicit in the European Holocaust, using the tautological argument that anyone who was a Nazi could not really have been a Christian.[41] Both sides in the current War on Terror seek transcendental authority for their actions, although this is more obvious for the radical Islamist side.

Four other crimes were studied with the 1971 and 1980 data, and they fall between larceny or homicide in severity: burglary, robbery, assault, and rape. Like larceny, burglary is a kind of stealing, but it involves breaking into a home or other building, and thus is more severe. It has a solid negative correlation with church membership, but weaker than the larceny correlation. Robbery is theft in which the criminal steals from the victim by force or the threat of force, and assault is a violent crime that does not cost the victim his or her life. In the 1980 data, controlling for the measure of social instability (percent of the population who moved in the past five years) erases the correlations entirely for burglary, robbery, and assault, as shown in appendix Table 5.1. Adding other control variables (percent of families that are in poverty, percent of the population that is African American, and the percent of adults who are divorced) restores those modest correlations. Thus, crimes of medium severity may possibly be deterred by religion, but religion's power against them is much weaker than it is against the very mild crime of larceny.

The story for rape is slightly different, in the 1980 data. Like the three crimes just described, rape loses its moderate negative correlation with the church member rate when a statistical control for social instability is introduced, but adding other control variables does not restore it. However, the most powerful variable explaining the rape rate is the divorce rate, and it is possible to argue that by holding families together religion may deter rape indirectly.

Writing in the *Journal of Law and Economics*, Paul Scott Heaton seeks to answer the question, "Does Religion Really Reduce Crime?"[42] His study explicitly replicates my study with the 1980 data, using data from 2000. Comparing his results with mine, he says, "The pattern of correlations is remarkably similar across the two studies despite the 20 year difference in time, with church membership negatively and significantly correlated with rape, assault, burglary, and larceny in both studies." But he then carries out a more sophisticated statistical analysis than I did. The result is that all the correlations vanish, and religion is left without any apparent ability to deter homicide, burglary, robbery, assault, rape, or even larceny in the most recent data.

I believe we should not yet give up on the hypothesis that religion has the power to deter larceny and some kinds of juvenile delinquency, at least under certain circumstances. I wish we had a greater variety of data on which to test religion's effects on serious crimes, if any. But at this point we should have no confidence that religion can prevent serious crimes.

Hedonistic Deviance

Some of the kinds of behavior discussed in this section are crimes, some have been considered criminal in the past but are not crimes today, and others are considered vices by many people but have seldom if even been criminalized. To the extent that some are illegal, they are victimless crimes.[43] They are also behaviors about which different cultures disagree to some extent. Probably all cultures, secular as well as religious, discourage theft and murder, but not all discourage alcohol, recreational drugs, or sexual experimentation. Religious traditions may differ on these issues, even as religious people may differ from the non-religious.

For example, the General Social Survey has asked a number of questions about attitudes toward various sensual or hedonistic behaviors, and in a few cases about whether the respondent engages in the particular behavior. Figure 5.1 illustrates the complexity of the differences. The first two questions concern alcohol: "Do you ever have occasion to use any alcoholic beverages such as liquor, wine, or beer, or are you a total abstainer?" "Which answer comes closest to how often you go to a bar or tavern?" Interestingly, the first row of figures shows the Protestants are less likely to drink alcohol than Catholics or Jews, whereas the differences between Catholics, Jews, and non-religious people are insignificant. The pattern for going to a bar or tavern is quite complex. The percent who never do this is highest for Protestants, which makes sense given that fewer of them drink at all. Although almost identical percentages of the three other groups drink, they differ significantly in whether they do it in bars.

The GSS question asked respondents how often they go to bars. Among people having no religion, 42.2 percent visit bars at least once a month, and 17.2 percent do so several times a week. These figures compare with 32.3 percent and 11.7 percent for Catholics, 24.3 and 9.1 for Jews, and 21.6 and 7.6 for Protestants. Figure 5.1 does not distinguish different kinds of Protestants, but other research has shown that conservative Protestants are much less likely to drink, or to drink often, than liberal Protestants, in both the United States and Canada.[44]

Figure 5.1: Religion and Hedonism

Behavior	Religious Affiliation			
	Protestant	Catholic	Jewish	None
Uses any alcoholic beverages.	63.8%	84.3%	83.4%	84.9%
Never goes to a bar or tavern.	57.1%	42.5%	49.6%	32.8%
Believes too little is being spent dealing with drug addiction.	64.5%	61.7%	61.1%	54.6%
Believes marijuana should be made legal.	19.2%	23.9%	44.3%	51.8%
The person smokes.	33.5%	35.8%	26.3%	47.8%
Believes homosexual relations are always wrong.	77.2%	64.8%	30.3%	37.4%
Believes extra-marital sex is always wrong.	79.6%	75.3%	51.5%	53.5%
Has seen an X-rated movie in the last year.	19.7%	24.1%	29.5%	35.4%
Believes pornography should be illegal to all, regardless of age.	45.6%	37.0%	20.5%	18.5%

Source: General Social Survey

Historically, the nineteenth-century Temperance Crusade was a largely Protestant social movement, and religious opposition to drinking was a conservative Protestant phenomenon.[45] Liquor was not a specifically religious issue for Catholics. Of course, people in both religious traditions recognized that alcoholism could be disastrous for the individual and the family, but it had significant religious meaning only among Protestants.

One way to see this empirically is to compare General Social Survey respondents in each religious tradition who attend church more or less frequently. Table 5.2 in the appendix reveals that how frequently Catholics attend church does not predict whether they abstain from alcohol, but among Protestants church attendance is a powerful deterrent against drink. Interestingly, the effect does not operate across the full range of church attendance. Protestants who attend church two or three times a month are no more likely to abstain than Protestants who never attend, 28.2 percent versus 29.7 percent. But abstainers constitute 41.2 percent of Protestants who attend church nearly every week, 51.4 percent who attend every single week, and fully 77.2 percent of Protestants who attend church more than once a week. This reflects the temperance values of sectarian groups whose members attend church very frequently.

To prevent drinking by members, religion needs to oppose it explicitly, and to be a strong influence in the person's life. In the sampling of theories that began this chapter, I noted that religion can also organize the community against certain behavior, and prohibition laws were one of the ways conservative Protestantism organized against alcohol. The era of Prohibition in the United States, 1919–1933, has generally been dismissed as an ill-advised experiment that failed. However, there is extensive evidence that banning the sale and possession of alcohol significantly reduced the death rate from cirrhosis of the liver, automobile accidents, and pneumonia, as well as reducing disorderly conduct. On average, across 194 American cities, the death rate from cirrhosis of the liver was 15.1 per hundred thousand in 1916, shortly before Prohibition, but only 8.8 per hundred thousand in 1923 after it had become well established. In an average city of 100,000 population, that was an annual savings of more than six lives, or more than 88 lives over the duration of Prohibition.[46]

Figure 5.1 has two items about illegal drugs, and one about tobacco. The first of these refers to "many problems in this country" and asks, "Are we spending too much, too little, or about the right amount on dealing with drug addiction?" People with no religion were less likely to feel that more should be done. The second of these questions asked, "Do you think the use of marijuana should be made legal or not?" On this issue, all the groups differ, with more than half of irreligious respondents favoring legalization, versus progressively lower fractions of Jews, Catholics, and Protestants. We also see that nearly half of those without religion smoke, compared with lower percentages for Catholics and Protestants, and only about a quarter of Jews.

Jews are slightly less willing than the non-religious to condemn sexual experimentation ("sexual relations between two adults of the same sex" and "a married person having sexual relations with someone other than the marriage partner"), whereas the two Christian groups are much more ready to condemn it. With respect to having seen a X-rated movie in the past year, the groups are arranged in descending order: None, Jewish, Catholic, Protestant. The ranking is reversed for believing pornography should be illegal.

Given that more than three quarters of Protestants believe homosexual relations are always wrong, and nearly two third of Catholics agree, we might expect significant geographic differences across the United States, with lower rates of homosexuality where religion was strongest. The 1980 dataset on denominational membership included the Metropolitan Community Church, a gay denomination. Other data on the geographical distribution of homosexual organizations can be found in four guidebooks designed to help gay travelers find the subculture in cities they visit. Published annually for several years, these guides all seem to have achieved excellent coverage. I use the 1984 editions, because later editions are less reliable as a result of AIDS epidemic publicity.[47]

I tabulated all standard listings in *Bob Damron's Address Book*, but ignored what Damron calls "cruisy areas"—public places where gays can meet informally—because their number may reflect the diversity of public facilities in a town rather than the number of gays. Three guides have classified sections: *The Gay Yellow Pages*, *Places of Interest*, and *Gaia's Guide*. Because they contain duplicate listings, and the overlap between them is imperfect, I created a unified dataset based on the telephone numbers of the organizations and businesses. In addition to total listings, I consider two subclassifications: (1) bars and restaurants and (2) bookstores and special interest groups. Bookstores and groups represent the social movement aspect of the gay subculture, and thus they have different social sources from the bars.

As shown in Table 5.3 in the appendix, the church member rate has significant negative correlations with the homosexuality variables, for 75 large metropolitan areas, but the social instability variable (living in a different house from the home five years ago) reduces them to insignificance. A multiple regression statistical analysis suggests that it is really college attendance and divorce that are related to high rate of gay-oriented advertisements in the guidebooks. Many listings in the gay guides have an obvious connection with higher education, notably the bookstores. Colleges have often permitted gay student groups to form and, through giving them free use of facilities, have effectively subsidized them.

For three of the five gay rates, divorce achieves the highest coefficients, suggesting that homosexuality greatly represents a disintegration of relations between the sexes, and it remains possible that weakness of organized religion has contributed to this. But with college education and divorce in the equation, religion has no direct effect on the gay rates. This seems to contradict the survey research that shows a consistent negative correlation between religion and deviant sexuality. However, the surveys generally fail to control for social and family disruption variables, and I did find significant negative correlations between religion and the gay rates before applying statistical controls for the other variables. Furthermore, the surveys measure mere attitudes toward sexuality, not actual social behavior as the geographical indicators do.

As usual, the picture is complex, suggesting that the ability of religion to deter hedonistic deviance may be real but weak and variable. However, one complexity does not arise here, namely the Stark effect. Studies of young people consistently find that religiousness is negatively correlated with using alcohol, recreational drugs, or sexual experimentation, even in secular communities.[48] For example, Table 5.4 in the appendix shows results from my questionnaire study of University of Washington students.[49] Respondents who attend church frequently are much less likely to drive a car under the influence of alcohol, to drink more than once a week, to use cocaine or marijuana, or to engage in sexual intercourse.

Why should this be true? Why is there no Stark effect for hedonism? Although I am not sure, I have two theories. First, religious beliefs may have a cognitive *advisory function*, guiding people away from choices that would be dangerous to them personally. Even without strong social support today, a student may avoid drugs or sexual experimentation, because he or she learned to fear these things earlier in life, in connection with religious teachings. In larceny, there is a victim, but for these victimless acts primarily the perpetrator is at risk.

Second, drugs, sexual relations, and even alcohol are in large measure social activities, and a person who engages in them thereby follows *subcultural norms* that are inconsistent with religious teachings. Although all human activities have some kind of social dimension, burglars are not part of a distinctive subculture, whereas marijuana users are.[50] Belonging to the marijuana subculture pulls one away from church, almost to the extent that belonging to one denomination precludes belonging to another.

Conclusion

It is easy to be confused by the complex results we have seen in this chapter and the two previous ones. Despite many theories suggesting that religion could deter crime and deviant behavior, we see only very inconsistent evidence that it does. The influence against crime operates only against relatively mild offenses, as if religion were saying, "Thou shalt not steal, but killing is okay." Of course, this commandment is crazy. One way to think about it is to note that, thankfully, the most serious crimes are also rare. The converse of that principle is, larceny is common and not very harmful. Religion may have a mild power to deter many people from committing acts like theft that harm other people. Violent acts of passion, or acts performed by abnormal individuals, may not be deterrable.

We cannot be entirely sure about the Stark effect, and all the questions of these three chapters would benefit from much more high quality research. Indeed, in reviewing recent literature before writing this book, I was struck by how many important topics have been the focus of so little good research. However, we have seen much evidence that the influence of religion is highly variable and often depends upon social support of some kind. This suggests, again, that the supernatural explanation of religion is false—indeed that religious beliefs themselves are false. If God were real, and was anything like how many Christians imagine him, his influence to guide the individual along a path of righteousness would be constant across behaviors and social contexts.

Whether beliefs are true or not, they can have consequences. Given the support of community consensus and the institution of the church, these consequences can be significant. It is understandable why some people want to use religion as a tool of correction in prisons.[51] But the poor showing of religion in preventing serious crime suggests that secularization will not unleash an unendurable crime wave upon society. We have good reason to worry that minor crimes would increase, along with juvenile delinquency. This might require a greater secular investment in community centers, real rehabilitation in institutions for juvenile offenders, and other reforms.

The idea that religion is the basis for morality is certainly false. Exchange theory suggests that norms arise largely in the interaction between individuals. In stable exchange systems, individuals must be trustworthy, for other people to trust them. Not a fantasy about supernatural influences, but the actual give and take of life builds communities of exchange partners who value each other and therefore treat each other well.[52] But in chaotic and insecure societies, people wish there were more law and order, so they pray to gods to serve as divine policemen and judges. This is consistent with exchange theory and suggests that much of religion's supposed power to support morality is really just a compensator. Faith provides hope and comfort, but not justice.

The findings on hedonistic deviance here loop back to the findings on health in the third chapter, and on fertility, in the fourth. If secularization does lead to religious decline, we may need new and better ways of integrating medicine and biotechnology into our lives. That is, we will not only need more powerful health and fertility technologies, which we can reasonably expect in the coming years. We will also need healthier and more fertile lifestyles. Innovation in that area is more problematic.

6

The New Age

> Once did one believe in
> soothsayers and astrologers;
> and therefore did one believe,
> "Everything is fate:
> thou shalt, for thou must!"
> —*Thus Spake Zarathustra*,[1]
> Friedrich Nietzsche

In ancient days, perhaps soothsayers and astrologers worked in relative harmony with the dominant religions of their societies, satisfying people's needs for certainty and a sense that events were under control. Today, however, they belong to a diffuse New Age subculture offering hope instead of certainty, and liberation rather than control. John A. Saliba has noted that the New Age "has no central organization and no commonly accepted creed."[2] However, J. Gordon Melton has argued that its historical heart was a millenarian movement that coalesced in the 1960s, when popular culture proclaimed the dawning of Age of Aquarius.[3]

The Aquarian Age

Whether the Age of Aquarius dawned in the 1960s, as suggested by the musical *Hair*, or much earlier in the twentieth century when many astrological and occult movements arose, we have presumably entered the full sunshine of the New Age by now.[4] New Age ideas permeate many tiny religious movements, but we have not seen the major upsurge in such groups that some scholars expected. More than twenty years ago, Rodney Stark and I suggested we should distinguish religious cult movements from client and audience cults, and it may be that the New Age is properly understood as a parareligious or pseudoscientific phenomenon, rather than fully religious.[5]

A *religious movement*, as Stark and I defined it, is a deviant religious organization.[6] Alternately, one could say that a religious movement is a form of social movement. In particular, it is an organized group that seeks to cause or prevent change in the religious life of members or of society at large.[7] At a first approximation, religious movements may be categorized either as *sects* (promoting traditional beliefs and practices) or *cults* (promoting novel beliefs and practices). The heart of every religion is a set of general compensators based on supernatural assumptions. Sects and cults tend to add specific compensators, such as a feeling of being a special person based on intense religious practices or a mystical sense of being part of a transcendent spiritual community.

Client and audience cults are similar to religious cult movements, in that they promote novel beliefs and practices, but they are far less organized. An *audience cult* may have no discernable organization at all, consisting for example of isolated individuals who read UFO contactee books or watch television programs about parapsychology, and authors of those books and programs who may have little or no contact with each other or with their audiences. A *client cult* has rudimentary organization, in that individual practitioners serve a clientele, such as astrologers casting horoscopes or mediums staging séances. Some clients recruit others through their friendship network, but they do not constitute a congregation or membership that meets collectively. The professional practitioners may learn from each other and share various cultural resources, but their work is not coordinated by a formal organization. Of course these differences are all matters of degree, and Chapter 3 already described the birth of the Process, an occasion in which a group of client-cult clients socially imploded into a small cult movement.[8] Thus, the three kinds of cult are different points along a dimension representing the degree of formal social organization they possess, from audiences with no organization to cult movements with much.

Individual intellectuals are constantly trying to synthesize New Age or "alternative" ideas to create a new orthodoxy. For example, many authors are consciously or unconsciously guided by the concept of fate, which plays a conspicuous role in astrology, numerology, and biorhythms and appears again and again throughout the New Age, even in the very concept of an Age of Aquarius. At a relatively high intellectual level, Duane Elgin has written *Awakening Earth*, describing future eras of spiritual enlightenment, increasing compassion, and world unity.[9] For a wider audience, James Redfield wrote *The Celestine Prophecy*, a novel depicting a spiritual quest, from which many readers have gained a new sense of spiritual possibilities in life.[10] Redfield asserts that each person will briefly meet a series of spiritual guides, from which the person can learn lessons to guide him or her on the proper path. Both of these books blend a sense of preordination with a sense of freedom, suggesting that for the entire world and for each person in it there is a proper path that has already been laid down, but humans need spiritual awareness to follow the path. Redfield took a long step toward the organization of a religious movement by publishing an instructional manual for applying the Celestine perspective to aspects of one's daily life.[11] However, the books remain largely in the territory of audience cults, with some Celestine-oriented teachers also serving clients.

Client and audience cults compete obliquely with organized religion rather than directly. That is, a member of a conventional religious denomination may on occasion consult a professional astrologer (client cult) or read astrological predictions in the newspaper (audience cult), rather than of necessity converting to an astrology-promoting religion such as The Rosicrucian Fellowship[12] or an astrology-accepting religion like The Family (Children of God).[13] However, conventional Christian denominations discourage involvement with the occult, and the Bible contains numerous stories concerning cultic supernatural phenomena that are in one way or another opposed by the main Judeo-Christian tradition. For example, Saul violates God's laws when he tells the Witch of Endor to raise the spirit of Samuel from the dead (1 Samuel 28). Thus, within the Western religious traditions at least, one may hypothesize:

> Hypothesis 1. Involvement in conventional religion discourages involvement in unconventional parareligion, because conventional religion competes with parareligion.

Stark and I offered much empirical evidence in support of this proposition. New Age stores and restaurants, professional psychics and astrologers, and writers of letters to an occult magazine tend to be in U.S. states where the church membership rate is low.[14] With metropolitan areas as the unit of analysis, powerful negative correlations between the church member rate and rates of occult letter writers or Transcendental Meditation meditators survive reasonable statistical controls.[15] A similar geographic pattern is found in Canada.[16] Ideally, one would like to compare individual-level data with such ecological data, and a survey of

1,439 college students found that respondents who lacked religious af-filiation were more likely to be interested in occult literature or horo-scopes, and to agree with statements like: "Some occult practices, such as Tarot reading, séances, or psychic healing, are probably of great value."[17]

However, one could also argue the opposite of the first proposition. Some secular critics of religion would say that both religious faith and the New Age depend upon belief in the supernatural. Put more neutrally, both assume a universe in which the world is organized around features of the human personality, as traditionally conceptualized, such as a tran-scendental self and a mystical connection between the self and the cos-mos. Both exist in some degree of tension with science and secular soci-ety. Thus, a second, apparently competing proposition can be stated:

> Hypothesis 2. Conventional religion encourages unconventional parare-ligion by promulgating supernatural assumptions about the nature of humanity and the universe.

The first hypothesis predicts a negative correlation between conven-tional religion and unconventional parareligion, and the second hypothe-sis predicts a positive correlation. A simplistic scientific study could col-lect relevant data, look at whether the correlation was negative or positive, and declare one hypothesis the winner over the other. However, a more sophisticated approach would explore the possibility that both hypotheses are correct. Strictly speaking, they are not logical opposites of each other. In some ways, traditional religion may have prepared the ground for novel parareligion, even though they will compete with each other. Religious effects often have to be understood in terms of the bal-ance of conflicting forces.[18] To do so, we need ample, appropriate data. Now I will introduce a survey that contains the needed items and has a sufficiently large number of respondents to permit the necessary analysis.

New Age Items in *Survey2001*

Survey2001 was a major international questionnaire with about 2,000 items in many modules presented to randomly selected subsets of re-spondents, administered on the World Wide Web by a team led by James Witte with sponsorship from the National Geographic Society and the National Science Foundation.[19] *Survey2001* was the successor to *Sur-*

vey2000, that contributed to Chapter 2, so the research team was already quite experienced with online questionnaires. Although the respondents were not a random sample of the population, the size and complexity of the dataset make it ideally suited for exploratory research, the results of which could potentially be confirmed in future surveys administered to random samples and through comparison with results of studies that employed entirely different rigorous methodologies. As a practical matter, it would have been prohibitively costly to collect these data from anything like a random sample of the population. Theoretical analysis links the results to findings from studies that employed very different methods, and it would be possible in future to verify the key results of this study by adding just a small subset of items to the General Social Survey or a similar national data collection effort.[20]

One section of *Survey2001* consisted of 30 agree–disagree items, including some about technology and 20 that relate to pseudoscience, parareligion, or what might be called New Age ideology. The statements were written in pairs, one expressing acceptance of a general idea, and the other expressing rejection. For example, two statements concerned telepathy or extra-sensory perception: "Some people really experience telepathy, communication between minds without using the traditional five senses." "Extra-sensory perception (E.S.P.) probably does not exist." Respondents could choose one of five responses: strongly disagree, disagree, do not know, agree, or strongly agree. The following analysis focuses on the 3,909 English-language respondents who answered all 30 agree–disagree items.

A standard statistical technique called factor analysis determined that the 20 New Age statements really did hang together. (See Table 6.1 in the appendix of this book.) People who agreed with one positively-phrased item tended to agree with the other positive statements and to disagree with the negative ones. But it was also possible to see three dimensions or groups of items that had somewhat different qualities. Because all 20 do measure acceptance of an underlying New Age subculture, they do not separate cleanly, but Figure 6.1 gives a reasonable division of 18 statements into three groups of six, with three positive and three negative statements in each.

For sake of simplicity, we can describe each cluster of six items with a name: General New Age, Mental Power, and Alien Beings. Each of these three groups meets the usual statistical standards for being a reliable psychological measurement scale. That is, you could put the six

Figure 6.1: Questionnaire Items for Three New-Age Clusters

General New Age	
Positive:	There is much truth in astrology—the theory that the stars, the planets, and our birthdays have a lot to do with our destiny in life.
	Some people can hear from or communicate mentally with someone who has died.
	Some scientific instruments (e.g., e-meters, psionic machines, and aura cameras) can measure the human spirit.
Negative:	Psychic mediums who claim they can communicate with the dead are either frauds or mentally ill.
	Numerology, biorhythms, and similar attempts to chart a person's life with numbers are worthless.
	Astrologers, palm readers, tarot card readers, fortune tellers, and psychics can't really foresee the future.
Mental Power	
Positive:	Some techniques can increase an individual's spiritual awareness and power.
	Dreams sometimes foretell the future or reveal hidden truths.
	Some people really experience telepathy, communication between minds without using the traditional five senses.
Negative:	Extra-sensory perception (E.S.P.) probably does not exist.
	Yoga, meditation, mind control, and similar methods are really of no value for achieving mental or spiritual development.
	Analyzing dreams is a waste of time because they are random fragments of thought and memory.
Alien Beings	
Positive:	Some UFOs (Unidentified Flying Objects) are probably spaceships from other worlds.
	Scientifically advanced civilizations, such as Atlantis, probably existed on Earth thousands of years ago.
	Some people can move or bend objects with their mental powers.
Negative:	All ancient people were less advanced than modern civilization in science and technology.
	Perpetual motion machines, anti-gravity devices, and time travel machines are physically impossible.
	Intelligent life probably does not exist on any planet but our own.

statements in a questionnaire, asking respondents how much they agreed or disagreed with each. Then, you could add up how many of the positive statements a person agreed with, plus how many of the negative statements a person disagreed with, and get a number representing how much the person believed in the particular kind of New Age tenets.

The General New Age group could represent the entire New Age subculture, but with moderate de-emphasis of the ideas expressed by the two other groups. In fact, at least 13 of the 20 items would be very happy in the General New Age group (as marked by the statistical criterion that their factor loadings are greater than 0.40), and all 20 items measure acceptance of the New Age. The Mental Power group concerns paranormal mental, psychic, or spiritual abilities. It suggests that some people have these abilities naturally, or that proper spiritual training can endow a person with these powers. The Alien Beings group expresses belief in aliens, such as extraterrestrials or Atlanteans, and the advanced technologies they possess.

The table lists 18 statements, but the remaining 2 of the 20 connect to the others as well, and were excluded merely because our immediate goal was to assemble equal numbers of items representing the three dimensions of the New Age. This statement would be quite comfortable in the General New Age group: "Every person's life is shaped by three precise biological rhythms—physical, emotional, and intellectual—that begin at birth and extend unaltered until death." Scientists have noted roughly daily cycles in living organisms, often called circadian rhythms, but this item refers to an unrelated pseudoscience devised by Wilhelm Fliess, a friend of Sigmund Freud. It asserts that each person's life is powerfully shaped by three precise cycles that began at the moment of birth: a 23-day physical cycle, a 28-day emotional cycle, and a 33-day intellectual cycle.[21] Like astrology, biorhythms claims to be able to predict aspects of an individual's life on the basis merely of data about his or her birth date.

The twentieth statement actually is connected to all three groups, especially General New Age and Mental Power: "It's not possible to influence the physical world through the mind alone." It is the negative statement corresponding most closely in topic to the following positive statement: "Some people can move or bend objects with their mental powers." These two refer to what believers call *telekinesis* or *psychokinesis*, the power of mind over matter. This pair has close affinities with the two ESP statements that wound up in the Mental Power group. Anyone who actually possessed telekinetic powers would be considered very strange by the average person, and thus a kind of alien, so there is also a connection to the Alien Beings group. Chapter 9, on cognitive science, will have more to say about telepathy, telekinesis, and other ideas from parapsychology.

If one is looking for the heart of the pseudoscientific New Age, then there are at least two places to look for it. Astrology is one candidate, because the factor analysis revealed that the two statements about astrology most strongly connect all the items of the first group, which represents the New Age in general. Extra-sensory perception is another candidate, because the two statements about telepathy and ESP are strongly connected with all three groups in the statistical analysis, even though here we have assigned them to the Mental Power group. It is also worth noting that the two statements about extraterrestrials bracket the Alien Beings group, and thus express an important topic for many New Age believers.

Religious Implications of the New Age

Now we can consider our competing hypotheses. Is religion connected to the New Age positively or negatively? At first, the data look complicated, until the right methods are used to analyze them. Among all 3,909 respondents there tends to be a slight negative correlation between the positively-phrased New Age items and church attendance, implying that conventional religion discourages belief in the New Age, but only very slightly. However, there are small positive correlations between New Age beliefs and how often the respondent prays, suggesting that religious urges support New Age beliefs, but, again, only weakly.

The picture clarifies considerably when we look at the 1,011 respondents who never attend religious services. Among them, people who pray often are significantly more likely to agree with the positive New Age items, and to disagree with the negatively-phrased items. Among all 3,909 respondents, 46.4 percent who never attend church believe in telepathy, compared with 52.8 percent of those who attend several times a year and 39.0 percent who attend several times a week. In other words, the New Age is situated on the boundaries of religion. It appeals to people who are half-religious, those who may have religious urges but are not firmly bound into congregations of conventional faiths. In such a situation, relationships between the New Age and religion may be *curvilinear*.

Alan Orenstein may have been the first to observe this clearly.[22] Orenstein employed data from a mailed questionnaire survey, based on responses from 1,765 Canadians who closely approximate a representative sample of the population. It would seem very difficult indeed to obtain a more representative sample of respondents to answer questions about our topic. The Canadian survey contained 6 items about "paranormal beliefs" covering ESP, psychic powers, precognition, astrology, communication with the dead, and reincarnation. With the exception of reincarnation, these items cover very much the territory of the items in the dataset described here. Controlling for frequency of church attendance, Orenstein found a strong positive association between a scale created from the paranormal belief items and a scale created from items about conventional religious belief in Heaven, Hell, angels, God, life after death, and experiencing God's presence. As in the present study, Orenstein found that different aspects of religion may have different relationships to paranormal belief or what we are calling the New Age.

A particular finding that encouraged Orenstein to look at the effects of religious belief and church attendance separately is a curvilinear relationship between church attendance and paranormal belief. Among Canadians who seldom if ever attend church, just 27.0 percent score high on Orenstein's paranormal belief scale. Among those with high church attendance, the proportion scoring high is even lower, only 20.6 percent. But among Canadians with medium frequency of church attendance, fully 34.6 percent score high on paranormal belief. This remarkable finding harmonizes with the analysis presented here and inspires us to look for a similar curvilinearity in the *Survey2001* dataset.

Figure 6.2 graphs three representative positively-phrased New Age statements against responses to a question that asked, "How would you describe yourself?" Seven responses were offered: extremely religious, very religious, somewhat religious, neither religious nor non-religious, somewhat non-religious, very non-religious, or extremely non-religious. People who described themselves as "somewhat religious" were most likely to agree with these three statements: "Some people really experience telepathy, communication between minds without using the traditional five senses." "Some UFOs (Unidentified Flying Objects) are probably spaceships from other worlds." "There is much truth in astrology—the theory that the stars, the planets, and our birthdays have a lot to do with our destiny in life."

One way that a curvilinear relationship could arise is in the interstitial or border territory between two competing cultures. Each culture

may be coherent within itself, and supported by established societal institutions, yet they contradict each other. This situation could characterize a
transition period between two eras, as in conventional secularization theory, because that implies that one of the cultures is replacing the other—
perhaps science replacing religion. Even if there is no secularization
trend, two competing cultures may exist, one religious and the other not,
and the people caught between them are receptive to a variety of beliefs
that have a deviant religious character. Indeed, telepathy, UFOs, and astrology are pseudoscientific ideas, on the border of modern science yet
excluded from it, reflecting the ambivalence of people caught between
religious and scientific cultures.

Figure 6.2: Religiousness and Three New Age Beliefs

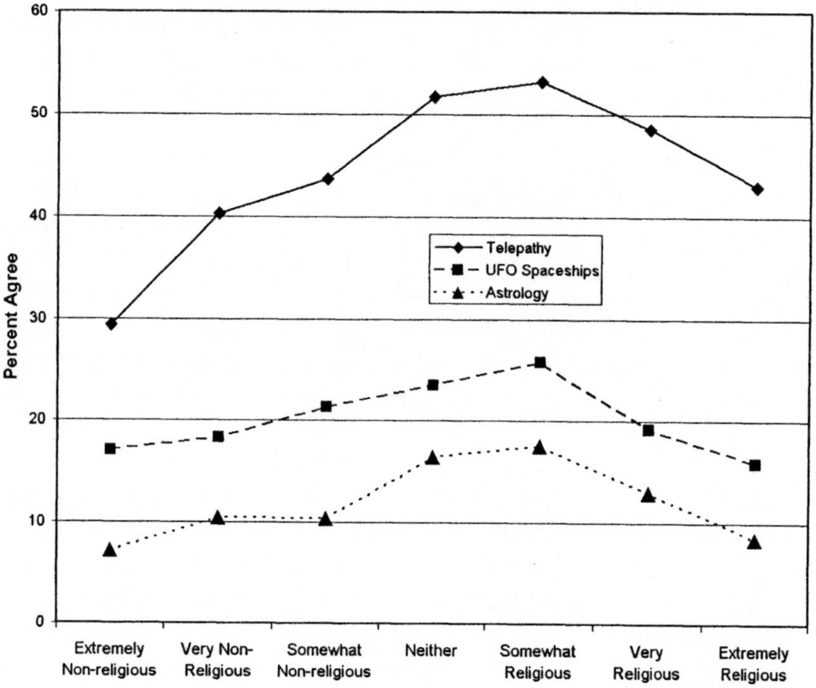

Charting Astrology

Astrology is interesting for the social science of religion in many ways. It
was the original parent of the science of astronomy, and it exploits data

from that real science, notably records and predictions of the locations of the planets. It featured in several ancient religions, such as the Babylonian state religion and Mithraism that was one of the chief competitors to Christianity.[23] In recent years, it has become a central feature of the New Age movement, and it well illustrates the connection between new religious movements and client or audience cults.

More than a quarter century ago, I collected data on the geographic distribution of astrologers in the United States by counting the number of them listed in the classified telephone directories of the nation's metropolitan areas. Ample time has passed to compare changes over time, and the availability of national online telephone directories suggests that the research could be done better today.

In 2005, I decided to repeat this analysis using the Infobel.com online telephone number database, that would be national in scope and hopefully easier to handle than the old-style paper phone books. This national "Internet yellow pages" has a classification called "Astrologer" or "Astrologers Psychic Consultants etc." As the data were assembled, it was obvious that many listings were duplicates. A few of these were telephone-based psychic services that advertise nationally and were included in each state's classified listings. Examples include Psychic Maria (Florida), Psychic Mariam (California), Awareness Psychic Center (Maryland), Psychic Readings by Tina (New Jersey), Angie's Psychic Readings (New York), and Morris Fonte Telepsychic (New York). A national service called Psychic Solutions, which we know is in Florida because of its 305 area code, needed to be distinguished from local services of the same name in Arizona, California, Nebraska, Nevada, North Carolina, and Texas.

In cleaning out duplicates based on phone numbers, I discovered that many phones are shared by an astrologer or psychic and a conventional small business. I was not surprised to see cases in which the business was an antique store, bookstore, candle shop, flower shop, gift shop, or vitamin store, because I imagined that they could be serving the same clientele. More challenging to understand were examples of astrologers or psychics whose phone numbers also were listed under asphalt maintenance, auto service, child care, cleaning service, construction, cosmetics training, custom doors, dating service, dentist, graphics, interior design, massage parlor, mufflers, office products, party clown, paving company, pet store, photographer, property management, recreational vehicle sales, scrap metal dealer, seamstress, software, stump removal, and tanning salon. Perhaps the conventional business is run by a family, and one family member happens to be an astrologer. But in some cases, individuals may be pursuing two different career paths simultaneously and might choose to be full-time psychics if there were enough business to support them. This is illustrated by a small business in Hutchinson, Kansas, that is listed both as Newage Gypsy Seers and as interior decorators called Two Chicks & A Ladder. This suggests that many astrologers and similar psychic practitioners work only part-time, either in conjunction with other, non-spiritual jobs or from the basis of retirement.

The total number of listings that could be placed in states or the District of Columbia, after deleting duplicates, was 3,859. These data are displayed in Table 6.2 in the appendix. In descending order, the ten states with the largest number of listings are California (838 listings), Florida (346), New York (300), Texas (269), New Jersey (182), Illinois (147), Massachusetts (130), Pennsylvania (118), Arizona (115), and Ohio (105). But, of course, these include many of the most populous states, so we might want to compare standardized rates. The ten states with the highest rates per million are Hawaii (26.1), Nevada (26.1), California (23.4), New Jersey (20.9), Massachusetts (20.3), Arizona (20.0) Florida (19.9), Alaska, (16.8), Colorado (16.7), Connecticut (16.0), New York (15.6), And New Hampshire (15.4).[24] For the nation as a whole, including Washington DC, the rate is 13.14 listings per million population. Every state has at least one listing, including North Dakota which has only one, giving it the lowest rate of 1.6 per million.

Figure 6.3 maps the rates for the 9 "divisions" of the United States and reveals that there are real regional differences. The Pacific region of the country (which includes Alaska and Hawaii although they are not shown on the map), has the highest rate. The East South Central Region (Kentucky, Tennessee, Alabama, Mississippi) is lowest. The difference between these two extremes is a ratio of about 3.5. Like the adjacent Pacific area, the Mountain region is also higher than the national average, but so, too, are New England and the Middle Atlantic region. The South Atlantic region is nearly as high as the national rate, but this is a reflection of high rates in Florida and the District of Columbia. Removing these two extreme areas leaves the remaining eight states of the South Atlantic Region with a combined rate of only 6.1 per million, identical to the adjacent East South Central region.

In the 1980s, Stark and I found that many measures of cultism and the occult correlated negatively with the rate of church membership.[25] In areas of the country where the churches are strong, the cults are weak. There are probably several reasons. For one thing, where churches are strong, most people's religious needs are already satisfied. For another, the social influence of church members discourages members of the community from experimenting with deviant alternatives. And for a third, we know that social instability is one of the key factors that can erode church membership, and instability favors experimentation.[26] Thus, the Pacific region of the United States, where church membership is weak and high rates of geographic mobility destabilize society, is the area where astrologers and other cultic phenomena are most common.

Figure 6.3: Astrologers and Psychics per Million in 2005

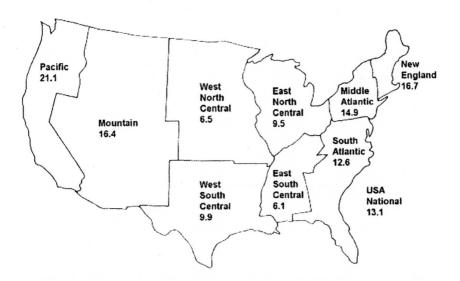

Having data spanning a quarter century, I compared the geographic pattern in 1979 with that of 2005. The more recent data concern not just astrologers but also psychic consultants, so I combined the 1979 astrologer data with listings of psychics from a 1979 guide.[27] When I compared the regional rates across time, two things were very clear. First, all the rates had increased significantly. Second, the rates have evened out across the regions to some extent. The Pacific region had 6.9 astrologers and 9.3 psychics per million in 1979, for a combined rate of 16.2, and a rate of 21.1 per million in 2005.[28] In contrast, the region with the lowest rate was the East South Central, with only 1.5 per million in 1979 rising to 6.1 in 2005. Relative to the rest of the nation, the Pacific region dropped, even as the absolute numbers of astrologers and psychics in it grew. This is what we would expect to happen if the western part of the country were a bellwether, reflecting trends that hit the rest of the country later. The general picture is one in which astrologers and psychics have become more significant for the society as a whole over the 26 years.

Astrology Books

Having charted astrology in time and space, we can begin to map it according to very different dimensions, those of culture. The data from *Survey2001* examined how astrology related to other New Age topics, and we can use data from Amazon.com, the most popular online bookseller, to begin to chart its internal structure and to see what human motivations it serves. This site offers two very different ways to classify books, an ontology and a recommender system. As the term is commonly used by information scientists, an *ontology* is a principled classification scheme in which the categories are usually arranged hierarchically and are mutually exclusive at any one level, although a given item may be assigned to multiple categories.[29] A *recommender system* is an information database that suggests items to consider for use or purchase, based on advice from other users or purchasers—what was originally called a *collaborative filtering system*.[30]

Entering the word *astrology* into the books part of the Amazon.com website on September 22, 2005 turned up 27,653 results, with the advisory that "Customers who searched for astrology ultimately chose:" *The Only Astrology Book You'll Ever Need* and *Sexual Astrology: A Sign-by-Sign Guide to Your Sensual Stars*, both by Joanna Woolfolk, and *Chart Interpretation Handbook: Guidelines for Understanding the Essentials of the Birth Chart* by Stephen Arroyo.

For the moment we will ignore the two books by Woolfolk, because they will turn up later from a different search that illustrates the recommender system. Instead we can focus on the somewhat technical *Chart Interpretation Handbook* to examine the ontology. Amazon.com assigns the *Handbook* to three categories, one of which is "Psychology & Counseling," which suggests a social function that astrology currently serves for the people interested in it. Indeed, it is my observation that the popular books one finds in the Psychology section of mass market bookstores have precious little to do with academic or experimental psychology, but are largely self-help books based on dubious theories with little empirical support, thus analogous to astrology or to religious inspiration. I have long argued that the various psychotherapies are magical client cults that appeal to better-educated people, but are in no substantive way better than the cults that appeal to the less educated. Astrology books are largely a subcategory of quasi-religious inspirational literature, appealing to people with a different educational background from those who like the equally insubstantial psychology and psychotherapy books.

The two other categories to which the *Handbook* is assigned are related subcategories of the "New Age" category within "Religion & Spirituality:" "New Age > General" and "New Age > Astrology > General." Here are Amazon's New Age labels: General, Astrology, Chakras, Channeling, Divination, Dreams, Goddesses, Meditation, Mental & Spiritual Healing, Mysticism, New Thought, Reference, Reincarnation, Self-Help, Theosophy, and Urantia. The Astrology subcategory contains four sub-subcategories: General, Chinese, Horoscopes, and Vedic.

On the same level of abstraction as New Age, there is also an Occult category, which includes such things as ESP, Parapsychology, Spiritualism and UFOs. The competing bookseller, Barnes & Noble, combines all these in a global Religion category under the label "New Age & Alternative Beliefs." Thus it would be interesting to see whether astrology books at Amazon are often categorized under Occult as well as New Age. To explore such issues, I manually downloaded the data for the first 100 books that Amazon presented as bestsellers in its "Astrology > General category," data tabulated in appendix Table 6.3.[31]

Fully 56.2 percent of bestsellers in the "New Age > Astrology > General" category also are assigned to "New Age > General," reinforcing the fact that astrology is culturally central to the New Age. A total of about 7.1 percent of the categorizations went to other subcategories within New Age, as opposed to just 3.0 percent to Occult. Another 2.6 percent of the astrology books belong to the "New Age > Divination" category, which contains the following prognosticatory cousins of astrology: Crystals, Fortune Telling, Graphology, I Ching, Numerology, Palmistry, Prophecy, Runes, and Tarot. Notably, about 12.9 percent of the categorizations are under "Health, Mind & Body," largely self-help books in these three areas: "Psychology & Counseling," "Relationships," and "Sex." An additional 1.8 percent of the books concern use of astrology to make business or investment decisions.

Amazon's recommender system, unlike its ontology, is based on the actual book purchasing behavior of customers, and thus it reflects widespread cultural conceptions that make certain pairs of books seem similar to each other.[32] On September 11, 2005, in the astrology category, Amazon was promoting *Sextrology: The Astrology of Sex and the Sexes* by Stella Starsky and Quinn Cox, which at that point ranked 2,175th in sales among all books. The page selling *Sextrology* reported that customers who bought this book also bought six others, all of them astrological best sellers:

Love on a Rotten Day: An Astrological Survival Guide to Romance by Hazel Dixon-Cooper
Born on a Rotten Day: Illuminating and Coping with the Dark Side of the Zodiac by Hazel Dixon-Cooper
Sexscopes: How to Seduce, Stimulate, and Satisfy Any Sign by Stuart Hazleton
Astrologically Incorrect: Unlock the Secrets of the Signs to Get What You Want When You Want! by Terry Marlowe
The Astrological Guide to Seduction and Romance: How to Love a Libra, Turn on a Taurus, and Seduce a Sagittarius by Susan Sheppard
Sexual Astrology: A Sign-by-Sign Guide to Your Sensual Stars by Joanna Woolfolk

Note that four of these are clearly related to love, sex, and personal relationships, whereas *Born on a Rotten Day* and *Astrologically Incorrect* concern wider issues of coping with life. The Amazon data on customer purchases can be used in many valid ways to do social-scientific research, because they reflect real human behavior and reveal the shape of culture as defined by the book-reading public. The data consist of links between pairs of books that people tended to buy together because they conceptualized their subjects together. The network of connections between books has very much the structure of a social network.

Having identified six books that are connected to Sextrology in people's buying patterns, I then inspected the web page for each of them in the same manner. Here are the other books they themselves added to the network:

How to Spot a Bastard by His Star Sign: The Ultimate Horrorscope by Adele Lang
Love and War Between the Signs: Astrological Secrets to Emotional Compatibility by Amy Keehn
Darkside Zodiac by Stella Hyde
Seduction by the Stars: An Astrological Guide To Love, Lust, And Intimate Relationships by Ren Lexander

Erotic Astrology by Olivia (no last name given)
*Sex Signs: Every Woman's Astrological and Psychological Guide to
   Love, Health, Men and More!* by Judith Bennett
The Only Astrology Book You'll Ever Need by Joanna Woolfolk
Linda Goodman's Love Signs: A New Approach to the Human Heart
   by Linda Goodman
Linda Goodman's Sun Signs by Linda Goodman

Figure 6.4 maps the connections among the 16 books. Clearly, all 16 books mapped here are about astrology, and most of them are self-help books concerning how astrology can give guidance for love, sex and personal relationships. It is interesting to note that the six books on the right side of the map all concern conflict in love and the "dark side" of intimate relationships. Books on the left blend over into general popular astrology books that are not so narrowly focused on romance.

Figure 6.4: Book-Buying Links from Amazon.com

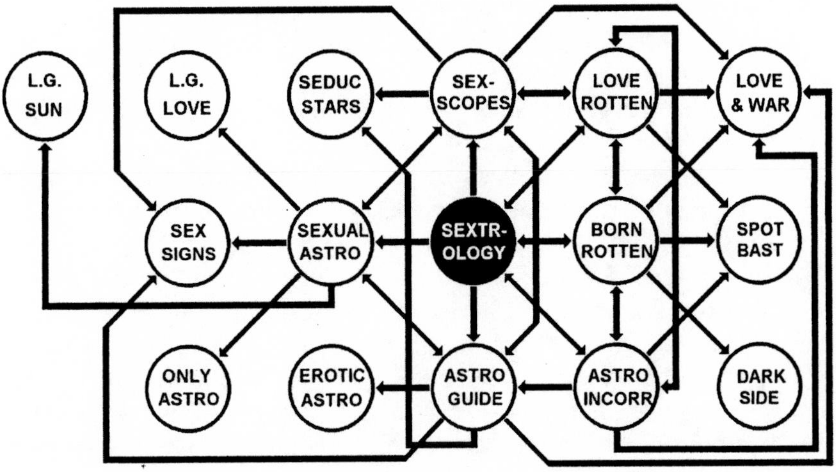

Dawning of the New Age

The Amazon.com results suggest that an excellent measure of the audience-cult dimension of astrology is book publishing, and one of the most valuable online information resources is the catalog of the Library of Congress (www.loc.gov). Although the information about any given book is sparse, it is useful for categorization and for charting changes over time. The primary Library of Congress classification scheme places astrology in Class B, under Philosophy, Psychology, and Religion, in the BF subclass for Psychology, with call numbers BF1651-1729. Numbers BF1001-1389 are labeled Parapsychology, and BF1404-2055 (including astrology) are labeled Occult sciences. Indeed, given the great current emphasis on character analysis and love life advice, astrology does seem to function largely as an alternative personality theory or folk psychology, rather than an alternative astronomy.

The LoC also assigns books to multiple subject headings.[33] An online search of the catalog for "astrology" turned up fully 288 subject headings. Appendix Table 6.4 shows the numbers of books in the top 30 categories, all those containing at least 20.[34] Although the main tradition of western astrology is rooted in Babylonian and Greek history, 512 astrology books and other items were classified as Hindu, and many others were classified Chinese, Tibetan, Japanese, and Thai, emphasizing the importance of astrological beliefs in Asian traditions. Other categories suggest the interests that people seek to satisfy through astrology, including 56 books about astrology and sex, 40 on medical astrology, 37 on astrology and marriage, 30 on astrology and child rearing, 24 on astrology and business, and even 22 on astrology and pets. There are also substantial libraries relating astrology to art, literature, poetry, and the Bible. Given its ancient origins, it is not surprising to see 76 books about the history of astrology.

The history of the field can be charted in a rudimentary way by examining the publication dates of books. I copied the many pages of listings for the two main general astrology categories, including 1,618 and 658 books, then deleted a small number of duplications to arrive at a total of 2,212, keeping multiple editions of a work if they had different publication data. The earliest book in the catalog dated from 1502, and there were a total of 13 published in 1500–1599. Another 38 date from 1600–1699, 13 again from 1700–1799, and 85 from 1800–1899. Whether the dip in the 18th century reflects the Enlightenment, I cannot say. Presumably all kinds of book publishing increased greatly in the 19th century, so one would be reluctant to attribute the growth to Romanticism. Fully 1,896 astrology books were listed for the years 1900–1999, and another 167 had been published in 2000 through September 2005. Figure 6.5 graphs the 20th century books by decade, along with books from Parapsychology and God categories.[35]

J. Gordon Melton has written about the growth of astrology publishing in the late 19th century and early 20th century, noting that interest in the subject was passed to a new generation in the 1960s.[36] But the remarkable surges in the graph demand further explanation. Philip Jenkins suggested a cyclical theory of phenomena related to new religions, and proposed that two of these cycles occurred at about the years in the 20th century indicated by Figure 6.5.[37] However, the data on book publishing and professional astrologers listed in telephone directories imply there is also a long-term upward trend, conceivably "pumped" upward each time one of Jenkins's cycles takes place.

Figure 6.5: Books per Decade Listed in the Library of Congress

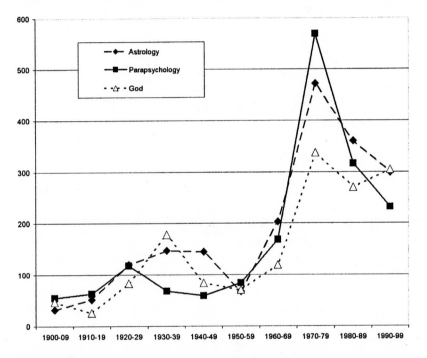

It is important to be aware, however, of the larger context in which astrology publishing takes place. The 1950s marked a major shift in popular culture, the most visible part of which was the rapid diffusion of television that had reached two-thirds of all American households by the middle of the decade. Pulp fiction magazine publishing collapsed in response, marked by the termination in 1954 of *Weird Tales*, the premiere fantasy magazine, and the break-up of the chief national distributor, the American News Company, in the same year.[38] If many astrology books were horoscope guides sold on newsstands, with relatively weak markets, then the disruption of the magazine business could have cost them dearly.

In understanding the apparent decline after the 1970s, one should note that publishers often overshoot the mark in a growing market, producing too many titles in a given genre and having to correct by publishing fewer after a boom that they themselves have exaggerated. Popular books stay in print for many years after they are first published, competing with new books. Two well documented cases in American popular publishing are science fiction magazines and comic books, both of which underwent exaggerated booms that peaked in the 1950s, just when astrology was in a slump.[39] Conceivably, readers with an interest in vivid fantasy could have been lured from horoscope guides to the two fiction genres, although I mention them here as examples of excessive booms in publishing genres, followed by busts that represented consolidation in an industry rather than a loss of customers.

In the same manner as the astrology listings, I tabulated 1,731 parapsychology books published in 1900–1999, and 1,519 books about God. The three curves are quite similar, but there is a slight tendency for astrology and parapsychology books to track each other more closely than they do books about God.[40] One could speculate that the deprivations caused by the Great Depression of the 1930s are shown in the rise of astrology and God books, above the parapsychology books. Both astrology and conventional religion offer compensators for deprivations, whereas parapsychology merely supports the notion of the human soul rather than offering specific compensators. The 1970s peak in publishing for the two New Age measures is remarkable. However, the fact that books about God track the other two measures suggests that we are not simply seeing a two-stage rise in the importance of the New Age, but also reflections of general market and spiritual trends.

A future research project could examine religious and parareligious publishing trends, on the basis of richer data and more fully developed theories. It is interesting to speculate that the rise of publishing about God reflects the fact that God became a contested concept during the twentieth century, that needed to be argued about rather than merely taken for granted. On the other hand, it may be that the curves for astrology and parapsychology largely reflect simply the growth in book publishing, coordinated with the more general rise of the mass media. However, clearly both topics had been solidly established as familiar if somewhat peripheral elements of western culture. A total of 3,627 books in the two categories constitutes a significant library, even before we add all the books about other New Age topics.

Angels and Aliens

The ancient Greek school of philosophers known as Epicureans believed that the universe contained many worlds beyond the one we inhabit, and this idea took on real substance when astronomers of the seventeenth century first studied the other planets through telescopes.[41] In 1758, the Swedish mystic, Emanuel Swedenborg, claimed to have communicated with angels living on other planets.[42] Despite the absence of direct evidence, the uniformity of physical laws and the diversity of the universe suggested to many modern scientists that life exists on other planets and could occasionally evolve intelligence comparable to our own. More important in the current context, they have vigorously communicated this view to the general public for more than half a century.[43] In the late 1940s and early 1950s, the flying saucer craze reported many sightings believed to be alien spaceships, and a few cases in which people claimed direct contact with the extraterrestrials.[44] Some New Age writers claimed that ancient extraterrestrial astronauts were the actual founders of human civilization.[45] In recent years, bona fide astronomers have cataloged more than 100 planets outside the solar system, thereby adding to the plausibility of extrasolar intelligences, and humans have sent robot probes to seven of the planets inside the solar system.

Thus, the idea that unidentified flying objects might be spaceships has some connection to real science. But it also has religious roots. Logically, extraterrestrial civilizations could be vastly older than our own, and some of them therefore would be more advanced technologically. It is a short step from this reasonable deduction to the hope that extraterrestrials (ETs) are spiritually more advanced, either something like angels or prophets of a superior creed. Their powers may border on the supernatural, and thus they can deliver religious compensators to us in their spaceships. A study of the alleged UFO crash at Roswell, New Mexico, has shown how the myth grew rumor-like, in a way not very different from the subculture-evolution model of cult innovation.[46] Here we will consider how belief in extraterrestrials fits between science and religion in modern culture.

One of the agree-disagree statements in *Survey2001* expressed disbelief in extraterrestrial intelligence: "Intelligent life probably does not exist on any planet but our own." People who disagree with this statement thereby express some willingness to believe that extraterrestrial intelligence does exist, but they do not necessarily believe that ETs dwell near the Earth or have traveled here. Another item concerns this possibility: "Some UFOs (Unidentified Flying Objects) are probably spaceships from other worlds." If we set aside the people who replied "do not know" to either of the two questions, there are four possible viewpoints, only three of which are logical. The illogical viewpoint is to deny that ETs exist but to assert that UFOs could be spaceships. Less than one percent of respondents are in this category, and we will ignore this tiny minority because they apparently made an error in reading the statements or in responding. That leaves three groups that deserve analysis.

People who do not believe extraterrestrials exist, in this vast universe, might be called *Geocentrists*, because they consider the Earth to be central to existence, or at least unique among the trillions of trillions of planets. Among English-speaking respondents to *Survey2001*, just 300 reject the possibility of extraterrestrials and (logically enough) deny that UFOs are spaceships. Those who believe extraterrestrials might exist can be assigned to two groups, depending on whether they think UFOs are spaceships. The 806 respondents who were inclined to think UFOs might be spaceships can be called *Ufophiles*. Using a term from biology that refers to geographically separated species, the remaining 754 respondents are *Allopatrists*. They think extraterrestrials could exist but do not routinely visit the Earth, perhaps because their civilizations are at a vast distance from Earth.

Earlier research showed that religion is a very powerful variable affecting attitudes and beliefs concerning extraterrestrials, with highly religious people being especially likely to reject the idea.[47] The *Survey2001* Geocentrists are more traditionally religious than the two other groups. Among Geocentrists, 45.3 percent attend religious services nearly every week or even more frequently, which is often. In contrast, 10.7 percent of Ufophiles and 15.6 percent of Allopatrists attend church often. Fully 69.7 percent of Geocentrists say they are at least somewhat religious, compared with 51.0 percent of Ufophiles and 38.5 percent of Allopatrists. Here we see again that people oriented toward the New Age, namely Ufophiles, come from the middle of the spectrum of religious beliefs, but are somewhat unchurched.

Conclusion

Kendrick Frazier has called the topics covered by this chapter the *paranormal borderlands of science*.[48] We have seen that they are also borderlands of religion. The New Age is a somewhat diffuse subculture that partially serves religious motives yet draws upon science for many of its metaphors. It appears to have grown during the twentieth century, and has become a familiar if minority viewpoint. Like any contested territory lying between two superpowers, its future potential depends largely upon the outcome of the competition between them.

If the world is passing through a period of gradual secularization, and science is destined to vanquish religion, the New Age conceivably could remain constant in size, yet move across the cultural map, following the retreat of religion. There are good reasons to doubt that it can invade territory currently held by either religion or science. First of all, the compensators it offers appear to be somewhat vague and may not be as convincing as those offered by intense religious sects, because it lacks the degree of social organization that could provide strong support for beliefs. Secondly, like the magic practiced in pre-industrial societies, it makes many claims that are susceptible to testing by science, and which are likely to be proven false.

Yet the New Age has advantages. Especially for poorly educated people who do not understand the real principles of science, it provides apparently scientific interpretations that connect the individual person with cosmic realities. Avoiding the authority structure that constrains faith within conventional denominations, it allows the individual to pick and choose among beliefs and practices, to find the ones that are personally most satisfying. If organized religion is anachronistic, and science too emotionally cold, the New Age conceivably could invade both of their territories. In so doing, it could undercut the functionality of both societal institutions.

Religion, as we saw in chapters 3 through 5, has some power to provide community ties that are supportive, nurturant, and moral. The New Age seems to be a cluster of ideologies designed for isolated individuals, offering compensatory hope for lack of rewards, but not rewards themselves. For example, much of astrology is about romantic relationships and other intimate social bonds, yet it does not provide or sustain those bonds in the way that a religious congregation can. Interactions with astrologers and other New Age client cult practitioners tend to be fleeting. A person reading his or her horoscope may subjectively feel that somebody is paying attention to him or her personally, but in fact he or she is engaged in a lonely activity. In the following chapter we will consider the possibility that new religious movements may arise out of the New Age milieu, and begin to provide social benefits and controls, but in its present form the New Age is more a mythology than a movement.

New Age beliefs may conceivably discourage young people from developing the analytical skills required to learn the principles of science and engineering. In particular, they may develop a romanticized image of the human mind that would prevent them from becoming attracted to the very different perspective of cognitive science. New Agers do not like the idea that the mind is neither a soul nor a spirit, but a cognitive mechanism. Alternately, New Age ideas may invade science, wherever the social organization of research happens to be weak, or where the actual findings of science cause the most discomfort for ordinary people. Again, the cognitive area is a likely battleground. The history of psychology is replete with client cults, of which Psychoanalysis is but one of the most successful examples.

If the borderlands metaphor is valid, then the New Age may function as a cultural buffer between science and religion. Certainly, many people could suffer if open hostility breaks out between secular and sacred factions, and anything that bridges between these competing subcultures would help unify society. One could also make a free market argument, that the New Age must be socially valuable since so many people are involved in it. The counter-argument to functionalism is the idea that many features of human life are accidental, and the New Age may merely be the cultural chaos that occurs when one coherent civilization is giving way to another. It may be that the New Age marks the gradual death of religion, but the next chapter will consider the possibility that it instead is a rebirth.

7
Scientistic Religions

> When walking around the top of an abyss,
> or crossing a deep stream on a plank,
> we need a railing,
> not to hold onto
> (for it would collapse with us at once),
> but rather to achieve
> the visual image of security.
> —*Human, All Too Human*,[1]
> Friedrich Nietzsche

Many tiny quasi-religious movements are supported by professional people and the upper social classes, whereas the "cults" most often criticized by the mass media are comparable to religious sects in recruiting among deprived populations and making great demands upon their members. Whether any of these diverse groups build the strong social bonds required to sustain the morality and fertility of a large community is an unanswered question. Movements like Scientology and Transcendental Meditation make claims comparable to those of science, so they are likely to have an uneasy relationship to it, harmonizing to the extent they draw upon metaphors from the sciences but conflicting in their empirical claims. Both their vitality and their vulnerability will come from the fact that their "science" is not mere theory but supports allegedly powerful spiritual technologies.

Low-Tension Quasi-Religions

Some innovative movements that combine science and religion are respectable even to the point of being bland, and were created by people who enjoy favored positions in society. The popular image of a religious cult, inflamed by journalistic exposés, is extremely negative. Not only do most people despise the beliefs and practices of the cults, but they also imagine that members are stupid, deprived, neurotic, violent, brainwashed, and duped. However, as noted in Chapter 4, the chief result of my questionnaire study of 1,025 members of the Children of God, a very high-tension communal and millenarian group, was the finding that members have very similar attitudes to those of the general public, except in a few specific areas connected to the group's distinctive beliefs. Another finding was that members possess a range of attitudes on most topics, just as other people do, rather than being fanatic slaves to a single, radical ideology. The truth notwithstanding, people expect cults to be strange and loathsome. One consequence is that a large number of innovative religious or quasi-religious movements founded by respectable people are never recognized as such, neither by the general public nor by social scientists—nor, indeed, often by members themselves.

Much of the research on religious movements has focused on radical groups that reject the norms and values of the society, to some degree or other, and thus are deviant subcultures. Following earlier work by Benton Johnson, Stark and I reconceptualized such groups in terms of a dimension of variation called *sectarian tension*.[2] The groups commonly called *sects*, that are solidly rooted in the standard religious tradition but are much more intense in their beliefs and practices, stand in high tension to secular society. The *mainstream churches*, which have accommodated themselves to secular society, are in low tension. A movement that seeks to shift a religious group toward higher tension is a *sect movement*. One that seeks to shift it toward lower tension is a *church movement*. When a group splits, in a painful schism that divides more religious members from more secularized members, a sect movement may be battling a church movement, and the two discover they cannot cohabit in the same congregation.

Stark and I argued that a third kind of movement was important in contemporary religion: *cult movements*. We defined these as supernaturally-oriented social movements with novel or exotic beliefs and practices. To a greater or lesser extent, they dissent from the prevailing religious tradition. Thus, they are religiously deviant. Science-related examples we will consider below include Scientology and Transcendental Meditation. Stark and I assumed that cults must of necessity exist in high tension, and much of our research compared cults with sects. However, this assumption presumes that the society actually has a dominant

religious tradition, and this may no longer be true in many modern societies. Once secularization has achieved a complete separation of church
and state, and the public is comfortable with religious diversity, it becomes possible for some cult movements to exist in low tension, just as
mainstream churches do. Mindful of the fact that their leaders are often
well-educated, prosperous, and respectable, we can call these innovative,
low-tension movements *elite cults.*

Here is an example having an ironic connection to my work with
Stark. When I joined Stark at the University of Washington in 1975, one
of our more impressive colleagues in the sociology department was Professor Stuart C. Dodd. An independent thinker and prolific writer on
many topics, Dodd kept aloof from the most influential schools of sociological thought. A search of sociology articles archived at JSTOR, turns
up 34 articles he published from 1939 through 1958, but none afterward.
Several concerned the methodology of public opinion research, or
mathematical models in *sociometry* (social network analysis).[3] The catalog of the Library of Congress lists 9 books published from 1927 through
1975, the year he died. Several of his books and articles offer an idiosyncratic theory of society, in which social relations are represented mathe-
matically with the hope that precise scientific understanding would overcome human conflict and other social problems. The one publication by
Dodd that I frequently cited over the years was a 1961 article published
in an Indian philosophy journal, "Can Science Improve Praying?"[4]

Thirty years after Dodd's death, I happened to attend the annual
meetings of the World Future Society in Chicago, where to my aston-
ishment I encountered three leaders of the Stuart C. Dodd Institute for
Social Innovation. The connection to religion was immediately apparent
in the fact that one was a clergymen, the second was a lay preacher (and
founder of a fast-food chain), and the third led one of the conference sessions in spiritual breathing exercises. The clergyman, Dr. Richard Kirby,
who also leads the World Network of Religious Futurists, refers to associates of the Institute as a "community of deutero-Doddites" and uses a
"social quantum theory" to bridge from social science to spirituality.[5]
Aside from a website offering several essays, the main intellectual product of the group is a book, *The Leadership of Civilization Building,* that
applies Dodd's principles in explaining how to build a better civilization.[6] It is fairly common for elite cults to focus their efforts on providing
advice to societal leaders about how to rule more ethically and effectively.

Another example, that I studied ethnographically in the period 1972–1974 was the Committee for the Future (CFF). The CFF was founded by Barbara Marx, daughter of a wealthy toy manufacturer, who frequently experienced bouts of depression and anomie. Spending her junior year of college abroad, she met Earl Hubbard, an artist who told her he was "in search of a new image of man commensurate with our new power to shape the world."[7] They married and retired to a life of raising children and living off the benevolence of Barbara's father. When the children were grown or in the custody of her housekeeper, her longing for transcendence reasserted itself. A love affair with Dr. Jonas Salk, which Barbara described as "a constant torture," partial estrangement from her brother and sisters, and a difficult period with Earl laid the basis for an emotional experience which she calls her *epiphany*. In February 1966, she took a walk, wondering what to do next:

> I asked myself. what do we have to announce of comparable concreteness to the birth of the Christ-child? I walked on "auto-drive" around the hill at our home in Lakeville, lost in thought, unaware of time. Then the answer came in a flash: what we have to announce is, precisely, a birth. A new child *is* born: mankind. Our birth had been heralded by the wise men of the ages—*we are one*. But until our nervous system linked up to create a common awareness, a consciousness of ourselves as a whole, we were prenatal, growing in the womb of history. Now we're born into the universe, awakening to ourselves, seeking our role in universal affairs. The commandment was so clear: "Go tell the story of the birth of mankind!" I felt transfigured by this awareness.[8]

Awakening as if from a trance, she ran across the hill, tears streaming from her eyes, thankful that her prayers to become like the saints and gurus had been fulfilled, possessor of a new state of consciousness and a sacred mission. Her first practical task was to edit a book out of Earl's philosophical ramblings about the future of humanity in outer space.[9] She interpreted her epiphany as one of Abraham Maslow's peak experiences, established a personal friendship with Maslow, and energetically developed a number of other relationships with intellectuals who possessed grand images of the future.[10]

She does not footnote in her autobiography all the intellectual influences that shaped her thinking, but among the participants in early CFF activities was anthropologist Roger W. Wescott of Drew University, who wrote a book extrapolating the future of human evolution toward divinity:

Man himself, of course, is "the divine animal." But he is so only when viewed in such long-range perspective that "the human condition" is seen as a brief, if painfully obtrusive, transition from man's beast-like origins to his godlike potentialities. In this perspective, the Christian concept of God the Son and the Jewish concept of the Son of Man are telescoped, yielding a hopefully fruitful hybrid: *God the Son of Man.*[11]

In 1970, Barbara announced the birth of an organization to promote her grand goals: "We, The Committee for the Future, believe that the long range goal for mankind should be to seek and settle new worlds. To survive and to realize the common aspiration of all peoples for a future of unlimited opportunity, this generation must begin now to find the means of converting the planets into life support systems for the race of man."[12] One of her first recruits was John Whiteside, a former Air Force information officer who designed a conversion ritual called *syncon.* The name stands for *synergistic convergence,* an amalgam of concepts drawn from Buckminster Fuller and Teilhard de Chardin.[13]

Syncon was an attitude-transforming convention format, using a *social technology* to bring participants together over a few days of intensive interaction. Before a syncon, each participant would sign up for one of several task forces, each of which would plan the future of some sector of civilization, such as technology, social needs, government, production, environment, or space. Several hours would be spent in vigorous brainstorming about a particular topic, then task forces would be combined in pairs, for example giving the environment and space people the assignment to find the common ground uniting their fields. This was done in a physical space, called the *wheel,* in which seminar rooms were separated by folding walls that could be removed. Then, an "all walls down" ceremony brought everyone into a single group that would proclaim the unity of their consciousness that a marvelous future could be created. The final moment of a syncon had a powerful religious quality, with singing and such expressions of joy as a snake-dance around the segments of the wheel. Fully twenty-five syncons were held, and Barbara Hubbard continues to play a prominent role among American visionaries of the early twenty-first century.

Groups like the Dodd Institute and CFF have strong mystical qualities, but their participants are often very respectable people with solid records of accomplishments. They generally accept the legitimacy of conventional secular institutions, but seek to guide them toward creation of a better world, employing insights or techniques they believe to be scientific. Another, very different category of science-related movement that often appeals to both average citizens and some members of the elite are some of the milder Asian spiritual movements that spread throughout western civilization during the twentieth century, and that we already noted have connections to the New Age.

Asian Spiritual Techniques

The cultures of Asia include many ritual practices that are essentially religious technologies: techniques like meditation and yoga intended to achieve verifiable goals such as health, mental equilibrium, or improved abilities in daily life. Although often couched in religious terms, these are technical procedures to achieve goals without significant supernatural intervention. In contrast, within the Christian tradition, there has been an emphasis on seeking a personal relationship with God, or with his divine representative, Jesus. Priests and faith healers serve as intermediaries between the divine and the less spiritually adept members of society, but there has long been some ambivalence about the cure of bodies and souls. To the extent that a person suffered from an identifiable disease, whether physical or mental, it is often easy to determine if he or she has been cured. Thus, religions that claim to cure diseases put themselves at risk, because too many visible failures could discredit their entire belief system.

As Stark and I pointed out in *A Theory of Religion* this is the reason why the most bureaucratically organized religions tend to distance themselves from magic. We defined magic rather broadly as "specific compensators that promise to provide desired rewards without regard for evidence concerning the designated means."[14] This was meant to cover Psychoanalysis and dubious mind-control practices connected to secular ideologies, as well as religious healing that invoked supernatural forces. Magic, we noted, is more vulnerable than religion to empirical disconfirmation. People never return from the afterlife to report that Heaven does not exist. By definition, the supernatural cannot be tested, unless its proponents make specific predictions about implications for the natural world that can be observed. While religious specialists such as priests may use stories about miracles to build the enthusiasm of their congregations, it is not in their interests to risk disconfirmation of the compensators they supply by promising to do miracles on the spot, outside of the most extreme sects. Thus, others in society tend to play the role of magicians, but as Stark and I explained, this will be a relatively unstable and powerless role:

> The roles of religious specialist and magician will tend to be differentiated, as will religious and magical culture generally.
> Magicians cannot require others to engage in long-term, stable patterns of exchange.
> In the absence of long-term, stable patterns of exchange, an organization composed of magicians and a committed laity cannot be sustained.
> Magicians will serve individual clients, not lead an organization.
> Magicians are much less powerful than are religious specialists.[15]

Inheriting the centralized bureaucracy of the Roman Empire, the Christian church always had a tendency to limit its involvement with magic. In the early modern period, the rise of nation states increased the importance of ideological unity, and one consequence was the infamous witch trials of western Europe that persecuted people who were largely magical folk healers operating outside or on the margins of Christianity.[16] The Reformation and Counter-Reformation, in which Protestantism and Catholicism competed for Christian purity, further marginalized magic. I hypothesize that secular education and the progress of technology further reduced the attractiveness of supernaturally-based magic, opening the spiritual marketplace for Asian imports and for treatments like psychotherapy that were based on secular ideologies.

It is worth noting that the influx of Asian practices, such as Transcendental Meditation and yoga, were accomplished by a number of somewhat isolated individuals, rather than great bureaucracies. Historians tend to mark the turning point for America at the World's Parliament of Religions in Chicago in 1893, where several gurus spoke.[17]

By 1919, psychologist James H. Leuba was ready to analyze yoga in a scientific journal. He dismissed the notion that the postures and exercises of yoga could really provide omniscience and omnipotence, but he acknowledged that the subjective side of the experience involved strong feelings:

> During the early stages of the emptying process the Yogin enjoys a *sense* of unlimited power and the delights of imagination freed from the checks of critical reason. Physical pain is allayed and, when a trance is sufficiently profound, altogether removed, moral pain also vanishes, the dread of sickness and age, the wearisome struggle to keep up with the demands of society and of one's better self, the wickedness of duplic-

ity, pride, and hatred, disappear when the mind has become concentrated upon an "objectless content." Sensuous raptures so conspicuous in drug ecstasy seem also in some measure at least to add their delights to the Yogin's experience.[18]

Liberalization of American immigration laws in the 1960s, plus the countercultural ferment of that decade, helped one Indian guru, Maharishi Mahesh Yogi, achieve spectacular success with his simplified Indian spiritual discipline, Transcendental Meditation (TM). He had studied physics, and presented TM as a scientifically-based practice rather than a religion, the Science of Creative Intelligence. In 1965, TM recruited at the University of California, Los Angeles, consolidating this success through establishment of the Students International Meditation Society (SIMS). In 1967, the Maharishi spoke at UCLA, Berkeley, Harvard, and Yale, and subsequent growth in the United States was spearheaded from the universities.[19] In 1972, Maharishi International University was launched in Santa Barbara, California, to teach advanced courses to Transcendental Meditation trainers, and this institution later moved to Fairfield, Iowa.

Despite cultural connections to Hinduism and frequent references to Brahma, Lord of Creation, TM offered a westernized brand of meditation from which most Indian cultural elements had been stripped. In 1970, I myself attended the pair of free introductory lectures at the Cambridge, Massachusetts, center, but I did not avail myself of the moderately costly individual session to learn the meditation technique. Ten years later, I collaborated with graduate student, Daniel H. Jackson, in writing a study based on his extensive experience as a TM trainer and on quantitative data about rates of initiation he obtained from the central TM organization.[20]

The one-on-one training session began when the TM teacher performs a brief ritual, expressing gratitude to the Hindu tradition from which TM derived, but the student was not expected to participate or to view this as a religious invocation. The key point in training was to assign the student a distinctive, secret mantra that would be used as the "mental vehicle" to focus the student's meditating. During his or her 20-minute meditation sessions, perhaps twice daily, the new meditator was supposed to contemplate the sound of the mantra. The mantras were said to be scientifically chosen to match the individual's nervous system, but they were in fact taken from a list of just 16 Sanskrit words, and assigned largely on the basis of the meditator's age. In the training session, and in three subsequent "checking" sessions, the teacher discussed the student's experience in meditating.

Given its initial targeting of college campuses, it is not surprising that TM was able to promulgate its message at least briefly through essays in standard publications. Noteworthy were articles by Robert Keith Wallace in the journal *Science* and by Wallace writing with Herbert Benson in the monthly magazine, *Scientific American*.[21] These apparently authoritative publications asserted that TM created a new "state of consciousness" that could alleviate stress and increase energy. A number of popular writers mistakenly assumed that these claims for TM rested on a solid scientific basis.[22] Subsequently, *Science* published a debunking article by Robert Pagano and others reporting that TM really seemed to be indistinguishable from ordinary rest in which the meditator could even fall asleep.[23]

Further critiques drove TM out of the scientific arena.[24] Nonetheless, today the TM website asserts that 600 scientific studies have validated its claims to provide increased intelligence, improved memory, reduced blood pressure and blood cholesterol, decreased alcohol and tobacco use, better social relationships, decreased anxiety and depression, and improved job performance.[25] I once observed one of these studies go through the review process at a journal that decided not to publish it, and I have discussed some of the TM studies with scientists likely to be reviewers. The chief problem the scientific reviewers seemed to have was the implausibility of the causal mechanisms claimed for the effects, which implied the existence of spiritual forces that are not part of any scientific theory currently under discussion in university research labs. There seemed to be some willingness to grant that TM might reduce stress through the calming effect of peaceful rest, and through the placebo effect. This raises the interesting question of whether many people need a spiritually transcendent justification to rest and take their minds off their troubles.

The data on TM initiations obtained by Daniel Jackson revealed that fully 919,300 Americans took TM training from 1966 through 1977, but not at a constant rate. About 1,000 were initiated the first year, 4,459 the second year, 9,847 the third, and so on up to 292,517 in 1975. Then the fad peaked, and the rate of initiations collapsed. The peak month was November 1975, in which 39,535 were initiated, but November 1977 brought in only 2,735 new meditators, a fall of 93 percent. This posed a severe problem for the many TM trainers, who now had little to do to justify their existence and were forced into stark competition with each other. The movement responded by offering trainers advanced spiritual training for themselves, a "new breakthrough in human potential" called the *siddhis*. A picture in an ill-advised press release showed an advanced meditator levitating in mid air, suggesting that the siddhis brought supernatural powers. Legal pressures forced TM to back off from its attempt to hold classes in public schools, because it was primarily a religious movement despite its scientific pretensions.

Whether it is a client cult or a religious movement, TM offers compensators and rewards that might substitute for those available at churches. Geographical analysis supports this hypothesis. Figure 7.1 graphs the 132 American metropolitan areas with populations over 250,000, outside New England where county boundaries make it impossible to calculate comparable rates of church members. It shows rates of initiations for the peak year of 1975, by the percentage of the population who are members of conventional religious groups. The top ten cities are labeled, and the presence of Madison, Wisconsin, reflects the TM success at the university there. The line through the points is a trend line, summarizing the statistical tendency of TM to be most successful in cities with low church member rates. Indeed, extending the line off to the right makes it hit a zero rate of TM meditators in a hypothetical city where all citizens belong to churches. Thus, TM is a substitute for religion in a secularizing society.

Another way to look at the data, one that includes New England, is to compare rates for the nine "divisions" (or regions) of the United States. Table 7.1 in the appendix presents such rates, along with four similar variables. Much previous research has found that religious cults and many kinds of client cults were strongest in the Pacific Region, but the TM data show a higher rate in New England, 255 people initiated per 100,000 urban population in 1975—urban because the TM data listed only people living in urban areas. In contrast, the Pacific rate was only 227, with the Mountain region third (206). Research like the astrologer analysis in the previous chapter generally shows that the Deep South is weak in client cults, and indeed the TM initiation rates are lowest in the East South Central (61 per 100,000) and West South Central (73) divisions of the country.

While we lack recent data on TM initiations, the movement continues to exist. There are 15 Maharishi centers in Canada, and 178 in the United States. Needless to say, the center in Fargo, North Dakota, is hardly equal to the one in New York City, yet counting centers can provide a rough sense of TM's current geographical distribution. Again, more than thirty years later, New England has the highest rate, 0.22 centers per 100,000 (or 2.2 per million) total population. The Pacific rate is second-highest at 0.10, and the Mountain and West North Central regions are tied for third and fourth place, with rates of 0.07 centers per 100,000 population.

Figure 7.1: 1975 TM Initiations in Large Metropolitan Areas

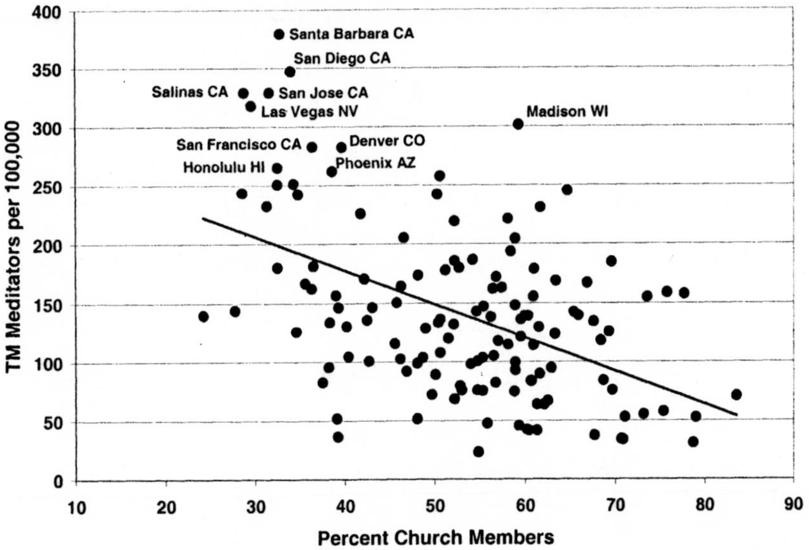

If yoga is similar to TM in its social reception, we might expect a similar geographic pattern. The International Kundalini Yoga Teachers Association, which originated from the Healthy-Happy-Holy Organization (3HO) of Yogi Bhajan, is in many ways comparable to TM. Its website lists 3HO yoga teachers.[26] The group has no yoga teachers in India, but fully 747 in the United States. The Mountain region has the highest rate, with 0.69 teachers per million, but this is the result of the fact that the group's headquarters, in Espanola, New Mexico, has 34 teachers. Again, New England leads the Pacific region, 0.48 to 0.45, and the East South Central is lowest with 0.03. Other nations with more than ten are Canada (111), Germany (24), Australia (19), Spain (15), the United Kingdom (14), Italy (13), Brazil (12), Netherlands (12), and Sweden (11). The group recognizes a connection between yoga and the New Age, saying "Kundalini Yoga is the yoga of the Aquarian Age."

An English-language website called Yogaserve lists teachers of yoga who have chosen to register.[27] As of March 23, 2006, fully 3,847 were listed for the United States. The New England rate is by far the highest, 6.29 yoga teachers per 100,000, with the Pacific region in fifth place (0.87) behind the Middle Atlantic (2.06), the Mountain (1.33), and the South Atlantic (1.14) regions. The site also lists 338 yoga teachers in Canada, 335 in Britain and Ireland (England 290, Ireland 19, Wales 14, Scotland 12), 73 in Australia, and 9 in New Zealand. India, the home of yoga, listed 106 teachers. Other non-English speaking countries with more than ten were Germany (with 31 yoga teachers), France (22), Mexico (21), Brazil (20), Italy (19), Netherlands (19), Argentina (18), Israel (12), and Switzerland (11).

The website of the Yoga Alliance lists 12,166 teachers in the United States, more than three times the number in Yogaserve.[28] Again, New England comes first, with 8.17 yoga teachers per 100,000, followed by the Mountain (6.17), the Middle Atlantic (6.04), the South Atlantic (4.44) and Pacific (4.13) regions. The 522 Canadian yoga teachers are distributed across the provinces as follows: Ontario (232), British Columbia (194), Quebec (46), Alberta (35), Nova Scotia (6), Manitoba (4), Prince Edward Island (2), Northwest Territories (2), Newfoundland (1), and none in Saskatchewan. Only one teacher is listed for India, but more than ten for each of these: Britain and Ireland (235), Australia (34), Germany (34), Japan (26), Hong Kong (24), New Zealand (19), and Mexico (18).

Clearly yoga has spread throughout modern civilization. The comparable Chinese practice, Qigong or Tai Chi, is spreading, as well, some of it promoted by the Falun Gong organization that has been the victim of severe persecution in China, although the data available are not yet sufficient for geographical analysis.[29] Writing in *The Journal of Asian Studies*, Jian Xu commented that Qigong has experienced a "difficult romance" with science, claiming objective health benefits and conceptualizing a field of forces around the human body.[30] It has long been recognized that all of these practices are analogous to psychotherapies, in that a trained professional leads a seeker through a series of experiences that may bring wisdom and probably relieve stress.[31]

As we saw with respect to astrology in the previous chapter, the Pacific region is no longer the unchallenged leader in these phenomena. The preeminence of New England in the meditator and yoga teacher rates is reminiscent of the stereotype among American political conservatives that there are actually two centers of radical liberalism in the country, San Francisco and Boston. In our 1985 book, *The Future of Religion*, Stark and I noted that New England seemed especially receptive to client cults that had a mystical quality but fell short of being fully religious.[32] The passage of two decades has only strengthened that tendency. But we should not expect to find the same degree of Bostonian receptivity for a novel spiritual practice that emphatically asserts its religious status.

Scientology

Scientology is the most-studied example of a science-oriented faith.[33] It is a "technological religion"[34] that employs an electronic device called the *e-meter* in its confessional and was founded by· L. Ron Hubbard, an adventurer and science-fiction writer. First introduced in 1950 as Dianetics, a form of psychotherapy, Scientology emerged in the 1950s as a religion offering spiritual technology intended to increase a person's abilities in this life, as well as providing a new understanding of the life to come. Of all the twentieth-century science-oriented religions, it appears to be the most successful in terms of sustained membership and impact on the surrounding culture. Examination of data about this particular group will illustrate scientific issues concerning the entire category of faiths.

The mass media have constantly excoriated Scientology for the past fifty years, so it is hard for readers to get past the negative propaganda to understand the reality. In 2001, the Religion and Public Life Survey asked Americans' reactions about a number of different religious groups "applying for government funds to provide social services to people who need them." Of 1,023 respondents, just 26.2 percent favored the idea for Scientology, 52.5 percent were opposed, and 21.3 percent did not know or refused to answer. All other religious groups showed higher favorable ratings, and lower "don't know" responses, suggesting that those Americans familiar with Scientology tend to have unfavorable attitudes, while many are not familiar. For sake of comparison, the numbers for "The Church of Jesus Christ of Latter-day Saints, or Mormon churches" are 50.9 percent favorable, 40.8 unfavorable, and 8.3 percent "don't know." The favorable responses were 62.2 percent for ordinary Catholic churches, and 61.7 percent for Protestant churches. The more education respondents had, the more likely they were to be familiar with Scientology, and the more likely they were to oppose it.[35] European hostility toward Scientology is illustrated by government criticism of the church in such nations as France and Germany.[36]

Scientology is so very different from the standard biblical faiths, that it appears strange to many people. One of the factors that determines whether a religious movement succeeds is the degree of continuity it has with the prevailing culture.[37] In a largely Christian society, for example, Christian sects have a greater chance of growing than do religious movements rooted in an alien tradition. This would seem to be a disadvantage for Scientology, which is not a Christian group, but Scientology's connection to Western science and technology may provide the necessary cultural continuity.[38] The first Dianetics book was subtitled, "the modern science of mental health."[39] The second Dianetics book claimed scientific evidence that the treatment could increase a person's intelligence.[40] Unconnected to Christianity, this technological religion does not seek the aid of Jesus or any other supernatural savior. Rather, it asserts that people can save themselves and each other while bringing science fiction hopes to reality.

A sense of the socio-cultural location of Scientology can be derived from a geographic analysis of where it is strong. In 1998, Scientology launched 15,693 personal websites in 11 languages for members in 45 nations. Of the total, 8,762 or 55.8 percent were residents of the United States. Other nations where at least a hundred Scientologists had personal websites were Italy (with 1,154), the United Kingdom (1,144), Australia (772), Germany (588), Russia (401), France (379), Mexico (369), Switzerland (314), Denmark (258), South Africa (241), Japan (153), Spain (131), Hungary (129), Taiwan (120), Netherlands (109), New Zealand (102), and Sweden (100). Another source of geographic data concerns Scientologists who have attained the high status in the church called *clear*.[41] A tabulation of how many Scientology *clears* lived in each 3-digit postal zip code area of the United States was provided by the Church of Scientology in 1985.

Table 7.2 in the appendix shows that Scientology has spread throughout the entire United States, but is strongest in the Pacific region. In 1985, there were 15.44 clears per 100,000 in the Pacific region, and in 1998 there were 9.60 websites per 100,000. The Mountain region was in second place with much lower rates, whereas New England was in third or fourth place. Essentially all new religious movements are extremely weak in the East South Central region, and Scientology is no exception, with rates of only 0.15 and 0.37. For comparison, the table also includes the 1990 church member rate, which was 40.1 percent in the Pacific states versus 59.7 in New England. This measure was calculated on the basis of a comprehensive tabulation of denominational membership and is expressed as the percentage of the population who formally belong to a church or other religious group.[42]

For the fifty U.S. states (excluding Puerto Rico and Washington, D.C.), the dataset comprises 9,021 clears and 8,654 websites. Data on the 50 American states allow us to look at statistical correlations between different variables, with states as the unit of analysis. Much social scientific research shows that new religious movements tend to be most successful in communities where people's religious needs are not satisfied, as measured by a low church member rate,[43] and we just saw a similar pattern for Transcendental Meditation. For the 50 states, there are strong negative correlations between the church member rate and the rates of clears and websites.[44] Thus, Scientology is more active where traditional churches are weak.

This illustrates the general finding that novel religions tend to thrive where conventional religious organizations are failing. Thus, there is some evidence that the decline of older faiths could stimulate the emergence of new, science-oriented churches like Scientology. However, new religions have not made up the membership deficit in the Pacific region of the United States, and there is good reason to doubt whether spiritual innovation can overcome secularization in the modern world of science.

Techniques of the Process

A logical way to conclude this chapter, and prepare the way for later ones, is to provide an ethnographic overview of the spiritual techniques employed by The Process Church of the Final Judgement, an example of a technological religion packaged in especially poetic religiosity. This was an extremely dramatic, even theatrical movement of the late 1960s and early 1970s, that drew upon Asian meditation, Scientology, Adlerian psychoanalysis, Rosicrucianism, and a variety of other systems that sought to transform personality through symbolisms and precise psychological techniques. In Chapter 3, it provided an example of the subculture-evolution model of religious innovation. Founded by Robert and Mary Anne'de Grimston in London, the group moved to the United States and Canada, achieving considerable fame on both sides of the Atlantic. Over the 1970–1975 period, I carried out about two years' worth of participant observation within the Process, and have kept in touch with members over the three subsequent decades.[45] The core group still exists today in the American southwest, but under a different name.

The Process imagined that in the distant past God existed alone and unified. Then God decided to have a game, and like a shattered mirror broke himself apart into myriad fragments, greater and lesser, spinning through space and reflecting each other's brilliance. The three greatest of these fragments were the Gods, as described in the group's scripture:

> JEHOVAH, the wrathful God of vengeance and retribution, demands discipline, courage and ruthlessness, and a single-minded dedication to duty, purity and self-denial.
> LUCIFER, the Light Bearer, urges us to enjoy life to the full, to value success in human terms, to be gentle and kind and loving, and to live in peace and harmony with one another.
> SATAN, the receiver of transcendent souls and corrupted bodies, instills in us two directly opposite qualities; at one end an urge to rise above all human and physical needs and appetites, to become all soul and no body, all spirit and no mind, and at the other end a desire to sink *beneath* all human values, all standards of morality, all ethics, all human codes of behavior, and to wallow in a morass of violence, lunacy and excessive physical indulgence.

Human beings are among the lesser fragments of God, and each person reflects one of the gods more strongly and clearly than the others. Thus, the Gods are as much a typology of human personalities, as they are a theology. For the Processeans, the female god Jehovah, and the male god Lucifer are locked in the *conflict of the mind,* representing opposite strategies of life, like the Apollonian–Dionysian dichotomy of the philosopher Friedrich Nietzsche or the obsessive-hysterical diagnostic categories of psychoanalytic psychiatry.[46] Satan represented the principle of separation that creates all dichotomies and all conflict. The Universal Law states, "As you give, so shall you receive." So, because Satan separates, Satan is separated into higher and lower aspects. As the group evolved, Christ was elevated to the status of fourth god. The opposite of separation is unification, and Christ is the unifier who seeks to heal the wounds of the conflict of the mind, and to unite with his opposite:

> Christ said: Love your enemies.
> Christ's Enemy was Satan and Satan's Enemy was Christ.
> Through Love enmity is destroyed.
> Through Love saint and sinner destroy the enmity between them.

Through Love Christ and Satan have destroyed their enmity and come
together for the End; Christ to judge and Satan to execute the
Judgement.
The Judgement is Wisdom; the execution of the Judgement is Love.

Processeans actually used these god-patterns to understand their own
and each other's personalities, going so far as to develop questionnaire
instruments like those of their colleagues in conventional psychology, to
measure members' Jehovian, Luciferian, Satanic, and Christian tendencies. Members varied considerably in how they regarded the gods, and
some of the better educated among them considered them merely metaphors to describe different personality types. Like psychotherapists,
Processean leaders employed the theory to diagnose member's personal
problems. Each of the four "gods" gave a person a different set of
"lower-end" or negative traits. Jehovians could be cruel, arrogant, self-
righteous, blameful, and bullying. Luciferians were often too sentimen-
tal, indulged in self-pity or self-justification, and were slothful. The Satanic god-pattern could indulge in lust, abandon, violence, and every
kind of excess or indulgence. Even the Christian type had flaws, Processeans believed, notably compulsive-responsibility, masochism, and
feeling weak or ineffective.

Another part of the Processean religious science was a theory and a
method about member's subconscious goals. The theory was derived
from the work of schismatic psychoanalyst Alfred Adler, who postulated
that each person possesses—or is possessed by—an overriding goal.[47]
Obsessed by this goal, but failing to understand it properly, the individual becomes caught in ever more self-defeating compulsions to achieve
it. This was not the origin of the god pattern theory of personality types,
but operated parallel to it, and there was no short list of subconscious
goals that people might have. Rather, the Process adapted the Scientology e-meter, an electronic device used in religious confessionals, calling
their similar device the *p-scope*, and employed this lie-detector device to
hunt for each individual's unique subconscious goals.

The p-scope incorporated a Wheatstone bridge circuit that causes a
highly sensitive galvanometer needle to move, as the electrical resistance
of a person fluctuated. The Processean therapist would operate the device
and give the patient instructions or ask questions. The patient would wear
a glove that touched electrodes to the patient's skin, and passed a very
weak electric current through his or her body. During a therapy session,
the person's emotions will vary, causing changes in the electrical resis-

tance of the person's skin, what psychologists call the *galvanic skin re-sponse*. The therapist would be guided by the p-scope readings.

For example, in seeking a subconscious goal, the patient could be asked, "What are your goals?" Together, the therapist and patient would list many possible goals, then the patient would speak them aloud several times, while the therapist watched the p-scope needle. When it reacted, the therapist would mark the particular goal the person was at that moment naming. They would go through the list again several times, eliminating goals that received no reaction. Eventually they would be down to just one goal, such as "to die." Then, depending upon the particular therapy process they were working on, the therapist might ask, "What would you do if you failed to die?" They would start a new list, of all the things the person said they might do if they were unable to die. Similarly, p-scope reactions would be used to whittle down this list, perhaps ending with a single secondary goal like, "to destroy people." This particular example, which happens to be from a real session, indicates the person has a compulsion associated with violence directed either inwards or outwards. Other sessions could fill in the details, until the patient understood what his or her fundamental goal was and what self-defeating compulsions needed to be avoided in order to achieve it.

A final example shows the variety of techniques the Process experimented with. Although the following exercise can be done by a lone individual, it was typically done in Midnight Meditation group sessions. There would be three chants, such as the following:

The Wrath of the Lamb has come,
The great Spirit of the Son.
To heal the wounds
That the conflict of the mind
And the power of death
Brought to the sacred land of the Gods.

Between chants there would be two meditations, the first focusing on a negative concept like confusion. For perhaps ten minutes, meditators were supposed to open themselves to all the confusion in their psyches, letting it come up to the surface and be fully felt. The second meditation would similarly focus on the positive opposite of the first concept. The opposite of confusion is clarity; the first is a burden, the second, a blessing. Meditators were supposed to draw upon their reservoirs of clarity, allow it to flow into the confusion and dissolve it. Over a period of weeks, the meditations would cover a list of 25 burden-blessing pairs, shown here in Figure 7.2.

Figure 7.2: Twenty-Five Pairs of Burdens and Blessings

Burden	Blessing	Burden	Blessing
Unawareness	Awareness	Misery	Happiness
Blame	Acceptance	Confusion	Clarity
Hatred	Love	Cowardice	Courage
Doubt	Certainty	Arrogance	Humility
Vulnerability	Invulnerability	Tension	Relaxation
Futility	Purpose	Insecurity	Security
Ignorance	Knowledge	Stupidity	Intelligence
Anxiety	Serenity	Hypocrisy	Honesty
Inhibition	Freedom	Greed	Generosity
Frustration	Satisfaction	Pessimism	Optimism
Weakness	Strength	Cruelty	Kindness
Apathy	Enthusiasm	Insensitivity	Sensitivity
Exhaustion	Energy		

Note that this is a very different conception of meditation from that promoted by TM. Transcendental Meditation is said to reduce stress, and the individual relaxes in a uniform experience of mentally repeating the sound of a one-word mantra. Perhaps this has the psychological effect of getting the person into a relaxed mood, within a familiar and reliable spiritualized context. Process meditation is quite different, challenging the individual to confront a series of twenty-five negative feelings, dissolving each with its positive opposite. TM meditations are done alone, whereas Process meditations were typically done in groups. The Midnight Meditation was a relatively brief ritual, but in some longer Process group activities the individuals were encouraged to share their meditation results with each other, thus entering into a kind of group therapy.

Conclusion

Why should we believe the faith of an ancient peoples, who lived and wrote their holy books before the rise of science? If an all-knowing God inspired the Bible, why didn't he give the ancient Hebrews any hint of the existence of the Americas, the fact that the planets are worlds, or confirmation of the Greek suspicion that matter is composed of atoms? Thinking of current debates between religion and science, why did God not explicitly admit that humans arose through a process of evolution by natural selection, or that the human mind reflects the operation of the neural network in our brains? If we have decided to keep faith with ancient traditions, why should we pick the religion of a minor country in the ever-troubled Middle East, rather than the faiths and philosophies of the great civilization of Greece and Rome, or perhaps that of the Egyptians? Indeed, why should we not preserve the religious traditions of our own people, whatever those might be, for example the English reviving the creeds associated with Stonehenge? Or, as this chapter implies, does not a scientific age require a scientistic religion?

Of course there are potential answers to these rhetorical questions. Christianity is powerful precisely because it is *not* entirely in tune with this or any other century. It offers a supernatural alternative to secular society, compensating people for the deprivations of mundane existence. Presumably incorporating the moral wisdom of generations of lived human experience, it offers a stable guide to behavior that is not overturned by current fads. Crucially, Christianity has become well-established, such that the mass media and public discourse do not constantly criticize it.

The mass media frequently imply that Scientology is some kind of fraud, but the media do not dare to suggest the same of Christianity. If we do not believe in the literal resurrection of Jesus, what are our options to understand the biblical reports? Were they socially-shared delusions, a conspiracy of lies, or metaphors that consolidated into supposed facts through a process of repeated retelling, what Peter Berger called "a rumor of angels"?[48] In any case, we avoid accusing Christian ministers of lying, on the basis that they believe what they are saying, none of us were witnesses to the original events, and there is no profit to be gained by offending the majority of fellow citizens. Again, the surrounding culture provides a cover of plausibility for the Christian claims, but the culture is changing in such a way that it provides ever-greater plausibility for scientistic religions as well. From a tiny subculture in the 1950s, science fiction has grown to become a major genre in books, movies, television programs, and video games. As science-based technology plays ever greater roles in our daily lives, it gives ideas like those embodied in scientistic religions ever increasing familiarity, without necessarily supporting them scientifically.

Although people in developing nations lead more insecure lives, there is much stress in advanced post-industrial society as well, and we must assume that future forms of society will have their own distinctive stressors. Transcendental Meditation seemed precisely designed to relieve stress. One source of stress today is low social status in a highly competitive world. Scientology, with its system of levels of training, is a separate system of honor that provides subjective status for members. New religions in general can exploit feelings of frustration, shame, guilt, and other negative emotions, so long as they encourage members to express them within an ideology that confers meaning on the members' lives.[49]

If a scientistic religion attempts to go beyond such subjective benefits, promising for example to give members higher status in the world at large, or to cure easily diagnosed physical diseases, it risks disconfirmation. Throughout history, well-established religious organizations have tended to reduce the amount of magic they offer, because magic can be disproven empirically, discrediting the entire belief system.[50] By claiming to be scientific, scientistic religions become vulnerable, so we may well wonder whether they can become as thoroughly established as traditional religions have done. Perhaps an era of scientistic religions is also an unstable one, marked by a multiplicity of movements that rise and fall rapidly, as they make magical claims, and these claims are disproven. The net result might be further discrediting of religion in general.

8
Atheism

Is man merely a mistake of God's?
Or God merely a mistake of man's?
—*Twilight of the Idols*,[1]
Friedrich Nietzsche

There are many species of doubt, and this chapter will follow a very simple distinction between Atheists, Agnostics, and people with no religion who do not choose to describe themselves with either of these words. The important point is that many people lack religious conviction, and some among them have developed one or another somewhat clear way of thinking about the issue. Atheists are those who are convinced that God does not exist. Agnostics are not sure, and they may believe it is impossible to decide about the nature of God. People who check the "no religion" box on a questionnaire, but who do not claim to be either Atheists or Agnostics, probably are a miscellaneous group. Some may be indifferent to religion and uninterested in thinking deeply about it. Others may have their own set of beliefs that fall outside the standard categories. Still others may be strong disbelievers who choose not to proclaim Atheism for fear of social reprisal.

What is Atheism?

In a religious society, Atheists are objects of ridicule. Jokes abound: "Atheism is a non-prophet organization." "Pray for the success of Atheism." "Atheists celebrate Christmas on April 1." "They have Dial-a-Prayer for Atheists now. You call, and it rings and rings but nobody answers." "How many Atheists does it take to screw in a light bulb? An infinite number, because they don't believe in light." Even some serious aspects of Atheism may seem like a joke to many religious people. For example, one of the missions of the National Cemetery Administration, part of the U.S. Department of Veterans Affairs, is to place memorial headstones on the graves of Americans who had served in the military. Among the "emblems of belief" that can be inscribed on a headstone are a Christian cross, a Jewish Star of David, and a Buddhist Wheel of Righteousness. The emblem for Atheists is the traditional symbol of an atom with the letter A in place of the nucleus.[2]

All joking aside, it would be useful to know about the social characteristics of contemporary Atheists, Agnostics, and others lacking religion. Such knowledge could provide some hint of what a more fully secular society would be like. It is possible that secularization will lead to a loss of relevance for religion, leaving people uninterested rather than Atheistic. After God is not only dead but buried, no one may need to reject him. Yet two factors suggest a continuing relevance for Atheism. First, religion will not wink out like a dead light bulb, so for a very long time there will be religious movements in society that Atheists may oppose. Second, to the extent that science succeeds in offering a comprehensive explanation of existence, those who accept it would tend to reject any supernatural alternative.

A dictionary will define Atheism as disbelief in the existence of deities, but that definition does not locate the concept sociologically. A fresh but frankly unproven approach is to map the words in a semantic space defined by their use in websites. Perhaps the most fundamental way to categorize websites is in terms of their domains. In North America, there have been primarily six classifications of websites ending in one of six domain codes: .edu (educational institutions), .com (businesses), .gov (US federal government), .net (mostly personal websites hosted by Internet service providers), .org (non-profit organizations), and .mil (the US military).

Figure 8.1 maps *Atheism, Atheist, Agnostic* and three religion-related words on the basis of how many web pages in different domains contain the word. In Google and several other search engines, one can restrict the search to one domain at a time, for example by entering "atheist site:edu" or "atheist site:com." Google estimates that fully 7,660,000 web pages contain the word "atheist," 118,000 in the .edu domain, and 4,740,000 in the .com domain. Arguably, websites in the .edu domain represent the intelligentsia of universities and colleges, thus a kind of intellectual orthodoxy. In contrast, .com sites serve the general public's commercial needs, and thus are more populist. A similar but not identical distinction

can be made between .gov and .net sites, the former representing the orthodoxy of the federal government, and the latter the informality of ordinary citizens. For each word we can calculate two ratios: .edu/.com and
.gov/.net, and together the two ratios measure the degree of elite orthodoxy of the concept, in comparison with its popular interest. For example, the .edu/.com ratio for "atheist" is 2.5 percent, and the .gov/.net ratio
is 0.2 percent. Table 8.1 in the appendix gives the numbers for all six
words.[3]

Figure 8.1: A Google-Based Semantic Map

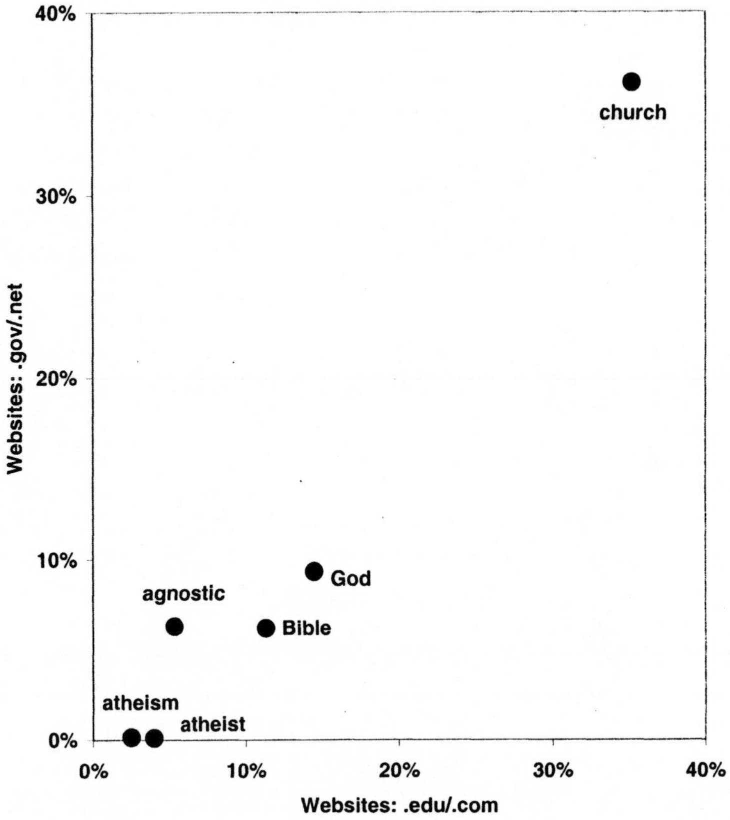

The lower-left corner of the concept map represents words that are
extremely remote from the educational and governmental institutions that
define non-religious orthodoxy in American society. Yet that is where

we find *Atheism, Atheist* and *Agnostic.* A little further out of the corner we find *Bible* and *God.* That is where we might expect to find these religious concepts in a formally secular society that has a long tradition of separation of church and state. Then we find the word *church* in the upper-right corner. Many universities and colleges have churches on campus, and the government must recognize the existence of churches because they represent a major institution of the society. Note that the map could continue far up and to the right, and any word less than 100 percent on both of the dimensions is somewhat underrepresented in .edu and .gov websites, so *church* is underrepresented, although less so than the other five words. We can read the map thus: religion is far from central to the nation's educational and governmental institutions, although formal religion as represented by *church* enjoys some recognition. Religious concepts like *Bible* and *God* are extremely marginalized, but not so completely marginalized as anti-religious concepts like *Atheism, Atheist* and *Agnostic.*

George H. Smith distinguished *implicit atheism,* in which a person simply lacks belief in gods, from *explicit atheism* that consciously rejects the existence of gods.[4] People who check the Atheist box on a questionnaire are explicit Atheists. When I capitalize the word *Atheism,* I mean to suggest that it is a system of beliefs, deserving social recognition comparable to that of Protestantism, Catholicism, or Confucianism. In a religious society, Atheism is a system of beliefs that rejects the consensus of most citizens, thus standing in opposition to the dominant culture. This may cause many Atheists to conceal their beliefs, in fear of formal or informal punishment. This may lead to a *spiral of silence,* in which Atheists think they are a smaller minority than they really are, thereby gaining even more motivation to conceal themselves, and the majority never confronts the fact that many of their friends and neighbors are unbelievers.[5] As we consider social characteristics of Atheists, we should keep in mind that the religious situation today may shape Atheism in ways that a fully secular society would not.

Over several recent years, 8,027 Americans have told the General Social Survey what they believe about God, through the very limiting means of checking a box. Just 2.5 percent selected the Atheistic option, "I don't believe in God." Another 4.0 percent expressed Agnosticism: "I don't know whether there is a God and I don't believe there is any way to find out." But, then, another 8.4 percent said, "I don't believe in a personal God, but I do believe in a Higher Power of some kind." What should we call this third alternative? Often the word *Deist* is used for somebody who believes God made the world then withdrew and no longer intervenes in its affairs, but the word has other connotations as well. What is a "a Higher Power of some kind" if it is not God? A clear definition of Atheism assumes we already have a clear definition of God, but in any modern, cosmopolitan society this is probably not the case.

In a polytheistic society, an Atheist might be a person who does not believe in enough gods. Some contemporary "flying saucer cults" and other new religious movements believe in a hierarchy of progressively higher beings, but may be quite vague on whether there is a supreme being above them all. *Pantheists* believe that God manifests throughout the universe, but if God is the universe, then there is no God outside it, and a Pantheist is a kind of Atheist. The Process Church of the Final Judgement, described in the previous chapter, asserted that God broke himself into parts (Lucifer, Jehovah, Christ, Satan, and a host of lesser beings including ourselves) in order to play a game, so in a sense God does not exist now and will not until the shattered fragments of God come back together.

Another definitional issue is the problem of certainty. Western, monotheistic religions stress faith in one God, represented by one religion. Despite the great latitude in belief that mainstream liberal denominations grant their members, the fundamental principle is that people should have conviction. Adherents of a religion should be loyal to it. Indeed, the words *true* and *faithful* can mean *loyal*, quite apart from their connection to belief. When I set out to model religious belief in artificial intelligence computer simulations, as described in the following chapter, I found that the best way to do it was in terms of probabilities and relative strength of feelings, rather than absolute conviction or pure Atheism. Using the approach called neural nets and machine learning, I modeled human minds in terms of networks of variable strengths of associations between data and ideas. Real people are constantly hedging their bets, and complete conviction is unnatural. An Atheist, by this standard, would be somebody who strongly doubts the existence of God, is highly critical of arguments people make in favor of God, and is not prepared to bet his or her life on the assumption that God exists. But, then, few devout church goers are really prepared to bet their lives on their faith. The claim that there are no Atheists in foxholes leaves open the possibility that there are many of them in church.

Who Are the Atheists?

We know surprisingly little about Atheism, from a social-scientific per-spective. One would think that it would have been studied extensively, for comparison with religiosity, but this is not the case. Historical studies exist, chiefly written within the History of Ideas,[6] and there is a fairly large and disputatious literature in which Atheists and their opponents argue matters of belief. But systematic attempts to understand Atheism as a social or psychological phenomenon, employing rigorous theory and quantitative research methods, are rare. For example, the online database of the National Science Foundation lists abstracts of no research grants at all containing the words "Atheism" or "Atheist."

Avowed Atheists are admittedly somewhat rare, although they may be increasing. Some nations include a question about religious affiliation in the census. The population of Canada rose 9.8 percent from 1991 to 2001, to a total of 29,639,030, but those claiming no religion rose 43.9 percent to 4,796,325, a much more rapid increase. Although most Cana-dians have a religious affiliation, the "no religion" group is the second largest, falling well behind the Roman Catholics but well ahead of the two largest Protestant denominations, the United Church of Canada and the Anglican Church. However, Atheists are a small fraction of the non-religious, just 18,605 in 2001, which is an increase of 37.7 percent over the decade before.[7] The proportion of Australians reporting no religion increased from 6.7 percent in 1971 to 16.5 percent in 1996, but the 7,496 self-avowed Atheists among them constituted only 0.04 percent of the 17,892,409 population in 1996.[8]

The relative dearth of survey research about Atheism has three very practical causes, quite apart from any dereliction of duty on the part of scholars who have simply failed to survey it. First, Atheists are rare in the populations that typically have been surveyed, so unless one has a very large number of respondents, the data will simply not support statis-tical analysis. Second, perhaps partly in response to the first problem, there has been a tendency to lump Atheists along with Agnostics and people who are simply indifferent to religion in an undifferentiated "No Religion" category, the infamous *nones* named long ago by Vernon.[9] Third, surveys with large numbers of respondents are quite expensive, every additional item is costly, and one cannot identify Atheists without including at least one specialized item like the GSS question about God, quite apart from the other items one needs to explore the correlates of Atheism.

However, two recent studies have offered interesting findings about Atheism, based on international surveys, and thus provide a good starting point for the present study. With data from the 1994 Eurobarometer survey and the 1994 American General Social Survey, Bernadette Hayes identified correlates of being a "religious independent," and part of her analysis distinguishes Atheists from Agnostics and the nondescript nonreligious.[10] Hayes reports that religious independents (including Atheists) tend to be young, male, unmarried, and well-educated. She comments that the gender difference is especially consistent across nations.

Wolfgang Jagodzinski and Andrew Greeley, in a study published on Professor Greeley's website, have employed data from the International Social Survey Program, to test the "supply side" theory that the demand for religion is relatively constant over time and space, in contrast with a simple secularization theory that predicted a decline over time.[11] Jagodzinski and Greeley chiefly used Atheism as an inverse indicator of the demand for religion in a national market, but they also suggested data-based hypotheses about Atheism itself.

For example, Jagodzinski and Greeley defined hard-core Atheists as people who firmly rejected the idea of life after death, as well as denying the existence of God. They report that 83 percent of this group claimed they never believed in God during their lives, and 61 percent never attended church when they were eleven or twelve years old. From these and other findings they conclude that hard-core Atheism was a personal choice made early in life. In the ISSP dataset, age shows a curvilinear relationship, with the very young and very old less likely to be Atheists. Men are significantly more likely than women to be Atheists, except in nations where Atheism is especially rare.

Given how rare Atheists are in the General Social Survey, and that most of the interesting questions one might want to correlate with Atheism were asked in different administrations of the survey that lack the God item, there is relatively little we can learn from it. The GSS does show that 3.7 percent of males claim to be Atheists, compared with only 1.7 percent of females. The corresponding numbers for Agnostics are 6.0 percent and 2.5 percent. Table 8.2 in the appendix also documents that Atheism is more common among the never-married GSS respondents, and those who have no children. These facts hint that Atheism may possibly be associated with weak social attachments or interpersonal obligations, an idea that will now receive theoretical justification.

Theories of Atheism

Probably, Atheism has many causes. Logically, some people could have been raised Atheists; others may have had early traumatic experiences with religion; a few may have resolutely unmystical personalities; a few may have by chance made religion the focus of adolescent rebellion; and many may have been socialized in adulthood to anti-religious professional ideologies (as sociology, anthropology, and psychology may be). Jagodzinski and Greeley make the interesting assumption that Atheists experience no need for religion, but they do not in their essay say how this might come to be. Here we will explore this further, beginning with a consideration of how religion meets social expectations, human needs and cognitive habits. Consider how the three scientific theoretical perspectives on religion might explain Atheism.

From the societal perspective, an Atheist might be someone who exists outside the society, *egoistic* or *anomic* to use Durkheim's terms. Durkheim wrote at the very beginning of the twentieth century, and later writers developed similar ideas into sophisticated explanations of deviant behavior. Many writers in the so-called *Chicago School* of sociology argued that individual deviance is caused by *social disorganization*, when society becomes so chaotic that the individual is cast adrift.[12] Notably, Faris and Dunham argued in 1939 that social disorganization could often cause mental illness, so presumably it could even more easily cause mild forms of mental deviation, such as Atheism might be in a predominantly religious society.[13] In the 1960s, criminologists like Travis Hirschi developed the related *control theory*, which argued that people are free to deviate if their social attachments and investments are weak or broken.[14] This line of reasoning suggests that Atheism may be a form of deviance, possibly connected with other forms.

Religious people often assume that Atheists are immoral, untrustworthy, or willfully antisocial. The King James Version of the Bible translates the first verse of Psalm 14 thus: "The fool hath said in his heart, There is no God. They are corrupt, they have done abominable works, there is none that doeth good." The Contemporary English Version published in 1995 by the American Bible Society puts it this way: "Only a fool would say, 'There is no God!' People like that are worthless; they are heartless and cruel and never do right." Some modern dictionaries give *wickedness* as a synonym for *atheism*.

According to the 2002 Religion in Public Life Survey, 44.5 percent of American adults believe, "It is necessary to believe in God in order to be moral and have good values."[15] A greater fraction, 52.1, said, "It is not necessary to believe in God in order to be moral and have good values." As we might expect, religious people are more likely to distrust atheists. Of those who attend religious services more than once a week, fully 65.0 percent believe it is necessary to believe in God in order to be moral. A slight majority, 52.8 percent, of those who attend once a week feel the same way. But even 25.7 percent of those who never attend hold the same negative stereotype of Atheists. So, the majority think Atheists could be moral, but a very large minority, even a majority of very religious people, are convinced Atheists are immoral. Notice that both statements are consistent with the view that Atheists are more likely to be immoral, and thus the survey shows very powerful prejudice against Atheists.

Other questions in the survey asked people whether their views on various groups are favorable or unfavorable. Probably, the familiar religious group that faced the most serious prejudice and discrimination in western civilization during the past century was the Jews, so we can compare their current public-opinion situation with that of Atheists. Charles Glock and Rodney Stark carried out a landmark study of how Christian beliefs contributed to anti-Semitism.[16] One factor they cited was the view that Jewish priests or the Jewish public were partly responsible for the crucifixion of Jesus, and another was the failure of Jews to convert to Christianity over the centuries. Another sociologist, Alan Edelstein, has noted a countervailing tradition of philo-Semitism, that could be based either upon a realistic assessment of the accomplishments of Jews or on religious romanticization of the ancient Hebrews.[17] One would imagine that fewer people today conceptualize Jews as characters in a religious drama—whether heroes or villains—but see them realistically as human beings. The same may be less true for Atheists.

Figures 8.2 and 8.3 compare the opinions of men and women about Atheists and Jews, based on the 2002 Religion in Public Life Survey. The results are striking. Altogether, 34.3 percent of Americans express favorable attitudes toward Atheists, whereas fully 75.4 percent have favorable attitudes toward Jews. A majority, 53.8 percent, have unfavorable attitudes toward Atheists, compared with only 8.1 percent who have negative opinions of Jews. It is possible that some latent anti-Semitism lurks among the slightly larger fraction who declined to express an opinion about Jews, but however one looks at the figures, prejudice against Atheists is remarkably strong, and stronger among women than among men. In his influential book *Protestant, Catholic, Jew*, half a century ago

Figure 8.2: Men's Attitudes toward Atheists and Jews

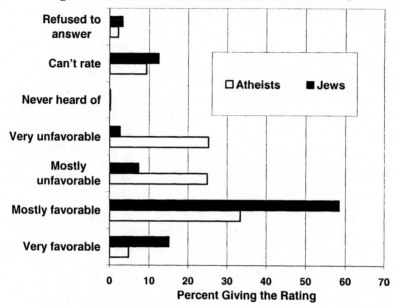

Figure 8.3: Women's Attitudes toward Atheists and Jews

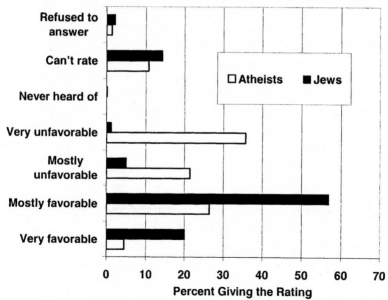

Source: Religion in Public Life Survey, 2002

Will Herberg argued that being Jewish had become an equally respectable way of being an American, but the same cannot be said today for Atheists.[18]

Unlike the societal theory, exchange theory does not necessarily say that Atheism is a form of deviance, but it does build much of its analysis on how humans interact with each other to get rewards and avoid costs. As animals living in a hazardous but resource-rich world, we must seek rewards and attempt to avoid costs. But more than any other animal, we posses powerful brains capable of language, analysis, and planning. Through social interaction, humans exchange explanations about how to obtain rewards. In the absence of a desired reward, explanations often will be accepted which posit attainment of the reward in the distant future or in some other non-verifiable context. Compensators are postulations of reward according to explanations that are not readily susceptible to unambiguous evaluation. Religion is the societal institution dedicated to the exchange of general compensators based on supernatural assumptions.

A person who had all the rewards he or she could ever want would have no need for compensators, and thus could be an Atheist. Religion is at least somewhat costly, so by the calculus of rewards and costs, a person would not be religious unless the person perceived it rewarding to be so. People who are especially healthy, prosperous, and untroubled in their personal relations may have little or no need for specific compensators, and both kinds of compensators play important roles in most religious traditions. As we reported in Chapter 3, Norris and Inglehart argue that the weaker religiousness of people in postindustrial societies stems from their higher level of social, economic, and political security.[19]

This is an explanation for the intensity of religiosity in sects: Their members are relatively deprived, even within prosperous societies, and thus they have greater need for specific compensators. For example, the Church of the Nazarenes and the Holiness churches are sectarian movements in the Methodist tradition. Data from the General Social Survey reveal that just 26 percent of regular Methodists had failed to graduate from high school, compared with 41 percent in the Nazarenes and 51 percent in smaller Holiness groups.[20] Among Jehovah's Witnesses, a major sect in the Adventist tradition, 43 percent have never graduated.[21] But all people face death, so at some level all people are objectively deprived and are therefore open to general compensators.

This observation may provide an explanation for the common but not entirely consistent finding that Atheists (or the larger category of non-religious people) tend to be somewhat young. Old people know that their own, personal deaths loom in the very near future, and throughout their long lives they have suffered the deaths of valued friends and family members. Thus, general compensators based on supernatural assumptions should be especially salient for them.

The suggestion by Jagodzinski and Greeley that Atheists tend to adopt their belief system in youth would seem logical in this light, because young people may not sense the reality of death as vividly as old people. In the rebelliousness of youth, a few may reject the beliefs of their elders. Once psychologically committed to their Atheism, these people may be reluctant to abandon it even as they learn some of the harsh lessons of life with the passage of years.

The cognitive theory of religion offers an alternative causal explanation of why some individuals are Atheists, but most are not. As we summarized this theory in Chapter 2: The human brain evolved to facilitate social interaction and to deal with predators or prey, so it naturally assumes that complex phenomena result from the actions of aware beings, incidentally favoring belief in gods. However, the human gene pool contains considerable variation, short people and tall, thin people and stout, sociable people and antisocial. Conceivably, people with an innate weakness in the part of the brain responsible for social attachments, if there is such a part, would attach less strongly to supernatural beings as well as natural ones.

Let us assume that some people have a weak propensity to develop social obligations, whether because their brains are different, their social experiences have not rewarded interaction, or for some other reason. Given a psychological difference, there can be social consequences. The compensator theory of religion is not merely psychological; it is social. In examining the ways that religion gains strength through intimate interactions between people, it can be valuable to distinguish two kinds of compensations:[22]

> Primary compensation substitutes a compensator for a reward that people desire for themselves.
> Secondary compensation substitutes a compensator for a reward that a person is obligated to provide to another person.

Primary compensation is psychological, satisfying the emotional need of the believer. Secondary compensation is social, sustaining a relationship when one party to it is empirically unable to provide a reward to the other, that the other either expects or desperately wants. For the obligated person, the compensator assuages guilt for failing to deliver the reward, especially if the person expecting it endorses the religious system of which the compensator is a part. For the person to whom the obligation exists, the compensator sustains trust that the exchange partner is benevolent, committed to the relationship, and willing to provide other rewards in future.

In an earlier publication, I described how my great-grandmother sang hymns to her brother over the painful weeks that he died from typhoid.[23] It would require a very dogmatic Atheist in such a situation to say, "Well, I'm sorry there's no God or afterlife, but we'll really remember you fondly after you've died."

This example perhaps suggests why studies tend to find that women are less likely to be Atheists (or non-religious) than men. Traditionally, and perhaps rooted in our biological natures, females are more nurturant and more concerned with intimate social relations than men. They have a more direct obligation for care-giving within the family. Thus, they may have more occasion to resort to secondary compensation, when they cannot materially provide the help or other rewards they are obligated to give.

Secondary compensation may be a major factor in the creation and maintenance of religious organizations, even though the literature on the subject has concentrated on primary compensation. If religious compensators actually do not satisfy sufferers' needs very well, they might still satisfy their exchange partners' obligations to provide assistance. I am not here asserting that religious primary compensation is ineffective, merely raising the theoretical point that it might be, and suggesting we should examine scientifically how much of the success of religious organizations is due to secondary compensation.

This line of argument suggests that Atheism may be most common among people who lack intimate, personal obligations of the kind that might benefit from secondary compensation. Someone upon whom no one else is dependent, someone who lacks strong social bonds of a kind to incur such obligations, is more free to espouse Atheism. The same may be true, but perhaps with lesser strength, for people who call themselves Agnostics, say they are non-religious, or who evidence no interest in religion. However, these people have not committed themselves, in the manner of someone who publicly professes Atheism, so they are more able to draw upon religion as needed over the course of time.

Religion in the *Survey2001* Dataset

The primary source of data for this chapter is *Survey2001*, the online
questionnaire we used extensively in Chapter 6. One *Survey2001* question asked, "What is your religious preference?" The available responses
were: Protestant, Catholic, Jewish, Muslim, none, other, and don't know.
The web pages of the questionnaire were generated dynamically, and the
program was set to ask follow-up questions for some items. Any respondent who said his or her religion was "none" or "don't know" was given
another question: "Individuals who do not have a religious preference, or
who do not know how to describe it, often categorize themselves in other
ways. How would you describe yourself?" The respondent was asked to
choose one of four responses: non-religious, Agnostic, Atheist, and none
of these.

The questionnaire's sponsor, *National Geographic*, publishes for-
eign-language editions, and social-scientists active in nations speaking
Spanish, German, and Italian were responsible for promoting the versions of the questionnaire in those languages, so the non-English speakers are not merely odd minorities who happened to stumble into the survey's website. However, because the respondents are far from a random
sample, it is important to focus on differences across the categories of
whatever independent variable we are looking at, rather than the absolute
level of the variables. Atheists constituted 11.7 percent of those responding in German and smaller fractions of those in Italian (8.8 percent),
Spanish (5.2) and English (5.1). The pattern was different for Agnostics,
with 6.7 percent of English speakers selecting this choice compared with
Italian (6.5 percent), Spanish (5.2), and German (4.3). English speakers
led again in the non-descript "non-religious" category with 11.0 percent,
followed by those responding in German (10.7 percent), Italian (8.2), and
Spanish (7.9).

Jagodzinski and Greeley made much of the unusually high level of
Atheism in East Germany, and here for German-speakers in general we
see double the rate of English-Speakers and Spanish-speakers, and
somewhat more than among Italian-speakers. Some of that German
Atheism seems to come at the expense of Agnosticism. There is a fine
line between the two, and it is possible that public pro-Atheism rhetoric
in German-speaking Europe could relatively easily have shifted some
respondents from the Agnostic to the Atheist response. Conversely, the
proverbial religiousness of the United States, and perhaps the lesser public visibility of Atheism in English-speaking nations (compared anyway

with Germany) could account for the larger fraction who are Agnostics rather than Atheists among the respondents who answered the questionnaire in English.

In Chapter 4, we suggested that the fertility collapse in advanced industrial nations may be connected to secularization. Thus it is worth comparing the questionnaire's estimates of Atheism with national fertility, for the nations with a significant number of respondents. Nine nations contributed at least 100 respondents who answered the religion questions, and Figure 8.4 includes two others (Argentina and China) that fell just below this threshold. There were neither Hindi nor Mandarin versions of the questionnaire, so respondents from India and China answered in English. China remains officially a Marxist–Leninist–Maoist nation, and continues to do much to suppress religion of all kinds. At the same time it is unusual among developing countries to have had a successful program to reduce the birth rate. The fertility rates came from the 2004 edition of the *World Factbook* published by the Central Intelligence Agency, and they are estimates of the average total number of children born to woman who have completed the childbearing years.[24]

A glance at the chart suggests that Atheists are relatively more numerous in nations with low fertility rates, and indeed there is a substantial negative correlation between the two variables.[25] There are, of course, at least three ways to interpret this association, and it is possible that all three are correct. First, low fertility could cause Atheism, which is in line with the argument of this chapter. Second, Atheism could cause low fertility, although it seems unlikely that such a small minority of the population could alone be responsible for such a large demographic phenomenon. Third, both Atheism and low fertility could be the results of a third factor, such as secularization.

Having anchored our discussion of Atheism in earlier topics of this book, we can now focus more closely on social life. In what follows, I will focus just on the English-language respondents who answered key questions. For sake of concision, I will seldom comment on the Agnostics and non-religious respondents, but will offer their data as well for the reader's inspection. In many of the tables, these two groups show a pattern that is indeed similar to that for Atheists. At times their patterns are more complex, and I suspect that may partly result from the fact that for some respondents Agnosticism is simply a "don't know" response that will associate with moderate responses to the other variable, and the non-religious are a heterogeneous group.

Figure 8.4: Atheism and Fertility in 11 Nations

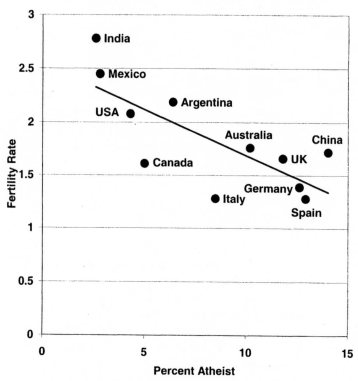

Family Obligations and Sociability

As reported by Hayes and noted above, studies tend to find that men are more likely to be non-religious or Atheists than women.[26] In the English-language *Survey2001* data, 6.4 percent of men who answered the questions report being Atheists, in comparison with 5.0 percent of women. The difference, 1.4 percentage points, may seem small, but keep in mind that Atheism is rare. The ratio of these numbers is not so small, men being nearly 1.3 times as likely to be Atheists as women are, which could be expressed as a rather more impressive 130 percent. Again, this can be interpreted as reflecting women's greater need for secondary compensation within family obligations, but of course that is an inference rather than a fact.

The next obvious step in evaluating the impact of family obligations is to look at marital status. Our theory of secondary compensation predicts that Atheists are more common among single persons than among the married, and among *Survey2001* respondents, 6.1 percent of single people are Atheists, compared with 5.0 percent of those who are married. People who are cohabiting without benefit of marriage are much more likely to be Atheists, 9.1 percent of them. The theory of secondary compensation is about using religion to fulfill obligations, and it suggests that Atheists will have fewer serious family obligations to other people. The theory does not say that Atheists are anti-social hermits. Cohabiters are certainly social—they share intimate domestic life with another person—but they have explicitly failed to take on the obligations of marriage. Thus the fact that Atheism is most common among cohabiters strongly supports the theory of secondary compensation.

In the *Survey2001* dataset, only 3.8 percent of divorced people are Atheists. Divorced persons may possibly have fewer family obligations—not the case if children are involved—and thus might have less need of secondary compensation. However, the divorced respondents, as is typical in survey research, are the divorced people who have neither remarried nor are cohabiting. Thus it seems likely that they suffer deprived social lives. However difficult marriage was for them—and many will not have wanted to get divorced—they have experienced the rewards of married life and now are deprived of those rewards. Thus, arguably, they will have unusually great need of primary compensation. It is hard to guess the balance between reduced secondary compensation and increased primary compensation, but divorced persons actually are less likely to be Atheists than the three other groups. Fuller statistics are available in appendix Table 8.3.

Having looked at marital status, the next logical variable is the presence or absence of children in the household. One *Survey2001* item asked, "How many people in your household are children under 18?" Naturally, the prediction is that the presence of children, and of more children, increases family obligations and reduces Atheism. Among respondents living in childless households, 6.2 percent are Atheists, compared with 5.8 percent in households having one child, and 3.9 percent in households with two or more children. As Table 8.4 in the appendix shows, the effect is greater for women. Among men, the proportion Atheist among those living with no children is about 1.3 times that of men living with two or more children. But the ratio is almost 2.7 among women, more than twice as great. Males without children are fully 3.2

times as likely as women with children to be Atheists—6.8 percent versus 2.1 percent. This is a really big difference, and further strengthens our confidence that a lack of need for secondary compensation is at least an important part of the explanation for Atheism.

Atheists' attitudes about having children can be measured roughly with a traditional "alienation" item, in the form of a statement with which the respondent could agree or disagree: "With how things look for the future, it's not fair to bring children into the world." Of those who strongly disagreed, thus being relatively favorable toward having children, 5.2 percent were Atheists. This compares with 5.9 percent among those who merely disagreed, 6.7 percent among those who responded "don't know," 10.9 percent among those who agreed, and fully 14.3 percent among those who strongly agreed.

One set of fully 40 items asks the respondents, "How much would you like to do the following activities?" Four of the stimuli are especially relevant here: a large family reunion, a family history field trip, preparing a festive meal, getting together with friends. Clearly, the first two of these concern family relations, and a festive meal might often mean Thanksgiving or some other family gathering. Getting together with friends implies nothing about family. Table 8.5 in the appendix examines Atheism across the response categories for the four items: not at all, not really, mixed feelings, would like, like very much.

The item about a family reunion gives really striking results. Among people who would not at all like a family reunion, fully 15.9 percent are Atheists, compared with only 3.4 percent among those who would like a reunion very much. This difference is a ratio of nearly 4.7! The pattern for a family history trip is also quite strong, and would have been remarkable in itself, were it not overshadowed by the somewhat stronger pattern for family reunion. The results for a festive meal also suggest that people who uninterested in this kind of social occasion are more apt to be Atheists. Responses about getting together with friends do not show a clear Atheism pattern. Atheists do not lack friends. The question then becomes: What is the quality of these friendships?

One *Survey 2001* item was part of a batch headed, "When I am with my friends" and stated: "They always take the time to talk over my problems." Another item said, "No matter what happens I know that my friends will be there for me." The available responses were: never, rarely, sometimes, often, always. Among respondents whose friends never "take the time," 8.9 percent are atheists, compared with 6.3 percent among those who friends always do. Few people admitted their friends never "are there for me," but among those who friends are rarely there, 11.6 percent are atheists, compared with 6.1 percent among those whose friends are always there. Both measures of friendship obligations show that Atheism is more common at the low obligation end of the scale.

Geographic Mobility

A substantial body of research exists that infers geographic differences in the stability of friendships from rates of migration. As earlier chapters noted, instability of social relationships, as measured by migration, tends to reduce membership in religious congregations, and has complex inter-relationships with religion in affecting a variety of kinds of deviant behavior. This can be illustrated for Atheism with data from the 1911 Australian census, giving religious affiliation by birthplace for each state (and the Capital Territory) for each sex, including Atheists, Agnostics, Freethinkers, and those with "no religion."[27] These data can be reorganized to compare the religious affiliations of migrants with those of people who still live in their state of birth.

The number of self-professed Australian Atheists in 1911 was quite small, only 238 men and 47 women, out of 1,814,897 male and 1,800,782 female native born Australians, only 0.013 percent and 0.003 percent. We would guess that significantly larger minorities privately held Atheistic sentiments but were discouraged by the cultural context from expressing their views. Keeping in mind that *Survey2001* respondents are not a random sample, it is still worth noting that Figure 8.4 reported that fully 10.2 percent of Australian respondents professed Atheism 90 years after the 1911 census.

Importantly, Atheism and similar forms of religious deviance were more common among migrants. Among males counted by the 1911 census in the same state in which they were born, 9 per 100,000 were Atheists, compared with 43 per 100,000 for males born in another state from where the census found them. This is a ratio of 4.8 in favor of migrants. This ratio is higher for Atheists than for the other forms of deviant belief: Agnostics (3.8), Freethinkers (3.8) and "no religion" (2.8). Similar ratios obtain for the small number of women as well: Atheists (3.0), Agnostics (2.9), Freethinkers (2.4), and "no religion" (1.5).

Several *Survey2001* items measured migration. One asked, "How long have you lived at your current address?" and offers a range of responses from "less than one year" to "10 years or more." Although we are generally avoiding elaborate statistical controls in this book, it is necessary to note that migration is a variable strongly connected to age, and we may need to take account of that factor. Abstractly, perhaps each person has a certain probability of moving in any given year, so whether they have moved will partly be a result of how many years they have lived. More concretely, there are points in life, such as graduating from college, getting married, or retiring that may increase the probability of moving, and these points accumulate over the years.

The item about how long the respondent has lived at his or her current address had fully eleven response categories, so for intelligibility and to preserve high numbers of respondents in each column, appendix Table 8.6 collapses them into six. Both with and without an age control, the pattern is uneven, but clearly Atheists are more common among very recent migrants who have lived in their current homes for less than one year.

Within the United States, a good proxy for migration is whether the respondent lives in the five states that the US Census Bureau places in its Pacific division of the country: Alaska, California, Hawaii, Oregon and Washington. As we have seen, church membership rates are unusually low in this region, and perhaps in consequence rates of cults are high. It will be interesting now to see whether rates of Atheism, Agnosticism and nondescript non-religiousness are high, as we might predict. They indeed are. Whereas 6.2 percent of the 1,129 *Survey2001* respondents from the Pacific region are Atheists, only 3.9 percent of the 5,279 respondents from the rest of the United States are. For Agnostics, the proportions are 9.0 percent versus 6.6 percent, and for non-religious, 13.0 percent versus 7.9 percent. Adding these three categories together, we find that the difference is 28.2 percent versus 18.4, or a ratio of more than 1.5.

Because all General Social Survey respondents are coded in terms of the region of the United States they live in, we can compare Atheism in the Pacific region between the GSS and *Survey2001*. In the GSS data, 3.7 percent of Pacific respondents were Atheists, versus 2.1 percent in the rest of the nation, which can be compared with the figures from *Survey2001* which are 6.2 percent and 3.9 percent. As we expected, respondents to this web-based questionnaire include more Atheists, but for present purposes the important thing to note is that the regional difference is essentially the same. Both datasets show that Atheists are more common in the Pacific region, by ratios of about 1.8 and 1.6, respectively.

Conclusion

The evidence considered in this chapter generally supports the hypothesis that an important source of Atheism is lack or weakness of social obligations, and thus reduced need for secondary compensation. A subtheme of the chapter is the concern that social obligations may be too weak in many societies to sustain them demographically. This suggests a fresh way of looking at secularization. A decline in interpersonal social obligations, associated with a collapse of fertility but perhaps also with the rise of modern institutions that have taken obligations away from individual citizens, is a very different but possibly more accurate statement of the secular trend. This may partly explain why religion seems stronger in the United States, where government has taken over fewer social obligations than in more secular Europe.

According to Stark, one of the key virtues that Christianity brought was increased fertility and increased emphasis on nurturance obligations between people,[28] thereby setting a good basis for both revival of civilization and a faith strengthened by secondary compensation. But Christianity did not prevent the fall of Rome, and the rebuilding took hundreds of years. Modern secular society may not be demographically viable in the long run, and the early symptoms of its fall may have ambiguous implications for Atheism.

The relevance of the fertility collapse to secondary compensation is that a failure to reproduce means fewer social relationships carrying family obligations. This tendency could be magnified in societies with a welfare state, or where at least many of the former nurturance obligations people have had with each other are taken over by the state or by such things as health maintenance organizations, extensive public education, and the mass entertainment industry. To reduce secondary compensation, the state does not need to fulfill the obligations it takes on; it merely needs to take those obligations away from its citizens. I am suggesting the possibility of a pernicious feedback loop, in which a decline of religion leads to reduced fertility, which in turn reduces the secondary compensation that is at least partly responsible for religion's strength.

Because we are early in the history of public Atheism, any analysis must be tentative. However, we have seen good evidence in earlier chapters, as well as this one, that a decline of religion would be associated with a decline of social relationships and obligations. Perhaps humanity could endure greater superficiality in social life, so long as it remains possible to produce and raise a sufficient number of children. But probably an Atheistic society would need to find alternative sources of the benefits religion traditionally offered. Atheism may possess the truth, but it remains to be seen how it can inspire hope.

9

Cognitive Science

And when you look for a long time
into an abyss,
the abyss also looks
into you.
—*Beyond Good and Evil,*[1]
Friedrich Nietzsche

Cognitive science offers more than merely a fourth theory of religion. It also offers research methods for testing religious claims scientifically, and the evidence to date is very unfavorable to religion. Through new cognitive technologies and through convergence with information technology, cognitive science can also contribute new ways to address problems over which religion has enjoyed a traditional monopoly. Notably, if people come to conceptualize themselves as dynamic patterns of information, they will find it plausible that their personalities can be transferred to computers and there achieve a kind of immortality. Long before that immense cultural shift, even today, cognitive science is directly challenging ancient faiths. Indeed, cognitive science challenges our very concept of who we are.

Human Fallibility

Five million years ago, an unremarkable group of monkeys fell out of the trees and began blundering around. After spending most of its existence as an insignificant wandering breed, it stumbled into technology and conquered the world. Of course, I am referring to human beings. I will suggest that dramatic further progress is inhibited by the fact that we do not understand ourselves, and from some perspectives there is less to us

173

than meets the eye. Religion, that channeled our urge for transcendence when alternatives were few, may block our ability to leap forward now that technology has given us many alternatives.

Seriously, it may be that all "intelligent" species in the cosmos share the same limitations. Once a species has developed the characteristics needed to develop a technological civilization, it will do so very quickly, too quickly for it to evolve biologically in response to that development.[2] That is, every technological species will be just barely intelligent enough to develop the technology, and not one bit smarter. Each such species will be burdened by an accidental set of biases that hamper its understanding of the truth.

Someone who was simultaneously an elitist and an optimist might conclude from such logic that civilization required only perhaps ten percent of the population to be smart enough, and thus ninety percent are incapable of thinking usefully and must be followers. However, an argument from division of labor indicates that the proper estimate of sufficiently intelligent individuals is not ten percent but zero.

Intelligence is embodied in communication and teamwork, more than individual cogitation. Humans have depended upon socially distributed intelligence since soon after the dawn of time. What are the factors associated with the origin of human civilization? We had some technology already, between 20,000 and 50,000 years ago, of which stone tools are best known because they are best preserved. Art appeared about 100,000 years ago, so we can assume that humans already possessed some degree of symbolic thinking expressed in language as well as visual images. Most importantly, social structures larger than the single hunter-gatherer band had probably evolved, loosely linking bands into tribes. Given our individual stupidity, we needed a division of labor to advance, including communications that would allow an invention developed by one band to diffuse to others and blend with other inventions to create an entire tradition of innovation. Shared superstitions may have served powerful functions for the tribe, binding members together and setting limits for their behavior.

The dramatic jumping-off point for civilization, of course, was the Neolithic Revolution marked by development of agriculture, military-political structures to defend agricultural land, writing initially to manage economic exchange then applied to religion and other areas of culture, an increasing population size, and concentration of people in towns and cities where they could develop specialized professions with the skills needed to practice them.[3] Already by the establishment of the first cities, human knowledge was greater than any one person could master, and the progress of civilization depended upon socially distributed intelligence, rather than upon the brilliance of individuals. Individual intelligence and social interaction evolved in the hunter-gatherer phase, and may be poorly adapted to postindustrial society.

Psychic Research

Historically, the first really influential cognitive science approach to religion was *psychic research*, a discrediting episode in the early history of psychology that psychologists would prefer to forget. One source of this deviant scientific tradition was the spiritualism movement that swept America in the middle of the nineteenth century.[4] Since ancient days, psychic mediums claimed to be able to communicate with the dead. Near the beginning of the nineteenth century in France, Franz Anton Mesmer claimed to have discovered *animal magnetism*, supposedly linking spiritual phenomena to physical science, with a technique that came to be called *Mesmerism* or *hypnotism*.[5] Rapid scientific and technological change, notably the spread of the telegraph and other electrical devices, provided spiritualists with a host of scientistic metaphors and a general optimism that empirical research could uncover the mysteries of life to the benefit of mankind. Thus, by the latter decades of the century, a foundation existed in both Western Europe and the United States on which a new science of the spirit could be built. Establishment of the Society for Psychical Research in Britain in 1882 was a watershed event, launching a program "to examine allegedly paranormal phenomena in a scientific and unbiased way."[6]

Early in the twentieth century, several prominent psychologists were interested in ESP. At Harvard University, hugely influential psychologist and philosopher, William James, began studying psychic phenomena as early as 1869.[7] Harvard professor of psychology, William McDougall, was active in psychic research around 1920. The most famous series of research studies was begun around 1930 at Duke University by McDougall and J. B. Rhine. Rhine's 1934 book, *Extra-Sensory Perception*, remains the classic in the field.[8] But critics like C. E. M. Hansel have charged that Rhine's evidence for ESP was based entirely on sloppy research procedures and fakery by some of his research subjects.[9] In 1974, Rhine's successor at the independent Institute for Parapsychology near Duke University resigned after admitting that he had falsified data. A

debate has continued between authors who claim that research demon-
strates the reality of paranormal phenomena,[10] and others who argue that
the apparent positive results are the result of error, poor experimental
design, and even occasional fraud. In recent years, the parapsychology
journals themselves have published studies raising serious questions
about the reality of the very phenomena they are dedicated to studying.[11]

The most noteworthy fact about parapsychology is that it has been
completely exiled from the domain of psychology. Some hint of how
thoroughly conventional science has banished parapsychology can be
ascertained by visiting the website of the National Science Foundation
(www.nsf.gov) and searching the awards database for keywords like *telepathy*. This database offers abstracts of every single one of the thousands of research grants made by NSF since 1989. As of 2004, not a single abstract contained any of the following words: telepathy, telepath,
precognition, clairvoyance, psionic, telekinesis, psychokinesis, or extra-
sensory. The only hit for "extra-sensory" (with a hyphen) is the phrase
"extra sensory organs" (lacking the hyphen) in a biology study of bugs
with supernumerary eyes. There were no hits for "E.S.P." but a couple of
dozen for "ESP." However, these do not concern extra-sensory perception. Instead, they toy with the familiar acronym: an Environmental
Sample Processor to test water samples for microbes, an Experience
Sampling Program to track what people do during the day, and an "ESP"
program to Enhance Secondary Mathematics Teacher Preparation. The
NSF database appears to contain only one research award that really relates to ESP as we mean the term. It is the only hit that arises from putting *parapsychology* in the search engine, and is a tiny $7,500 doctoral
dissertation enhancement grant.

Parapsychological research has an amateur quality, probably for
three reasons, two of which we have just encountered. First, the research
methodologies used tend to be incompetent. Second, the researchers and
their publications exist outside the critical communication channels of
science, such as the central journals of psychology or the annual meetings of scientific organizations like the American Psychological Association. The third reason is perhaps more interesting: The research is largely
based on the populist notions of everyday people, rather than the abstract
theories of science. Another way of putting this is to say that parapsychology plays into the same images and motives that fuel religion. Many
parapsychologists proclaim no connection to religion, but their field
could justly be called *parareligion*.[12]

Many parapsychology experiments use cards, either ordinary playing cards or the special "Zener cards" designed by Rhine's colleague, Karl Zener. The point here is that many people play card games, and they often wish they could see their opponent's cards, or foresee the order in which their own cards will be dealt. Much telepathy research tries to duplicate every-day situations in which people sometimes report paranormal feelings, such as guessing the caller when a telephone rings, or the uncanny feeling of being stared at.[13]

Similarly, much research on alleged powers of the mind to move physical objects—psychokinesis, telekinesis, or teleportation—have exploited popular interests rather than testing scientific theories. Rhine and his collaborators had research subjects try to influence rolling dice, rather than using a sensitive physical instrument to measure rigorously any tiny forces the human mind could exert.[14] Stage magician Yuri Geller convinced many audiences he really could bend spoons with his mind, although professional scientists never in a million years would have thought of spoon-bending as a rigorous way to detect mental forces.[15]

It is worth thinking through the logic of the dice influencing experiments, beginning with the attraction of the idea as a fiction premise. What may be the most famous short story about psychokinesis, "Report on the Barnhouse Effect" by Kurt Vonnegut, was originally published in the popular magazine *Collier's* in 1950.[16] The story was dramatized on the radio program, *Dimension X*, on April 22, 1950, and much more recently a one-act play has been adapted from it.[17] The story is told from the standpoint of a graduate student of psychology who is the teaching assistant for Professor Arthur Barnhouse of Wyandotte University. In confidence, the professor reveals to the student that he has developed a new mental discipline which he calls *dynamopsychism*, and which allows him to roll sevens with dice as often as he wishes. The professor finds that his mental powers are increasing to the degree that he can demolish distant objects, so he innocently tells the United States government, which immediately imprisons him in a top-secret project to transform the professor into a weapon.

After a very dramatic demonstration of his powers, Professor Barnhouse escapes and begins using dynamopsychism to destroy the major weapons of all nations of the world. In the radio play version, he is captured by enemy agents, and just as they are flying him back to their own country to exploit him for evil, he uses his powers to commit suicide in a most spectacular manner, thus saving the world from the danger that he himself represents. Both 1950 versions end, however, as the graduate

student is about to go into hiding, after having rolled dice for fifty con-
secutive sevens. The story not only deals with the familiar artifact of
dice, but one of modern humanity's greatest *desires*: the end to weapons
of mass destruction.

The operative word is *desire*. Telepathy and telekinesis are about
how human beings *want* the world to be, not how it really is. Humans
want direct meeting of the minds to be possible, and desire itself seeks
the power of mind over matter. Supernatural concepts abound in this research, such as the idea that living beings exude some kind of transcendental life force. In one study, mental energies were supposed to make
plants grow, and in another they were supposed to kill fungus.[18] One
telekinesis experiment seemed to use more reasonable equipment, by
having people influence a pendulum, but often the research subjects
could not see it to know when mentally to push or pull, and they tended
to focus on the counter that measured their success.[19] Another study, exploring a connection between ESP and psychokinesis, had people try to
make a particular dog win, in a dog race displayed on a computer
screen.[20]

Scientists notice a huge conceptual gap in experiments like these.
The parapsychologists offer not a clue how the experiment could work,
even if paranormal powers really existed. In the dice experiments, even if
the mind could exert force on a falling die, the human mind cannot react
fast enough or calculate precisely enough to force the dice to roll lucky
seven. In the computerized dog racing experiment, it would take an expert programmer a long time to figure out which bytes in the machine's
memory needed to be changed to make a particular dog win. The concept
of telepathy ignores all the evidence that thought consists in complex
patterns of connections between neurons in the brain, that are undoubtedly different from person to person, and so small and numerous that
reading them out by any physical means seems quite implausible. Perhaps the unverified concept of life force gives a certain ring of rationality
to the plant growth experiments, but it is still difficult to believe that
people would have the psychic skill to change the readings on two lie
detectors hooked up to a pair of philodendron plants, as was done in one
study.[21]

The answer to the mystery is clear. The conceptual framework within
which these parapsychology experiments were designed was not one of
physical objects and forces. Rather, it concerned human desires, goals,
and wishes. The experiments take it for granted that phenomena are organized in ways that fit ordinary human ways of thinking. The dice and

the computerized dogs are part of humanly-meaningful games, in which the research subject wants to win. Telepathy is about direct communication between transcendent souls, not data exchange between neural networks. This is the province of religion, and we can understand it better by looking more deeply at how contemporary cognitive scientists approach the phenomenon of faith.

Cognitive Science

It has been very exciting, over the past decade, to see the rapid development of new cognitive approaches to religion, and one theme of this book is that great progress can be made by connecting the cognitive, exchange, and societal theories. However, there are at least two deficiencies in the work on religion that has been carried out within cognitive science. First, the leading authors have studiously avoided connecting their work with the older traditions that center in sociology. Second, the leading books in the cognitive science of religion refer to precious little systematic empirical research. Some of the authors developed their ideas while doing anthropological studies, a field that has become largely interpretive, but rigorous quantitative studies are largely lacking.

This is not a scientific disaster, because careful testing of theories can come later. We can look upon the past decade as a useful brainstorming session in which anthropologists and psychologists adapted cognitive ideas to religion. At this point, the theories sell themselves largely on their intellectual fascination, novelty, and cogency. How important each one will actually prove in explaining human religious behavior remains to be seen. Exactly how we can assemble these ideas into a comprehensive theory, giving each idea its proper role, challenges our current scientific capabilities. Notably, some ideas concern the traditional concept of immortal soul, whereas others concern belief in deities, without either explaining its connection to the other.

Perhaps the most direct threat to religious faith coming from cognitive science is the doubt it casts on the notion that each individual has a spiritual core of being, a soul. One approach is through the variety of research indicating that humans traditionally have misunderstood their own minds, including the way our nervous systems operate upon very fragmentary information. Using the obsolete term *psychology*, philosopher Daniel Dennett notes:

One of the surprising discoveries of modern psychology is how easy it is to be ignorant of your own ignorance. You are normally oblivious of your own blind spot, and people are typically amazed to discover that we don't see colors in our peripheral vision. It *seems* as if we do, but we don't, as you can prove to yourself by wiggling colored cards at the edge of your vision—you'll see motion just fine but not be able to identify the color of the moving thing. It takes special provoking like that to get the absence of information to reveal itself to us.[22]

Perhaps the most forceful demonstrations of the poverty of human awareness can readily be found by searching for "change blindness" sites on the World Wide Web. A video on the website of the Visual Cognition Lab of the University of Illinois shows a young man sitting at a desk. He gets up, and the camera cuts to a different shot, as he answers a wall telephone. Less than 30 percent of people viewing this video notice that in fact it is two different men, wearing different clothing.[23] We assume continuity in events and ignore facts that conflict with our interpretation of them. The Visual Cognition Lab of the University of British Columbia offers ten pairs of pictures, that flicker between images in each pair, in which it is difficult to notice substantial changes.[24] We do not really perceive things unless we have our attention on them. Evolution has shaped our brains to deal with problems that typically are most important, and to ignore distractions from these vital challenges.

To be aware of everything would not only be distracting but also would require much greater investment in mental apparatus. Our eyes would need sharp focus over the entire visual field, rather than just in the center. The brain would need to be able to handle the greatly increased input. The low-definition peripheral vision we actually possess alerts us to movement and may prepare us to interpret the scene quickly when we shift our gaze, but it provides very little information and thus makes negligible demands on the brain.

Half a century ago, psychologist George Miller pointed out that humans can hold about seven items in short-term memory, and can assign sensory inputs such as musical tones to a maximum of about seven categories.[25] Notably, he analyzed these observations in terms of information theory and explained how humans can handle somewhat larger numbers of data bits by learning to treat some groups of bits as chunks that count as units. "Chunking" was one of the central principles of artificial intelligence work developed in the subsequent decades.[26] Out of the limited information about events ever held in short-term memory (or "working memory"), only a small fraction persists beyond a few minutes and becomes part of autobiographical memory.[27] Based on insights like these, Herbert A. Simon has argued:

> Human beings, viewed as behaving systems, are quite simple. The apparent complexity of our behavior over time is largely a reflection of the complexity of the environment in which we find ourselves.[28]

Like many pioneers of artificial intelligence, however, Simon had a narrow view of human mentality, focusing almost entirely upon our limited power to carry out logical deductions. This ignored talents that computers still cannot equal, such as the ability to recognize a very large number of objects visually, the ability to understand speech and other manifestations of language, and the complex interplay of many mental functions that produce religion.

The fact that early artificial intelligence enthusiasts like Simon thought the human mind was simpler than it really is does not mean it is extremely complex. And much of the complexity it does possess seems to be a reflection of the complexity of the environment, as Simon said it was, but built into the human brain via evolution rather than learned by the individual. Given that perceptions are fragmentary, it is not surprising that the perceiver is a loosely connected set of fragments as well. Numerous functions are localized in various parts of our brains, and the unity of an individual's consciousness may be another illusion stemming from ignorance.[29] Paul Bloom explicitly says the idea humans have souls is a delusion, resulting from the fact that the brain is not aware of its own operation.[30]

The most widely used idea in the new cognitive science literature about religion concerns the human propensity to impute agency to complex events.[31] That is, we tend to assume somebody is responsible for the things that happen. Pascal Boyer says, "Our minds are not general explanation machines. Rather, minds consist of many different, specialized explanatory machines... more properly called *inference systems.*"[32] Like many other writers, Boyer says the human mind contains a very powerful module that interprets the perceptions and intentions of other intelligent beings. Some cognitive scientists think this is located in a particular brain structure, and Asperger's Syndrome or Autism Spectrum Disorder may be caused by a defect in this area. Whether a localized structure or a diffuse function, this *mind reading* ability may have evolved to help proto-humans anticipate the behavior of predators or prey, other animals they encountered daily that presented either dangers or opportunities. Or, we developed this ability to support complex cooperative exchanges with other humans, and to distinguish trustworthy from untrustworthy exchange partners. Belief in supernatural beings, from this vantage point, represents hyperactivity of this mind-imputing function of the human brain.

Justin Barrett put it this way. Humans have a "hypersensitive agency detection device" in their brains, defining an agent as a "being that does not merely respond mechanistically to environmental contingencies but initiates action on the basis of internal, mental states."[33] Barrett devotes a chapter of his book, *Why Would Anyone Believe in God?*, to the sorry plight of Atheists, who are doomed, he says, to be greatly outnumbered by religious people: "Only privileged minorities enjoy atheism. If religion is the opiate of the masses, atheism is a luxury of the elite."[34] He argues that disbelief in God is most likely among people who are comfortable, intellectually reflective, and capable of thinking in terms of complex statistical concepts. That is, Barrett believes that the human agency detection device is such a strong categorizer in the human brain that only special training can counteract it.

However, modules in the brain like Barrett's agency detection device are hypothetical constructs, that have not yet been precisely described, localized, or measured. We certainly are not currently able to compare how strong this tendency is, compared with others such as the ability to identify events that have purely mechanistic causes, or the ability to estimate statistical probabilities. Psychological research with small children shows that social tendencies that look very much like a agency detection device are natural features that emerge early in life, and cultural anthropologists report that all societies have beliefs in supernatural beings. However, those facts do not equal belief in a single all-powerful God, such as promoted by modern religious organizations. Arguably, not modern theistic religion but primitive animism is the natural human faith.

Other cognitive theories also abound. Porter Abbott suggests that human thought organizes things in terms of narratives—stories in which protagonists face obstacles and take actions in pursuit of goals—and thus the scientific theory of evolution cannot compete with religious stories because it is *unnarratable*.[35] Pascal Boyer and Justin Barrett focus on the characteristic that religious beliefs have that facilitates their communication and memorization, calling them *minimally counterintuitive*.[36] They are similar to real phenomena, so they are easily remembered and discussed, but they are enough different to be memorable and remarkable.

Scott Atran has shown that such hypotheses can be tested experimentally.[37] It is also possible that belief in an afterlife reflects the fact that we develop mental models of the feelings, beliefs, and intentions of the individual people closest to us, and the models persist after the deaths of the people.[38] Presumably, a complete theory of religion might make use of all these ideas.

Now that many cognitive hypotheses have been proposed, it is time to carry out systematic studies to compare their explanatory powers, and to test them against the wealth of existing sociological data on religion. One of the most striking dimensions of variation within religion is the *sectarian tension axis* that arranges religious groups from the mildest, liberal denominations comfortable with the dominant secular institutions, to the extreme sects in high tension with secular institutions. The standard sociological explanation holds that sectarians are relatively deprived of rewards in comparison with members of mainstream denominations that serve the prosperous middle classes, and thus they have greater need for religious compensators.

Recently, Harvey Whitehouse and associates have proposed an alternative but potentially compatible cognitive analysis, suggesting that these two modes of religiosity exploit different forms of memory in the human brain.[39] Mainstream religion, relatively intellectual and involving a host of symbols, is rooted in *semantic memory* that learns through constant repetition of logically connected ideas. Sectarian religion is more emotional and rooted in *episodic memory* that is activated by emotionally intense but rare religious experiences. The two modes of religiosity, according to Whitehouse, spread socially through very different forms of communication, and future research will need to elucidate the connection between episodic memory and specific compensators for relative deprivations. Several authors have applied Whitehouse's ideas to ethnographic and historical data,[40] so it is time to frame quantitative studies to evaluate this theory in comparison with others.

As we noted in Chapter 4, among the most important issues facing the world today is the collapse of fertility among the most prosperous and educated populations, and the offsetting high birth rate among religiously fundamentalist populations. Thus, while semantic memory may be the basis of our civilization, emotional sectarian movements that activate episodic memory appear to have a great evolutionary advantage.

Intelligence

The simplest and least flattering cognitive theory of religion is this: Religion is an expression of human stupidity. I hasten to report that empirical data do not provide strong support for this theory, but intelligence is a variable that may interact with other factors to shape the kinds and strength of religious beliefs. Indeed, intelligence would seem related to the inference systems that Boyer and others claim compose the human mind. That is, a person with a larger number of well-functioning inference systems, and the ability to switch from one to another when needed, would be a more intelligent person. Such a person would also be able to avoid interpreting complex, natural events as the result of supernatural beings. In the second half of the twentieth century, intelligence tests were subjected to many kinds of criticism, and we cannot here recapitulate or resolve those debates. Rather, I will briefly use data from the General Social survey to show both that intelligence needs to be factored into cognitive studies of religion, and that stupidity cannot in itself explain religion.

My first piece of evidence is so clear that it should disarm readers who are constitutionally opposed to intelligence tests. One GSS item is the statement, "Astrology—the study of star signs—has some scientific truth." A set of GSS multiple-choice items asks respondents the meanings of ten words, and the number of right answers is a variable called WORDSUM. This is a very simple short-form verbal intelligence test, certainly not nearly so reliable as a much larger test might be, but serviceable in the context of the General Social Survey. Of 1,617 respondents who answered the astrology question and completed the WORDSUM test, 52.0 percent said that the astrology statement was either definitely or probably true, and the remaining 48.0 percent said it was definitely or probably not true. Among those who got 8 or more of the 10 word definition questions correct, just 30.4 percent thought the astrology statement was true, compared to 54.4 percent of those scoring 5 through 7, and fully 72.6 percent of those scoring lower. That is a huge difference of 42.2 percentage points, from low to high scorers. We should not make much of the 6 poor people who completely flunked the test, getting no answers right, but all of them professed to believe astrology was scientific. So, clearly, the WORDSUM test can distinguish something potentially powerful about an individual's cognition that is related to the topics of this book.

A total of 21,608 people took the word test and reported their religious affiliation, with substantial numbers getting each of the test scores from 0 through 10. Interestingly, the percentages who have no religion hardly vary from those who scored 0 (8.3 percent of them having no religion) through those who scored 7 (8.5 percent). But the three higher scores showed increasing fractions who were non-religious: 10.1 percent of those scoring 8, 13.6 percent of those scoring 9, and 17.7 percent of those scoring 10.

The GSS items about belief in God can be discussed best by comparing the average test score of people holding each different view about the deity's existence. The lowest average score, 5.83, was earned by people who said, "I know God really exists and I have no doubts about it." But an almost identical average score, 5.84, was earned by people who selected the wishy-washy and ungrammatical response, "I find myself believing in God some of the time, but not at others." Next come Atheists, with an average of 6.13. A better score, 6.29, was earned by those who said, "While I have doubts, I feel that I do believe in God." Much higher was the vaguely Deist position, "I don't believe in a personal God, but I do believe in a Higher Power of some kind," averaging 6.82 on the word test. The highest average score, 7.05, was earned by Agnostics.

Thus, Atheists are not an intellectual elite, leading humanity into a Bright Age. However, traditional religious faith appeals to people with weaker intellectual skills, and the smartest people tend to have nuanced and uncertain views about God. This situation could change, if progress in cognitive science and related fields strengthens the scientific basis for rejecting traditional religious beliefs, and if convergence of all scientific and technical fields provides ever more complete answers to the questions that religion pretended to address. Under those circumstances, being Atheist could become what it now is not, evidence of being smart and well educated.

Computer Simulation of Religion

I believe I was the first scientist to make a serious attempt to apply artificial intelligence techniques to religion, first in *Sociology Laboratory*, a software-textbook package I published in 1987, then in a 1995 journal article, and finally in my 2006 book, *God From the Machine*.[41] This most recent project builds on two decades of programming research to create a community of 44,100 simulated human beings, organized in what is often called a *massive multi-agent system*. Each run of the computer program tested a theory under one or another set of circumstances, and the entire set explored a wide range of topics in the social science of religion. To give a rough sketch of the entire project, I will describe a fresh computer run using somewhat stupid "intelligent agents," then write briefly about the most advanced experiments that gave the agents much more complex minds.

Figure 9.1 shows part of the display on my computer screen at two points in time. The top half of the picture depicts a neighborhood consisting 315 of the 44,100 agents. Each one represents a human being, depicted as a square. Of course, I could have put 315 tiny faces on the screen, but that would not have made their behavior any more realistic. The lines connecting some of the squares are social bonds, the friendship ties conventionally represented as a social network. Around the edge, some lines reach out to other agents who are not shown in this small fraction of the community. Each agent belongs to one of ten religious groups, depicted by the shading or symbol inside the square. At the beginning of a computer run such as this, the program gives me various choices. I selected a social network density of about 50 percent, meaning that each possible social bond between adjacent agents had a 1/2 chance of existing. By chance, the precise starting density this time was 49.91 percent. I told the machine to distribute membership in the ten religious groups at random, each agent having a 1/10 chance of winding up in a particular group. We will focus on the religious sect depicted as a black square, and initially its membership was 4,379 or 9.93 percent of the whole population.

This particular computer run involved three theories from the standard social-scientific literature:

1. Sutherland's Differential Association Theory
2. Heider's Balance Theory
3. Stark and Bainbridge's Network Recruitment Theory

In its simplest form, Edwin Sutherland's Differential Association Theory describes human behavior as the result of social influence.[42] Sutherland himself offered it as an explanation for juvenile delinquency, and it is best known among criminologists. However, it really applies very broadly. Many sociologists blithely think the *associations* in the theory refer to social relationships. Indeed, one way to interpret it is to

Figure 9.1: Agents at Start (Top) and after Ten Turns (Bottom)

say that you will commit crimes if most of your friends are criminals, influenced by them to behave in a criminal manner. But that is not how Sutherland himself presented the theory. He couched it in terms of an influential school of thought often called *symbolic interactionism* that especially focused on how people *define* situations.[43] That is to say, it is really a cognitive theory. The associations refer to mental associations favorable to violation of the law, and to socially acquired knowledge about how to violate it.

Yes, a person will become criminal if he or she has many criminal friends, but it is the communications of information from those associates that shape the mental associations, rather than the mere fact of their criminality. Cognition is at the very heart of the theory and the sociological perspective on which it is based. Here, we represent Differential Association Theory as a simple rule. Agents take turns at random. If Differential Association Theory is in effect on a given turn, the agent will take a vote of the other agents to which he or she has a social bond, and shift to the plurality religious affiliation if there is one. I set the particular computer run so that Differential Association Theory is in effect exactly half the time, at random, for all the agents, and Balance Theory is in effect the other half the time.

Fritz Heider's Balance Theory is a form of cognitive consistency theory.[44] It is not very different from the very famous Cognitive Dissonance Theory proposed by Leon Festinger, but it focuses on situations involving at least two people.[45] Heider's analysis was framed in terms of triads, which could be two people and a thing. If two people have a strong social bond between them, and thus communicate information frequently with positive emotions, they should tend to develop a similar attitude toward the thing. If not, the triad is imbalanced. Or, in Festinger's terms, each person should experience at least a little cognitive dissonance. In my simulation, the thing is religious affiliation.

If two people are friends, but belong to different denominations, they experience imbalance. If two people are neighbors but happen not to be friends, and they belong to the same denomination, there is also imbalance. On a turn when Balance Theory is in effect, an agent will check each of his or her neighbors, looking at their religious affiliations and inspecting whether there is a friendship tie or not. If the agent finds a neighbor of the same denomination who is not already a friend, the agent will build a friendship. If the agent finds a friend who belongs to a different denomination, the agent will break off the friendship.

The Stark-Bainbridge Network Recruitment Theory is a small part of our general theory, but it is not based on the concept of compensators, and it really ignores the distinctive features of religion. Presented in an article published in the *American Journal of Sociology*, it argues that much about religion can be explained merely as a consequence of the dynamics of recruitment through social networks.[46] In particular, we argued that the best way a religious movement could grow was to have members make friendships with non-members, even investing great effort in building those friendships, and not proselytize for the faith until after the friendships were solidly established. At that point, Differential Association Theory could take over and complete the religious conversion of the friends. *Outreach* is the standard term for a religious group's efforts to develop social relations with non-members.

For the computer run described here, I set the program so that only one of the ten groups practiced outreach, the religious sect marked by black squares. At the end of a turn, fifty percent of the time at random, a member of this sect will build social bonds with all eight neighbors, regardless of their affiliations. Members of the other nine denominations never do this. Thus, the simulation is an experiment to see what happens if one group practices outreach. The simulation does not claim the sect has more effective compensators, more charismatic clergy, or beliefs that communicate more easily than the beliefs of the other groups. The context is the community I have described, with ten denominations, a social network, and a back-and-forth play between Differential Association and Balance.

As the lower part of Figure 9.1 clearly shows, after ten turns, members of the ten religious groups have started to clump together, showing the joint effects of Differential Association and Balance. But it also shows that the sect marked by black squares has begun to grow. After the tenth turn, it is no longer 9.93 percent of the total 44,100 population, but 22.58 percent.

Figure 9.2 graphs how that percentage rises over the first fifty turns, to 56.34 percent, represented by the dashed line. If I had allowed the graph to run further to the right, you would see that the sect had grown to 95.54 percent after the 1,000th turn, and 96.31 percent after the 2,000th. It never quite reaches 100 percent, because isolated knots of surviving members of other denominations embrace each other so tightly it is impossible to invade their tiny enclaves. But, clearly, the sect has triumphed, with the single advantage of outreach.

The solid line in Figure 9.2 graphs how the density of the social net-work changes over the first 50 turns. At first it drops, from 49.91 percent to 24.43 percent after the third turn. Balance Theory is making agents break off relationships with neighbors belonging to other denominations, more rapidly than Balance Theory builds new friendships with neighbors who belong to the same denomination. With ten denominations distrib-uted at random, most near neighbors are of different denominations. But as the sect grows, so does the density of social bonds in the network, un-til it passes the original density on turn 24. Both the solid and dashed curves are bent, getting progressively less steep for most of their length, and if we could look way to the right beyond the edge of the graph, we would see that they become horizontal just short of 100 percent.

Figure 9.2: Sect Membership, Network Density: 50 Simulation Turns

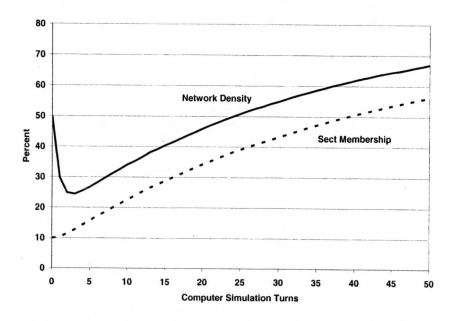

In *God from the Machine*, I explore how outreach works with differ-ent numbers of groups with different sizes, and indeed for two groups of equal size it does not confer any advantage on the group that practices it. The book is filled with other examples of interesting principles about religious cognition that computer simulation can help us understand. I cannot devote much space here to that point. However, a very brief discussion of the most advanced program can conclude this section by hinting that this methodology has great potential.

Late in my series of simulation experiments, I gave the computerized agents much more intelligence than they had for the simulation I just described. Each agent was a neural network having several parallel modules, each structured on two levels. For the record, they were "variance-maximizing hierarchical direct reinforcement neural networks," although *God from the Machine* tried to avoid too much technical language in order to communicate to a variety of readers. The agents interacted in an economy, where each agent produce rewards of value to the others, and sought rewards from them in turn.

At the start, the agents understood little of the world they lived in. They knew that the other agents belonged to groups, but they did not know whether there were two, three, or four groups. They knew that different groups supplied different rewards, but they did not know which. Their task was to develop a theory of how many groups there were, and which group provided which reward. That is, the computer program employed machine learning to help the agents master the cognitive challenge they faced. Success meant a functioning and reasonably efficient economy, and survival for the individual agent.

However, the agents wanted one reward they could not in fact get from each other, namely extended life. On each turn, an agent would tend to go in search of the reward he or she has least of. To start with, each agent had a fairly high life-expectancy, but as they took their turns they used up their lives. Following the same rules they followed for the available rewards, they tried to figure out which group could provide eternal life. But every time they tried to get it from another agent, they failed, thereby learning that that theory, like all the others, was false.

In the end, the artificial intelligent agents came to believe in supernatural beings, whom they were capable of imagining with their little neural net minds, but whom they could not empirically interact with in order to learn if they really provided life or not. You will have to read *God from the Machine* if you want more detail, but I can give a brief glimpse of the kind of theory they wound up with: "For eternal life, go to members of the fourth of three groups." This is a contradiction. If there are only three groups, what does it mean to talk about the fourth group? This, I suggest, is the same kind of contradiction in talking about the supernatural, something that exists but does not exist inside nature. Agents in the fourth group, when there are only three groups, are precisely the "minimally counterintuitive" beings that religion postulates.

Cyberimmortality

The fact that artificial intelligence can simulate religious faith, when it is clear that neural net agents inside a computer lack souls, raises profound issues in the relationship between science and religion. As the twentieth century drew to a close, individual visionaries began realizing that it might some day be feasible to transfer human personalities into information systems, computers, or robots where they could experience second lives. Furthermore, most of the objections against the technological feasibility of personality transfer were based on questionable assumptions about the nature of human consciousness. However, most people probably hold these assumptions, so personality transfer will seem both impossible and undesirable to the majority of those who hear about the idea. This could become a major battleground between religion and science, as science competes with religion to overcome mortality, and religious people mock the idea and may even seek to prevent research.

One of the pioneers in this field, robotics expert Hans Moravec, sought to disarm critics by calling cybernetic copies of human personalities *mind children*—cybernetic offspring rather than cyberimmortality of the individual himself—setting aside the issue of whether they really are the person they were based on.[47] I prefer to address the problem in different ways. Under the assumption that a supernatural afterlife does not really exist, we might as well do the best we can to give our personal thoughts, feelings, commitments, and memories a future beyond our biological deaths. At present, we can make a low fidelity copy of a personality, and reanimate it rather crudely, but a crash research program should enable us to achieve much higher fidelity rather quickly. For the foreseeable future, something will be lost when a personality is transferred from a human body to an information system, but something can be gained, as well. Already, we could give the personality many new abilities, from vast stores of information to the ability to operate via robotic telepresence in environments like outer space where a human body cannot survive.

For over twenty years I have been exploring practical methods for personality capture, based on computerizing traditional methods in psychology and sociology. My first publication in this series was a very simple program bundled with *Experiments in Psychology* in 1986 that allowed the user to create short questionnaires, answer them, and archive the answers.[48] My 1989 textbook and software package, *Survey Research: A Computer-Assisted Introduction*, included a more complex set of modules for computerized questionnaire administration.[49] In the 1990s, I began writing journal articles and book chapters that explicitly addressed one or another of the technical challenges or cultural hurdles that will need to be overcome.[50] As a natural part of the research, I administered computerized questionnaires to myself, and have long since passed the point at which I had answered fully 100,000 questions. This is not actually as difficult as it sounds, especially if one carries a pocket computer or wearable computer, responding to a few questions at otherwise wasted times during the day, such as standing at a bus stop.

Computer visionaries like Ray Kurzweil and Hugo de Garis have predicted that computers will take on ever more of the cognitive tasks performed by humans, and grow exponentially in their intelligence, until they have the real potential to replace us within a few decades.[51] I believe that the development of general-purpose artificial intelligences rivaling human abilities in a range of tasks will take longer than they think, and that our present ignorance about how our own minds operate leaves us unaware of many difficult scientific challenges that lie ahead. However, progress in computer-related cognitive science could gradually have two very significant influences on religion.

First, as people experience more and more practical examples of specialized artificial intelligence, they will lose the traditional sense that intelligence is something mystical requiring supernatural explanations. Second, the ability of machines to assist humans in their day-to-day lives will gradually give the machines mental characteristics like those of their individual users, increasing the plausibility of future methods to achieve cyberimmortality and thus rivaling religion as a source for transcendental hopes. For artificial intelligence technologies to undercut religious faith in these two ways, it is not necessary that they be fully successful, merely that they be moving in the general direction prophesied by Moravec, Kurzweil, de Garis and myself.

We can distinguish three interrelated tasks that lead step-by-step from simple tools assisting humans in their ordinary lives to a radical redefinition of what it means to be human:

Personality Enhancement: Increasing the cognitive, affective, and social functioning and scope of a person through artificial means like information technology.

Personality Capture: Entering substantial information about a person's mental and emotional functioning into a computer or information

system, sufficiently detailed to permit a somewhat realistic simulation.

Personality Emulation: Allowing a captured personality to act and perceive in the world, by means of artificial intelligence, robotics,
sensors, or possible biological embodiment.

The convergence of cognitive and information technologies will
promote the convergence of enhancement, capture, and emulation. As
humans use ever more sophisticated information systems, their tools become extensions of themselves, their personalities expand into cyber-
space, and they can begin to transcend location in bodies that exist only
briefly in a limited domain of space. Information technology applications
must become knowledgeable about the user in order to serve him or her,
so systems will perform personality capture incidentally to doing other
work. This path leads in small, practical steps from minor human en-
hancements, to self-transformation, to cyberimmortality.

Henry Kautz of the computer science department of the University of
Washington, is a leader in developing computer systems for *assistive
cognition*. The aim is to help people suffering from cognitive disorders
like Alzheimer's Disease, which requires the computer to become aware
of the context surrounding the user, to learn how to interpret the user's
behavior and to offer appropriate help when it appears that the person is
failing to reach a goal. One project employs a pocket computer with
Global Positioning System for users traveling around the city of Seattle,
not merely to monitor where the user is but to deduce where the user
wants to go and guide him if he gets lost.[52] Another research study employs a glove with radio frequency identification equipment to infer from
the movements of a person's hand what activity he is engaged in.[53] A
new research project funded by the National Science Foundation is comparing sensor methodologies for mapping social interactions among a
number of people, to understand the dynamics of their social network
and their individual positions in it.[54]

At the University of Michigan, Martha Pollack has been working
with several colleagues in developing automatic methods for helping
elderly people plan their activities, which requires the computer to learn
the habits and preferences of the users.[55] Also at Michigan, Edmund Durfee had been involved in projects to develop computerized planning approaches and methods to coordinate the actions of multiple artificial intelligence agents. Now, with NSF support, Durfee and Pollack have
teamed up to develop *socio-cognitive orthotic systems*, designed to help
individuals and groups manage their social relations.[56] The elderly have

one set of problems with social relations, but young people who are strangers to each other have other problems. At the New Jersey Institute of Technology, Quentin Jones is developing a system for students that will map users in time and space, identifying opportunities to introduce students with similar interests to each other.[57]

Rosalind Picard is a pioneer in the field of *affective computing*, developing artificial intelligence systems that sense and respond appropriately to human emotions, and she has established an affective computing research group in the Media Laboratory of the Massachusetts Institute of Technology.[58] Picard envisions a time when an artificial intelligence software agent might be able to help a recovering drug addict by providing constant attention, based on a deep understanding of the user's feelings and challenges.[59] Picard's current NSF research grant supports development of a *social-emotional intelligence prosthetic* that would help people who have difficulty reading the feelings and reactions of other people, those sometimes diagnosed with Asperger's Syndrome or Autism Spectrum Disorder. A portable system that is alert to nonverbal cues would observe people the user is interacting with, then unobtrusively advise the user.[60]

These are only a few of the research projects that are developing new technologies to assist the disabled, and potentially to assist anyone, in conducting some of the difficult personal business of life. Importantly, these systems would be impossible without artificial intelligence, and the AI must adapt to the individual user. Thus, the intelligent agent in the device becomes a reflection of the user, possessing intimate information about the user's feelings and activities. A somewhat different approach involves systems designed to record everything a person experiences, while moving through the complex real world, either to gather information of practical value to other humans, or to assemble an archive of the individual's life.

The Experience on Demand Project, led by Howard Wactlar at Carnegie Mellon University in the late 1990s, was funded by the Defense Advanced Research Projects Agency of the U.S. government. This project developed "tools, techniques and systems allowing people to capture a record of their experiences unobtrusively, and share them in collaborative settings spanning both time and space."[61] Specific applications included rescue workers, crisis managers, and military scouts who gain detailed information rapidly in operational settings and must share it with other members of the team. For example, the system would be able to connect a dynamic map of someone's movements with pictures of what the person saw at each point in time and space.

Steve Mann's Personal Imaging Lab at the University of Toronto "is a computer vision and intelligent image processing research lab focused on the area of personal imaging, mediated reality and wearable computers."[62] The central idea is that a person would wear a lightweight computer with an optical input-output device over one eye, the *eyetap*. The person would see his or her surroundings perfectly well, but the eyetap could superimpose information on the scene as desired, achieving *augmented reality*, for example the names of people the individual meets. At the same time, the eyetap would be taking in the scene and storing it in detail for analysis, long-term archiving, and whatever use the person would want to make of it.

Gordon Bell's MyLifeBits project at Microsoft combines experience capture with many other kinds of data.[63] The project's website explains, "Gordon Bell has captured a lifetime's worth of articles, books, cards, CDs, letters, memos, papers, photos, pictures, presentations, home movies, videotaped lectures, and voice recordings and stored them digitally. He is now paperless, and is beginning to capture phone calls, IM transcripts, television, and radio."[64] Another interesting approach records perceptions and behaviors of people as they play videogames, including games designed for educational purposes and games specifically created to record people's reactions to realistic scenarios.[65]

Already, commercial videogames include somewhat convincing artificial intelligence, although as a programmer I know that the AIs in the games are really stupid and the game developers use a variety of tricks, including flashy graphics, to make the character seem more intelligent. Among the most interesting examples is the PlayStation 2 videogame *The Thing*. The original story, "Who Goes There?" was written in 1938 by John W. Campbell, Jr., most important editor of the golden age of magazine science fiction. Set in Antarctica, the story imagined that an alien spaceship crashed, and was found by an American team. Rather than being dead, the extraterrestrial pilot was merely in suspended animation, and began to attack the humans as soon as it revived. The innovative idea of this story was that the creature could morph itself to resemble any other living being, including humans. As the Americans fight the monster, they can never tell when one of their own people might turn out to be the alien in disguise. When the story was originally filmed in 1951, this complexity was dropped and the setting was moved to Alaska. John Carpenter's 1982 version returned the story to Antarctica and restored the alien's ability to transform itself. The game takes off where Carpenter's movie ended, sending the player into Antarctica, to discover what happened to the exploration outposts that have fallen silent.

The player's character is assisted by as many as three artificial intelligence team members: a commando who fights well, an engineer who can fix broken equipment, and a medic who can heal wounds. Depending on the situation, the player can leave these assistants in a safe place, or order any of them to follow him. Unfortunately, the AIs may not trust the player, either suspecting him of being an alien or worrying about his military competence, and their distrust increases when they see horrible things. The player can increase an assistant's trust by giving him a weapon, ammunition, or medical treatment. An alien, presumably, would not do this. Also, the player's character or an AI character can take a blood test, derived from Campbell's original story in which blood from an alien would try to escape from a test tube when given an electric shock. The player can assess an assistant's level of trust by observing his movements or listening to what he says. When the player is not watching, a team member may be taken over by the monster, so the player's trust in the AIs is a crucial variable in the game. Despite the simple way in which it is programmed, this videogame goes a long way toward convincing artificial intelligence, because trust is so human an issue.

On October 8, 2005, news flashed from the Nevada desert that a robot car named Stanley had just achieved the remarkable accomplishment of driving 133 miles across difficult terrain, in less than seven hours, without a human driver. This feat won a two million dollar prize for the builders of Stanley, a team from Stanford University headed by Sebastian Thrun.[66] The race was sponsored by the U.S. Defense Advanced Research Projects Agency, which wanted proof that a practical automated system could be developed for delivering supplies or remotely operating weapons in territory such as Iraq. Stanley was not "intelligent" in a general sense, and did not understand the goal of the race. Indeed, part of the guidance was a series of many, dumb pre-defined geographic points located with the Global Positioning System. But absolutely essential to success was a computer vision system that could find its own way down a poorly-marked road and around obstacles in its path. Impressively, three other teams using different computer vision systems also completed the race. Before too many years, we can expect safety-enhancing computer vision accessories for civilian automobiles, if we do not entirely hand the driving over to the machines.

A longstanding proverb of the artificial intelligence field is, "Once you understand how it works, it isn't AI any more." This expresses the very human tendency to feel that intelligence somehow transcends logic. Once a machine can do it, the magic is lost. Thus, even before computers can emulate full human intelligence, they will begin to erode people's feeling that the human mind can supernatural qualities, and from there it may be a short distance to doubting that God's soul is supernatural either.

Conclusion

The idea that human personalities could be ported to information systems, and there survive indefinitely, may seem unrealistic to many people. But many of our every-day assumptions are false or arbitrary, as physicists of the twentieth century delighted in demonstrating repeatedly. Now it is the turn of the cognitive scientists. We may be wrong to imagine that we have immortal souls, that our memories are vast, and that we possess qualities like "free will" that a "mere machine" could never possess. Perhaps each of us would like to believe he or she is an unfathomable mystery, rather than the simple child of a monkey that fell out of a tree not so long ago in the evolution of life on Earth.

Since I first started creating computer programs to administer questionnaires more than twenty years ago, I have been exploring the ways in which conventional social-science research methods might be adapted for use in personality capture. As tools for personality capture, the mobile and ubiquitous information technologies have the disadvantage that they collect vast amounts of data that the person may not have perceived and does not remember, and it will be difficult to base emulation on such datasets until we have carried out many empirical studies on what people actually perceive and remember. The much more traditional social-science approaches are more ready to support emulation in the near term.

For example, one line of semantic differential research has developed a grammar of emotions, such that a mathematical model would accurately predict how a person reacted to a complex situation based on how the individual reacts to its separate parts.[67] Altogether, eleven personality capture modules I have created gather 44,000 measurements of the user's attitudes, preferences, beliefs, and self-conceptions.[68] Another software system I developed collects more than 40,000 other measurements of the person's emotional reactions to situations.[69] Existing computational methods can predict how the person would respond to other questions and to some kinds of real situations, which is one good step toward being to emulate the personality.

However, mobile AI systems that help people in their daily lives will have very significant roles to play in personality capture and emulation. To the extent that an artificial intelligence learns the user's preferences and acts successfully in the real world on behalf of the user, it takes on some of the user's identity. Feedback from the user guides the system to incorporate the user ever more accurately, and accomplishment of the user's goals is an excellent test of the authenticity of the AI surrogate.

My own current projects focuses on the combination of personality capture and personality emulation, what I call *personality transfer*. One set of studies concerns how people remember and evaluate events that happen in their lives, research in the areas of episodic memory and affective computing, and the social-psychology of video games. Another concerns the way in which online recommender systems can capture human preferences, in such a way that statistical modeling or artificial intelligence can emulate the given individual's decision-making habits. We need a wide range of scientific research and engineering development efforts, not only to develop distinct ways of assisting people that incidentally archive their personalities, or to study personalities through focused studies, but also to combine multiple modalities through convergence of methods rooted in separate disciplines. Only thus will we be able to capture, preserve, and emulate human personalities in all their natural complexity—or simplicity.

10
Technological Transcendence

> I teach you the Superman.
> Man is something that is to be surpassed.
> What have ye done to surpass man?
> —*Thus Spake Zarathustra,*[1]
> Friedrich Nietzsche

At the beginning of the twenty-first century, science-based technologies are massing at the border of religion, preparing to invade territory that traditionally has been the province of faith. Many very recent writers suggest that advanced technologies will overcome some of the problems that have motivated human religious hopes. Some believe that the combination of biotechnology and nanotechnology will reverse aging and extend life almost to the point of immortality.[2] Others believe that cognitive science and artificial intelligence will upload human personalities for new lives within artificial intelligence information systems and robots.[3] Advocates of such human metamorphosis are called Transhumanists or Convergenists. Whether such hopes will be realized or not, religion has a vital interest in preventing research and technology development in this area. This chapter documents religious opposition to human reproductive cloning and other technologies advocated by technological transcendentalists, and it describes how a broadly-based cultural movement is laying the ideological groundwork for resistance against any religious attempt to suppress the technology.

Transhumanism

Transhumanists believe that we have reached the point in history at which fundamental changes in our very natures have become both possible and desirable. When humans can improve their own minds and bodies technologically, then they will gain the intelligence and longevity to devise even more methods for self-improvement. In a positive feedback loop that vastly accelerates evolution, humans could become like gods, and in so doing may put conventional religion out of business. Thus it is in the vital interests of Christianity and the other great world faiths to prevent human technological transformation.

Oxford philosopher Nick Bostrom, who co-founded the World Transhumanist Association in 1998, notes that some Transhumanists might consider Friedrich Nietzsche to be a precursor. Bostrom asserts, "What Nietzsche had in mind, however, was not technological transformation but rather a kind of soaring personal growth and cultural refinement in exceptional individuals (who he thought would have to overcome the life-sapping 'slave-morality' of Christianity)."[4] This observation points to two unresolved issues for Transhumanists. First, will philosophical or spiritual training contribute in any substantial way to human transformation, or will the technologies require no special effort on the part of individuals? Second, will all of humanity evolve together to a higher level, everybody benefiting roughly equally from the new technology, or will a very few individuals advance, leaving the remainder of humanity behind?

Nietzsche famously postulated a higher form of human, the *Übermensch*, but then posterity distorted his vision in ways both tragic and comic. After his death, with the complicity of his sister, the Nazis misappropriated some of Nietzsche's ideas, and only long after the Second World War was it possible for Walter Kaufmann and other scholars to rehabilitate this philosopher.[5] Nietzsche's word *Übermensch* was often translated into English as *superman*, but in the 1930s two science fiction fans, Jerry Siegel and Joe Shuster, appropriated this name for the hero of the *Superman* comic books. Importantly, both the Nazi and comic book versions of supermen implied that one could not become superior but had to be born that way. Recently, some translators of Nietzsche have avoided the word *superman*, for example using *overman* instead.

Throughout the middle of the twentieth century, science fiction writers explored implications if some form of *homo superior* were actually to emerge. Interestingly, novelists as diverse as Olaf Stapledon (*Odd John*, 1935), Robert A. Heinlein (*Stranger in a Strange Land*, 1961), and A. E. van Vogt (*Slan*, 1946) concluded that ordinary humans would try to kill any superior mutants.[6] Van Vogt was one of a number of people from the science fiction subculture who have hoped to bring the fantasies to reality, and his word *slan* is occasionally employed to describe humans with unusual mental powers. He was impressed by the possibility that Alfred Korzybski's General Semantics could transform humans, and wrote *The World of Null-A* to describe a future society based on this philosophical system.[7] Van Vogt considered founding a Church of General Semantics, and when his friend and colleague, L. Ron Hubbard, created Dianetics, van Vogt worked in its California branch for a number of years.[8]

Science fiction also played a major role in creation of the Cryonics Movement, that today is directly allied with Transhumanism. Many stories of the 1930s concern human beings who come back to life after being frozen, such as "The Jameson Satellite" by Neil R. Jones and "The Resurrection of Jimber-Jaw" by Edgar Rice Burroughs.[9] At least two classic science-fiction movies incorporate this idea, *Buck Rogers* (1939) and *The Thing* (1951). In 1964, Robert C. W. Ettinger published the book, *The Prospect of Immortality*, suggesting that freezing could actually be used to preserve human bodies until medical technology had advanced sufficiently to cure their diseases and overcome the ill effects of the freezing process itself.[10] As an indication of his connection to the science-fiction subculture, Ettinger contributed an article to the science-fiction magazine *If*, on how cryonics could be used for long-duration spaceflight.[11] In 1972, he published his second book, *Man into Superman*, suggesting that technology could not only preserve human life but vastly improve it.[12]

Today, among the formal affiliates of the World Transhumanist Association are three organizations that actually realize Ettinger's original vision by freezing clients for future possible resurrection: The Alcor Life Extension Foundation, The Cryonics Institute, and The American Cryonics Society. Another affiliate, The Immortality Institute, has published a collection of essays, *The Scientific Conquest of Death*, about other promising biological or computational technologies that might, in principle, extend life indefinitely.[13]

Since the 1970s, a few visionaries have been propagandizing for technological transcendence, prominent among them the son of an Iranian diplomat, Fereidoun M. Esfandiary who renamed himself *FM-2030* to symbolize that he was a citizen of the future with no primitive ethnic or national connections. His 1989 book, *Are You a Transhuman?* did much to popularize the concept of Transhumanism.[14] FM-2030 proclaimed himself neither left-wing nor right-wing, but an "up-wing" revolutionary. In 2000, FM-2030 succumbed to pancreatic cancer at the age of 69, but he was immediately frozen and is currently held in cryonic suspension at the Alcor Foundation in Scotsdale, Arizona. Apparently, FM-2030 is dead, but it is literally correct to say, "He does not consider himself to be dead." Either he really is dead, and is not capable of considering anything, or he will be revived at some future time when his hope to survive will be fulfilled.

In 1988, two graduate students at the University of California at Los Angeles, Max More and T. O. Morrow, founded *Extropy*, intended to be the opposite of entropy, to promote human transformation. More later teamed up with an associate of FM-2030, Natasha Vita-More.[15] More became influential in promoting the ideals of *Extropianism*, and Vita-More developed an artistic style oriented toward post-humans. For a number of years, they headed the Extropy Institute. A theme of the Extropians has been an emphasis on the individual's freedom to choose what to become, and a concern that governments and other traditional institutions might try to restrict this freedom. While advocating transcendence, they rejected religious traditions: "Extropy means favoring reason over blind faith and questioning over dogma. It means understanding, experimenting, learning, challenging, and innovating rather than clinging to beliefs."[16]

The World Transhumanist Association, with currently about 3,000 members, is the moderate but influential center of the Transhumanist Movement. Many of the leaders are academics or graduate students, including a number of philosophers. The home page of the group's website explains its goals: "The World Transhumanist Association is an international nonprofit membership organization which advocates the ethical use of technology to expand human capacities. We support the development of and access to new technologies that enable everyone to enjoy better minds, better bodies and better lives. In other words, we want people to be better than well."

The organization offers an extensive news service from its website and launched *The Journal of Evolution and Technology*, currently published by the Institute for Ethics and Emerging Technologies and edited by Professor James Hughes of Trinity College in Connecticut. The August 2005 issue was dedicated to the similarities and differences between religion and Transhumanism. For example, an article by professor Patrick Hopkins of Millsaps College explains that Transhumanism and religion are similar, in that they both seek transcendence, but Transhumanism believes humans can achieve transcendence through their own technological efforts, whereas religion relies upon supernatural belief, obedience, or practices. Hopkins foresees the very real possibility of antagonism between Transhumanism and religion, as particular faiths reject specific technical means Transhumanists adopt to achieve transcendence.[17] In a later issue, Professor Gregory Jordan of the University of South Florida analyzed the possibilities that religious movements might incorporate some of the principles of Transhumanism, a topic that would take us back to Chapter 7.[18]

Other issues have contained occasional articles about the public's response to Transhumanism. John Schloendorn proposed a psychological *terror management theory*, that predicts people will reject novel messages about overcoming death because the topic elicits terror, and terror causes people to fall back on culturally traditional modes of response.[19] An article by W. Scott Badger, based on an Internet questionnaire, detected religious opposition to cryonic suspension, comparable to our finding in Chapter 8 that Atheists tend to be weak in social obligations: "Christians were more disposed to perceive cryonics as unnatural, selfish, and immoral than either Agnostics or Atheists. Agnostics and Atheists had fewer concerns with the negative perceptions of family and friends toward cryonics than Christians. They were also less concerned about waking up in a future time without family and friends around than either Christians or Jews."[20]

In his book, *Citizen Cyborg*, analyzing the techno-political challenges of the twenty-first century, James Hughes argued that much of the immediate opposition to Transhumanism has been religiously motivated.[21] He reports that two Christian organizations are very active in criticizing Transhumanists, the Center for Bioethics and Culture, and the Center for Bioethics and Human Dignity.[22] It is less clear how strong the religious influences may be in The President's Council on Bioethics that has argued against technological enhancement of human beings and against cloning in its reports *Beyond Therapy* and *Human Cloning and Human Dignity*.[23] In any case, Council member Francis Fukuyama has asserted that Transhumanism is one of the "world's most dangerous ideas," and has argued that we must not allow "transhumanists to deface humanity."[24]

Convergenism

Over many decades, science became progressively more specialized, fragmenting into numerous separate domains that had trouble even talking with each other. This was comfortable for religion, because a problem for faith in one realm was isolated from all the rest of science. For example, Darwin's theory of evolution had no consequences for most subfields of biology, let alone for physics, chemistry, or sociology. Thus, a scientist in another field could ignore Darwin at no peril to his or her own research, and ordinary citizens who respected much of science could continue to reject the theory of evolution by natural selection.

However, this situation challenged the best minds in science to seek bridges across disciplinary boundaries, and much of the most exciting research occurred at the margins between fields. Interdisciplinary fields arose, such as biochemistry, astrophysics, social-psychology, and most recently cognitive science. Sciences distant in theories and subject matters nonetheless use the same mathematics, and the introduction of scientific computing gave them many of the same analytic tools. By the end of the twentieth century, many observers sensed that science had begun to go through a significant phase change. Edward O. Wilson has called the unification of the sciences *consilience*. Wilson himself exemplifies consilience, because he is not only an entomologist but contributed significantly to the creation of sociobiology, a field that combines ethnology, genetics, and other fields to study animal social behavior.[25]

A broadly-based movement to unify science crept forward inside the laboratories, observatories, and universities, but with limited implications for the wider culture. Then it became obvious that technologies were unifying as well, and would have powerful direct impacts that the public could not ignore. The launch site for a comprehensive convergence movement turned out to be nanotechnology, with its growing connections to biotechnology and information technology.

On September 28–29, 2000, a major workshop was held at the National Science Foundation to explore the societal implications of nanoscience and nanotechnology. Dozens of scientists, engineers, and policy makers reported on recent developments and projected future trends. The first sentence of the book-length report summarized their key point thus:

> A revolution is occurring in science and technology, based on the recently developed ability to measure, manipulate and organize matter on the nanoscale—1 to 100 billionths of a meter. At the nanoscale, physics, chemistry, biology, materials science, and engineering converge toward the same principles and tools. As a result, progress in nanoscience will have very far-reaching impact.[26]

NSF scientists immediately got to work organizing a second major meeting to examine convergence directly, and after much preparation it also was held at NSF, December 3–4, 2001. The title of the book-length report, *Converging Technologies for Improving Human Performance*, made it clear that the prime goal was to expand the scope for human action and enhance human abilities. In addition to plenary sessions surveying the overall potential of converging technologies, the conference hosted five workshops on distinct themes: expanding human cognition and communication, improving human health and physical capabilities, enhancing group and societal outcomes, national security, and unifying science and education. The executive summary introduces the fundamental principle of convergence:

> In the early decades of the 21st century, concentrated efforts can unify science based on the unity of nature, thereby advancing the combination of nanotechnology, biotechnology, information technology, and new technologies based in cognitive science. With proper attention to ethical issues and societal needs, converging technologies could achieve a tremendous improvement in human abilities, societal outcomes, the nation's productivity, and the quality of life. This is a broad, crosscutting, emerging and timely opportunity of interest to individuals, society and humanity in the long term.

> The phrase "convergent technologies" refers to the synergistic combination of four major "NBIC" (nano-bio-info-cogno) provinces of science and technology, each of which is currently progressing at a rapid rate: (a) nanoscience and nanotechnology; (b) biotechnology and biomedicine, including genetic engineering; (c) information technology, including advanced computing and communications; (d) cognitive science, including cognitive neuroscience.[27]

Since then, three other major Converging Technologies conferences have resulted in books, plus a re-examination of the societal implications of nanotechnology in the light of five years of progress emphasized the importance of convergence.[28] The leading scientists and engineers who participated offered many predictions about future technological possibilities. For example, Brian Pierce of the Raytheon Corporation and Rudy Berger of the MIT Media Lab said new nano-enabled sensor systems could improve human cognition.[29] Sherry Turkle of MIT explained how robots and computers could become companions rather than mere tools, by being transformed into sociable technologies.[30] Computer graphics pioneer Warren Robinett argued that full understanding of how the brain works could vastly improve human senses, memory and imagination.[31] Patricia Connolly of the University of Strathclyde predicted that nano-bio convergence could extend the lifespan significantly.[32]

The conference participants offered not merely prophecies but also accomplishments. For example, one area of radical potential is direct connection between the human brain and computers, essentially thought transfer between people and machines. Many teams and individual researchers are working in this area, partly in order to help paralyzed people gain more control in this lives, and partly motivated by military needs to achieve quicker reaction times from aircraft pilots. Among the Converging Technologies researchers working in this area are Britton Chance at the University of Pennsylvania, Edgar Garcia-Rill at the University of Arkansas for Medical Sciences, and Miguel Nicolelis at Duke University. Another, Rodolfo Llinás at New York University Medical School, has been developing nanoscale-diameter wires to reach inside the living brain through blood vessels to record the detailed interactions among individual neurons.[33] My point is not to claim that these specific lines of research will be successful, but to reinforce the fact that the dreams of the Transhumanists could possibly be achieved in the coming decades by practical researchers, as convergence energizes science and technology across a broad front.

Religious Rejection of Cloning

Of all the technologies with the potential to transform human life radically, cloning is most likely to be achieved in the near future and has been discussed most extensively. The popular image concerns *human reproductive cloning*, in which a genetic duplicate of someone is brought to life. This concept relates to Transhumanism, because cloning could be a step toward immortality if a means were found to transfer a person's memories to the new body. Achievement of that goal, if it is possible at all, would probably require all four NBIC fields of technological convergence, presumably with the intermediate step of transferring the memories to an information system.

Public concepts have probably been shaped not by science but by a host of horror novels and movies, including Ira Levin's *The Boys from Brazil* about cloning Adolf Hitler, and John Darnton's *The Experiment* about raising clone children only to harvest their organs for transplants.[34] However, real medical applications of cloning might be developed in the very near future that do not create viable individuals but merely produce replacement tissues or organs, thereby avoiding most of the moral or religious issues. This far more limited application of the technology is often called *therapeutic cloning.*

The movement to ban human reproductive cloning appears to draw strength from traditional religious beliefs, and one way to conceptualize this hostility is in terms of evolutionary competition.[35] Four decades ago, the influential sociologist Talcott Parsons argued that religion was an evolutionary universal, found in all societies and necessary for the emergence of civilization.[36] However, even if this were true, religion might be destined for extinction as humanity ascended to a higher stage of development. Just as humans lack the gills and tail possessed by their remote ancestors, they might do without faith at some time in the future.[37]

As we have seen, religion historically may have performed beneficial functions for humanity. Thus, religion has evolutionary implications, notably because some varieties of it encourage fertility, thereby outbreeding competing cultural alternatives. This is where cloning enters the debate, because technological means of reproduction directly challenge religion's demographic advantage. In trying to defeat cloning, religion may be fighting for its life against a whole host of secular reproductive technologies.

Large majorities in many opinion polls oppose cloning, but it is widely reported that opposition is greatest among religious people. For example, an ABC poll carried out in 2001 asked a random national sample of American adults whether human cloning should be legal.[38] Fully 95 percent of evangelical Protestants wanted it to be illegal, compared with 91 percent of Catholics, 83 percent of non-evangelical Protestants, and 77 percent of non-religious respondents.

Other polls agreed. The Pew Research Center found that 88 percent of white evangelical Protestants oppose "cloning experimentation," compared with 79 percent of "mainline" Protestants, 75 percent of Catholics, and 56 percent of "secular" respondents.[39] A Gallup poll asked whether respondents approved or disapproved of "cloning of human embryos for use in medical research." Fully 72 percent of those who attend church weekly disapproved, compared with 66 percent of those who attend nearly weekly and only 50 percent of those who attend church less often.[40]

To explore this issue further, I placed a number of religion items and three questions about cloning in *Survey2001*, the web-based questionnaire we have used in earlier chapters. Because they were recruited through *National Geographic* and the academic networks of the social scientists who created *Survey2001*, the respondents are probably more aware of issues related to science and technology than the average person. Because the survey was administered online, they were probably richer and better educated than the average.[41] However, research has found that such online surveys can do a good job of charting the relationships between variables, even if they cannot specify the exact value of each variable in the general population.[42]

Two of the questions asked how much the respondent agreed or disagreed with these statements: "Research on human cloning should be encouraged, because it will greatly benefit science and medicine." "There should be a law against cloning human beings." The third cloning-related item presented the two statements again and offered a space where the respondent could write his or her views on their topic freely. This approach combines both quantitative and qualitative methodologies in a manner that is especially effective in pilot studies designed to open up a new area of social-scientific research. Figure 10.1 shows how different religious and non-religious groups responded to the two fixed-choice questions, combining those who responded "agree" or "strongly agree."

Altogether, only 31.7 percent feel that research on human cloning should be encouraged, and fully 52.3 percent want human cloning banned by law. The two largest groups, the 1,116 Protestants and 650 Roman Catholics, favor a law against cloning and are not enthusiastic about supporting cloning research. The small number of Buddhists tend to agree with the Christians. Jews show considerably less opposition to cloning, although many of them may be secularized people for whom being Jewish is a cultural heritage rather than a faith. Like the Jews, the non-religious respondents and the agnostics are ambivalent. Atheists are far more favorable toward cloning than any of the religious groups, and noticeably more favorable even than agnostics and the non-religious. Indeed, Atheists are the only group in which more respondents encourage cloning research than want a law against human cloning.

A person's religious preference is an informative measure of religiousness, but it is good to compare this measure of group affiliation with measures about the individual's own religious behavior and self-conception. Perhaps the most potent single variable in social science survey research on religion is the respondent's frequency of church attendance. Religion is a social phenomenon, and by associating with believers, a person becomes socialized to the norms and beliefs of a particular religious tradition. Therefore, *Survey2001* included this extensively used question: "How often do you attend religious services?" Figure 10.2 shows a very strong religious effect on attitudes toward cloning.

Figure 10.1: Cloning Attitudes by Denomination

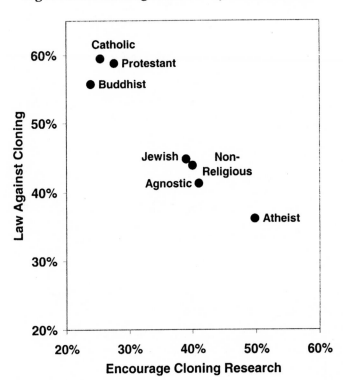

Among respondents who never attend church, support for cloning research is almost three and a half times as great as among those who attend most frequently, 37.7 percent compared with only 11.1 percent. The fraction supporting research declines by 26.6 percentage points from the most secular to most religious group. Agreement with a legal ban on cloning is higher is all categories, but rises from 45.7 percent to 78.5 percent, a gap of fully 32.8 percentage points attributable to religion. So many of the *Survey2001* respondents never attend church, that this question does not distinguish people well at the low end of the religion spectrum. Another question asked people to say how religious they were, and among those 333 who said they were "extremely non-religious," fully 51.4 percent wanted to encourage cloning research, and only 38.1 percent wanted a legal ban.

Figure 10.2: Church Attendance and Cloning (percent agree)

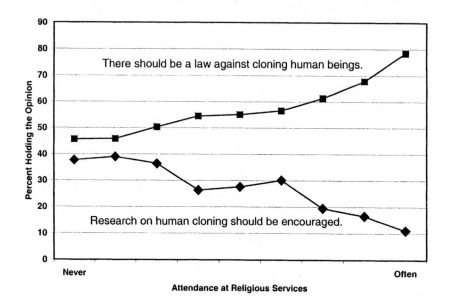

Religious Conceptions of Cloning

Having documented the significance of religion in shaping the cloning attitudes of respondents to *Survey2001*, we can examine responses to the open-ended item. *Survey2001* was administered online by a sophisticated computer system, and it was set so that people responding to the science items would be divided at random into four groups, each to receive three open-ended items from a set of twelve. Thus, something approaching 1,000 English-language respondents were offered the chance to answer the third cloning item, and 749 of them took the opportunity to do so.

One way to conceptualize religious faith is to take what believers say literally. A person who believes in God, according to this view, considers God to be real in the sense that a chair is concretely real. Although in some way transcending the material plane, God has personality, will, and desire, in the minds of such people. He can speak to a human being or forcefully intervene in a person's life. Being God, he is tremendously important to all aspects of life, so all of a literal believer's other beliefs must harmonize with the central tenets of his or her faith. People whose religion is like this are called "literalists." For example, those who consider the stories of miracles in the Bible to be historically factual are called "biblical literalists." Atheists sometimes have difficulty recognizing that many other people really do believe in the concrete, factual existence of God.

Fully 32 of the *Survey2001* respondents said that cloning was "playing God," and many others expressed similar ideas. For people who believe in a literal God, changing the factors shaping life and death usurps the divine prerogative. Other respondents called cloning "blasphemous" and "morally wrong," some saying: "Creating human life is God's job, and His alone." "We are not the creator, only the creation." "Human cloning is going too far and trying to take God's place in our creation." "The Bible tells us that 'it is he who made us and we are his' (Psalm 100), and I do not believe we have been given any permission to compete or override God's act of creation." "Cloning humans is Science presuming to have rights that belong only to our Creator."

In his classic statement of the societal theory, Emile Durkheim defined religion as concerning a sacred realm where humanity may not trespass and where supernatural beings rule.[43] One respondent wrote, "Cloning is messing with the sanctity, the magic that is life." Another said "It goes against everything holy." To another, cloning is "an attempt to deny that God exists (despite the wonderful evidence of creation)."

Several respondents described a power struggle: "Scientists shouldn't receive government funding to satisfy their own god-complexes." "Humans should never become more powerful than God." "Our Lord has made it very clear that only He can create human life. He is very upset with scientists' efforts with regard to stem cell research and cloning." "The punishment should be harsh, so that no scientist on a power trip would try it." "The scientists that are experimenting are on a power trip and should leave well enough alone. God will have His day with them."

For many respondents, God is the unifying principle of nature's beneficence: "I believe that God created human beings, and it is for Him and Him alone to create life. When man dabbles in the realm of the Divine, he threatens the entire balance of life as we know it. We are like children playing in a tide pool, thinking that because we have lingered there, we understand the complexities of the vastness of the entire ocean. Danger lurks in the depths, and it threatens our very humanity."

Some respondents connect cloning with abortion, an issue having powerful negative connotations for religious conservatives.[44] One argued, "Stop killing our children before they are born if you want to increase the population." Another agreed: "I see no real value in creating a spare parts source to prolong human life. We are busily destroying life every day in the name of 'Pro Choice.' If we subscribe to killing a million unborn babies each year, how can we justify cloning even one human?" To the extent that many firm believers associate cloning with other religiously charged issues, it may be nearly impossible to convince them to change their minds about it.

The Christian notion of an immortal, righteous soul offers hope in return for moral behavior. One respondent asked, "Where does the 'soul' or 'spirit' of a human being fit into the cloning process?" Others brooded: "We don't know enough about our souls and the psychology behind it." "I am very wary of the idea of cloning an entire human because of the whole question about the human spirit/soul." "Since we will never be able to clone the soul, why even try humans?" The assumption that clones would lack souls seems to be widespread: "I don't believe that a person made by man can have a soul." "We are God's creation, and while man may be able to create the heartbeat and physical body, the spirit and soul can only come from God." "Life—the spirit/soul—comes from God when a sperm and an egg combine to create a human. I can't resolve this with cloning where you lack one of these elements."

Not all self-consciously religious people believe in the literal existence of God. For many, God is a metaphor, albeit a precious one that should not be deflated by acknowledging its figurative quality. The God metaphor may mean different things at different times, and a person may often be confused about whether to apply it to a given situation or to use a different metaphor. For example, several respondents said that cloning was contrary to *nature*: "For all I have to say is NO ONE SHOULD PLAY GOD!!!!! Nature intended us to be as we are, by birth to our parents." One respondent exclaimed, "Leave such matters to GOD and don't monkey with nature!" Others argued that human cloning "goes against nature" or would be "against the laws of nature," "messing with nature," "upsetting the balance of nature," "against every law of nature that exists," or even "against the natural elements in nature."

In a sense, religion is the death business, and it cannot tolerate any technology that would take away its market: "I do not believe that cloning should be opened up to any egotistical rich individual who thinks that cloning is the next best thing to immortality." "Rich people want to buy immortality" "Do we want the 1,000 most powerful and rich people to live forever?" Religion compensates people psychologically for the losses they suffer and the rewards they never gain. Hope for eternal life is one of these supernatural compensators, but another is compensatory social status.[45] Thus the idea that rich people could buy immortality through cloning is doubly galling to people whose religion is rooted in socio-economic deprivations.

One religious respondent could not locate the boundary of sacred territory: "I do not feel that it is right for humans to play the role of God. Only he decides what should be alive or dead. Cloning organs so that they can be used to replace malfunctioning organs is a different story. Although if we go there then we are cheating death, or did God make us able to figure that out so we could live longer? Vaccinations are in a way impeding the plan of death, because the people who get the disease would have died unless we came up with a vaccination. It is all very confusing to me, and I wish that life could be simpler."

Many ancient legends, notably the expulsion from the Garden of Eden, imagine a time when humanity lived comfortably with nature, ending with an abrupt estrangement that required labor and technology to make a living.[46] Tool-making probably emerged over millions of years, and the birth of agriculture took thousands, but the legends have a certain poetic truth. The religious question then becomes whether with cloning (and genetic engineering more broadly) we face a second temptation to eat the fruit of the tree of knowledge, that may lead to a further estrangement from God. When theologians debate this point, they would do well to remember that the Bible itself endorses artificial selection in Genesis 30–31, where Jacob breeds sheep and goats for desirable characteristics.

The Transhuman Heresy

I carried out an initial scientific reconnaissance of the relationship between religion and technological transcendence, with a pilot questionnaire study of attitudes toward radical technological possibilities that was distributed initially at the 2003 Transvision conference of the World

Transhumanist Association, then through classes at religious colleges and a secular university. The 435 respondents were by no means a random sample of the population, but included a number of Transhumanists, others who might be sympathetic to the idea of human enhancement, and religious people who were recruited because they presumably have very different beliefs and attitudes from those of Transhumanists. The primary point was to administer the pilot questionnaire to people with strong views who were thus likely to highlight any deficiencies in the items so that they could be improved for a future study that sought a broader and more representative sample. However, until such time as we have more reliable data, the results of this pilot study offer tentative but clear insights.

The questionnaire included seven brief stories about people who are exploring some of the new technological possibilities for transcendence, asking respondents to read each one and judge whether the plans of the person in the story are good or bad. There were actually eight versions of each story, varying three dichotomous variables, and at random a given respondent received just one. Here, the questionnaire was prototyping material following a standard method for incorporating experiments in questionnaires, called the *vignette method*.[47] For example, here are two versions of a story about cryonic suspension:

> Story I, Version 1: Michael is a senior scientist in a medical research laboratory who has an incurable disease. He has become interested in a process called cryonic suspension. This involves carefully freezing a person's body, perhaps for as long as several decades, then thawing and reviving the person to continue his life. Michael has decided to enter cryonic suspension himself, so that his disease can be cured by the medical science of the future.

> Story I, Version 2: Mary is a high school health teacher who is perfectly healthy. She has become interested in a process called cryonic suspension. This involves carefully freezing a person's body, perhaps for as long as several decades, then thawing and reviving the person to continue her life. Mary has decided to enter cryonic suspension herself, so that she can see what the future will be like.

For each of the seven stories, half of the respondents read a story about a man, and half read a story about a woman. There were three reasons why gender was varied in this way. First, respondents might identify more closely with a protagonist if he or she were of the respondent's own gender. Second, if we asked just about one gender, then we would not know if the results generalized to the other. Third, research supports the common stereotype that males are more likely to take physical risks than females,[48] so by varying gender at random we can explore whether this applies to futuristic risks like cryonic suspension. The stories also varied in whether the person was an expert in the field, and thus able to make an informed decision—here whether the person was a senior medical research scientist or a high school health teacher. And a third variable differed across stories, but often gave the person a special motivation for taking the risk, such as having a currently incurable disease.

In fact, the different experimental manipulations appeared to have very little impact on respondents' judgments of the stories. About 21 percent of people who read the story about Michael think cryonic suspension would be a good idea, compared with 18 for those who read about Mary. This is a small difference, and could easily be due to chance. Indeed, averaging across all seven stories to get more stable statistics, respondents thought the ideas were good for a male protagonist 31 percent of the time, and 33 percent if the protagonist were female. The difference between expert protagonists and non-experts is coincidentally about the same, 31 versus 33. Although many published vignette studies have reported significant differences, the experimental manipulation often proves far weaker than other variables, notably the personal characteristics of respondents.[49]

This is important for the present analysis, because it suggests that the ideology of the respondent could overpower any specific details of the concrete situation described in a story. If the expertise of the protagonist in the story does not matter to respondents, then we may wonder whether the respondents are willing to grant protagonists the right to decide their own fate. After briefly explaining the content of the other stories, we will see whether respondents' religious views are a more powerful determinant of reactions.

The second story concerned using advanced multi-media computer technology to record all of one's experiences, which could be a step toward cybernetic immortality but was described blandly enough that it did not provoke negative reactions. So many respondents thought the person had a good plan that differences in opinion cannot be correlated with other variables. The third story stimulated more disagreement, because it took that idea to an extreme conclusion:

Story III, Version 1: Albert is a very successful brain surgeon. He reads a lot about both computers and the human brain, and he believes it is possible to transfer a person's mind from the brain to a computer. Recently he has become involved in a research project to accomplish this, by having his own mind scanned in, using a process that will destroy his brain.

The fourth story drew moderate reactions, and describes a method of personality capture somewhat between stories two and three in terms of how radical the technological idea is:

Story IV, Version 1: Elizabeth is the head of a computer science laboratory. She has become interested in the concept of uploading a human personality to a computer, using a variety of psychological tests and opinion surveys. She has assembled a huge computerized collection of questionnaires and has already answered forty thousand questions. She hopes that progress in information technology and artificial intelligence will allow her ideas to influence people even after her death.

The fifth story concerned human reproductive cloning, and the previous section already addressed this issue. Story number six was about nanotechnology:

Story VI, Version 1: Martin is a nanotechnologist who designs microscopic devices on the molecular scale. Recently, he has become interested in nanites. These are tiny nanotechnology robots that could go into the human body to repair organs or even individual cells. In a few days, he will have specially designed nanites inserted into his blood stream to clean and repair his circulatory system, and later on he expects to have other nanotechnology treatments for other parts of his body. He has recently suffered a heart attack, and he hopes that these treatments will greatly extend his life.

The final story builds on the earlier items and explores an idea I presented in a book published by NASA:[50]

Story VII, Version 1: Carl is an electrician working for an airline who has always dreamed of traveling through space to another star. He has joined a group that believes it is possible to record an individual's personality and genetic code, send them to a distant planet, and reconstitute the person there to begin a new, extraterrestrial life. He is very excited about the most recent advances in the space program, and has volunteered to have himself recorded for launch on a future interstellar mission.

The seven stories do not directly attack religion, but they have two qualities that might offend religious sensitivities. First, they suggest that it may be possible to improve human nature to a significant degree, thus implicitly faulting God's handiwork in creating humans. Second, they hint that it may be possible to achieve technological immortality, thus stealing one of God's supposed prerogatives.

One of the miscellaneous items in the survey gives us a measure of the intensity of the respondent's religious faith. It was the God item from the General Social Survey, that we used in earlier chapters. Given that we intentionally oversampled religious conservatives (in the relatively religious United States), fully 56.2 percent said "I know God really exists and I have no doubts about it." In Figure 10.3 we compare them with the 43.8 percent who selected any of the other options.

Among people who selected one of the five choices indicating some doubt in the existence of God, 28 percent felt that cryonic suspension was a good idea, compared with only 13 percent among those having complete faith in God. Discounting the second story, which was too bland to elicit strong opinions, we see a solid tendency for religiously faithful people to reject the other transcendent technologies as well. On average, only 26 percent of highly religious respondents think the plan in a story is good, compared with 39 percent of those with a range of religious views. In a larger study, with sufficient numbers of respondents to compare across all different beliefs in God, we would expect to find an even greater range of reactions to the stories.

The pilot questionnaire also included 20 agree–disagree statement items. One stated, "Cryonics (freezing a person's body until medical science is able to cure its diseases) will enable people to survive otherwise fatal accidents and illnesses." Among people having complete faith that God exists, only 17 percent agreed, compared with 31 percent who have some degree of doubt about God. Another agree–disagree item said, "Technological convergence—combining nanotechnology, biotechnology, information technology, and cognitive science—will greatly improve human abilities." Here agreement levels were higher, with 40 percent of the faithful agreeing, compared with 59 percent of doubters.

There were also four confidence questions taken from the General Social Survey, one of which measures attitudes toward religion in a very

Figure 10.3: Percent Saying the Idea is Good by Belief in God

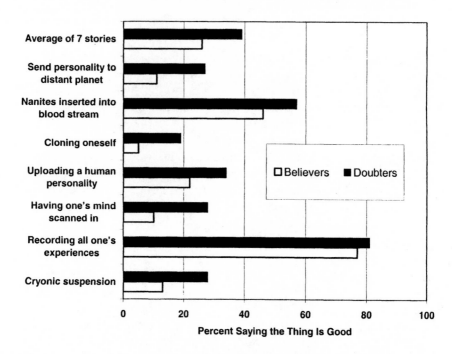

different way. "Organized religion" was one of a set of "institutions in this country," the other three being medicine, the scientific community, and major companies. The instructions asked: "As far as the people running these institutions are concerned, would you say you have a great deal of confidence, only some confidence, or hardly any confidence at all in them?" Table 10.1 in the appendix shows how confidence in religion versus science affects enthusiasm for the seven kinds of technological transcendence. We should not expect huge differences, because data from the General Social Survey itself show that people who are confident in religious leaders tend to be confident in scientific leaders as well. Some people tend to support all the standard institutions of society, in contrast to other people who distrust them all. Nonetheless, people who have a great deal of confidence in organized religion think the ideas in the seven stories are good only 26 percent of the time, compared with an average of 38 percent among those with hardy any confidence in religion. In contrast, 42 percent of people having a great deal of confidence in the scientific community favor the ideas, compared with 25 percent among those with hardly any confidence in science.

Religious Conceptions of Technological Transcendence

After each of the seven stories, the respondent was encouraged to write comments, and many availed themselves of this opportunity.[51] Again, some religious respondents felt that the technology violates God's plan for us. That would be bad not only because it defies the Lord—as they see it—but also because they believe all human life gains its meaning from God's plan. "Cryonic freezing is something I disagree with. God put us on this earth at a certain time for a certain reason." On the same topic, others wrote, "We as humans do not have the right to play God in such a manner;" "I don't believe in altering God's plan;" "You are messing with God's work and his plan for you." "This is wrong, to continue life like this is against everything I believe in. When God gives you a time to die it is your time. This is acting too God like in my opinion." The same objection was leveled against interstellar colonization: "Other planets are not made for humans to live on. If God wanted us to live on those planets he would have put us there."

On brain scanning, one worried, "I don't see that happening, and if it does that will be very scaring. Will we be doing God's work?" Another complained, "It is wrong to play God with mind, body, or spirit." About computerized personality capture through question-answering, one said, "From a religious point of view, I see this as 'playing God.' I feel that God ultimately decides how long one is here and I'm relatively certain that the development of such technology (God willing) would lead to the demise of all humanity." Another asserted, "It is corrupt to think someone wants their human personality to be alive after they die. You should just leave all that stuff alone and let God do his work."

Several of the stories suggest not merely enhancement but technological immortality, and religious respondents think the problem of human death has already been solved, but by God, not by human inventiveness. On recording all one's experiences, one religious respondent wrote, "For educational purposes about his life it is ok, but to achieve immortality? That is only done by accepting Jesus." In response to two of the personality capture items, another commented, "Only God gives eternal life through His son Jesus . . . There is no way to become immortal in this world, unless you believe in a loving God who sent His son to die for you." A third respondent offered a more complete analysis: "While recording and documenting one's personal life experiences is something I find realistic and even interesting, I don't see the connection between that and achieving a kind of immortality. While we analyze and often relive our memories, the things we go through are merely experiences through which our characters and faith in God are enhanced. If we were meant to be immortal on earth, God would've created us so."

A religious conception implies a very different way of thinking about human personality, that may render technological solutions implausible to the religious person. One said, "Immortality is a matter of the spirit, not the physical. The mind is more than a collection of electrical impulses and neurotransmitters or neurons. It's linked to the spirit, which isn't transferable to a database." Another thought cryonic suspension would fail: "If one believes that a human being is made up of both soul and body, then no matter what is done to the body, if a man's soul departs, then he is dead. There's nothing wrong with wanting to have a long life, but when a man's time is up, it's up and no amount of scientific advancement can prevent the soul from leaving the body." "A person's being is not just his brain, but his soul. Unfortunately, the soul needs the brain to exist on Earth." "I think the human soul and mind is something that could never be contained in any computer, no matter how sophisticated or advanced." "You may be able to transfer one's personality to a computer, but not their soul, and that is what counts."

Some respondents explained that a soul or spirit is what gives us many fundamental human characteristics. "Her ideas may remain in the computer, but her soul is in her body. Even if she lives on mentally, she will be dead and it won't be here, just her thoughts (no feelings or emotions)." "The mind is not solely a collection of ones and zeros processing data and spewing out results. That is one function, but there is also the spirit of a man that sustains him. Without a man's spirit the mind would be a mere 'super computer' without life, free-will and choice."

Belief in the soul poses a difficulty as well for interstellar travel in the form of an information pattern: "Duplicate her? So there's a copy on another planet? Don't think so. Nor would it really be her. Again the missing ingredient is the spirit that God gives to a person and they develop, some more, some less. That's not copyable. If this means 'deconstitute' Carol to reconstitute her, again it doesn't work. It's like suicide. If physically possible, her mind would be there, and the mind is an integral part of the soul of a person!" "A person's soul cannot be reconstituted, so this plan of reconstituting a person—even if they have their personality and genetic code—is flawed. 'The body without the spirit is dead.'"

Finally, to some respondents pursuing these technologies for personal gain would not serve appropriate spiritual goals. "It's man's attempt to achieve the spiritual or eternal life on his own without having to go through the proper channels.—Probably so he can say 'I did it myself without God'—which basically is pride, and pride in my opinion is the opposite of true, sacrificial love." "Why waste your life working towards a false sense of eternity, when there is so much to cherish, learn and love in the life we are given?"

Conclusion

Many technological advances could be achieved within a few years that reduce the value of religion for ordinary people, by enhancing their lives technologically. Thus, Transhumanism offers the hope that traditional Atheism lacks. Religion is likely to respond to this challenge by coercing governments into forbidding some of the necessary research and the deployment of some technologies. It may do this by outright legal prohibition, by influencing governments and corporations to withhold funding for research and development, and by stigmatizing the technologies such that few young people are attracted to careers dedicated to advancing them. The failure of schools to teach simple but profound ideas like evolution and relativity in the early grades steals future scientists from the world and breeds an electorate uninterested in supporting the needed research. The faith that God will welcome dying believers into Heaven saps energy from real efforts to conquer death and to explore the heavens. Humanity needs a sense of urgency to drive it out into the universe.

The church is the last remaining absolute monarchy—God, after all, is its Lord—and its loyal defenders will oppose any attempt to establish a republic. Transhumanism asserts that each individual has the right to become whatever he or she wishes, so long as this does not compromise the equal rights of other people to become what they wish. Convergenists are building the technological basis for realizing those rights. True human freedom would violate the divine right of kings, or the rites of divine kings, so all but the most secularized forms of religion will brand it sacrilegious.

However, people who belong to highly secularized conventional religious denominations, the New Age, or scientist religions may be temporary allies of Transhumanists and Convergenists, at least concerning some issues. Also, it is still possible to make progress inside standard scientific and technological organizations. The time for overt conflict against religion has not yet come.

Already, some kinds of research are opposed by conservative churches and the politicians who cater to them. Most striking are attempts to ban human reproductive cloning and forms of research that might lead to it. Those who want to develop banned technologies face a dilemma. Should they invest considerable effort into a rational and respectable campaign to present their views, in hopes that open-minded policy leaders will refrain from instituting bans? Or should they sharpen their bayonets in preparation for total conflict against religion? If religion and other reactionary forces do institute legal bans, innovators will face a situation described by a Transhumanist bumper sticker: "When evolution is outlawed, only outlaws will evolve."

Fertility collapse and an inability of the world to cooperate in the best use of technology probably doom our present civilization, and the only course is to seek new principles on which to build a better one. A civilization that is not viable has no moral claim against efforts to create another. Any government that seeks to prevent technological transcendence thereby renders itself illegitimate. Clearly, many readers will not want to go very far along the line of this argument, but for sake of clarity I should state the conclusion: Well-intentioned people seeking to develop the means for transcendence of the current human condition have the right to defend themselves against any government or institution that seeks to prevent them.

11
An Age of Transition

Man is a rope stretched between
the animal and the Superman—
a rope over an abyss.
—*Thus Spake Zarathustra,*[1]
Friedrich Nietzsche

So far, we have used the word *secular* to refer to a society where the influence of religion is weak, and *secularization* to mean the weakening of religion. But there is another meaning of *secular*, one found on the American dollar bill: "*Novus ordo seclorum.*" Novelist Dan Brown is wrong to say this phrase means "New Secular Order" and expresses the opposition of Illuminati scientists to religion.[2] *Seclorum* is a poetic form of *seculorum* (or *saeculorum*), and the motto is usually translated, "a new order of the ages" implying that the foundation of the United States transcended the defects of earlier societies. Christians may recognize this phrase from Ephesians 3:21: "*in omnes aetates seculi seculorum*" which the King James version renders "throughout all ages, world without end." In social science, a *secular trend* is a gradual change over time, but the motto on the dollar is clearly millenarian, announcing a radical transformation of human existence. That is the issue, really: Are we nearing a singularity in history, when everything changes radically, or are we nearing the end of history when the only change is the end of change? Perhaps both outcomes are possible, and our own actions today will determine which future is realized. We shall now consider a collection of scenarios that suggest the range of possible outcomes, as we teeter on the end of the secular abyss.

225

Scenarios for the Future

Many clergy, theologians, and members of moderate or mainstream denominations today seem to think it is possible to be content with a distant
God. For example, Karen Armstrong wonders whether the idea of God is
"an idea of the past" that will pass away. She concludes, "Human beings
cannot endure emptiness and desolation; they will fill the vacuum by
creating a new focus of meaning."[3] Armstrong rejects fundamentalism,
and imagines people will be satisfied by a demythologized, distant deity
who avoids intervening in their lives. However immune from empirical
debunking a useless god may be, he offers nothing and thus can demand
nothing. That is, a fully Deist religion cannot serve significant social
functions, such as sustaining fertility or preventing crime and suicide. At
best, it is the impotent nostalgia of a generation experiencing an advanced stage of secularization, for the more religious culture that it has
lost.

The compensator exchange theory of religion absolutely does not
assert that secularization is unreal or unimportant. Rather, it merely rejects the simplistic notion that the grand sweep of history runs inexorably
from a religious to a non-religious era, and that scientific and social progress are destined to eliminate the need for faith. Indeed, secularization
does take place, within particular organizations, denominations, and religious traditions. Within a well-established tradition, such as Protestantism, some churches become highly secular and lose membership, but
sects will arise, expand and fill the gap.[4] Thus, so long as a religious tradition remains vigorous, secularization is a circular process that leads to
no net loss in faith, because the falling denominations are balanced off
by rising ones. Revival sustains the tradition.

However, at certain points in history an entire religious tradition
loses faith. Over the long run, the theory argues, secularization is self-
limiting, because it creates conditions suitable for religious innovation,
cult formation, and the establishment of a new religious tradition. It is
difficult to specify where in such a course of development western civilization currently finds itself. Will Christendom be sustained for generations to come by revival? Or is secularization eroding the basis of Christianity, gradually opening up substantial opportunities for new cults?
Perhaps both are happening in different parts of western civilization
(more secularization in Europe than in the Americas). Furthermore, religious innovation is a very difficult business. Really new successful religious traditions are rare, and they may require a substantial level of so-

cial disorganization to get a foothold in society. Innovation can establish a new tradition, but only with difficulty and the passage of considerable time.

Integrating the cognitive theory with exchange theory changes the equation, for two reasons. First, it identifies religion even more strongly as a set of cognitive errors, and thus deserving critical scrutiny rather than blind faith. Second, in combination with information technologies, it suggests that it might indeed be possible to abandon religion, but only at the point in human history when science and technology can effectively solve the problems that religion pretended to address. Have we reached that point in time? Or are we entering a period of social crisis that drives vigorous religious revival, religious innovation, and even repression of anti-religious forces like science?

Near the beginning of this book, we examined eight scenarios for the future of religion. Many serious writers use the scenario method to explore the human meanings of possible futures. For example, Robert Constanza sketched four visions of the year 2100, depending upon whether technology will make it possible to overcome limitations in natural resources:[5]

1. Star Trek: Public policies are optimistic, assuming that technology will overcome limitations, and in fact technology does achieve this, leading to expansion into the solar system.
2. Mad Max: Public policies are optimistic, assuming that technology will overcome limitations, but technology fails to achieve this, so civilization crashes.
3. Big Government: Public policies are pessimistic, assuming there are strict limits to economic growth, but in fact technology could have overcome these limits, so progress is unnecessarily suppressed.
4. Ecotopia: Public policies are pessimistic, assuming there are strict limits to economic growth, and this assumption is correct, so civilization achieves a necessary harmony with the environment.

Rather more ambitious were the three scenarios sketched for the year 3000 by the Millennium Project of the American Council for the United Nations University:[6]

1. Human civilization still exists in the year 3000, in a form similar to the year 2000, but with numerous specific changes.
2. The human species has become extinct by the year 3000, but robots and other machines originally built by humans have evolved into the dominant form of intelligence.

3. Human civilization has given birth to several different kinds of intelligence: one similar to traditional Homo sapiens, others that have merged humans with computers, and others that are artificial life forms.

Three scenarios suggested by political scientist Benjamin Barber highlight the question of whether we will be able to choose our future:[7]

1. Pangloss: Market forces will naturally ensure that new technologies benefit humanity.
2. Pandora: Governments will use new technologies to enforce standardization, control, and repression.
3. Jeffersonian: Citizens will be able to decide among technologies, developing only those that are beneficial.

When I carried out a sociological study of science fiction literature, employing factor analysis to make sense of rich questionnaire data, I found three schools of thought about the future of science and technology:[8]

1. Hard-science: A positive future for humanity can be achieved by advancing physical science and technology, following rational plans based on objective knowledge.
2. New-wave: Technological development will be harmful, and humanity needs to emphasize social science, the humanities, and critical perspectives.
3. Fantasy: The future will be shaped not by physical science or social science, but by magic, supernatural forces, and unknowable dangers.

All these ideas suggest that we are at a crossroads, or indeed a tangle of roads that might cause historical gridlock, unless we can find our way through the maze. At a high level of generality, we have considered three major possibilities for the future of religion in an age of unprecedented scientific and technological possibilities. The idea that religion and science can coexist peacefully, Gould's magisteria, seems unlikely to me, but as I examine the two other scenarios the reader can periodically reflect upon this other alternative.

More likely, I think, over the long run either religion will triumph over science, or science will triumph over religion. The long run could mean a thousand years or more, or perhaps a little as two hundred. Over the next couple of centuries, there is a real possibility that religion will triumph initially, driving significant portions of science underground. Progressive convergence across the sciences, energized by hard-won progress in exactly those sciences suppressed by religion, could then lead to a revolution in which religion was toppled from power. This latter possibility is important to consider, because Convergenists, Transhumanists, plus scientists and engineers more generally, may need to prepare for a period in which their work is explicitly opposed by governments in league with religion.

Any reasonable analysis will need to acknowledge that other factors, only indirectly related to religion and science, will also play crucial roles. Conflict between nations, exhaustion of natural resources, erosion of democratic institutions, and exaggeration of economic inequalities are among them. I have particularly emphasized demographic collapse in the advanced industrial nations as a factor that has historical connections to secularization, but that in the future might be largely autonomous. Societies undergoing many stresses may not only turn to religion, but also allow anti-democratic forces to gain political ascendancy under the purloined banner of faith, producing a union of church and state that amounted to a dictatorship despite the support of many citizens.

Scenarios for Disaster

For decades, social scientists and ordinary citizens have been concerned about rising divorce rates and other signs that the traditional family may be disintegrating. In many industrialized nations, the divorce rate increased gradually over a long period of time, until changes in divorce laws and employment opportunities for women allowed the rate to leap suddenly upward. For example, in the United States, about 1 married woman per 1,000 became divorced in the year 1860, 5 per 1,000 in 1915, and more than 20 per 1,000 in 1975.[9] Writing in the *American Sociological Review*, Clem Brooks reports that concern about the decline of the family is much greater among evangelical Protestants who attend church frequently, and that this group has been contributing to a deepening political cleavage.[10] Therefore, we should consider the kinds of fears people have, that might motivate a religious transformation of politics away from secularization.

Survey2000 respondents have a wide variety of opinions about the future of the family, but many expect the cohesion of the family and its stabilizing influence on society to disintegrate even further.[11] By 2100, traditional family life will have largely dissolved, some fear. Family structure will be weak, with many single parent homes and little involvement with grandparents, aunts, and uncles. Society will be too busy and fast paced to attend to important matters such as family and child rearing. People will not be able to stay married for very long, because they are used to fast changes. Divorce rates will be above fifty percent, and most children will be raised in single-parent homes. The typical person will experience multiple divorces and remarriages.

Because of divorce and non-marital pregnancies, some *Survey2000* respondents believe, the rate of single parenthood will be high. Perhaps single parent families will contribute toward the decline of morals and an increase in crime and poverty.[12] Children's lives will be unstable, because of a high level of divorce and lack of extended families. People will have little contact with family members who are separated by more than one generation, and they will know little about their families' histories. Grandparents will have very little significance in the lives of their grandchildren.

In this scenario, the breakdown of the traditional nuclear family will cause increasing social problems. Youth violence will increase, as family members continue to spend less and less time interacting with one another. A decrease in family closeness will result in a breakdown in the work ethic. Society will consist of less caring, less devoted and less dedicated people.

Families will cease to be units of love and comfort. The individual will be alienated from friends and family. Marriages will decrease drastically in occurrence as fewer individuals share intimate relations with one another. This will be a vicious circle in which family disintegration in one generation fails to prepare the members of the next generation to create strong families. Indeed, young people will lack guidance and support, so they will be forced to invent their own ways of life. Many children will be left to their own devices. After school, many children will return home unsupervised, due to the economic need for both parents to work. They will have little experience of childhood, having to take responsibility and fend for themselves. Children will leave home at a very young age.

In consequence, young people will rebel against parental authority. They will be disrespectful, rude, lazy, and ill mannered. Youth society will be outrageous in an attempt to be different from the previous generation. Adolescents will find new music to irritate their parents with. Raising of children and moral instruction may be done by the peer groups and by technology, not by the family. At the extreme, there will packs of children living together without schooling or adult supervision.

More and more young girls will abuse alcohol and drugs during their pregnancies. Children will be desensitized to brutality through violent videos, news broadcasts, and computer games. Perhaps society will be so desensitized to violence that school shootings will no longer make the news. Lacking healthy forms of stimulation, children will be less and less creative. Many will largely stay indoors and have virtually no experience with the world of nature. Such is the long list of worries *Survey2000* respondents feel concerning the future of the family.

Both social critics and ordinary people often associate secularization with hedonism. In the 1960s, futurologists Herman Kahn and Anthony J. Wiener argued that the fundamental trend was toward a more *sensate* culture, which they defined as "empirical, this-worldly, secular, humanistic, pragmatic, utilitarian, contractual, epicurean or hedonistic."[13]

Pitirim A. Sorokin had already foreseen this thirty years earlier. The entire rise-and-fall cycle of civilization which he wrote about can take many centuries to complete, but he believed that western society was approaching a crisis point. Ultimately, a sensate civilization is likely to crash, ushering in a new period of intense cultural chaos out of which a new ideational civilization may be born. Sorokin wrote, "Neither the decay of the Western society and culture, nor their death, is predicted by my thesis. What it does assert . . . is simply that one of the most important phases of their life history, the Sensate, is now ending and that we are turning toward its opposite through a period of transition. Such a period is always disquieting, grim, cruel, bloody, and painful."[14]

Survey2000 respondents foresaw a number of ways in which the year 2100 could be hedonistic. Perhaps formerly illicit drugs will be socially accepted, and be as legal as alcohol. Marijuana, narcotics and mood elevator drugs will be widely available and very popular. In time, all non-medical drugs could become legalized, and new psychoactive substances will be invented in order to take people even higher. Psychedelic drugs with long-lasting beneficial effects will also have been invented. Emotional reality will be emphasized more than practical reality. Having superficial fun will be more important than being profoundly happy.

Some *Survey2000* respondents thought that early in the twenty-first century, a vaccine to prevent AIDS will have unleashed a second sexual revolution which will dwarf the first in magnitude and scope. The customs people live by will continue to relax, and acceptance of sexuality will permeate society. Prevailing customs will value frankness, and no topics will be taboo in either public or private settings.

Sexual puritanism that once repressed erotic behavior will be replaced by the view that many varieties of sexual interaction can be life-enhancing. Pornography and the general marketing of sex will increase. Total nudity and sex acts will be shown on television. Sex with animals will be common. Children will be sexually active at young ages.

As the twenty-first century progresses, respondents suggested, many people will have problems with intimacy. Interpersonal emotional relationships will be very difficult, although casual sex will be easy to get. Many people will prefer cybersex to the traditional pleasure of two bodies touching. For others, sex will be reduced to using simple machines for self gratification. Science will even develop an orgasm pill.

However, for some people sexuality will develop into a new form of spirituality. For example, the Roman Catholic Church will no longer have a rule requiring priests to be celibate. In several religions, sexual intercourse will become a ritual, paying homage to creation.[15]

In this scenario, moral decay and post modernism will lead to a loss of social values. Over a century ago, sociologist Emile Durkheim predicted that this *anomie*, as he called it, would become endemic in modern society.[16] The world will become a less civilized place, as the social contract breaks down. People will be extremely lax in their morals, and this could lead to a total loss of moral values. Perhaps by 2100, morality will have degenerated to such a degree, that the most shocking radicals are those few people who possess honor, values, dignity, and responsibility.

Fast technological progress will create chaos. Cultures will be challenged by this rapid and disruptive change. Enlightenment positivism will completely disappear, and people will realize that reality is negotiated and socially constructed.[17] Many will believe that there is no such thing as truth. In such a cultural wasteland, it will become harder and harder for the individual to find correct and truthful information. Technology and social outlook will have altered history to the point that no one will know the truth about the past. History will constantly be revised, to keep it compatible with the prevailing politically correct ideology.[18]

Optimists predict that the golden age of science may have ended, but the age of conceptual logic and relative thinking will have just begun. Pessimists worry that people will hold onto superstitions and myths all the more strongly, as the gap widens between science and public understanding of it. For better or worse, highly educated people will tend to have anti-intellectual and anti-technological sentiments.

Previously stable cultural bedrocks of society, such as religion and law, will break down and be replaced by trendy norms and bureaucratic whims. Situational ethics will grow in popularity, asserting that right and wrong are not objective but are relative to the particular situation. Moral relativism will reverse all standards, making what once was considered evil to be the norm and what used to be good to be considered outdated. Moral values and religion will be meaningful only to the old people. The moral standards of all civilized societies will continue to weaken until almost everybody will think that right and wrong are relative.

With no basis for acquiring character, the individual will drift in a maelstrom of confusion. Life will be a baffling experience. Meaning will be stripped from art and literature by academicians, the media, government, and popular culture. Honesty will not be considered an important value. There will be no respect for privacy or individual rights. The rule of law will be considered less and less important in society. These were among the conjectures of the respondents.

Long before Durkheim wrote about anomie and egoism, social scientists conjectured that modernization inflicts increasing psychological stresses on people, driving some of them insane. Way back in 1842, Edward Jarvis warned that the United States would see increasing rates of insanity, because "in the highest state of civilization and metal activity there is the greatest danger of mental derangement."[19] More than a century and a half later, several *Survey2000* respondents predicted that mental illness will be very common a century in their future.

Loneliness will be the most prevalent disease in the world. Depression will be the leading disease, due to technological isolation of the individual. People will be lonely, unappreciated, and lack recognition. People will be very introspective and self-conscious. People will be bombarded with too much information to the point of mental information overload. Nervous breakdowns due to the strain of constant information overload will be common. Daily lives will be very hectic and emphasize material gain. People will smile less, because life will be valued less.

Anxiety disorders will be a persistent, worldwide psychological problem. Adults will be exceedingly insecure in personal relationships, because of life-long histories of moving from one community to another. Social skills will decline as people will have less and less face to face contact with fellow employees, friends, and relatives. There will be a global feeling of dissatisfaction, frustration, and selfishness.

Schools will have grave problems with restless children. School children will be rude, disrespectful, and unable to concentrate. Young people will have poor social skills. Adults will become more and more adolescent in their behaviors. People will be technically proficient but socially immature.

Assisted suicide will be legal for the elderly and those with incurable medical conditions. It will be considered proper for people to decide when, where and how they will die. Euthanasia and suicide will be customary, because medical science will prolong life such that the world would become overcrowded without intentional death.

In the past twenty years, a new factor has been introduced with great significance for any analysis involving secondary compensation, namely the fertility collapse in most (possibly all) advanced industrialized societies that we discussed in Chapter 4. Almost every advanced nation today has a fertility rate below the replacement level, and analysis of the few exceptions (notably the United States) is inconclusive because of the difficulty of factoring in such things as the second-generation impact of immigrants and the differential fertility in culturally and religiously diverse segments of the population. Evidence at both the individual and societal level indicates that strong religion supports fertility, so the widespread fertility collapse may at least in part be a symptom of secularization.

It is worth remembering that the Roman Empire did not become Christian merely through refined intellectual debates in the Forum. Rome was in the slow but dramatic process of falling. The edicts of Diocletian imply population declines in critical areas, the liberty and frankly the innovativeness of Roman citizens had declined, and for a host of reasons individuals were ready for a new faith. St. Augustine's influential book *On the City of God* is partly a rebuttal of the charge that the sacking of Rome by the Visigoths in 410 was punishment for abandoning its pagan gods, but it famously recognized that the Roman civilization might be past saving, so the priorities should be shifted toward saving souls.[20]

Against the Fall of Night

Can science prevent reactionary religion from bringing a new Dark Age? After fifteen years serving in various roles in a federal science agency, and nearly four decades of research, I have formed an ambivalent opinion about this: Science could evaluate many of the questions associated with religion, including the existence or non-existence of God, but with very, very few exceptions it strenuously avoids doing so. Naturally, I cannot refer to any specific incidents, for reasons of confidentiality. So, let me state my observations as hypotheses:

1. Most science deals with very limited questions of no philosophical significance, so neither the results nor the scientists themselves raise any issues for religion.
2. It is in the interests of scientists to preserve the decades-long "truce" with religion, because they rely upon government grants and similar sources of funding that might be endangered if politicians or the public perceived that the particular kinds of science had negative implications for religion.
3. The philosophically significant results that do occasionally result from science, and the mental orientation associated with them, are only very poorly communicated to the public, perhaps because they often are counter-intuitive and uncomfortable.[21]
4. The status of science in society is precarious. History teaches us that few societies of the past have supported science, and research has become largely captive to large corporations and governments whose commitments are to their own power rather than to truth.[22]
5. Funding for cognitive science and the social sciences is remarkably weak, in significant measure because such research contradicts Christian dogma, and Christians have great influence in the political and economic system of western civilization.
6. The potential for a future collision between science and religion is great, however, both because new technologies such as computers embody some of the challenging scientific ideas, and because a marked convergence of sciences and technologies appears to be taking science to a new and more unified level.

Having cited Pitirim Sorokin's theory that any sensate society is destined to crash in a Dark Age, it is worth citing his counter-balancing theory that out of decades of obscure cultural conflict, a new *ideational* culture could arise, establishing the basis for a new civilization. It is an open question how deep the darkness must become, before the spark of the new culture can be seen clearly. Perhaps eagle-eyed Transhumanists already see it, in their vision of human transcendence through technology.

The unification of science and technology, over the next two or three decades, could produce a global scientific-technical culture. This has been the aim of the four Converging Technologies conferences and the four books that resulted from them. Concerted action could accelerate convergence, but it is happening gradually even without having a high priority for funding.

It is interesting to speculate about the central principles of the future unified scientific worldview, although it is certainly too early to state them with any confidence. In two publications I have suggested that eight, high-level, somewhat abstract concepts could organize a very large number of mathematical, physical, and cognitive principles that apply across fields of science and engineering:[23]

> *Conservation*: Many properties are conserved, through symmetries, parity laws, and feedback-regulated stabilities in complex adaptive systems.
>
> *Indecision*: Inconsistency, undecidability, uncertainty, chance, deterministic chaos and similar concepts are fundamental principles in the dynamics of systems over time.
>
> *Configuration*: Detailed, dynamic structures of objects determine their properties, notably the unity of nature at the nanoscale.
>
> *Interaction*: Elements of a system influence each other, generating higher-level dynamics and other emergent phenomena.
>
> *Variation*: Statistical distributions of properties are caused by the combination of chance and divergent processes of interaction.
>
> *Evolution*: Marked by drift, natural selection, and a trend toward greater complexity, evolution exploits variation to develop new configurations that compete through interactions.
>
> *Information*: Scientific laws can be analyzed in terms of information content and flow, while the doing of any science today relies heavily upon information technology.
>
> *Cognition*: Mental or computational process are the dynamic aspect of information, and fundamental to the human practice of science.

Edward O. Wilson, the sociobiologist who called the unification of the sciences *consilience*, has expressed skepticism that religion could find a way to participate in the coming intellectual consensus.[24] I myself have argued that the unification of all sciences and technologies would leave religion no room to breathe.[25] Where could a God of the Gaps live, if there were no significant gaps in human knowledge? How could faith in the supernatural survive if every piece of knowledge was securely tied to a universally shared model of nature? The fantasy writer, H. P. Lovecraft, possessed a refined sensitivity for the horrors that science could conjure. In the remarkably prescient first paragraph of "The Call of Cthulhu," Lovecraft recognized that consilience could impel people to reject science in favor of superstition:

The most merciful thing in the world, I think, is the inability of the human mind to correlate all its contents. We live on a placid island of ignorance in the midst of black seas of infinity, and it was not meant that we should voyage far. The sciences, each straining in its own direction, have hitherto harmed us little; but some day the piecing together of dissociated knowledge will open up such terrifying vistas of reality, and of our frightful position therein, that we shall either go mad from the revelation or flee from the light into the peace and safety of a new dark age.[26]

I can imagine my own scenario for the year 2100, a world in which the New Dark Age has begun. To be sure, the technical level will remain higher than the previous Dark Age, and everywhere people will read, use electricity, and kill each other with advanced weapons rather than spears and swords. But the Dark Age will not be limited to western Europe, and would involve every society on the Earth. Samuel Huntington has suggested we face a Clash of Civilizations, but I see it more as a clash of religions, especially if the current War on Terror decays into a general conflict between fundamentalist Christendom and fundamentalist Islam. The result could be the same, even if that disaster does not occur, merely taking longer to consolidate.

The Americas will be Christian. The Middle East, North Africa, Indonesia, and parts of south Asia will be Islamic. Both blocs will be poor, since the oil will have been exhausted, technical progress will have ceased, and the ideology-based governments will be incompetent. Public health will have declined, and periodic pandemics will overwhelm health care. Crime rates will be high, despite the religiousness of the populace. However, barring nuclear war between them, Christendom and Islam will be demographically viable. It will be a matter of debate whether the rights of women have declined more than the rights of men, but in any case the fertility rate will be sufficiently high to sustain the population up at the level where poor nutrition and poor general welfare increase mortality just enough to offset fertility. That is, the demographic transition will have been reversed, and fundamentalist religion will play a central role in accomplishing that historic shift.

An issue for the Americas is whether the United States will play the role of Second Rome, using military force to control both continents through a mixture of direct rule and client states. It is possible that some of today's democratic institutions will survive, despite the terrible problems. It could be that religion continues to be manifested in hundreds of denominations. If so, the Americans will be completely Protestant. Indeed, Roman Catholicism could be simply the largest Protestant denomination. There is already much evidence that American Jews are becoming more and more Protestant, for example adopting Christian notions of the afterlife.[27] However, if American imperialism dominates the hemisphere, we would need to contemplate scenarios in which religious power consolidated and became established with the state, leading to a new American Byzantine Empire.

The questions that face Islam are numerous. For a long time, Britain, France, and the United States have done much to prevent a strong Islamic state from emerging, for example in helping make sure that neither side won the Iran–Iraq war. Perhaps a unified Islamic society will emerge democratically, through gradual consolidation of a common market, but we are very far from that development today. It is easier to imagine a period of protracted conflict, when the larger states competed with each other to absorb the smaller ones. A century may be too short for this difficult process to run to completion.

India is already demographically viable, and it is developing the technical basis to defend itself against a second domination by Islam, and against Chinese expansion. The extent to which religious organizations will become larger and more centrally controlled will be a prime question.

What ideology will dominate China remains a complete mystery, but one possibility might be that China will reassert its Marxism, after trade with a declining western world becomes unprofitable. Then China could be the only viable secular part of the globe, achieving sufficient fertility through coercion of its population. I could also imagine the following scenario: China begins to democratize, instituting freedom of religion, then world economic depression follows a surge in oil prices and the collapse of the dollar when foreign debts are called in. A Qigong movement, not peaceful like Falun Gong but comparable to the Boxers of a century ago, sweeps China, topples the government, and institutes an aggressive religious regime.[28] Japan and Russia east of the Urals become embroiled in this messianic revolution.

It is hard to imagine that Europe could avoid being absorbed into one of the clashing religious civilizations. However, perhaps the high level of education and technical accomplishment in Europe, combined with the advanced state of secularization in many European nations, could resist the encroaching darkness. Night might come in the form of Islamic immigration, or American attempts to "save Europe once again," and resistance would be difficult. The diversity of Europe suggests that it might achieve a "unity in diversity," experimenting with different forms of post-human life and disseminating the most successful ones throughout the world.

More important than the fate of any nation would be the fate of science. The gloomy scenarios above cover a century at least, and possibly several centuries, so there would be time for scientists to react. Of course, the standard, surprise-free scenario is that none of these terrible things will happen, but I think it more likely that science will face increasing pressures to conform to popular ideologies that are mobilized for political action. Therefore, I will offer one more scenario, one that is based in my research on personality transfer, and on the section of Chapter 9 about spiritual machines.

An Experimentalist Scenario

I sense that western civilization is not very hospitable to fresh ideas of wide scope, even as consumers gobble up new consumer electronics and mass media fads. Let me suggest in all earnestness that there is a high likelihood that progress in cognitive science and artificial intelligence really could develop technologies over the next century to archive, transfer, emulate, and indeed resurrect human personalities with the help of computers and biotechnology.

Replacement of religion's fanciful hopes for immortality with real technical solutions will entail a difficult transition. It will be necessary to create entirely new social institutions, as well as the technology itself. We cannot record our personalities without both creating a progressive civilization willing to sustain our existence in a diversity of future forms, and honoring our ancestors for having given us the means to take this revolutionary step. *To be remembered, we must remember.* Cyberimmortality will not succeed if it is done for purely selfish motives. In a chapter in a NASA book, I argued that personality transfer could be the motive for human expansion to the stars. *To become immortals, we must escape the Earth.* The remainder of this section is a scenario I published in the 1993 annual *Religion and the Social Order*, perhaps a little playful in style, but fully serious in intent.[29]

As every student of new religions knows, the Experimentalist Church was founded by Anson MacDonald, an electronics engineer with the space program. Experimentalism was first introduced as a new science, through the aegis of the Institute for Spiritual Exploration (ISE, pronounced ice), and only later transformed into a church. ISE was founded on January 1, 2000, and The Experimentalist Church on January 1, 2001. Thus the mix of science and religion that is Experimentalism has a millennial quality, born at both the popular and the calendrical beginnings of the new millennium. The cult's familiar symbol, of course, is the letter X, representing eXperimentalism, eXploration, and the unknown.

Originally named Don A. Stuart, Anson MacDonald experienced a transformational experience after years of frustration attempting to contribute to the space program (MacDonald, 2020).[30] His first job in the 1970s was on a NASA project to place a powerful radar in orbit around Venus, to chart the geological features of the planet through its dense atmosphere. When that was canceled, he drifted from job to job for five years, in the burgeoning microcomputer industry, before gaining employment with NASA again. Colleagues joked that he was jinxed, because project after project was canceled out from under him: two separate attempts to develop an upper stage for the Space Shuttle, a probe to Halley's comet, and the SETI-X multi-channel high-sensitivity receiver intended to search for radio signals from extraterrestrial civilizations. His autobiography states that throughout the 1990s, feelings of personal inadequacy and hatred of humanity grew. Then, in the deepest pit of suicidal despair, he experienced Aricibo.

Aricibo is a remote valley in Puerto Rico containing a large radio telescope, where MacDonald had been sent to install some equipment, just as Congress cut funding for the SETI project once again. While he was a highly talented engineer, who could have found employment almost anywhere, his entire identity and self-esteem were invested in spaceflight, and the psychohistorian Paul French (2026) has argued that MacDonald was on the verge of a psychotic break, when he stepped out on the vast, bowl-shaped antenna of the telescope, ringed by rugged hills that could only dimly be seen in the midnight darkness of December 31, 1999.[31]

In retrospect, we can see where MacDonald got the pieces of his great idea. His commitment to colonization of the galaxy dates from early adolescence, when he was a fanatical science fiction reader, but his professional career had given him a deep understanding of what would actually be required to accomplish this transcendent goal. Those five years wandering from one foundering software company to another had given him both experience programming video games and contact with the idea that human beings' psyches could be measured. At one point he had been hired to write a people-matching program for a dating service, and another time he was part of a team producing educational psychology software. There is reason to believe that in youth he attended one of Barbara Hubbard's syncons, and speculation persists that he may have tried Scientology and experienced E-Meter auditing.

It is quite certain, however, that MacDonald was greatly influenced by the anthropic argument as presented in *The Anthropic Cosmological Principle,* by Barrow and Tipler (1986).[32] MacDonald went a step further than Barrow and Tipler, deciding that the universe was created by us, through our act of observing it. Teilhard de Chardin had written about the *omega point,* a spiritual goal equivalent to God, standing at the end of time or outside of material existence altogether. MacDonald substituted the *omicron point,* standing in the very middle of time, at the moment when an intelligent being first asked why the universe was conducive to his own existence, and realizing that only in such a universe could the question be asked.[33] From the beginning of time up to the omicron point, chaotic processes generated a vast range of conditions, only one of which would produce intelligence. At the omicron point, The Key Observer appeared, entirely by chance, and by asking and answering the great question of existence he would act as the pivot of universal history. After the omicron point, The Key Observer would lead other intelligent beings on a quest to realize their greatest potentials and bring all the universe into their grasp.

Through Barrow and Tipler, MacDonald had also learned of John von Neumann's idea that robot spacecraft could be sent to distant stars where they would build copies of themselves to be sent onward to still other stars. When planets capable of supporting life were found, the probes would construct people from samples of human DNA, who would establish colonies. To this, MacDonald added the astonishing plan of giving these manufactured people the memories and personalities of members of the Experimentalist movement. Thus, he promised a new kind of immortality (MacDonald 2002).[34] Much of the Experimentalists' energy is devoted to recording themselves by a variety of means, in hopes that centuries hence they could be brought back to life on distant planets. The rest of their energy supports projects designed to further the space program and build a world capable of launching von Neumann probes.

Initially, MacDonald's followers were mainly elderly people frantic for any possibility of immortality and ambitious young intellectuals of a somewhat obsessive sort. At first, they worked with every existing psychological questionnaire, which MacDonald incorporated into an elegant set of computer programs. For hundreds of hours, each member would sit at a computer, answering questions that flashed on the screen, building up a vast file of data that supposedly captured the person's psyche in a manner that could be sent to the stars and used to bring him or her back to life.

Then around the year 2005, MacDonald had a series of four insights that gave his movement much wider appeal. First, he introduced a number of recording techniques based on social interaction in sessions reminiscent of group therapy, adding measurement of the individual's social psychology and far more exciting to the members than merely answering written questions. Second, members were subjected to many highly intense experiences, from the sensual to the adventurous, so that their emotional reactions could be tested. Third, Experimentalism began to claim that all the testing actually improved its members in their current lives, transforming them into superhumans. Fourth, the most advanced members began reporting clairvoyant glimpses of the planets they would live on in future lives, and this was taken as proof both of the ultimate success of the movement and of the superiority of these members (MacDonald 2011).[35]

There is no evidence that MacDonald had ever studied the sociology of religion, but perhaps instinctively he understood how to build a cult. Members were drawn into powerful social relationships with each other, emotionally dependent on the local congregation and perceiving everything that happened in terms of the shared ideology. The extreme hostility the cult suffered around 2020 probably strengthened it still further. Not only were several members killed by mobs, but data archives were also destroyed. The Experimentalists considered this even worse than murder, because they believed a person was immortal so long as his or her data were preserved.

An accommodation was achieved greatly by geographic separation. Few Experimentalists live near big cities, today, unless one counts the industrial complexes they have built for themselves in several remote areas. A substantial fraction of the world's science and engineering is done by the few million members of the movement, and with the decline in prestige of science and invention, they have become a pariah caste, living apart from ordinary people but in a symbiotic economic relationship with society. They talk a good deal about a coming dark age, in which they will preserve learning and prepare the way for a new civilization that will eventually colonize the galaxy. Sociologists of religion must recognize the substantial success of this deviant cult, both in terms of membership size and the capacity to defend their subculture against erosion from secular society.

New Challenges

Let us imagine that ample grant funds were available to support objective, scientific research on some of the religion-related topics covered in this book. What should be done?

We should answer definitively the questions raised by suicide rates. For the cost of just a few hundred thousand dollars, a team of social scientists and graduate students could create a comprehensive dataset of all available church membership data with corresponding suicide statistics and control variables. Using the same control variables over the decades, does the apparent power of religion to deter suicide really decline to practically nothing? What new approaches could be used to collect other data that could replicate results from official data? For example, it might be possible, with appropriate confidentiality controls and the cooperation of the Canadian government, to create a dataset of all Canadians, noting their cause of death or their survival through a given year, and linking to their religious affiliation as recorded in the Canadian census. This would not only let us calculate suicide rates for different religious groups, but help us understand which other causes of death were reduced by faith or religiously-supported healthy lifestyles.

We should understand better the mechanisms by which religion may support healthy lifestyles and reduce debilitating stress. One approach would be to carry out systematic health and lifestyle surveys of people who have already participated in such major questionnaire projects as the General Social Survey, the Panel Study of Income Dynamics, and the American National Election Studies. Then their religious beliefs and behavior in past years could be used to predict their health status today. A particularly exciting approach would be to do a comprehensive religion and lifestyle survey in a nation with a national health service and excellent record-keeping, so that the health over time of a million or more people could be examined in the light of their degree and kind of faith. Comparing across nations would also be important, because some nations like the United States might need religion more than other nations did, and some countries might have distinctive non-religious health-supporting factors that could substitute for religion.

The reality and extent of the Stark effect needs to be documented. Is it generally true that individual religiousness has the power to deter property-crime delinquency only in religious communities? Or, is this apparent deterrence effect merely the spurious result when religiousness has become a marker of social conformity? And, does individual religiousness deter hedonistic delinquency even in communities that are very secular? Whatever the truth turns out to be, what does it say about the validity of religious beliefs quite apart from their utility? Clearly, we know how to do such studies. A major, international questionnaire survey, involving parents as well as adolescents, backed up with behavioral reports from schools and the police, could be extremely valuable.

Especially crucial will be studies to understand whether religion, or indeed any socio-cultural factors, could sustain human fertility at the population replacement level. It is possible that religion connects to fertility only in poor, traditional societies, or among peripheral minorities within modern societies. These are groups that tend to prefer intense forms of religion, because it offers them powerful emotional compensators for insecurity, powerlessness, and low social status. Do highly secularized "mainstream" religious denominations also support fertility? Can we identify factors or invent institutions that could sustain fertility without religion? I believe these questions will be especially difficult to answer, although existing scientific research, such as covered in Chapter 4, suggest how to start.

Research on the New Age and about scientistic religions will be useful, partly to help us understand the processes by which the tides of secularization erode the shores of religion, but also to see how people attempt to integrate science-oriented metaphors into unscientific worldviews. A radical idea would be to employ experimental methods as well as the traditional research methodologies of field observation, interviews, questionnaires, and historical documents. The idea of creating a new mythology or a new religion primarily as a scientific experiment may seem outrageous, but people create them all the time for other motives that are even less admirable. Alternatively, if a new religion might benefit humanity, what would be wrong in consciously engineering it, if indeed our research suggests that all religious are false but some can be beneficial?

Cognitive research on religion and Atheism is in its infancy. After a decade or more of very exciting theoretical development, the cognitive approach to religion is ready to undertake substantial, carefully-designed empirical studies. To date, the primary methodology has been unsystematic example-taking from the anthropological or historical literature, augmented by a very small number of tiny experimental studies of communication. Thus, we could be standing on the threshold of a major period of cognitive research, employing many methodologies. It will be particularly interesting to learn how humans actually model the minds and intentions of other beings, and whether the mechanisms really bias us toward believing in supernatural beings.

Whereas physical science innovations aimed at achieving technological transcendence will be very interesting, I suggest we need to experiment with new social institutions of many kinds, seeking alternatives to twentieth-century models of the family, the corporation, the church, and the school. This notion arose in our discussion about what to do about collapsing fertility, in Chapter 4, but really was implicit in many other chapters. Perhaps the most noteworthy fact about FM-2030's book, *Are You a Transhuman*, is that it is a manual for social-scientific research in which you yourself are the object of study, and you want to know whether you are a being of the future or of the past.[36]

Our world is changing rapidly, for better or worse, largely out of control. We must change, hopefully with some degree of choice about what we shall become. We must become personal researchers, studying our personalities as we create them anew, experimenting with new forms of family and community. This requires taking risks, and overcoming societal resistance to our risk taking. It is an open question how much religion deters scientific research to solve human problems, but religion is a key factor in the political and cultural barrier that prevents our society from investing significantly in the social and behavioral sciences, and from doing research to document the actual good and harm performed by religion.

Conclusion

As the year 2006 drew to a close, the popular press discovered that a network of Atheist scientists was aggressively attacking the claims of religion, for example proclaimed in cover stories in the magazines *Time* and *Wired*.[37] At the 2005 meetings of the World Future Society, I suggested that a great conflict loomed between religion and cognitive science, one that would become especially acute and perhaps even bloody when scientists took their first significant strides toward cyberimmortality.[38] At the 2003 and 2006 meetings of the World Transhumanist Association, I suggested that science may be forced into opposition to the dominant institutions of society, if they work in league with religion to suppress research and experimentation with transcendent technologies.[39]

I envision what Herbert Blumer called a general movement, a bland term describing something grand.[40] A general movement is a transformation in consciousness based in multiple groups and overlapping social networks. Some parts of it will thrive inside standard societal institutions such as government agencies and industrial corporations. Some parts of it will be private scientific, communication, and educational organizations. Some parts will even be communities, whether you want to call them experimental, intentional, or utopian. There will also be many roles for independent individuals to play.

For a time, perhaps a decade or a century, progress will still be possible in public, but sooner rather than later the citizens of the future will also need to build a network of clandestine groups, separating from retrograde society in order to survive its destructiveness and its downfall, and to establish the basis of a new civilization. Even if a church-state alliance refrains from overtly repressing the needed kinds of scientific research, it will discourage support for them, entice scientists' attention in other directions through funding patterns, and impose negative stereotypes that prejudice young and creative people against them. Thus, even far short of theocratic dictatorship, secession may be necessary.

What will drive some progressive people into rebellion against the society? I can imagine three factors related to information. First, they may need to escape information monopoly by powerful institutions through creating a network to distribute industrial and governmental secrets. Today, information about scientific research is not greatly restricted. But at some time in the near future, it may become obvious that vital information is being withheld, and the only remedy may be information liberation. Second, scientists may be forced into rebellion in order to carry out research prohibited unnecessarily by powerful institutions. Current examples include research on psychedelics, human cloning, and some aspects of cryptography. Third, people may be forced to create a scientific counter-culture in reaction to episodes of overt repression. I call these three phases of rebellion the *Information Insurrection*.

Perhaps, as I have said many times before in this book, we need to understand the role of religion in society from multiple viewpoints. The supernatural theory of religion has been partly discredited by the research considered here, but it might predict that God himself would intervene to prevent scientists from "playing God." The societal theory would not lament the death of faith, so long as other institutions took over its functions. Both exchange theory and cognitive theory imply that supernatural beliefs are false. I have suggested that the cognitive approach, as part of a broad convergence of all fields of science and technology, could provide satisfactory solutions to the problems that religion only pretended to solve.

Until about this point in history, humanity was ignorant and beset by insoluble problems. Religion assuaged fears, motivated sacrifice, and strengthened social solidarity. People probably exaggerated how well religion served such functions, but it was almost certainly of some net value. However, now it has become an impediment to the full flowering of science and technology, and the transformation of humanity. Pre-industrial society was a viable option, the only one prior to the rise of modern science, and religion was an integral, functioning part. The industrial revolution launched humanity on a rapid flight toward an unseen destination, and contemporary society is probably not viable in the long run. The question becomes how we can create a new civilization, based on new principles, that will be progressive without being dangerously chaotic.

Humanity is crossing an abyss on a tightrope. Behind us is the old world of religious faith that compensated wretched but fertile people for the misery in their lives. On the other side, if we can only reach it, is a new land where we no longer need to live by illusions, where wisdom and procreation are compatible, where truth and life are one. Nietzsche warned that as we make this perilous crossing, we must look neither down nor backward, but forward.

Appendix

Tables

Table 3.1: Percent "Very Happy" by Religious Tradition

Nations	None	Catho-lics	Protes-tants	Ortho-dox	Muslim	Bud-dhist
Argentina	21.7%	26.2%				
Belgium	33.8%	38.6%				
Brazil	15.7%	20.7%				
Dominican R.	26.5%	33.5%				
France	21.0%	23.8%				
Mexico	31.4%	30.8%				
Portugal	8.5%	13.7%				
Slovenia	13.0%	10.3%				
Spain	14.3%	20.2%				
Uruguay	19.4%	22.5%				
Great Britain	33.5%		41.2%			
Belarus	5.3%			3.6%		
Bulgaria	6.2%			9.8%		
Ukraine	5.0%			5.0%		
Russia	5.9%	5.9%		5.3%		
Japan	32.4%					21.2%
Macedonia	15.7%			10.9%	14.6%	
Bosnia-Herz.	14.0%			11.0%	12.9%	

Source: World Values Surveys

Table 4.1: Control of Religion (correlations)

	Government Favoritism	Government Regulation	Social Regulation
All 193 Nations:			
Fertility	-0.15	0.15	0.13
Population Growth	0.00	0.25	0.24
141 Nations Outside Africa:			
Fertility	0.01	0.25	0.28
Population Growth	0.10	0.27	0.29

Table 5.1. Church Membership and Crime Rates

	Murder	Rape	Assault	Burglary	Larceny	Robbery
Mean rate per 100,000	11.0	44.9	317.7	1938.9	3660.5	276.0
Correlations:						
Church members	0.03	-0.38	-0.23	- .44	- .63	-.01
Different house	0.25	0.58	0.29	.60	.64	.04
Families in poverty	0.62	0.37	0.36	.38	-.02	.49
Blacks	0.55	0.32	0.29	.12	-.10	.44
Divorced	0.38	0.72	0.39	.60	.58	.21
Standardized betas:						
Church members	0.36	0.03	-0.06	-.05	- .36	.04
Different house	0.49	0.60	0.25	.57	.40	.07
Standardized betas:						
Church members	0.06	-0.11	-0.26	-0.22	-0.39	-0.23
Different house	0.03	0.10	-0.08	0.26	0.30	-0.31
Families in poverty	0.39	0.17	0.28	0.40	0.03	0.37
Blacks	0.34	0.33	0.24	0.03	0.08	0.29
Divorced	0.40	0.59	0.30	0.25	0.11	0.31

Table 5.2: Church Attendance and Alcohol

Attendance	Percent Who Do Not Drink Alcohol		Number of Respondents	
	Protestant	**Catholic**	**Protestant**	**Catholic**
Never	29.7%	24.4%	1,058	295
Less than once a year	23.1%	11.8%	853	228
Once a year	18.1%	11.8%	1,312	525
Several times a year	23.1%	10.0%	1,370	508
Once a month	24.2%	12.8%	828	344
2-3 times a month	28.2%	18.1%	1,160	326
Nearly every week	41.2%	17.2%	658	244
Every week	51.4%	16.8%	2,044	1,357
More than once a week	77.2%	24.6%	1,093	171

Source: General Social Survey

Table 5.3. Church Membership and Rates of Gay Groups

	MCC Members	Damron's Guide	Three Gay Guides		
			Total	**Bars**	**Groups**
Mean rate per 100,000	13.6	2.1	3.8	1.5	1.3
Correlations:					
Church members	-0.45	-0.27	-0.30	-0.23	-0.22
Different house	0.54	0.35	0.30	0.35	0.28
Attended college	0.33	0.35	0.53	0.31	0.60
Divorced	0.61	0.40	0.24	0.40	0.13
Standardized betas:					
Church members	-0.16	-0.06	-0.17	0.02	-0.06
Different house	0.43	0.31	0.18	0.36	0.23
Standardized betas:					
Church members	-0.06	0.03	-0.11	0.11	-0.02
Different house	0.01	-0.07	-0.15	-0.01	0.01
Attended college	0.19	0.31	0.52	0.26	0.59
Divorced	0.53	0.40	0.18	0.4	-0.02

Table 5.4: Church Attendance and Hedonistic Behavior

Hedonistic Behavior	How Often the Person Attends Religious Services					
	Once a Week or More	2 or 3 Times a Month	Once a Month	Only Holi-days	Hardly Ever	Never
643 Males:						
Driven under influence	39%	43%	60%	66%	62%	58%
Drinks more than once a week	12%	15%	40%	39%	33%	40%
Used cocaine	11%	23%	21%	27%	33%	33%
Used marijuana	44%	56%	61%	70%	72%	66%
Sexual intercourse	34%	65%	55%	57%	70%	68%
795 Females:						
Driven under influence	21%	37%	43%	43%	51%	42%
Drinks more than once a week	9%	22%	22%	20%	23%	23%
Used cocaine	7%	11%	22%	23%	29%	30%
Used marijuana	33%	59%	61%	64%	72%	64%
Sexual intercourse	27%	37%	58%	67%	58%	69%

Table 6.1: Factor Analysis of "New Age" Questionnaire Items

Statement	Agree	F. 1	F. 2	F. 3
There is much truth in astrology—the theory that the stars, the planets, and our birthdays have a lot to do with our destiny in life.	14.3%	0.76	-0.32	-0.06
Some people can hear from or communicate mentally with someone who has died.	23.4%	0.69	-0.38	-0.26
Some scientific instruments (e.g., e-meters, psionic machines, and aura cameras) can measure the human spirit.	9.1%	0.66	-0.19	-0.19
Some people can move or bend objects with their mental powers.	18.1%	0.61	-0.29	-0.39
Some people really experience telepathy, communication between minds without using the traditional five senses.	48.0%	0.56	-0.45	-0.41
Scientifically advanced civilizations, such as Atlantis, probably existed on Earth thousands of years ago.	34.8%	0.53	-0.10	-0.49
Every person's life is shaped by three precise biological rhythms—physical, emotional, and intellectual—that begin at birth and extend unaltered until death.	28.1%	0.46	0.14	-0.05
Some UFOs (Unidentified Flying Objects) are probably spaceships from other worlds.	22.2%	0.42	-0.13	-0.64
Dreams sometimes foretell the future or reveal hidden truths.	55.4%	0.33	-0.68	-0.23
Some techniques can increase an individual's spiritual awareness and power.	57.3%	0.27	-0.73	-0.08
Intelligent life probably does not exist on any planet but our own.	10.4%	0.21	0.09	0.75
Yoga, meditation, mind control, and similar methods are really of no value for achieving mental or spiritual development.	7.2%	-0.08	0.72	0.16
Analyzing dreams is a waste of time because they are random fragments of thought and memory.	16.0%	-0.11	0.75	0.11
Perpetual motion machines, anti-gravity devices, and time travel machines are physically impossible.	29.3%	-0.23	0.19	0.54
All ancient people were less advanced than modern civilization in science and technology.	32.9%	-0.39	0.15	0.40
It's not possible to influence the physical world through the mind alone.	30.5%	-0.45	0.44	0.29
Extra-sensory perception (E.S.P.) probably does not exist.	19.4%	-0.53	0.47	0.46
Psychic mediums who claim they can communicate with the dead are either frauds or mentally ill.	44.4%	-0.67	0.41	0.21
Numerology, biorhythms, and similar attempts to chart a person's life with numbers are worthless.	47.0%	-0.68	0.34	0.03
Astrologers, palm readers, tarot card readers, fortune tellers, and psychics can't really foresee the future.	60.5%	-0.71	0.34	0.10

Table 6.2: Astrologers and Psychic Consultants, 2005

State	Listed	Per million	State	Listed	Per million
Alabama	12	2.6	Montana	5	5.4
Alaska	11	16.8	Nebraska	9	5.2
Arizona	115	20.0	Nevada	61	26.1
Arkansas	18	6.5	New Hampshire	20	15.4
California	838	23.3	New Jersey	182	20.9
Colorado	77	16.7	New Mexico	22	11.6
Connecticut	56	16.0	New York	300	15.6
DC	14	25.3	North Carolina	61	7.1
Delaware	11	13.2	North Dakota	1	1.6
Florida	346	19.9	Ohio	105	9.2
Georgia	79	8.9	Oklahoma	14	4.0
Hawaii	33	26.1	Oregon	39	10.8
Idaho	16	11.5	Pennsylvania	118	9.5
Illinois	147	11.6	Rhode Island	13	12.0
Indiana	52	8.3	South Carolina	34	8.1
Iowa	18	6.1	South Dakota	6	7.8
Kansas	14	5.1	Tennessee	63	10.7
Kentucky	23	5.5	Texas	269	12.0
Louisiana	28	6.2	Utah	24	10.0
Maine	15	11.4	Vermont	4	6.4
Maryland	70	12.6	Virginia	68	9.1
Massachusetts	130	20.3	Washington	81	13.1
Michigan	88	8.7	West Virginia	10	5.5
Minnesota	40	7.8	Wisconsin	45	8.2
Mississippi	9	3.1	Wyoming	5	9.9
Missouri	40	7.0	USA	3,859	13.1

Table 6.3: 100 Astrology Books in Amazon.com

Category	Items
Religion & Spirituality:	
New Age > General	56.2%
New Age > Astrology > OTHER	2.7%
New Age > Divination	2.6%
New Age > OTHER	1.8%
Occult	3.0%
Authors, A-Z	2.5%
OTHER	5.8%
Health, Mind & Body:	
Psychology & Counseling	4.2%
Relationships	4.3%
Sex	2.1%
OTHER	2.3%
Miscellaneous:	
Business & Investing	1.8%
Entertainment	2.2%
Literature & Fiction > World Literature	1.7%
Nonfiction > Social Sciences	1.6%
Science	1.1%
OTHER	4.3%
TOTAL	100.0%

Table 6.4: Popular Astrology-Related LoC Subject Headings

Items	Headings	Items	Headings
1618	Astrology	40	Medical astrology
658	Astrology. [from old catalog]	37	Astrology and marriage
512	Hindu astrology	31	Astrology, Japanese
301	Astrology, Chinese	30	Astrology and child rearing
137	Astrology, Chinese. [from old catalog]	30	Astrology Periodicals. [from old catalog]
107	Astrology Early works to 1800.	26	Astrology Tables.
86	Hindu astrology Early works to 1800.	25	Astrology Poetry.
76	Astrology History	25	Astrology, Indic
68	Astrology and psychology	24	Astrology and business
60	Astrology, Tibetan	24	Astrology, Japanese. [from old catalog]
56	Astrology and sex	23	Astrology in art
51	Astrology in literature	22	Astrology and pets
43	Astrology (for children)	22	Astrology Dictionaries.
41	Astrology Periodicals.	21	Bible and astrology
40	Jewish astrology	20	Astrology, Thai

Table 7.1: TM and Yoga Rates per 100,000

Geographic Regions of the US	1975 TM Urban Initiations	2006 Centers TM	2006 Centers 3HO	Yoga Teachers Yoga Serve	Yoga Teachers Yoga Alliance
New England	255	0.22	0.48	6.29	8.17
Middle Atlantic	129	0.03	0.22	2.06	6.04
East North Central	124	0.04	0.08	0.82	3.20
West North Central	126	0.07	0.11	0.74	2.18
South Atlantic	123	0.05	0.19	1.14	4.44
East South Central	61	0.02	0.03	0.47	1.18
West South Central	73	0.03	0.19	0.52	2.11
Mountain	206	0.07	0.69	1.33	6.17
Pacific	227	0.10	0.45	0.87	4.13
USA	108	0.06	0.25	1.30	4.10

Table 7.2: Geographic Distribution of Scientology in the US

| | Scientology | | |
Geographic Regions of the US	1985 Clears per 100,000	1998 Websites per 100,000	1990 Church Membership*
New England	2.29	2.12	59.7%
Middle Atlantic	1.88	1.55	63.4%
East North Central	1.05	1.19	54.2%
West North Central	1.54	1.30	61.1%
South Atlantic	1.94	4.01	50.9%
East South Central	0.15	0.37	65.1%
West South Central	1.56	0.88	65.2%
Mountain	5.29	2.98	48.2%
Pacific	15.44	9.60	40.1%
USA	3.82	3.26	55.0%

*Source: Association of Religion Data Archives (www.thearda.com)

Table 8.1: Estimated Frequency of Words on Web Pages

| | Pages Containing the Word (thousands) | | | | | Ratios | |
Words	All Domains	.edu	.com	.gov	.net	.edu/.com	.gov/.net
agnostic	5,040	140	2,640	14	230	5.3%	6.3%
atheism	4,970	109	2,750	1	431	4.0%	0.1%
atheist	7,660	118	4,740	1	393	2.5%	0.2%
Bible	68,400	4,460	39,400	199	3,210	11.3%	6.2%
church	160,000	23,100	65,600	2,320	6,420	35.2%	36.1%
God	173,000	11,900	82,200	792	8,460	14.5%	9.4%

Table 8.2: Belief in God

| | Gender | | Married | | Has Children | |
	Male	Female	Never	Yes	No	Yes
Atheist	3.7%	1.7%	3.9%	2.2%	3.3%	2.2%
Agnostic	6.0%	2.5%	6.5%	3.5%	5.9%	3.3%
Believer	90.3%	95.8%	89.6%	94.3%	90.7%	94.5%
TOTAL	(3,467)	(4,551)	(1,740)	(4,102)	(2,241)	(5,769)

Source: General Social Survey

Table 8.3: Marital Status and Irreligion in *Survey2001*

Religious Preference	Single	Married	Cohabiting	Divorced
All respondents:				
Non-religious	11.3%	9.3%	15.3%	10.5%
Agnostic	6.5%	5.9%	9.6%	5.7%
Atheist	6.1%	5.0%	9.1%	3.8%
TOTAL	(4,863)	(4,396)	(806)	(684)
Males:				
Non-religious	11.8%	9.6%	15.1%	12.2%
Agnostic	7.1%	5.9%	8.4%	6.2%
Atheist	7.2%	5.3%	9.7%	4.2%
TOTAL	(2,431)	(2,526)	(391)	(260)
Females:				
Non-religious	10.9%	8.9%	15.6%	9.0%
Agnostic	5.9%	5.7%	10.5%	5.7%
Atheist	5.1%	4.5%	8.5%	3.3%
TOTAL	(2,423)	(1,849)	(411)	(420)

Table 8.4: Children in Household

Religious Preference	No Children	1 Child	2+ Children
All respondents:			
Non-religious	11.5%	9.7%	8.4%
Agnostic	7.0%	5.6%	4.6%
Atheist	6.2%	5.8%	3.9%
TOTAL	(7,499)	(1,678)	(1,570)
Males:			
Non-religious	11.8%	10.8%	8.2%
Agnostic	7.0%	7.0%	5.1%
Atheist	6.8%	6.6%	5.2%
TOTAL	(3,788)	(858)	(924)
Females:			
Non-religious	11.2%	8.6%	8.8%
Agnostic	7.0%	4.0%	3.8%
Atheist	5.6%	4.9%	2.1%
TOTAL	(3,690)	(815)	(634)

Table 8.5: Likes Social Activities

Religious Preference	Not at all	Not really	Mixed feelings	Would like	Like very much
Family reunion:					
Non-religious	12.3%	18.1%	11.7%	11.2%	7.2%
Agnostic	9.4%	8.7%	9.0%	6.9%	6.1%
Atheist	15.9%	9.8%	9.1%	5.7%	3.4%
TOTAL	(277)	(529)	(1,077)	(1,613)	(1,247)
Family trip:					
Non-religious	17.9%	14.8%	11.6%	11.3%	7.4%
Agnostic	6.6%	7.2%	9.4%	7.1%	7.4%
Atheist	14.4%	9.8%	7.3%	6.3%	4.9%
TOTAL	(257)	(580)	(784)	(1,802)	(1,319)
Festive Meal:					
Non-religious	14.4%	12.0%	11.9%	11.1%	10.3%
Agnostic	7.0%	4.6%	7.7%	8.0%	7.9%
Atheist	10.0%	9.5%	6.0%	7.2%	5.9%
TOTAL	(201)	(482)	(700)	(1,816)	(1,537)
With friends:					
Non-religious	-	-	9.1%	12.2%	10.5%
Agnostic	-	-	6.1%	7.7%	7.6%
Atheist	-	-	6.1%	8.4%	6.3%
TOTAL	(11)	(29)	(198)	(1,448)	(3,056)

Table 8.6: How Long at Current Home

Preference	<1 Year	1-2 Year	2-3 Years	3-6 Years	6-10 Years	10+ Years
All respondents:						
Non-religious	11.4%	11.2%	13.3%	11.2%	10.7%	9.4%
Agnostic	6.8%	10.1%	6.4%	6.7%	6.3%	5.0%
Atheist	6.9%	5.6%	6.0%	6.0%	4.6%	5.3%
TOTAL	(1,730)	(1,252)	(952)	(1,907)	(1,212)	(3,777)
Aged 30-49:						
Non-religious	8.3%	10.3%	13.9%	11.2%	11.5%	9.1%
Agnostic	6.4%	12.1%	5.7%	6.4%	6.4%	4.8%
Atheist	7.4%	5.2%	6.1%	6.6%	4.4%	5.5%
TOTAL	(530)	(522)	(476)	(1,024)	(608)	(1,276)

Table 10.1: Favor Idea by Confidence in Religion and Science

	Organized Religion			Scientific Community		
	A great deal	Only some	Hardly any	A great deal	Only some	Hardly any
Cryonic suspension	14%	16%	25%	33%	15%	9%
Recording all one's experiences	81%	80%	78%	85%	76%	72%
Having one's mind scanned in	9%	18%	25%	27%	14%	16%
Uploading a human personality	21%	29%	33%	39%	24%	19%
Cloning oneself	4%	11%	18%	16%	10%	9%
Nanites inserted into blood stream	44%	51%	57%	63%	49%	40%
Send personality to distant planet	10%	16%	27%	30%	52%	12%
Average of 7 ideas	26%	32%	38%	42%	34%	25%

Notes

Chapter 1:

1. Friedrich Nietzsche, *Thus Spake Zarathustra*, Prologue, Part 3; translated by Thomas Common, online at http://www.gutenberg.org/etext/1998; this chapter draws upon William Sims Bainbridge, "Religion and Science," Futures, 2004, 36: 1009–1023.

2. Chris Mooney, *The Republican War on Science* (New York: Basic Books, 2005).

3. Rodney Stark and William Sims Bainbridge, *The Future of Religion* (Berkeley, Ca.: University of California Press, 1985).

4. Rodney Stark and Charles Y. Glock, *American Piety: The Nature of Religious Commitment* (Berkeley, Ca.: University of California Press, 1968).

5. Samuel McMath Bainbridge, "The Last Great Shaking" (Penn Yan, N.Y.: S. C. Cleveland, 1856).

6. William Folwell Bainbridge, *Along the Lines at the Front: A General Survey of Baptist Home and Foreign Missions* (Philadelphia: American Baptist Publication Society, 1882); *Around the World Tour of Christian Missions* (New York: Blackall, 1882).

7. Helen S. Coan Nevius, *The Life of John Livingston Nevius* (New York: Fleming H. Revell, 1895); *Our Life in China* (New York: Robert Carter, 1869).

8. John L. Nevius, *Demon Possession and Allied Themes, Being an Inductive Study of Phenomena of Our Own Times*, third edition (New York: Fleming H. Revell, 1896)

9. William Folwell Bainbridge, letter to William Seaman Bainbridge, quoted in Chautauqua lecture, July 26, 1912.

10. Lucy Seaman Bainbridge, *Round the World Letters* (Boston: Lothrop, 1882); *Helping the Helpless in Lower New York* (New York: Fleming H. Revell, 1917); *Jewels From the Orient* (New York: Fleming H. Revell, 1920); *Yesterdays* (New York: Fleming H. Revell, 1924); A. H. McKinney, *Triumphant Christianity: The Life and Work of Lucy Seaman Bainbridge* (New York: Fleming H. Revell, 1932).

11. Louis Effingham de Forest, *Ancestry of William Seaman Bainbridge* (Oxford: Scrivener, 1950).

12. William Seaman Bainbridge, *The Cancer Problem* (New York: Macmillan, 1914).

13. William Seaman Bainbridge, *Report on Medical and Surgical Developments of the War*, special issue of *United States Naval Medical Bulletin*, January, 1919.

14. Louis Livingston Seaman, *From Tokio through Manchuria with the Japanese* (New York: Appleton, 1905); *The Real Triumph of Japan: The Conquest of the Silent Foe* (New York: Appleton, 1906).

15. Consuelo Andrew Seoane, *Beyond the Ranges* (New York: R. Speller, 1960); Rhoda Low Seoane, *The Whole Armor* (New York: R. Speller, 1965); *Uttermost East and the Longest War* (New York, Vantage Press, 1968).

16. John Seaman Bainbridge, *The Study and Teaching of Law in Africa* (South Hackensack, N.J.: F. B. Rothman, 1972).

17. Angus McIntosh, M.L. Samuels, and Michael Benskin, *A Linguistic Atlas of Late Mediaeval English* (New York: Aberdeen University Press, 1986); Michael Alexander Kirkwood Halliday, Angus McIntosh, and Peter Strevens, *The Linguistic Sciences and Language Teaching* (London: Longmans, 1964).

18. Christopher McIntosh, *The Rosicrucians: the History, Mythology, and Rituals of an Esoteric Order* (York Beach, Me.: S. Weiser, 1997); *The Rose Cross and the Age of Reason: Eighteenth-century Rosicrucianism in Central Europe and its Relationship to the Enlightenment* (New York: E.J. Brill, 1992); *Eliphas Lévi and the French Occult Revival* (London: Rider, 1972); *The Astrologers and their Creed* (London: Hutchinson, 1969); *Ludwig II of Bavaria, the Swan King* (London: I. B. Tauris, 1997); *Gardens of the Gods: Myth, Magic and Meaning* (London: I. B. Tauris, 2005).

19. William Sims Bainbridge, *The Spaceflight Revolution* (New York: Wiley Interscience, 1976).

20. Rodney Stark and William Sims Bainbridge, *The Future of Religion* (Berkeley, Ca.: University of California Press, 1985).

21. Rodney Stark and William Sims Bainbridge, *A Theory of Religion* (New York: Toronto/Lang, 1987).

22. Rodney Stark and William Sims Bainbridge, *Religion, Deviance and Social Control* (New York: Routledge, 1996).

23. William Sims Bainbridge, *Dimensions of Science Fiction* (Cambridge, Ma.: Harvard University Press, 1986).

24. William Sims Bainbridge, *Experiments in Psychology* (Belmont, Ca.: Wadsworth, 1986); *Sociology Laboratory* (Belmont, Ca.: Wadsworth, 1987); *Survey Research: A Computer-Assisted Introduction* (Belmont, Ca.: Wadsworth, 1989); *Social Research Methods and Statistics* (Belmont, Ca.: Wadsworth, 1992).

25. *Goals in Space: American Values and the Future of Technology* (Albany, New York: State University of New York Press, 1991).

26. Mihail C. Roco and William Sims Bainbridge, eds., *Societal Implications of Nanoscience and Nanotechnology* (Dordrecht, Netherlands: Kluwer, 2001); *Converging Technologies for Improving Human Performance* (Dordrecht, Netherlands: Kluwer, 2003); *Nanotechnology: Societal Implications*, two volumes (Berlin: Springer, 2006); William Sims Bainbridge and Mihail C. Roco, eds., *Managing Nano-Bio-Info-Cogno Innovations: Converging Technologies in Society* (Berlin: Springer, 2006).

27. William Sims Bainbridge, ed., *Encyclopedia of Human-Computer Interaction* (Great Barrington, Ma.: Berkshire, 2004).

28. William Sims Bainbridge, *The Sociology of Religious Movements* (New York: Routledge, 1997).

29. William Sims Bainbridge, *The Endtime Family: Children of God* (Albany, N.Y.: State University of New York Press, 2002).

30. William Sims Bainbridge, *God from the Machine* (Lanham, Md.: AltaMira, 2006).

31. Rodney Stark and William Sims Bainbridge, *The Future of Religion* (Berkeley, Ca.: University of California Press, 1985); William Sims Bainbridge, "The Religious Ecology of Deviance," *American Sociological Review* 54 (1989): 288–295.

32. Paul Bloom, *Descartes' Baby: How the Science of Child Development Explains what Makes Us Human* (New York: Basic Books, 2004).

Chapter 2:

1. Friedrich Nietzsche, *Thus Spake Zarathustra*, Part 30, translated by Thomas Common, online at http://www.gutenberg.org/etext/1998.

2. Will Herberg, *Protestant, Catholic, Jew* (Garden City, New York: Doubleday, 1955).

3. John Henry Barrows, *The World's Parliament of Religions* (Chicago: Parliament Publishing Company, 1893); Walter R. Houghton, *Neely's History of the Parliament of Religions and Religious Congresses at the World's Columbian Exposition* (Chicago: Neely, 1893); Richard Hughes Seager, *The World's Parliament of Religions* (Bloomington, In.: University of Indiana Press, 1995).

4. Emile Durkheim, *The Rules of Sociological Method* (Chicago: University of Chicago Press, 1938).

5. Emile Durkheim, *The Elementary Forms of the Religious Life* (London: Allen and Unwin, 1915); W. S. F. Pickering, *Durkheim's Sociology of Religion* (London: Routledge and Kegan Paul, 1984).

6. Terry N. Clark, *Prophets and Patrons: The French University and the Emergence of the Social Sciences* (Cambridge, Ma.: Harvard University Press, 1973).

7. Talcott Parsons, *The Social System* (New York: Free Press, 1951); Kingsley Davis, "The Myth of Functional Analysis as a Special Method in Sociology and Anthropology," *American Sociological Review* 24 (1959): 757–772.

8. Kingsley Davis and Wilbert Moore, "Some Principles of Stratification," *American Sociological Review* 10 (1945): 242–249.

9. Talcott Parsons, "Evolutionary Universals in Society," *American Sociological Review* 29 (1964): 339–357.

10. Alvin W. Gouldner, *The Coming Crisis of Western Sociology* (New York: Basic Books, 1970).

11. Rodney Stark and William Sims Bainbridge, *The Future of Religion* (Berkeley, Ca.: University of California Press, 1985); Rodney Stark and William Sims Bainbridge, *A Theory of Religion* (New York: Toronto/Lang, 1987).

12. Michael S. Gazzaniga, ed., *Cognitive Neuroscience: A Reader* (Malden, Ma.: Blackwell, 2000).

13. Harvey Whitehouse, *Modes of Religiosity: A Cognitive Theory of Religious Transmission* (Walnut Creek, Ca.: AltaMira, 2004).

14. William Sims Bainbridge, *God From the Machine: Artificial Intelligence Models of Religious Cognition* (Lanham, Md.: AltaMira, 2006).

15. Ronald Inglehart and Wayne E. Baker, "Modernization, Cultural Change and the Persistence of Traditional Values," *American Sociological Review* 65 (2000): 19–55.

16. There is no correlation between the year the respondent took the survey and strength of belief in god (gamma = 0.00, r = -0.02) or frequency of prayer (gamma = 0.00, r = 0.00), and only a very weak temporal correlation with attendance at religious services (gamma = -0.04, r = -0.05).

17. Michael Hout and Claude S. Fischer, "Why More Americans Have No Religious Preference: Politics and Generations," *American Sociological Review* 67 (2002): 165–190.

Notes

. A. D. White, *A History of the Warfare of Science with Theology in Christendom* (Gloucester, Ma.: Peter Smith, 1978 [1896]); Rodney Stark, "On the incompatibility of religion and science," *Journal for the Scientific Study of Religion* 3 (1963): 3–20.

19. Rodney Stark and Roger Finke, *Acts of Faith* (Berkeley, Ca.: University of California Press, 2000), 53.

20. Edward J. Larson and Larry Witham, "Leading scientists still reject God," *Nature* 394 (1998): 313.

21. Richard S. Westfall, *Science and Religion in Seventeenth-century England* (New Haven, Ct.: Yale University Press, 1958); Robert K. Merton, *Science, Technology and Society in Seventeenth-century England* (New York: Harper and Row, 1970).

22. William Sims Bainbridge, "Validity of Web-based Surveys," in *Computing in the Social Sciences and Humanities*, ed. O. Vernon Burton (Urbana, Ill.: University of Illinois Press, 2002), 51–66.

23. William Sims Bainbridge, *Survey Research: A Computer-assisted Introduction* (Belmont, Ca.: Wadsworth, 1989); *Goals in Space* (Albany, N.Y.: SUNY Press, 1991); *Social Research Methods and Statistics* (Belmont, Ca.: Wadsworth, 1992); "Religious ethnography on the World Wide Web," in *Religion on the Internet* (volume 8 of Religion and the Social Order), ed. Jeffrey K. Hadden and Douglas E. Cowan (New York: Elsevier, 2000), 55–80.

24. Margot Adler, *Drawing down the Moon: Witches, Pagans, Druids, Goddess-worshippers and Other Pagans in America Today* (Boston: Beacon Press, 1979); T. M. Luhrmann, *Persuasions of the Witch's Craft* (Cambridge, Ma.: Harvard University Press, 1989).

25. Cf. J. Gordon Melton, "New age," in *Encyclopedia of Millennialism and Millennial Movements*, ed. R. Landes (New York, Routledge, 2000), 285–288.

26. Jerry Adler, "In Search of the Spiritual," *Newsweek*, 29 August 2005, http://www.msnbc.msn.com/id/9024914/site/newsweek/

27. Cf. Christian Smith, *American Evangelicalism* (Chicago: University of Chicago Press, 1998).

28. Dean Kelley, *Why Conservative Churches are Growing* (New York: Harper and Row, 1972); Laurence R. Iannaccone, "Why Strict Churches Are Growing," *American Journal of Sociology* 99 (1994): 1180–1211.

29. Roger Finke and Rodney Stark, *The Churching of America, 1776-1990* (New Brunswick, N.J.: Rutgers University Press, 1992).

30. Rodney Stark, Bruce D. Foster, Charles Y. Glock, and Harold E. Quinley, *Wayward Shepherds* (New York: Harper and Row, 1971).

31. Rodney Stark and William Sims Bainbridge, *The Future of Religion*, (Berkeley, Ca.: University of California Press, 1985); *A Theory of Religion* (New York: Toronto/Lang, 1987).

32. James J. O'Donnell, "The Demise of Paganism," *Traditio* 35 (1979): 45–88; Rodney Stark, *The Rise of Christianity* (Princeton, N.J.: Princeton University Press, 1996).

33. William Sims Bainbridge, "The Omicron Point: Sociological Application of the Anthropic Theory," in *Chaos and Complexity in Sociology: Myths, Models and Theory*, ed. Raymond A. Eve, Sara Horsfall, and Mary E. Lee (Thousand Oaks, Ca.: Sage Publications, 1997), 91–101.

34. Sigmund Freud, *The Future of an Illusion* (Garden City, N.Y.: Doubleday, 1927 [1961]); Anthony F. C. Wallace, *Religion: An Anthropological View* (New York: Ran-

dom House, 1966); Herman Kahn and Anthony J. Wiener, *The Year 2000* (New York: Macmillan, 1967).

35. Ferdinand Tönnies, *Community and Society* (East Lansing, Mi.: Michigan State University Press, 1957).

36. Emile Durkheim, *The Division of Labor in Society* (New York: Free Press, 1933).

37. Claude Lévi-Strauss, *The Raw and the Cooked* (New York: Harper & Row, 1969).

38. Edward Jarvis, *The Autobiography of Edward Jarvis* (London: Wellcome Institute for the History of Medicine, 1992); Gerald N. Grob, *Edward Jarvis and the Medical World of Nineteenth-century America* (Knoxville, Tenn: University of Tennessee Press, 1978).

39. Edward Jarvis, "Statistics of Insanity in the United States," *Boston Medical and Surgical Journal* 27 (1842): 116–121, 281–282.

40. Edward Jarvis, *Report on Insanity and Idiocy in Massachusetts* (Boston: White, 1855); August B. Hollingshead and Fredrick C. Redlich, *Social Class and Mental Illness* (New York: Wiley, 1958).

41. Michael Young and Peter Willmott, *Family and Kinship in East London* (Glencoe, Ill.: Free Press, 1957); *The Symmetrical Family* (New York: Pantheon Books, 1973).

42. Peter Laslett, *The World We have Lost* (London: Methuen, 1965).

43. William Foote Whyte, *Street Corner Society* (Chicago: University of Chicago Press, 1943); Herbert J. Gans, *The Urban Villagers* (New York: Free Press, 1962); Reo F. Fortune, *Sorcerers of Dobu* (New York: E. P. Dutton, 1932); Jules Henry, *Jungle People* (New York: J. J. Augustin, 1941); Robert Knox Dentan, *The Semai* (New York: Holt, Rinehart, and Winston, 1968).

Chapter 3:

1. Friedrich Nietzsche, *The Antichrist*, translated by H. L. Mencken (New York: A. A. Knopf, 1920), p. 51.

2. Stephen Jay Gould, "The Median Isn't the Message," *Discover* 6 (June 1985): 40–42.

3. Stephen Jay Gould, *Rocks of Ages: Science and Religion in the Fullness of Life* (New York: Ballantine, 1999), 175.

4. Daniel C. Dennett, *Breaking the Spell: Religion as a Natural Phenomenon* (New York: Viking, 2006).

5. *Webster's Ninth New College Dictionary* (Springfield, Ma.: 1990), 736.

6. Charles Y. Glock and Rodney Stark, *Christian Beliefs and Anti-Semitism* (New York: Harper and Row, 1966), 3.

7. Viktor Frankl, *Man's Search for Meaning: An Introduction to Logotherapy* (Boston: Beacon Press, 1962), 164.

8. Peter L. Berger and Thomas Luckmann, *The Social Construction of Reality: A Treatise in the Sociology of Knowledge* (Garden City, N.Y.: Doubleday, 1966).

9. William Sims Bainbridge and Rodney Stark, "Cult Formation: Three Compatible Models," *Sociological Analysis* 40 (1979): 283–295.

10. Anthony F. C. Wallace, "Revitalization Movements," *American Anthropologist* 58 (1956): 264-281; Simon D. Messing, "Group Therapy and Social Status in the Zar Cult of Ethiopia, *American Anthropologist* 60 (1958): 1120–1126; Claude Levi-Strauss, "The

Sorcerer and His Magic," in *Structural Anthropology* (New York: Basic Books, 1963), 161–180; Ioan M. Lewis, *Ecstatic Religion* (Baltimore: Penguin, 1971).

11. Julian Silverman, "Shamans and Acute Schizophrenia," *American Anthropologist* 69 (1967): 21–32.

12. Maren Lockwood Carden, *Oneida: Utopian Community to Modern Corporation* (Baltimore: Johns Hopkins Press, 1969).

13. Stefan Zweig, *Mental Healers* (New York: Viking, 1932).

14. Ronald L. Numbers, *Prophetess of Health: Ellen G. White and the Origins of Seventh-day Adventist Health Reform* (Knoxville, Tenn.: University of Tennessee Press, 1992).

15. Jennifer Langston, "Bankruptcy May be Love Israel Family's Salvation," *Seattle Post-Intelligencer*, 1 March 2003, http://seattlepi.nwsource.com/local/110637_loveisrael01.shtml

16. http://www.loveisraelfamily.com/WE'RE%20ALL%20ONE!!.htm

17. Alan Rogerson, *Millions Now Living Will Never Die: A Study of Jehovah's Witnesses* (London: Constable, 1969); Melvin D. Curry, *Jehovah's Witnesses: The Millenarian World of the Watch Tower* (New York: Garland, 1992).

18. H. T. Dohrman, *California Cult* (Boston: Beacon, 1958).

19. Shoko Asahara, *The Day of Destruction* (Tokyo: Aum Publishing Company, 1989); T. R. Reid, "The Doomsday Guru," *Washington Post*, 24 March 1995, A25, A28; Nicholas D. Kristof and Sheryl WuDunn, "The Seer Among the Blind: Japanese Sect Leader's Rise," *New York Times*, 26 March 1995, 26, 1, 8.

20. Special thanks go to Erika Ohara Bainbridge, who translated several pertinent early articles from Japanese: anonymous, "Horrifying Aum Incident," *Asahi Weekly*, 7 April 1995, 22–31; "Fifteen Super Brains Supporting Aum," *Asahi Weekly*, 14 April 1995, 22–28; "Dictionary of Aum Shinryko," *Josei Jishin*, 18 April 1995, 63–66; Shoko Egawa, "Aum Shinrikyo: Memoir of a Fugitive," *Bungeishunju*, May 1995, 146–158, "Aum Shinrikyo: The Fraud of Mysterious Experiences," *Bungeishunju*, September 1995, 158–167; Shunsuke Serizawa, "Revolutionary Shoko Asahara: About His Satanic Element," *Chuo Koron*, June 1995, 68–77; Takeshi Yori and Tamotsu Aoki, "What Produced Aum?" *Chuo Koron*, June 1995, 56–67; Shinshuko Kenkyurkai (New Religion Study Group), *New Religion Guide Book* (Tokyo: Best Books, 1995).

21. Rodney Stark and William Sims Bainbridge, *A Theory of Religion* (New York: Toronto/Lang, 1987), 180.

22. William Sims Bainbridge, *Satan's Power* (Berkeley, Ca.: University of California Press, 1978).

23. Pippa Norris and Ronald Inglehart, *Sacred and Secular: Religion and Politics Worldwide* (Cambridge, England: University of Cambridge Press, 2004), 14.

24. Pippa Norris and Ronald Inglehart, *Sacred and Secular: Religion and Politics Worldwide* (Cambridge, England: University of Cambridge Press, 2004), 57.

25. Rodney Stark and Roger Finke, *Acts of Faith* (Berkeley, Ca.: University of California Press, 2000).

26. Gregory S. Paul, "Cross-National Correlations of Quantifiable Societal Health with Popular Religiosity and Secularism in the Prosperous Democracies," *Journal of Religion and Society* 7 (2005): http://moses.creighton.edu/jrs/2005/2005-11.html

27. James Banks, Michael Marmot, Zoe Oldfield, and James P. Smith, "Disease and Disadvantage in the United States and in England," *Journal of the American Medical Association* 295 (2006): 2037–2045.

28. http://nds.umdl.umich.edu/cgi/s/sda/hsda?harcWEVS+wevs

29. Robert J. Barro and Rachel M McCleary, "Religion and Economic Growth across Countries, *American Sociological Review* 68 (2003): 760–781.

30. Richard P. Sloan and Emilia Bagiella, "Claims About Religious Involvement and Health Outcomes," *Annals of Behavioral Medicine* 24 (2002): 14–21.

31. Robert A. Hummer, Richard G. Rogers, Charles B. Nam, and Christopher G. Ellison, "Religious Involvement and U.S. Adult Mortality, *Demography* 36 (1999): 273–285.

32. Darren E. Sherkat and Christopher G. Ellison, "Recent Developments and Current Controversies in the Sociology of Religion," *Annual Review of Sociology* 25 (1999): 363–394.

33. Randolph C. Byrd, "Positive Therapeutic Effects of Intercessory Prayer in a Coronary Care Unit Population," *Southern Medical Journal* 81 (1988): 826–829.

34. Herbert Benson, Jeffery A. Dusek, Jane B. Sherwood, Peter Lam, Charles F. Bethea, William Carpenter, Sidney Levitsky, Peter C. Hill, Donald W. Clem, Jr., Manoj K. Jain, David Drumel, Stephen L. Kopecky, Paul S. Mueller, Dean K. Marek, Sue Rollins, and Patricia L. Hibberd, "Study of the Therapeutic Effects of Intercessory Prayer (STEP) in cardiac bypass patients: A multicenter randomized trial of uncertainty and certainty of receiving intercessory prayer," *American Heart Journal* 151 (2006): 934–942.

35. Robert Crosnoe and Glen H. Elder, "Successful Adaptation in the Later Years: A Life-Course Approach to Aging," *Social Psychology Quarterly* 65 (2002): 309–328.

36. Neal Krause, Berit Ingersoll-Dayton, Jersey Liang, and Hidehiro Sugisawa, "Religion, Social Support, and Health among the Japanese," *Journal of Health and Social Behavior* 40 (1999): 405–421.

37. Marc A. Musick, "Religion and Subjective Health Among Black and White Elders," *Journal of Health and Social Behavior* 37 (1996): 221–237.

38. Christopher G. Ellison, "Religious Involvement and Subjective Well-Being," *Journal of Health and Social Behavior* 32 (1991): 80–99; Christopher G. Ellison and Jeffrey S. Levin, "The Religion-Health Connection: Evidence, Theory, and Future Directions," *Health Education and Behavior* 25 (1998): 700–720.

39. Timothy P. Daaleman, Subashan Perera, and Stephanie A. Studenski, "Religion, Spirituality, and Health Status in Geriatric Outpatients," *Annals of Family Medicine* 2 (2004): 49–53.

40. Linda J. Waite and Evelyn L. Lehrer, "The Benefits from Marriage and Religion in the United States: A Comparative Analysis," *Population and Development Review* 29 (2003): 255–275.

41. Adolph Heinrich Gotthilf Wagner, *Die Gesetzmässigkeit in den Scheinbar Willkürlichen Menschlichen Handlungen vom Standpunkte der Statistik* (Hamburg: Boyes und Geisler, 1864).

42. Henry Morselli, *Suicide: An Essay on Comparative Moral Statistics* (New York: Appleton, 1882 [1879]).

43. Thomas G. Masaryk, *Suicide and the Meaning of Civilization* (Chicago: University of Chicago Press, 1970 [1881]).

44. Emile Durkheim, *Suicide* (New York: Free Press, 1951 [1897]).

45. R. D. Goldney and J. A. Schioldann, "A Note Concerning Durkheim's Precedence in the Use of the Terms *Altruistic* and *Egoistic* Suicide," Suicide and Life-Threatening Behavior 31 (2001): 113–114; Hugh P. Whitt, "Durkheim's Precedence in the Use of the Terms *Egoistic* and *Altruistic* Suicide: An Addendum," *Suicide and Life-Threatening Behavior* 36 (2006): 125–127.

46. Andrew F. Henry and James F. Short, *Suicide and Homicide* (Glencoe, Ill.: Free Press, 1954).

47. Rodney Stark and William Sims Bainbridge, *Religion, Deviance, and Social Control* (New York: Routledge, 1996).

48. Steven Stack, "The Effect of Religious Commitment on Suicide: A Cross-National Analysis," *Journal of Health and Social Behavior* 24 (1983): 364.

49. Maurice Halbwachs, *Le Causes de Suicide* (Paris: Felix Alcan, 1930); Austin L. Porterfield, "Suicide and Crime in Folk and in Secular Society," *American Journal of Sociology* 57 (1952): 331–338.

50. Whitney Pope, *Durkheim's "Suicide"—A Classic Analyzed* (Chicago: University of Chicago Press, 1976).

51. Rodney Stark, Daniel P. Doyle, and Jesse Lynn Rushing, "Beyond Durkheim: Religion and Suicide," *Journal for the Scientific Study of Religion* 22 (1983): 120–131.

52. Douglas W. Johnson, Paul R. Picard, and Bernard Quinn, Churches and Church Membership in the United States—1971 (Washington, D.C.: Glenmary Research Center, 1974); Rodney Stark, "Estimating Church-Membership Rates for ecological Areas" (Washington, D.C.: U.S. Government Printing Office, 1980).

53. William Sims Bainbridge and Rodney Stark, "Suicide, Homicide, and Religion: Durkheim Reassessed," *Annual Review of the Social Sciences of Religion* 5 (1981): 33–56.

54. For the technically minded, Figure 2.3 is based on moving correlations that compensate for the city size difference. To make the curve for 1926, I calculated the association between church membership and suicide for the 75 largest cities. Then I dropped the largest one (New York) and added the city with the 76th largest population, (Fort Wayne, Indiana). I calculated the correlation for these 75 cities. Then I dropped Chicago and added Lynn, Massachusetts. Continuing down in population until I had exhausted the list, drew the 1926 line on the graph from right to left. I then did the same for 1980. The lines actually show the percent of variance explained. For the largest 75 cities in 1926, the correlation between church membership and suicide is -0.50, and the variance is the square of this, 0.25 or 25 percent. So, in 1926 differences in church membership explain 25 percent of the variation in suicide rates, which is a very substantial fraction. In 1980, the correlation for the 75 largest cities about which I had data was only -0.37, and the explained variance was 14 percent. On the face of it, this is a very large drop in the beneficial power of religion.

55. One limitation of city data for recent decades, is that it is impossible to calculate church member rates for New England, but this affects the 1971 data as well as 1980. The 1926 data on church membership are the best, but the 1980 data are probably better than 1971, and we used good corrections for 1971 and 1980 that were not necessary for 1926. The 1926 data allow one to correct for the differing fraction of children that various denominations count as full members, but the 1971 and 1980 data do not permit this, so I did not add an age correction to either year in Figure 2.3.

56. William Sims Bainbridge, *The Sociology of Religious Movements* (New York: Routledge, 1997), p. 290.

57. Robert D. Baller and Kelly K. Richardson, "Social Integration, Imitation, and the Geographic Patterning of Suicide," *American Sociological Review* 67 (2002): 873–888.

58. Roger Finke and Christopher Scheitle, "Accounting for the Uncounted: Computing Correctives for the 2000 RCMS Data," *Review of Religious Research* 41 (2005): 5–22.

59. The correlation between church membership and suicide was -0.32 for 50 states, whereas the correlation between residential stability and suicide was -0.55.

60. With both independent variables in a simultaneous regression analysis, standardized Beta for church membership was an insignificant -0.13, whereas the standardized Beta for residential stability was a strong -0.50.

61. Rodney Stark and William Sims Bainbridge, *Religion, Deviance and Social Control* (New York: Routledge, 1996), 34.

62. Recent increasing rates are reported by Jean Stockard and Robert M. O'Brien, "Cohort Effects on Suicide Rates: International Variations," *American Sociological Review* 67 (2002): 854–872.

63. Frans van Poppel and Lincoln H. Day, "A Test of Durkheim's Theory of Suicide—Without Committing the 'Ecological Fallacy,'" *American Sociological Review* 61 (1996): 500–507.

64. Bernice A. Pescosolido and Sharon Georgiana, "Durkheim, Suicide, and Religion: Toward a Network Theory of Suicide," *American Sociological Review* 54 (1989): 33–48.

65. Daniel E. Hall, "Religious Attendance: More Cost-Effective Than Lipitor?" *Journal of the American Board of Family Medicine* 19 (2006): 103–109.

Chapter 4:

1. Friedrich Nietzsche, *Thus Spake Zarathustra*, First Part, Section 9, translated by Thomas Common, online at http://www.gutenberg.org/etext/1998.

2. Pippa Norris and Ronald Inglehart, *Sacred and Secular: Religion and Politics Worldwide* (Cambridge, England: Cambridge University Press, 2004), p. 23.

3. *CIA World Factbook*, http://www.cia.gov/cia/publications/factbook/.

4. BBC News, "Japan Population Starts to Shrink," *BBC News*, 22 December 2005 at http://news.bbc.co.uk/2/hi/asia-pacific/4552010.stm.

5. www.cia.gov/cia/publications/factbook

6. Susan Greenhalgh, "Science, Modernity, and the Making of China's One-Child Policy," *Population and Development Review* (2003): 163–196.

7. Thomas Malthus, *An Essay on the Principle of Population* (London: J. Johnson, 1798), online at http://www.ac.wwu.edu/~stephan/malthus/malthus.0.html

8. United States Bureau of the Census, *Statistical Abstract of the United States* (2005) Online version at http://www.census.gov/statab/www/

9. Samuel H. Preston, "Mortality Trends," *Annual Review of Sociology* 3 (1977): 163–178; "Population Studies of Mortality," *Population Studies* 50 (1996): 525–536; United States Bureau of the Census, *Historical Statistics of the United States, Colonial Times to 1970* (Washington, D.C.: U.S. Bureau of the Census, 1975); Didier Blanchet, "Population Growth and Income Growth During the Demographic Transition: Does a Malthusian Model Help Explain their Relationship?" *Population: An English Selection* 2 (1990): 37–52.

10. CIA (Central Intelligence Agency), *The World Factbook*. Online 2005 version at http://www.cia.gov/cia/publications/factbook/

11. William Fielding Ogburn, *Social Change with Respect to Culture and Original Nature* (New York: B. W. Huebsch, 1922).

12. Kingsley Davis, "The World Demographic Transition," *Annals of the American Academy of Political and Social Science* 237 (1945): 1–11; "The Theory of Change and

Response in Modern Demographic History," *Population Index* 29 (1963): 345–366; cf. Dennis H. Wrong, *Population and Society* (New York: Random House, 1977).

13. Paul R. Ehrlich, *The Population Bomb* (New York: Ballantine, 1968).

14. Harry C. Bredemeier, "The Methodology of Functionalism," *American Sociological Review* 20 (1955): 173–180; Kingsley Davis, "The Myth of Functional Analysis as a Special Method in Sociology and Anthropology," *American Sociological Review* 24 (1959): 757–772.

15. Talcott, Parsons, "Evolutionary Universals in Society," *American Sociological Review* 29 (1964): 339–357.

16. George Caspar Homans, *Coming to My Senses: The Autobiography of a Sociologist* (New Brunswick, N.J.: Transaction, 1984).

17. Kingsley Davis, "Low Fertility in Evolutionary Perspective," *Population and Development Review*, Supplement 12 (1986): 48–65; John Knodel and Etienne van de Walle, "Lessons from the Past: Policy Implications of Historical Fertility Studies," *Population and Development Review* 5 (1979): 217–245.

18. Kingsley Davis, Mikhail S. Bernstam, and Rita Ricardo-Campbell, eds., *Below-Replacement Fertility in Industrial Societies: Causes, Consequences, Policies* (New York: Population Council, 1987).

19. Sarah F. Harbison and Warren C. Robinson, "Policy Implications of the Next World Demographic Transition," *Studies in Family Planning* 33 (2002): 37–48.

20. Ben J. Wattenberg, *The Birth Dearth* (New York: Ballantine, 1987).

21. http://www.profam.org/THC/xthc_faq.htm.

22. http://www.profam.org/THC/xthc_principles.htm

23. Leta S. Hollingworth, "Social Devices for Impelling Women to Bear and Rear Children," *American Journal of Sociology* 22 (1916): 19–29.

24. Kingsley Davis, "Low Fertility in Evolutionary Perspective," *Population and Development Review*, Supplement, 12 (1986): 59.

25. Ronald R. Rindfuss and Karin L. Brewster, "Childrearing and Fertility," *Population and Development Review*, Supplement, 22 (1996): 258–289

26. Thomas Buttner and Wolfgang Lutz, "Estimating Fertility Responses to Policy Measures in the German Democratic Republic," *Population and Development Review* 16 (1990): 539–555.

27. Nathan Keyfitz, "The Family that Does Not Reproduce Itself," in *Below-Replacement Fertility in Industrial Societies: Causes, Consequences, Policies,* ed. Kingsley Davis, Mikhail S. Bernstam, and Rita Ricardo-Campbell (New York, Population Council, 1987), 139–154.

28. Hans-Peter Kohler, Francesco C. Billari, and Jose Antonio Ortega, "The Emergence of Lowest-Low Fertility in Europe during the 1990s," *Population and Development Review* 28 (2002): 641.

29. Shireen J. Jejeebhoy and Zeba A. Sathar, "Women's Autonomy in India and Pakistan: The Influence of Religion and Region," *Population and Development Review* 27 (2001): 687–712; S. Philip Morgan, Sharon Stash, Herbert L. Smith, and Karen Oppenheim Mason, "Muslim and Non-Muslim Differences in Female Autonomy and Fertility: Evidence from Four Asian Countries," *Population and Development Review* 28 (2002): 515–537.

30. William Sims Bainbridge, "The Poverty of Nations," *Analog* 121 (March 2001): 47–56.

31. This particular analysis also leaves out parts of nations that the World Values study considered separately, East Germany and West Germany, and Britain and Northern Ireland. I was able to combine Serbia and Montenegro, because their World Values attendance rates are identical.

32. For all 54 nations, the correlation is 0.58, and for the 53 graphed, it is 0.45.

33. William Ray Arney and William H. Tresher, "Trends in Attitudes Toward Abortion, 1972–1975," *Family Planning Perspectives* 8 (1976): 117–124; B. Krishna Singh and Peter J. Leahy, "Contextual and Ideological Dimensions of Attitudes Toward Discretionary Abortion," *Demography* 15 (1978): 381–388; William Alex McIntosh, Letitia T. Alston, and Jon P. Alston, "The Differential Impact of Religious Preference and Church Attendance on Attitudes Toward Abortion," *Review of Religious Research* 20 (1979): 195–213; John H. Simpson, "Moral Issues and Status Politics," in *The New Religious Right*, ed. Robert C. Liebman and Robert Wuthnow (New York: Aldine, 1983); Carol Mueller, "In Search of a Constituency for the 'New Religious Right,'" *Public Opinion Quarterly* 46 (1983): 213–229; Mary Holland Benin, "Determinants of Opposition to Abortion," *Sociological Perspectives* 28 (1985): 199–216; Ted G. Jellen, "Changes in the Attitudinal Correlations of Opposition to Abortion, 1977–1985," *Journal for the Scientific Study of Religion* 27 (1988): 211–228; Robert F. Szafran and Arthur F. Clagett, "Variable Predictors of Attitudes Toward the Legalization of Abortion," *Social Indicators Research* 20 (1988): 271–290; Everett Carll Ladd, "A Debate on Abortion," *Public Opinion* 12 (1989): 3-8; Robin D. Perrin, "American Religion in the Post-Aquarian Age," *Journal for the Scientific Study of Religion* 28 (1989): 75–89; Eric Woodrum and Beth L. Davison, "Reexamination of Religious Influences on Abortion Attitudes," *Review of Religious Research* 33 (1992): 229–243.

34. U.S. Census Bureau, *Current Population Survey*, June 2004, Table S1.

35. The correlation between the church membership rate and children per 1,000 women is 0.11, and the correlation with children per 1,000 never-married women is 0.20; these are actual births, rather than estimated total fertility.

36. Brady E. Hamilton, Joyce A. Martin, Stephanie J. Ventura, Paul D. Sutton, and Fay Menacker, "Births: Preliminary Data for 2004," *National Vital Statistics Reports* 54 (29 December 2005): 1–18.

37. Brian J. Grim and Roger Finke, "International Religion Indexes: Government Regulation, Government Favoritism, and Social Regulation of Religion," *Interdisciplinary Journal of Research on Religion*, 2006, 2, 1, http://www.religjournal.com/

38. Shireen J. Jejeebhoy and Zeba A. Sathar, "Women's Autonomy in India and Pakistan: The Influence of Religion and Region," *Population and Development Review* 27 (2001): 687–712.

39. William Axinn and Jennifer S. Barber, "Mass Education and Fertility Transition," *American Sociological Review* 66 (2001): 481–505.

40. Victor Agadjanian, "Religion, Social Milieu, and the Contraceptive Revolution," *Population Studies* 55 (2001): 135–148.

41. Elihu Katz and Paul Lazarsfeld, *Personal Influence* (Glencoe, Ill.: Free Press, 1955); Mark Granovetter, "The Strength of Weak Ties," *American Journal of Sociology* 78 (1973): 1360–1380.

42. Charles F. Westoff and Elise F. Jones, "The Secularization of U. S. Catholic Birth Control Practices," *Family Planning Perspectives* 9 (1977): 203–207.

43. Elizabeth H. White, "Legal Reform as an Indicator of Women's Status in Muslim Nations," in *Women in the Muslim World*, ed. Lois Beck and Nikki Keddie (Cambridge, Ma.: Harvard University Press, 1978), 52–68.

44. Douglas L. Anderton and Rebecca Jean Emigh, "Polygynous Fertility: Sexual Competition Versus Progeny," *American Journal of Sociology* 94 (1989): 832–855.

45. Solene Lardoux and Etienne van de Walle, "Polygyny and Fertility in Rural Senegal," *Population* 58 (2003): 717–743.

46. Nels Anderson, "The Mormon Family," *American Sociological Review* 2 (1937): 601–608.

47. Marcia Guttentag and Paul F. Secord, *Too Many Women?: The Sex Ratio Question* (Beverly Hills, Ca.: Sage, 1983).

48. James C. Witte and Gert G. Wagner, "Declining Fertility in East Germany After Unification: A Demographic Response to Socioeconomic Change," *Population and Development Review* 21 (1995): 387–397.

49. John Humphrey Noyes, *History of American Socialisms* (Philadelphia: Lippincott, 1870); Charles Nordhoff, *The Communistic Societies of the United States* (London: John Murray, 1875); Rosabeth Moss Kanter, *Commitment and Community* (Cambridge, Ma.: Harvard University Press, 1972); Karen H. Stephan and G. Edward Stephan, "Religion and the Survival of Utopian Communities," *Journal for the Scientific Study of Religion* 12 (1973): 89–100.

50. John Humphrey Noyes, *History of American Socialisms* (Philadelphia: J. B. Lippincott, 1870).

51. William Sims Bainbridge, *The Endtime Family: Children of God* (Albany, N.Y.: State University of New York Press, 2002).

52. J. Milton Yinger, "Countercultures and Social Change," *American Sociological Review* 42 (1977): 833.

53. Steven M. Tipton, *Getting Saved from the Sixties: Moral Meaning in Conversion and Cultural Change* (Berkeley, Ca.: University of California Press, 1982).

54. William Sims Bainbridge, *The Endtime Family: Children of God* (Albany, N.Y.: SUNY Press, 2002), 125.

55. William Sims Bainbridge, *The Endtime Family: Children of God* (Albany, N.Y.: SUNY Press, 2002), 142.

56. Peter McDonald, "Sustaining Fertility through Public Policy: The Range of Options," *Population* 57 (2002): 417–446.

Chapter 5:

1. Friedrich Nietzsche, *Beyond Good and Evil*, Section 32, Part Two, "The Free Spirit," http://www.mala.bc.ca/~johnstoi/Nietzsche/beyondgoodandevil2.htm

2. Steven Stack and Mary Jeanne Kanavy, "The Effect of Religion on Forcible Rape," *Journal for the Scientific Study of Religion* 22 (1983): 67–74.

3. Dominic D. P. Johnson, "God's Punishment and Public Goods," *Human Nature* 16 (2005): 410–446.

4. Robert K. Merton, *Social Theory and Social Structure* (New York: Free Press, 1968), 185–214.

5. John Finley Scott, *Internalization of Norms* (Englewood Cliffs, N.J.: Prentice-Hall, 1971).

6. Rodney Stark and William Sims Bainbridge, *A Theory of Religion* (New York: Toronto/Lang, 1987).

7. William Sims Bainbridge, "Values," in *The Encyclopedia of Language and Linguistics* ed. R. E. Asher and J. M. Y. Simpson (Oxford, Pergamon, 1994), 4888–4892.

8. John D. Bransford, Ann L. Brown, and Rodney R. Cocking, eds., *How People Learn: Brain, Mind, Experience, and School* (Washington, D.C.: National Academy Press, 1999).

9. Travis Hirschi, *Causes of Delinquency* (Berkeley, Ca.: University of California Press, 1969).

10. Edward B. Reeves, "Morality," in *Encyclopedia of Religion and Society*, ed. William H. Swatos, Jr. (Walnut Creek, Ca.: AltaMira, 1998), web version at http://hirr.hartsem. edu/ency/Morality.htm

11. William F. Ogburn, "Factors in the Variation of Crime among Cities," *Journal of the American Statistical Association* 30 (March 1935): 12–34.

12. Rodney Stark, William Sims Bainbridge, Robert Crutchfield, Daniel P. Doyle, and Roger Finke, "Crime and Delinquency in the Roaring Twenties," *Journal of Research in Crime and Delinquency* 20 (1983): 4–23. Correlations of -0.44 and -0.43 respectively; controlling for population stability had little effect, leaving strong associations.

13. A correlation of -0.16.

14. Rodney Stark, Daniel P. Doyle, and Lori Kent, "Rediscovering Moral Communities: Church Membership and Crime," in *Understanding Crime* ed., Travis Hirschi and Michael Gottfredson (Beverly Hills, Ca.: Sage, 1980), 43–52.

15. Controlling for the percent of the population that was African-American; burglary -0.46, larceny -0.44, property crimes -0.45.

16. William Sims Bainbridge, "The Religious Ecology of Deviance," *American Sociological Review* 54 (1989): 288–295.

17. A correlation of -0.63 versus 0.44.

18. Christian Smith and Robert Faris, *Religion and American Adolescent Delinquency, Risk Behaviors and Constructive Social Activities* (Chapel Hill, N.C.: National Study of Youth and Religion, 2002).

19. Travis Hirschi, *Causes of Delinquency* (Berkeley, Ca.: University of California Press, 1969).

20. Robert K. Merton, *Social Theory and Social Structure* (New York: Free Press, 1968 [1938], 185–214; Richard A. Cloward and Lloyd E. Ohlin, *Delinquency and Opportunity* (New York: Free Press, 1960).

21. Edwin H. Sutherland, *Principles of Criminology* (Philadelphia: Lippincott, 1947).

22. Rodney Stark and Charles Y. Glock, *American Piety: The Nature of Religious Commitment* (Berkeley, Ca.: University of California Press, 1968); Charles Y. Glock and Rodney Stark, *Religion and Society in Tension* (Chicago: Rand McNally, 1965); *Christian Beliefs and Anti-Semitism* (New York: Harper and Row, 1966).

23. Travis Hirschi and Rodney Stark, "Hellfire and Delinquency," *Social Problems*, 17 (1969): 202–213.

24. Hugh Hartshorne and Mark A. May, *Studies in Deceit* (New York: Macmillan, 1928).

25. Steven R. Burkett and Mervin White, "Hellfire and Delinquency: Another Look," *Journal for the Scientific Study of Religion* 13 (1974): 455–462.

26. William Sims Bainbridge, "Crime, Delinquency, and Religion," in *Religion and Mental Health*, ed. John F. Schumaker (New York: Oxford University Press, 1992), 199–210.

27. William Sims Bainbridge and Robert D. Crutchfield, "Sex Role Ideology and Delinquency," *Sociological Perspectives* 26 (1983): 253–274.

28. Albert Lewis Rhodes and Albert J. Reiss, "The 'Religious Factor' and Delinquent Behavior," *Journal of Research in Crime and Delinquency* 7 (1970): 83–98; Paul C. Higgins, P. C. and Gary L. Albrecht, "Hellfire and Delinquency Revisited," *Social Forces* 55 (1977): 952–958; Stan L. Albrecht, Bruce A. Chadwick and David Alcorn. "Religiosity and Deviance: Application of an Attitude-Behavior Contingent Consistency Model," *Journal for the Scientific Study of Religion* 16 (1977): 263–274; Kirk W. Elifson, David M. Petersen, and C. Kirk Hadaway, "Religiosity and Delinquency," *Criminology* 21 (1983): 505–527; Charles W. Peek, Evans W. Curry, and H. Paul Chalfant," Religiosity and Delinquency over Time," *Social Science Quarterly* 66 (1985): 120–131.

29. Rodney Stark, Lori Kent, and Daniel P. Doyle, "Religion and Delinquency: The Ecology of a 'Lost' Relationship," *Journal of Research in Crime and Delinquency* 19 (1982): 4–24.

30. Rodney Stark, "Religion as Context: Hellfire and Delinquency One More Time," *Sociology of Religion* 57 (1996): 164.

31. Charles R. Tittle and Michael R. Welch, "Religiosity and Deviance: Toward a Contingency Theory of Constraining Effects," *Social Forces* 61 (1983): 653–682; Kirk W. Elifson, David M. Peterson, and C. Kirk Hadaway 1983 Religiosity and Delinquency: A Contextual Analysis," *Criminology* 21 (1983): 33–55.

32. For example, Calvin O. Butts III, George B. Stefano, Gregory L. Fricchione, Elliott Salamon, "Religion and its Effects on Crime and Delinquency," *Medical Science Monitor* 9 (2003): SR79–SR82.

33. Byron R. Johnson, Spencer De Li, David B. Larson, and Michael McCullough, "A Systematic Review of the Religiosity and Delinquency Literature," *Journal of Contemporary Criminal Justice* 16 (2000): 32–52.

34. Lisa D. Pearce and Dana L. Haynie, "Intergenerational Religious Dynamics and Adolescent Delinquency," *Social Forces* 82 (2004): 1553–1572.

35. Marc D. Hauser and Peter Singer, "Morality Without Religion," Project Syndicate, 2005, website of the Cognitive Evolution Laboratory, Harvard University, http://www.wjh.harvard.edu/~mnkylab/publications/recent/HauserSingerMoralRelig05.pdf

36. Rodney Stark and William Sims Bainbridge, *Religion, Deviance, and Social Control* (New York: Routledge, 1996), 56–65; the correlations are -0.16 for 1923 and -0.12 for 1971.

37. William Sims Bainbridge and Rodney Stark, "Suicide, Homicide, and Religion: Durkheim Reassessed," *Annual Review of the Social Sciences of Religion* 5 (1981): 33–56; the correlation between church membership is 0.02.

38. William Sims Bainbridge, "The Religious Ecology of Deviance," *American Sociological Review* 54 (1989): 288–295; the correlation is 0.03.

39. The correlation is -0.10, statistically insignificant.

40. Gregory S. Paul, "Cross-National Correlations of Quantifiable Societal Health with Popular Religiosity and Secularism in the Prosperous Democracies," *Journal of Religion and Society*, 2005, 7, http://moses.creighton.edu/jrs/2005/2005-11.html

41. Yaakov Ariel, "The Faithful in a Time of Trial: The Evangelical Understanding of the Holocaust," *Journal of Religion and Society*, 2001, 3, http://moses.creighton.edu/ JRS/pdf/2001-8.pdf

42. Paul Scott Heaton, "Does Religion Really Reduce Crime?" forthcoming in *Journal of Law and Economics*, draft online at http://home.uchicago.edu/~psheaton/workingpapers/religionandcrime.pdf

43. Edwin M. Schur, *Crimes without Victims* (Englewood Cliffs, N.J.: Prentice-Hall, 1965); James P. Spradley, *You Owe yourself a Drunk* (Boston: Little, Brown, 1970).

44. Rodney Stark and William Sims Bainbridge, *Religion, Deviance, and Social Control* (New York: Routledge, 1996), 93.

45. Joseph R. Gusfield, *Symbolic Crusade* (Urbana, Ill: University of Illinois Press, 1963).

46. Rodney Stark and William Sims Bainbridge, *Religion, Deviance, and Social Control* (New York, Routledge, 1996): 84–92.

47. William Sims Bainbridge, "The Religious Ecology of Deviance," *American Sociological Review* 54 (1989): 288–295.

48. Russell Middleton and Snell Putney, "Religion, Normative Standards, and Behavior," *Sociometry* 25 (1962): 141–152; Steven R. Burkett and Mervin White, "Hellfire and Delinquency: Another Look," *Journal for the Scientific Study of Religion* 13 (1974): 455–462; Robert Wuthnow, *Experimentation in American Religion* (Berkeley, Ca.: University of California Press, 1978); C. Kirk Hadaway, Kirk W. Elifson, and David M. Petersen, "Religious Involvement and Drug Use among Urban Adolescents," *Journal for the Scientific Study of Religion* 23 (1984): 109–128.

49. William Sims Bainbridge, "Crime, Delinquency, and Religion," in *Religion and Mental Health*, ed. by J. F. Schumaker (New York: Oxford University Press, 1992), 199–210.

50. Peter Letkemann, *Crime as Work* (Englewood Cliffs, N.J.: Prentice-Hall, 1973); Howard S. Becker, *Outsiders* (Glencoe, Ill.: Free Press, 1963).

51. Thomas P. O'Connor, "What Works, Religion as a Correctional Intervention, *Journal of Community Corrections* 14(1), (2004): 11–22, 27, 14(2), (2004): 4–6, 20–26.

52. George Caspar Homans, *Social Behavior: Its Elementary Forms* (New York: Harcourt, Brace Jovanovich, 1974; Robert Axelrod, *The Evolution of Cooperation* (New York: Basic Books, 1984); David Gauthier, *Morals By Agreement* (New York: Oxford University Press, 1986).

Chapter 6:

1. Friedrich Nietzsche, *Thus Spake Zarathustra*, Chapter 56, Part 9, translated by Thomas Common, online at http://www.gutenberg.org/etext/1998; this chapter draws upon William Sims Bainbridge, "After the New Age," *Journal for the Scientific Study of Religion* 43 (2004): 381–394.

2. John A Saliba, *Understanding New Religious Movements* (Walnut Creek, Ca.: AltaMira, 2003), 27.

3. J. Gordon Melton, "The New Age," in *Encyclopedia of Millennialism and Millennial Movements* ed. R. Landes (New York: Routledge, 2000), 285–288.

4. William Sims Bainbridge, "The New Age," in *The Sociology of Religious Movements* (New York: Routledge, 1997), 363–391.

5. William Sims Bainbridge and Rodney Stark, "Client and Audience Cults in America," *Sociological Analysis* 41 (1980): 199-214; Rodney Stark and William Sims Bainbridge, *The Future of Religion* (Berkeley, Ca.: University of California Press, 1985).

6. Rodney Stark and William Sims Bainbridge, *A Theory of Religion* (New York: Toronto/Lang, 1987), 124.

7. William Sims Bainbridge, "Collective Behavior and Social Movements," in *Sociology* by Rodney Stark (Belmont, Ca.: Wadsworth, 1985), 492–523.

8. William Sims Bainbridge, *Satan's Power* (Berkeley, Ca.: University of California Press, 1978).

9. Duane Elgin, *Awakening Earth* (New York: William Morrow, 1993).

10. James Redfield, *The Celestine Prophecy* (New York: Time Warner, 1993).

11. James Redfield and Carol Adrienne, *The Celestine Prophecy: An Experiential Guide* (New York: Warner, 1994).

12. Max Heindel and Augusta Foss Heindel, *The Message of the Stars* (Oceanside, Ca.: Rosicrucian Fellowship, 1922).

13. William Sims Bainbridge, *The Endtime Family: Children of God* (Albany, N.Y.: State University of New York Press, 2002).

14. Rodney Stark and William Sims Bainbridge, *The Future of Religion* (Berkeley, Ca.: University of California Press, 1985), 440.

15. William Sims Bainbridge, "The Religious Ecology of Deviance," *American Sociological Review* 54 (1989): 293.

16. Rodney Stark and William Sims Bainbridge, *Religion, Deviance and Social Control* (New York: Routledge, 1996), 118.

17. Rodney Stark and William Sims Bainbridge, *The Future of Religion* (Berkeley, Ca.: University of California Press, 1985), 385; William Sims Bainbridge, *The Sociology of Religious Movements* (New York: Routledge, 1997), 389.

18. William Sims Bainbridge, "Social Influence and Religious Pluralism, *Advances in Group Processes* 12 (1995): 1–18.

19. James C. Witte, "The Case for Multimethod Design, in *Society Online*, ed. Philip N. Howard and Steve Jones (Thousand Oaks, Ca.: Sage, 2003), xv–xxxiv; James C. Witte, L. M. Amoroso, and P. N. Howard, "Method and Representation in Internet-based Survey Tools: Mobility, Community, and Cultural Identity in *Survey2000*," *Social Science Computer Review* 18 (2000): 179–195; William Sims Bainbridge, "The Future of the Internet," in *Society Online*, ed. Philip N. Howard and Steve Jones (Thousand Oaks, Ca.: Sage, 2003), 307–324.

20. A classic example of this research strategy is a survey of northern California churches that was replicated by placing some of the questionnaire items into a national survey: Charles Y. Glock and Rodney Stark, *Christian Beliefs and Anti-Semitism* (Westport, Ct.: Greenwood, 1966), 188–206.

21. George S. Thommen, *Is This Your Day?* (New York: Avon, 1973); Barbara O'Neil and Richard Phillips, *Biorhythms—How to Live With Your Life Cycles* (Pasadena, Ca.: Ward Ritchie Press, 1975); Daniel Cohen, *Biorhythms in Your Life* (Greenwich, Ct.: Fawcett, 1976); Arbie Dale, *Biorhythm* (New York: Pocket Books, 1976); Robert E. Smith, *The Complete Book of Biorhythm Life Cycles* (New York: Aardvark, 1976); William Sims Bainbridge, "Biorhythms: Evaluating a Pseudoscience," *Skeptical Inquirer* 2(2) (1978): 40–56.

22. Alan Orenstein, "Religion and Paranormal Belief," *Journal for the Scientific Study of Religion* 41 (2002): 301–311.

23. Stephen Edelston Toulmin and June Goodfield, *The Fabric of the Heavens* (New York: Harper, 1961); Christopher McIntosh, *The Astrologers and their Creed* (New York: Praeger, 1969); David Ulansey, *The Origins of the Mithraic Mysteries: Cosmology and Salvation in the Ancient World* (New York: Oxford University Press, 1989).

24. Using state population estimates for July 1, 2004, from the US Census Bureau, online at www.census.gov/popest/states/tables/NST-EST2004-01.xls

25. Rodney Stark and William Sims Bainbridge, *The Future of Religion* (Berkeley, Ca.: University of California Press, 1985); William Sims Bainbridge, "The Religious Ecology of Deviance," *American Sociological Review* 54 (1989): 288–295.

26. William Sims Bainbridge, "Explaining the Church Member Rate," *Social Forces* 68 (1990): 1287–1296.

27. Donald A. McQuaid, *The International Psychic Register* (Erie, Pa.: Ornion Press, 1979).

28. It is possible that some people were listed in both the astrologer and psychic tallies for 1979, and the astrologer rate may be inflated somewhat because it is based just on metropolitan areas of the country. Thus, the increase over the 26 years may be a little greater than estimated here.

29. Christopher Welty, "Ontology," in *Encyclopedia of Human-Computer Interaction*, edited by William Sims Bainbridge (Great Barrington, Ma.: Berkshire, 2004): 528–531.

30. David Goldberg, David Nichols, Brian M. Oki, and Douglas Terry "Using Collaborative Filtering to Weave an Information Tapestry," *Communications of the ACM* 35 (December 1992): 61–70; Paul Resnick and Hal R. Varian, "Recommender Systems," *Communications of the ACM* 40 (March 1997): 56–58.

31. To make this table, I first removed all the "New Age > Astrology > General" categorizations, because all 100 books shared this characteristic, then used a spreadsheet to arrange and count all the other assignments in terms of fractions of books. Each book was counted as 1 categorization, so if it was assigned to 4 categories, each category was counted as containing 1/4 of a book; if it was assigned to 5 categories, then the tally for each was incremented by 1/5 of a book. The table reports the data as percentages of the total 100 books.

32. Zan Huang, Wingyan Chung, Thian-Huat Ong, and Hsinchun Chen, "A Graph-based Recommender System for Digital Library," in *Proceedings Joint Conference on Digital Libraries* (Portland, Oregon, 2002), 65–73.

33. Lois Mai Chan, *Cataloging and Classification* (New York: McGraw-Hill, 1994).

34. A given book may be assigned to two or more of the categories, and there has been no attempt to purge the table of duplications.

35. Technically, the twentieth century ran 1901–2000, but I thought the division into decades shown in the graph would be more immediately meaningful to readers.

36. J. Gordon Melton, "The Revival; of Astrology in the United States," in *Religious Movements*, ed. Rodney Stark (New York: Paragon House, 1985), 279–299.

37. Philip Jenkins, *Mystics and Messiahs: Cults and New Religions in American History* (New York: Oxford University Press, 2000).

38. Ron Goulart, *An Informal History of the Pulp Magazines* (New York: Ace, 1972).

39. William Sims Bainbridge, *The Spaceflight Revolution* (New York: Wiley-Interscience, 1976), 208.

40. As is often the case for time series data, the three variables correlate highly with each other, but the two New Age variables correlate more highly with each other than either does with books about God. Using separate years 1900–1999 as the units of analy-

sis, the astrology-parapsychology correlation is 0.85. The astrology-God correlation is 0.81, and the parapsychology-God correlation is 0.71. We could speculate that the common reaction to the Great Depression of the 1930s accounts for the greater astrology-God correlation.

41. Steven J. Dick, *Plurality of Worlds: The Origins of the Extraterrestrial Life Debate from Democritus to Kant* (Cambridge, England: Cambridge University Press, 1982).

42. Emanuel Swedenborg, *Earths In Our Solar System Which Are Called Planets, and Earths In The Starry Heaven Their Inhabitants, And The Spirits And Angels There* (Boston: New Church Union, 1950).

43. H. Spencer Jones, *Life on Other Worlds* (New York: Mentor, 1951); A. G. W. Cameron, ed., *Interstellar Communication* (New York: Benjamin, 1963); I. S. Shklovski and Carl Sagan, *Intelligent Life in the Universe* (New York: Dell, 1966)

44. Kenneth Albert Arnold and Ray Palmer, *The Coming of the Saucers* (Boise, Id.: Palmer Publishing, 1952); Desmond Leslie and George Adamski, *Flying Saucers Have Landed* (New York: British Book Centre, 1953); George Adamski, *Inside the Space Ships* (New York: Abelard-Schuman, 1955).

45. Erich von Däniken, *Chariots of the Gods?* (New York, Bantam Books: 1971); Erich von Däniken, *Gods from Outer Space* (New York, Bantam Books: 1972); Clifford Wilson, *Crash Go the Chariots* (New York: Lancer, 1970).

46. Benson Saler, Charles A. Ziegler, and Charles B. Moore, *UFO Crash at Roswell: The Genesis of a Modern Myth* (Washington, D.C.: Smithsonian Institution Press, 1997); William Sims Bainbridge, "Extraterrestrial Tales," *Science* 279 (1998): 671.

47. William Sims Bainbridge, "Attitudes Toward Interstellar Communication: An Empirical Study," *Journal of the British Interplanetary Society* 36 (1983): 298–304.

48. Kendrick Frazier (ed.), *Paranormal Borderlands of Science* (Buffalo, N.Y.: Prometheus, 1981).

Chapter 7:

1. Friedrich Nietzsche, *Human, All Too Human*, Chapter IX, Paragraph 600, Translation by Helen Zimmern, Published 1909–1913; this chapter draws upon William Sims Bainbridge, "Religion and Science," *Futures* 36 (2004): 1009–1023; "New Religions, Science and Secularization," in *The Handbook of Cults and Sects in America*, ed. David G. Bromley and Jeffrey K. Hadden. (Greenwich, Ct.: JAI, 1993), pp. 277–292.

2. Rodney Stark and William Sims Bainbridge, *The Future of Religion* (Berkeley, Ca.: University of California Press, 1985).

3. http://www.jstor.org/

4. Stuart C. Dodd, "Can Science Improve Praying?" *Darshana* 1(4) (1961): 22–37.

5. Richard S. Kirby, "The Future of Mathematical Sociology," website of the Stuart C. Dodd Institute for Social Innovation, http://www.stuartcdoddinstitute.org/mathematical-sociology.shtml, 2003.

6. Richard J. Spady and Richard S. Kirby, *The Leadership of Civilization Building* (Seattle, Wa.: Forum Foundation, 2002).

7. Barbara Hubbard, "From Meaninglessness to New Worlds," *The Futurist* (April 1971): 72.

8. Barbara Hubbard, *The Hunger of Eve* (Harrisburg, Pa.: Stackpole, 1976), 90–91, emphasis in original.

9. Earl Hubbard, *The Search Is On* (Los Angeles: Pace, 1969).

10. Abraham Maslow, *Religions, Values, and Peak-Experiences* (New York: Viking, 1970).

11. Roger W. Wescott, *The Divine Animal* (New York: Funk and Wagnalls, 1969) 14–15, emphasis in original.

12. *New Worlds*, the magazine of the Committee for the Future, April 1971, p. 2.

13. R. Buckminster Fuller, *Operating Manual for Spaceship Earth* (New York: Pocket Books, 1970); Pierre Teilhard de Chardin, *The Future of Man* (New York: Harper and Row, 1964).

14. Rodney Stark and William Sims Bainbridge, *A Theory of Religion* (New York: Toronto/Lang, 1987), 105.

15. Rodney Stark and William Sims Bainbridge, *A Theory of Religion* (New York: Toronto/Lang, 1987), 106–107.

16. Christina Larner, *Witchcraft and Religion: The Politics of Popular Belief* (New York: Blackwell, 1984).

17. Richard Hughes Seager, *The World's Parliament of Religions* (Bloomington: Indiana University Press, 1995).

18. James H. Leuba, "The Yoga System of Mental Concentration and Religious Mysticism," *The Journal of Philosophy, Psychology and Scientific Methods*, 16(8) (1919): 203.

19. William Sims Bainbridge, *The Sociology of Religious Movements* (New York: Routledge, 1997), 187–191.

20. William Sims Bainbridge and Daniel H. Jackson, "The Rise and Decline of Transcendental Meditation," in *The Social Impact of New Religious Movements*, ed. Bryan Wilson (New York: Rose of Sharon Press, 1981), 135–158.

21. Robert Keith Wallace, "Physiological Effects of Transcendental Meditation," *Science* 167 (1970): 1751–1754; Robert Keith Wallace and Herbert Benson, "The Physiology of Meditation," *Scientific American* 226 (February 1972): 84–90.

22. Jack Forem, *Transcendental Meditation* (New York: Dutton, 1973); Harold H. Bloomfield, Michael Peter Cain, Dennis T. Jaffe, and Robert E. Korey, *TM–Discovering Inner Energy and Overcoming Stress* (New York: Dell, 1975); Denise Denniston, Peter McWilliams, and Barry Geller, *The TM Book—How to Enjoy the Rest of Your Life* (New York: Warner, 1975).

23. Robert R. Pagano, Richard M. Rose, Robert M. Stivers, and Stephen Warrenberg, "Sleep During Transcendental Meditation, *Science* 191 (1976): 308–310.

24. John White, "A Critical Look at TM," *New Age Journal* (January 1976): 30–35; "Second Thoughts: What's Behind TM?" *Human Behavior* (October 1976): 70–71; Don Allen, "TM at Folsom Prison: A Critique of Abrams and Siegel," *Criminal Justice and Behavior* 6 (1979): 9–12.

25. http://www.tm.org/

26. http://www.kundaliniyoga.com/

27. http://www.yogaserve.com/

28. http://www.yogaalliance.org/index.html

29. http://www.nqa.org/

30. Jian Xu, "Body, Discourse, and the Cultural Politics of Contemporary Chinese Qigong," *The Journal of Asian Studies* 58 (1999): 961–991.

31. Jane Monnig Atkinson, "Shamanisms Today, *Annual Review of Anthropology* 21 (1992): 307–330; Joseph S. Alter, Francesca Bray, Abhijit Guha, P. C. Joshi, and Charles

Leslie, "Heaps of Health, Metaphysical Fitness," *Current Anthropology* 40 Supplement (1999): S43-S66.

32. Rodney Stark and William Sims Bainbridge, *The Future of Religion* (Berkeley, Ca.: University of California Press, 1985), 218.

33. William Sims Bainbridge, "Science and Religion: The Case of Scientology," in *The Future of New Religious Movements*, ed. David G. Bromley and Phillip E. Hammond (Macon, Ga.: Mercer University Press, 1987), 59–79.

34. Walter Braddeson, *Scientology for the Millions* (Los Angeles: Sherbourne Press, 1969).

35. The data used in this paragraph were made available by the American Religion Data Archive (www.thearda.com) and were originally collected by The Pew Research Center for the People and the Press.

36. James T. Richardson, ed., *Regulating Religion: Case Studies from Around the Globe* (New York, Kluwer, 2004).

37. Rodney Stark, "Why Religious Movements Succeed or Fail, *Journal of Contemporary Religion* 11 (1996): 133–146.

38. Roy Wallis, "Hostages to Fortune: Thoughts on the Future of Scientology and the Children of God," in *The Future of New Religious Movements*, ed. David G. Bromley and Phillip E. Hammond, (Macon, Ga.: Mercer University Press, 1987), 80–90.

39. L. Ron Hubbard, *Dianetics: The Modern Science of Mental Health, a Handbook of Dianetic Therapy* (New York: Hermitage House, 1950).

40. L. Ron Hubbard, *Science of Survival: Simplified, Faster Dianetic Techniques* (Wichita, Ka.: Hubbard Dianetic Foundation, 1951).

41. Church of Scientology, *What is Scientology* (Los Angeles: Bridge Publications, 1988).

42. Martin B. Bradley, N. M. Green, D. E. Jones, M. Lynn, L. McNeil, *Churches and Church Membership in the United States, 1990* (Atlanta, Ga.: Glenmary Research Center, 1992).

43. William Sims Bainbridge, "The Religious Ecology of Deviance," *American Sociological Review* 54 (1989): 288–295.

44. Pearson's *r* coefficients of -0.51 and -0.42, respectively.

45. William Sims Bainbridge, *Satan's Power: A Deviant Psychotherapy Cult* (Berkeley, Ca.: University of California Press, 1978): "Social Construction from Within: Satan's Process Pages," in *The Satanism Scare*, ed. James T. Richardson, Joel Best, and David G. Bromley (New York: Aldine de Gruyter, 1991), 297–310.

46. William Sims Bainbridge, "Social Construction from Within," in *The Satanism Scare*, ed. James T. Richardson, Joel Best, and David G. Bromley (New York: Aldine de Gruyter, 1991), 297–310.

47. Alfred Adler, *Understanding Human Nature* (Greenwich, Ct.: Fawcett, 1954).

48. Peter L. Berger, *A Rumor of Angels: Modern Society and the Rediscovery of the Supernatural* (Garden City, N.Y.: Doubleday, 1969).

49. Ari Kiev and John L. Francis, "Sabud and Mental Illness," *American Journal of Psychotherapy* 18 (1964): 66–78.

50. Rodney Stark and William Sims Bainbridge, *A Theory of Religion* (New York: Toronto/Lang, 1987), 104–109, 284–289.

Chapter 8:

1. Friedrich Nietzsche, *Twilight of the Idols*, Maxims and Arrows 7, http://www. hand-print.com/SC/NIE/GotDamer.html; this chapter draws upon William Sims Bainbridge, "Atheism," *Interdisciplinary Journal of Research on Religion*, 2005, http://www. bepress.com/ijrr/vol1/iss1/art2/.

2. http://www.cem.va.gov/hmemb.htm

3. This is one of the first attempts to use website information in this way, so I have tried to keep the methods simple. One might want to norm the ratios further by the total number of sites in each domain. As of January 31, 2006, Google counted 1,590,000,000 .edu pages, 4,020,000,000 .com pages, 1,060,000,000 .gov pages and 208,000,000 .net pages.

4. George H. Smith, *Atheism: The Case Against God* (Buffalo, N.Y.: Prometheus, 1979).

5. D. Garth Taylor, "Pluralistic Ignorance and the Spiral of Silence: A Formal Analysis," *Public Opinion Quarterly* 46 (1982): 311–335.

6. Colin Campbell, *Toward a Sociology of Irreligion* (New York: Herder and Herder, 1972); James Turner, *Without God, Without Creed: The Origins of Unbelief in America* (Baltimore, Md.: Johns Hopkins University Press, 1985).

7. http://www12.statcan.ca

8. Gerard Newman, "Census 96: Religion," Research Note 27 1997–98, Parliament of Australia Library, http://www.aph.gov.au/library/pubs/rn/1997-98/98rn27.htm

9. G. M. Vernon, "The Religious 'Nones': A Neglected Category," *Journal for the Scientific Study of Religion* 7 (1968): 219–229.

10. Bernadette C. Hayes, "Religious Independents Within Western Industrialized Nations: A Socio-Demographic Profile," *Sociology of Religion* 61 (2000): 191–207.

11. Wolfgang Jagodzinski and Andrew Greeley, "The Demand for Religion: Hard Core Atheism and 'Supply Side' Theory," no date, http://www.agreeley.com/articles/hardcore.html

12. Frederic M. Thrasher, *The Gang* (Chicago: University of Chicago Press, 1927); Clifford Shaw and Henry D. McKay, *Delinquency Areas* (Chicago: University of Chicago Press, 1929).

13. Robert E. L. Faris and H. Warren Dunham, *Mental Disorders in Urban Areas* (Chicago: University of Chicago Press, 1939).

14. Travis Hirschi, *Causes of Delinquency* (Berkeley, Ca.: University of California Press, 1969).

15. The data were downloaded from the Association of Religion Data Archives, www.TheARDA.com, and were collected by The Pew Research Center for the People and the Press.

16. Charles Y. Glock and Rodney Stark, *Christian Beliefs and Anti-Semitism* (New York: Harper and Row, 1966).

17. Alan Edelstein, *An Unacknowledged Harmony: Philo-Semitism and the Survival of European Jewry* (Westport, Ct.: Greenwood, 1982).

18. Will Herberg, *Protestant, Catholic, Jew: An Essay in American Religious Sociology* (Garden City, N.Y.: Doubleday, 1955).

19. Pippa Norris and Ronald Inglehart, *Sacred and Secular: Religion and Politics Worldwide* (Cambridge, England: University of Cambridge Press, 2004).

20. William Sims Bainbridge, *The Sociology of Religious Movements* (New York: Routledge, 1997), 85.

21. William Sims Bainbridge, *The Sociology of Religious Movements* (New York: Routledge, 1997), 111.

22. William Sims Bainbridge, "A Prophet's Reward: Dynamics of Religious Exchange," in *Sacred Markets, Sacred Canopies*, ed. Ted G. Jelen (Lanham, Md.: Rowman and Littlefield, 2002), 69.

23. William Sims Bainbridge, "Sacred Algorithms: Exchange Theory of Religious Claims," in *Defining Religion*, ed. David Bromley and Larry Greil (Amsterdam: JAI Elsevier, 2003), 30–31.

24. http://www.cia.gov/cia/publications/factbook/

25. $r = -0.76$.

26. Bernadette C. Hayes, "Religious Independents Within Western Industrialized Nations: A Socio-Demographic Profile," *Sociology of Religion* 61 (2000): 191–207.

27. G. H. Knibbs (ed.), *Census of the Commonwealth of Australia - 1911* (Melbourne: McCarron, Bird, and Company, 1914).

28. Rodney Stark, *The Rise of Christianity* (Princeton, N.J.: Princeton University Press, 1996).

Chapter 9:

1. Friedrich Nietzsche, *Beyond Good and Evil*, Part Four, Aphorisms and Interludes, Section 14, translated by Ian Johnston, http://www.mala.bc.ca/~johnstoi/Nietzsche/beyondgoodandevil4.htm

2. Kyle R. Skottke, "The Evolution of Human Intelligence: Increasing Importance of Domain-Specific Intelligence in the Modern Environment," Rochester Institute of Technology, http://www.personalityresearch.org/papers/skottke.html.

3. V. Gordon Childe, *Man Makes Himself* (New York: New American Library, 1951).

4. Ann Braude, *Radical Spirits* (Boston: Beacon Press, 1989).

5. Robert Darnton, *Mesmerism and the End of the enlightenment in France* (New York: Schocken, 1970).

6. Society for Psychical Research web page, http://www.spr.ac.uk/.

7. William James, *Essays in Psychical Research* (Cambridge, Ma.: Harvard University Press, 1986).

8. J. B. Rhine, *Extra-Sensory Perception* (Boston: Bruce Humphries, 1964 [1934]); *New Frontiers of the Mind* (New York: Farrar and Rinehart, 1937).

9. C. E. M. Hansel, *ESP - A Scientific Evaluation* (New York: Scribner's, 1966).

10. J. B. Rhine, ed., *Progress in Parapsychology* (Durham, N.C.: Parapsychology Press, 1971); John Beloff, ed., *New Directions in Parapsychology* (Metuchen, N.J.: Scarecrow Press, 1974); Hoyt L. Edge, Robert L. Morris, Joseph H. Rush, and John Palmer, *Foundations of Parapsychology* (Boston: Routledge and Kegan Paul, 1986).

11. Julie Milton, "Should Ganzfeld Research Continue to be Crucial in the Search for a Replicable PSI Effect?" *Journal of Parapsychology* 63 (1999): 309–333.

12. Joseph M. Felser, "Parapsychology Without Religion," *Journal of the American Society for Psychical Research* 93 (1999): 259–279.

13. Rupert Sheldrake and Pamela Smart, "Videotaped Experiments on Telephone Telepathy," *Journal of Parapsychology* 67 (2003): 147–166; Linda Evans and Michael A.

Thalbourne, "The Feeling of Being Stared At: A Parapsychological Investigation," *Journal of the American Society for Psychical Research* 93 (1999): 309–325.

14. Louisa E. Rhine, "PK in the Laboratory: A Survey," in *Progress in Parapsychology*, ed. J. B. Rhine (Durham, N.C.: Parapsychology Press, 1971), 72–85; Sara R. Feather and Louisa E. Rhine, "A Helper-Hinder Comparison," in *Progress in Parapsychology*, ed. J. B. Rhine (Durham, N.C.: Parapsychology Press, 1971), 86–96.

15. James Randi, *The Magic of Uri Geller* (New York: Ballantine, 1975); David Marks, *The Psychology of the Psychic* (Amherst, N.Y.: Prometheus, 2000).

16. Kurt Vonnegut, "Report on the Barnhouse Effect," in *Welcome to the Monkey House* (New York: Delacourte, 1968), 156–170.

17. Pat Cook, *The Barnhouse Effect* (Woodstock, Ill.: Dramatic Publishing, 1997); I recalling hearing the radio dramatization in 1950.

18. Bernard Grad, "A Telekinetic Effect on Plant Growth: II Experiments Involving Treatment of Saline in Stoppered Bottles," *International Journal of Parapsychology* 6 (1964): 473-494; Jean Barry, "Retarding Fungus Growth by PK," in *Progress in Parapsychology*, ed. J. B. Rhine (Durham, N.C.: Parapsychology Press, 1971), 118–121.

19. W. E. Cox, "PK on a Pendulum System," in *Progress in Parapsychology*, ed. J. B. Rhine (Durham, N.C.: Parapsychology Press, 1971), 97–101.

20. Chris A. Roe, Russell Davey, and Paul Stevens, "Are ESP and PK Aspects of a Unitary Phenomenon? A Preliminary Test of the relationship between ESP and PK," *Journal of Parapsychology* 67 (2003): 343–366.

21. Robert Brier, "PK Effect on a Plant-Polygraph System," in *Progress in Parapsychology*, ed. J. B. Rhine (Durham, N.C.: Parapsychology Press, 1971), 102–117.

22. Daniel Dennett, *Breaking the Spell: Religion as a Natural Phenomenon* (New York, Viking, 2006), p. 31.

23. http://viscog.beckman.uiuc.edu/djs_lab/demos.html; the different clothing is important, because when I examine screen shots of the men simultaneously I still can't be sure they are not the same person, granted that the hairstyles are somewhat different. This suggests to me another principle: The psychologists themselves have no difficulty distinguishing the two men, merely because they have had lots of experience with them, illustrating in a different way how limited our immediate powers of perception are.

24. http://www.psych.ubc.ca/~viscoglab/demos.htm

25. George A. Miller, "The Magical Number Seven, Plus or Minus Two: Some Limits on our Capacity for Processing Information," *Psychological Review* 63 (1956): 81–97.

26. Allen Newell, *Unified Theories of Cognition* (Cambridge, Ma.: Harvard University Press, 1990).

27. Martin A. Conway, "Sensory-perceptual Episodic Memory and Its Context: Autobiographical Memory," *Philosophical Transactions of the Royal Society, Biological Sciences* 356 (2001): 1505–1515.

28. Herbert A. Simon, *The Sciences of the Artificial*, third edition (Cambridge, Ma.: MIT Press, 1996), 53.

29. S. Zeki, "The Disunity of Consciousness," *Trends in Cognitive Sciences* 7 (2003): 214–218.

30. Paul Bloom, *Descartes' Baby: How the Science of Child Development Explains what Makes Us Human* (New York: Basic Books, 2004).

31. Scott Atran, *In Gods We Trust: The Evolutionary Landscape of Religion* (Oxford, England: Oxford University Press, 2002).

32. Pascal Boyer, *Religion Explained: The Evolutionary Origins of Religious Thought* (New York: Basic Books, 2001), 16–17.

33. Justin L. Barrett, *Why Would Anyone Believe in God?* (Walnut Creek, Ca.: AltaMira, 2004), 125.

34. Justin L. Barrett, *Why Would Anyone Believe in God?* (Walnut Creek, Ca.: AltaMira, 2004), 118.

35. H. Porter Abbott, "Unnarratable Knowledge: The Difficulty of Understanding Evolution by Natural Selection," in *Narrative Theory and the Cognitive Sciences, ed.* David Herman (Stanford, Ca.: Center for the Study of Language and Information, 2003), 143–162.

36. Pascal Boyer, *Religion Explained: The Evolutionary Origins of Religious Thought* (New York: Basic Books, 2001); Justin L. Barrett, *Why Would Anyone Believe in God?* (Walnut Creek, Ca.: Altamira, 2004).

37. Scott Atran, *In Gods We Trust* (New York: Oxford University Press, 2002).

38. Jesse M. Bering, "The Cognitive Psychology of Belief in the Supernatural," *American Scientist* 94 (2006): 142–149.

39. Harvey Whitehouse, *Modes of Religiosity: A Cognitive Theory of Religious Transmission* (Walnut Creek, Ca.: Altamira, 2004).

40. Harvey Whitehouse and James Laidlaw, eds., *Ritual and Memory: Toward a Comparative Anthropology of Religions* (Walnut Creek, Ca.: Altamira, 2002); Harvey Whitehouse and Luther H. Martin, eds., *Theorizing Religions Past: Archaeology, History, and Cognition* (Walnut Creek, Ca.: Altamira, 2004).

41. William Sims Bainbridge, *Sociology Laboratory* (Belmont, Ca.: Wadsworth, 1987); "Neural Network Models of Religious Belief," *Sociological Perspectives* 38 (1995): 483–495; *God from the Machine* (Lanham, Maryland: AltaMira, 2006).

42. Edwin H. Sutherland, *Principles of Criminology* (Philadelphia: Lippincott, 1947).

43. Charles Horton Cooley, *Human Nature and the Social Order* (New York: Scribner's, 1922); W. I. Thomas, *The Unadjusted Girl* (Boston: Little, Brown, and Company, 1923); Herbert Blumer, *Symbolic Interactionism: Perspective and Method* (Englewood Cliffs, N.J.: Prentice-Hall, 1969).

44. Fritz Heider, *The Psychology of Interpersonal Relations* (New York: Wiley, 1958).

45. Leon Festinger, *Theory of Cognitive Dissonance* (Evanston, Ill.: Row, Peterson, 1957).

46. Rodney Stark and William Sims Bainbridge, "Networks of Faith: Interpersonal Bonds and Recruitment to Cults and Sects," *American Journal of Sociology* 85 (1980): 1376–1395.

47. Hans P. Moravec, *Mind Children: The Future of Robot and Human Intelligence* (Cambridge, Ma.: Harvard University Press, 1988).

48. William Sims Bainbridge, *Experiments in Psychology* (Belmont, Ca.: Wadsworth, 1986).

49. William Sims Bainbridge, *Survey Research: A Computer-Assisted Introduction* (Belmont, Ca.: Wadsworth, 1989).

50. William Sims Bainbridge, "New Religions, Science and Secularization," in *The Handbook of Cults and Sects in America*, ed. David G. Bromley and Jeffrey K. Hadden (Greenwich, Ct.: JAI, 1993), 277–292; "A Question of Immortality," *Analog* 122 (May 2002): 40–49; "The Spaceflight Revolution Revisited," in *Looking Backward, Looking Forward*, ed. Stephen J. Garber (Washington, D.C.: National Aeronautics and Space Administration, 2002), 39–64; "Massive Questionnaires for Personality Capture," *Social*

Science Computer Review 21 (2003): 267–280; "The Future of the Internet: Cultural and Individual Conceptions," in *Society Online: The Internet in Context*, ed. Philip N. Howard and Steve Jones (Thousand Oaks, Ca.: Sage, 2004), 307–324 ; "Progress toward Cyberimmortality," in *The Scientific Conquest of Death: Essays on Infinite Lifetimes*, ed. Bruce J. Klein and Sebastian Sethe (Birmingham, Alabama: Immortality Institute, 2004), 107–122; "The Coming Conflict between Religion and Cognitive Science," in *Foresight, Innovation, and Strategy: Toward a Wiser Future*, ed. Cynthia G. Wagner (Bethesda, Md.: World Future Society, 2005), 75–8; "Cognitive Technologies," in *Managing Nano-Bio-Info-Cogno Innovations: Converging Technologies in Society*, ed. William Sims Bainbridge and Mihail C. Roco (Berlin: Springer, 2006), 203–226; "Strategies for Personality Transfer," *The Journal of Personal Cyberconsciousness* 1(4) (2006), online at http://www.terasemjournals.org/PC0104/bainbridge_01a.html.

51. Ray Kurzweil, *The Age of Spiritual Machines: When Computers Exceed Human Intelligence* (New York: Viking, 1999); Hugo de Garis, *The Artilect War* (Selden, N.Y.: Marilyn June Janson Literary Services, 1999).

52. Lin Liao, Dieter Fox and Henry Kautz, "Location-Based Activity Recognition using Relational Markov Networks," in *Proceedings of the Nineteenth International Joint Conference on Artificial Intelligence* (Edinburgh, Scotland, 2005).

53. Donald Patterson, Dieter Fox, Henry Kautz, Matthai Philipose, "Fine-Grained Activity Recognition by Aggregating Abstract Object Usage," in *Proceedings of the IEEE International Symposium on Wearable Computers* (Osaka, Japan, October 2005).

54. NSF award 0433637, "Creating Dynamic Social Network Models from Sensor Data;" http://www.nsf.gov/awardsearch/index.jsp.

55. Martha E. Pollack, "Intelligent Technology for an Aging Population: The Use of AI to Assist Elders with Cognitive Impairment," *AI Magazine* 26(2) (2005):9–24, 2005.

56. NSF award 0534280, "Multi-Agent Plan Management for Socio-Cognitive Orthotics," http://www.nsf.gov/awardsearch/index.jsp.

57. NSF award 0534520, "Using GeoTemporal Social Matching to Support Community," http://www.nsf.gov/awardsearch/index.jsp.

58. Rosalind W. Picard, *Affective Computing* (Cambridge, Ma.: MIT Press, 1997).

59. Rosalind W. Picard, "Helping Addicts: A Scenario from 2021," http://affect.media. mit.edu/pdfs/05.picard-RWJ.pdf

60. NSF award 0555411, "Social-Emotional Intelligence Prosthetic," http://www.nsf.gov/ awardsearch/index.jsp.

61. http://www.informedia.cs.cmu.edu/eod/index.html

62. http://www.eyetap.org/

63. Jim Gemmell, Lyndsay Williams, Ken Wood, Gordon Bell and Roger Lueder, "Passive Capture and Ensuing Issues for a Personal Lifetime Store," *Proceedings of The First ACM Workshop on Continuous Archival and Retrieval of Personal Experiences* (New York: Association for Computing Machinery, 2004), 48–55; Steven Cherry, "Total Recall," *IEEE Spectrum* 42 (November 2005): 24–30.

64. http://research.microsoft.com/barc/mediapresence/MyLifeBits.aspx

65. Kiyoung Yang, Tim Marsh, Minyoung Mun and Cyrus Shahabi, "Continuous Archival and Analysis of User Data in Virtual and Immersive Game Environments," *Proceedings of the ACM Multimedia Conference* (New York: Association for Computing Machinery, 2005).

66. Stanford Racing Team, "Stanford Racing Team's Entry In The 2005 DARPA Grand Challenge,"

http://www.darpa.mil/grandchallenge05/TechPapers/Stanford.pdf

67. David R. Heise and Brian Weir, "A Test of Symbolic Interactionist Predictions about Emotions in Imagined Situations," *Symbolic Interaction*, 22 (1999): 129–161.

68. William Sims Bainbridge, "Massive Questionnaires for Personality Capture," *Social Science Computer Review* 21 (2003): 267–280.

69. William Sims Bainbridge, "Cognitive Technologies," in *Managing Nano-Bio-Info-Cogno Innovations: Converging Technologies in Society*, ed. William Sims Bainbridge and Mihail C. Roco (Berlin: Springer, 2006), 203–226.

Chapter 10:

1. Friedrich Nietzsche, *Thus Spake Zarathustra*, Prologue 3, http://www.publicappeal.org/library/nietzsche/Nietzsche_thus_spake_zarathustra/pro3.html; this chapter drew upon William Sims Bainbridge, "The Transhuman Heresy," *Journal of Evolution and Technology*, 2005, 14, http://jetpress.org/volume14/bainbridge.html; "Religious Opposition to Cloning," *Journal of Evolution and Technology*, 2003, 13, www.jetpress.org/volume 13/bainbridge.html.

2. Bruce J. Klein and Sebastian Sethe, eds., *The Scientific Conquest of Death: Essays on Infinite Lifetimes* (Birmingham, Alabama: Immortality Institute, 2004).

3. Ray Kurzweil, *The Age of Spiritual Machines* (New York: Viking, 1999).

4. Nick Bostrom, "A History of Transhumanist Thought," *Journal of Evolution and Technology*, 2005, 14(1), http://jetpress.org/volume14/bostrom.html.

5. Walter A. Kaufmann, *Nietzsche: Philosopher, Psychologist, Antichrist* (Princeton, New Jersey: Princeton University Press, 1974).

6. Olaf Stapledon, *Odd John* (London: Methuen, 1935); Robert A. Heinlein, *Stranger in a Strange Land* (New York: Putnam, 1961); A. E. van Vogt, *Slan* (Sauk City, Wisc.: Arkham House, 1946).

7. A. E. Van Vogt, *The World of Null-A* (New York: Simon and Schuster, 1948).

8. Van Vogt, A. E., "Predisposition and the Power of Hidden Words," *Journal of the Dianetic Sciences* 1(1) (1961): 1–18.

9. Neil R. Jones, "The Jameson Satellite," *Amazing Stories* 30 (April 1956): 156–176, reprinted from the July 1931 issue; Edgar Rice Burroughs, "The Resurrection of Jimber-Jaw," *Argosy* (20 February 1937).

10. Robert C. W. Ettinger, *The Prospect of Immortality* (Garden City, N.Y.: Doubleday, 1964).

11. Robert C. W. Ettinger, "Interstellar Travel and Eternal Life," *If* 18 (January 1968): 109–114.

12. Robert C. W. Ettinger, *Man into Superman: The Startling Potential of Human Evolution—and how to Be Part of It* (New York: St. Martin's Press, 1972).

13. Bruce J. Klein and Sebastian Sethe, eds., *The Scientific Conquest of Death: Essays on Infinite Lifetimes* (Birmingham, Alabama: Immortality Institute, 2004); my own contribution is sandwiched between essays by those computational visionaries, Ray Kurzweil and Marvin Minsky.

14. FM-2030, *Are You a Transhuman?* (New York: Warner, 1989).

15. James Hughes, *Citizen Cyborg* (Cambridge, Ma.: Westview, 2004), 167.

16. From the page of the Institute's website presenting the principles of Extropy, http://www.extropy.org/principles.htm.

17. Patrick D. Hopkins, "Transcending the Animal: How Transhumanism and Religion Are and Are Not Alike," Journal of Evolution and Technology 14(2) (2005): 13–28; http://jetpress.org/volume14/hopkins.html

18. Gregory E. Jordan, "Apologia for Transhumanist Religion," *Journal of Evolution and Technology* 15(1) (2006): 55–72, http://jetpress.org/.

19. John Schloendorn, "Negative Data from the Psychological Frontline," *Journal of Evolution and Technology*, 2005, 14, http://jetpress.org/volume14/schloendorn.html.

20. W. Scott Badger, "An Exploratory Survey Examining the Familiarity with and Attitudes toward Cryonic Preservation," *Journal of Evolution and Technology* 3 (1998) http://www.jetpress.org/volume3/badger.htm.

21. James Hughes, *Citizen Cyborg* (Cambridge, Ma.: Westview, 2004), 107.

22. http://www.thecbc.org/; http://www.cbhd.org/.

23. President's Council on Bioethics, *Beyond Therapy: Biotechnology and the Pursuit of Happiness* (Washington, D.C.: President's Council on Bioethics, 2003); President's Council on Bioethics, *Human Cloning and Human Dignity: An Ethical Inquiry* (Washington, D.C.: President's Council on Bioethics, 2002).

24. Francis Fukuyama, "Transhumanism," *Foreign Policy* (September-October 2004), http://www.keepmedia.com/pubs/ForeignPolicy/2004/09/01/564801?page=4; *Our Posthuman Future: Consequences of the Biotechnology Revolution* (New York: Farrar, Straus, and Giroux, 2002).

25. Edward O. Wilson, *Consilience: The Unity of Knowledge* (New York: Knopf, 1998); *The Insect Societies* (Cambridge, Ma.: Harvard University Press, 1971); *Sociobiology: The New Synthesis* (Cambridge, Ma.: Harvard University Press, 1975).

26. Mihail C. Roco and William Sims Bainbridge, eds., *Societal Implications of Nanoscience and Nanotechnology* (Dordrecht, Netherlands: Kluwer, 2001), 1.

27. Mihail C. Roco, and William Sims Bainbridge, eds., *Converging Technologies for Improving Human Performance* (Dordrecht, Netherlands: Kluwer, 2003), ix.

28. Mihail C. Roco and Carlo D. Montemagno, eds., *The Coevolution of Human Potential and Converging Technologies* (New York: New York Academy of Sciences, 2004); Mihail C. Roco and William Sims Bainbridge, eds., *Nanotechnology: Societal Implications* (Arlington, Virginia: National Science Foundation, 2005); William Sims Bainbridge and Mihail C. Roco, eds., *Managing Nano-Bio-Info-Cogno Innovations: Converging Technologies in Society* (Berlin: Springer, 2006).

29. Brian M. Pierce, "Sensor System Engineering Insights on Improving Human Cognition and Communication," in *Converging Technologies for Improving Human Performance*, ed. Mihail C. Roco and William Sims Bainbridge (Dordrecht, Netherlands: Kluwer, 2003), 117–119; Rudy Burger, "Enhancing Personal Area Sensory and Social Communication Through Converging Technologies," in *Converging Technologies for Improving Human Performance*, ed. Mihail C. Roco and William Sims Bainbridge (Dordrecht, Netherlands: Kluwer, 2003), 164–166.

30. Sherry Turkle, "Sociable Technologies," in *Converging Technologies for Improving Human Performance*, ed. Mihail C. Roco and William Sims Bainbridge (Dordrecht, Netherlands: Kluwer, 2003), 150–158.

31. Warren Robinett, "The Consequences of Fully Understanding the Brain," in *Converging Technologies for Improving Human Performance*, ed. Mihail C. Roco and William Sims Bainbridge (Dordrecht, Netherlands: Kluwer, 2003), 166–170.

32. Patricia Connolly, "Nanobiotechnology and Life Extension," in *Converging Technologies for Improving Human Performance*, ed. Mihail C. Roco and William Sims Bainbridge (Dordrecht, Netherlands: Kluwer, 2003), 182–190.

33. Rodolfo R. Linás and Valeri A. Makarov, "Brain-Machine Interface via a Neurovascular Approach," in *Converging Technologies for Improving Human Performance*, ed. Mihail C. Roco and William Sims Bainbridge (Dordrecht, Netherlands: Kluwer, 2003), 244–251.

34. Ira Levin, *The Boys from Brazil* (Boston: G. K. Hall, 1976).

35. William Sims Bainbridge, "Cultural Genetics," in *Religious Movements*, ed. Rodney Stark (New York: Paragon House, 1985), 157–198; *The Sociology of Religious Movements* (New York: Routledge, 1997).

36. Talcott Parsons, "Evolutionary Universals in Society," *American Sociological Review* 29 (1964): 339–357.

37. Daniel C. Dennett, *Darwin's Dangerous Idea* (New York: Simon and Schuster, 1995).

38. Dalia Sussman, "Majority Opposes Human Cloning," *ABCNEWS.com*, 16 August 2001.

39. Pew Research Center, "Public Makes Distinctions on Genetic Research," press release 9 April 2002: http://people-press.org/reports/print.ph3?PageID=408.

40. Lydia Saad, "Cloning Humans Is a Turn Off to Most Americans," Gallup News Service, 16 May 2002.

41. Department of Commerce, *Falling Through the Net: Defining the Digital Divide* (Washington, DC: U.S. Department of Commerce, 1999).

42. William Sims Bainbridge, "Validity of Web-Based Surveys," in *Computing in the Social Sciences and Humanities*, ed. Orville Vernon Burton (Urbana, Ill.: University of Illinois Press, 2002), 51–66; cf. Samuel J. Best, Brian Krueger, Clark Hubbard, and Andrew Smith, "An Assessment of the Generalizability of Internet Surveys," *Social Science Computer Review* 19 (2001): 131–145.

43. Emile Durkheim, *The Elementary Forms of the Religious Life* (New York: Free Press, 1915 [1965]).

44. Mary Holland Benin, "Determinants of Opposition to Abortion," *Sociological Perspectives* 28 (1985): 199–216; Ted. G. Jelen, "Changes in the Attitudinal Correlations of Opposition to Abortion, 1977–1985," *Journal for the Scientific Study of Religion* 27 (1988): 211–228; Eric Woodrum and Beth L. Davison, "Reexamination of Religious Influences on Abortion Attitudes," *Review of Religious Research* 33 (1992): 229–243.

45. Liston Pope, *Millhands and Preachers* (New Haven, Ct.: Yale University Press, 1942).

46. Claude Levi-Strauss, *The Raw and the Cooked* (New York: Harper, 1970).

47. Cheryl S. Alexander and Henry Jay Becker, "The Use of Vignettes in Survey Research," *Public Opinion Quarterly* 42 (1978): 93–104; Paul M. Sniderman and Douglas B. Grob, "Innovations in Experimental Design in Attitude Surveys," *Annual Review of Sociology* 22 (1996): 377–399.

48. J Flynn, P. Slovic, and C. K. Mertz, "Gender, Race, and Perception of Environmental Health Risks," *Risk Analysis* 14 (1994): 1101–1108.

49. John B. McKinlay, Ting Lin, Karen Freund, and Mark Moskowitz, "The Unexpected Influence of Physician Attributes on Clinical Decisions: Results of an Experiment," *Journal of Health and Social Behavior* 43 (2002): 92–106.

50. William Sims Bainbridge, "The Spaceflight Revolution Revisited," in *Looking Backward, Looking Forward*, ed. Stephen J. Garber (Washington, D.C.: National Aeronautics and Space Administration, 2002), 39–64.

51. Wilma Alice Bainbridge transcribed their comments into a computerized database.

Chapter 11:

1. Friedrich Nietzsche, *Thus Spake Zarathustra*, Prologue 4, http://www.gla.ac.uk/~dc4w/laibach/nietzar.html or http://etext.library.adelaide.edu.au/n/nietzsche/friedrich/n67a/part3.html; this chapter draws upon William Sims Bainbridge, "Religion and Science," *Futures* 36 (2004): 1009–1023.

2. Dan Brown, *Angels and Demons* (New York: Pocket Books, 2000), 141; Latin scholars will recognize that *ordo* and *seclorum* are not the same case, so the phrase could not grammatically mean "secular order."

3. Karen Armstrong, *A History of God* (New York: Knopf, 1994), 377, 399.

4. Rodney Stark and William Sims Bainbridge, *The Future of Religion* (Berkeley, Ca.: University of California Press, 1985), *A Theory of Religion* (New York: Toronto/Lang, 1987); Roger Finke and Rodney Stark, *The Churching of America, 1776–1990* (New Brunswick, N.J.: Rutgers University Press, 1992); Rodney Stark and Roger Finke, *Acts of Faith* (Berkeley, Ca.: University of California Press, 2000).

5. Robert Constanza, "Four Visions of the Century Ahead," in *Exploring Your Future*, ed. Edward Cornish (Bethesda, Md.: World Future Society, 2000), 19–24.

6. Jerome C. Glenn, "Millennium Project's Draft Scenarios for the Next 1000 Years," *Futures* 32 (2000): 603–612.

7. Benjamin R. Barber, "Three Scenarios for the Future of Technology and Strong Democracy, *Political Science Quarterly* 113 (1998): 573–589.

8. William Sims Bainbridge, *Dimensions of Science Fiction* (Cambridge, Ma.: Harvard University Press, 1986).

9. Andrew Cherlin, *Marriage, Divorce and Remarriage* (Cambridge, Ma.: Harvard University Press, 1981); the rate has held roughly steady since then, however: "Monthly Vital Statistics Report," 43(9) supplement (Atlanta: Centers for Disease Control, 1995).

10. Clem Brooks, "Religious Influence and the Politics of Family Decline Concern: Trends, Sources, and U.S. Political Behavior," *American Sociological Review* 67 (2002): 191–211.

11. Frances K. Goldscheider, "Men, Children and the Future of the Family in the Third Millennium," *Futures* 32, (2000): 525–538.

12. Suzanne M. Bianchi, "Feminization and Juvenilization of Poverty: Trends, Relative Risks, Causes, and Consequences," *Annual Review of Sociology* 25 (1999): 307–333.

13. Herman Kahn and Anthony J. Wiener, *The Year 2000* (New York: Macmillan, 1967).

14. Pitirim A. Sorokin, *Social and Cultural Dynamics* (New York: American Book Company, 1937), volume 3, 537.

15. Already in the year 2000, some new religious movements had begun to evolve in this direction. For example, members of "The Family," also known as The Children of God, try to feel during sexual intercourse that they are making love to Jesus: William

Sims Bainbridge, *The Endtime Family: Children of God* (Albany, N.Y.: State University of New York, 2001).

16. Emile Durkheim, *The Division of Labor in Society* (New York: Free Press 1964 [1893]).

17. Ideas about how the "post-modern" malaise could be cured by futurology are offered by Pentti Malaska, "A Futures Research Outline of a Post-Modern Idea of Progress," *Futures* 33 (2001): 225–243.

18. George Orwell, *1984* (New York: Harcourt Brace Jovanovich, 1949).

19. Edward Jarvis, "Statistics of Insanity in the United States," *Boston Medical and Surgical Journal* 27 (1842): 116–121, 281–282; see also Adolph Heinrich Gotthilf Wagner, *Die Gesetzmässigkeit in den Scheinbar Willkürlichen Menschlichen Handlungen vom Standpunkte der Statistik* (Hamburg, Germany: Boyes und Geisler, 1864); Henry Morselli, *Suicide: An Essay on Comparative Moral Statistics* (New York: Appleton, 1882 [1879]); Thomas G. Masaryk, *Suicide and the Meaning of Civilization* (Chicago: University of Chicago Press, 1970 [1881]).

20. Arthur Edward Romilly Boak, *A History of Rome to 565 A. D.* (New York: Macmillan, 1955), 515.

21. National Science Board, *Science and Engineering Indicators, 2006* (Arlington, Virginia: National Science Foundation, 2006), Chapter 7, http://www.nsf.gov/statistics/seind06/pdf/c07.pdf

22. Joseph Ben-David, *The Scientist's Role in Society* (Englewood Cliffs, N.J.: Prentice-Hall, 1971).

23. William Sims Bainbridge, "Transformative Concepts in Scientific Convergence," in *Progress in Convergence*, edited by William Sims Bainbridge and Mihail C. Roco (New York: New York Academy of Sciences, 2007); "Technological Convergence from the Nanoscale," in *Handbook of Nanotechnology*, second edition, ed. Bharat Bhushan (Berlin, Springer, 2006), 1807–1822.

24. Edward O. Wilson, *Consilience: The Unity of Knowledge* (New York: Knopf, 1998).

25. William Sims Bainbridge, "Cognitive Technologies," in *Managing Nano-Bio-Info-Cogno Innovations: Converging Technologies in Society*, ed. William Sims Bainbridge and Mihail C. Roco (Berlin: Springer, 2006), 203–226.

26. Howard Phillips Lovecraft, *The Call of Cthulhu and Other Weird Stories* (Baltimore, Penguin, 1999).

27. Andrew M. Greeley and Michael Hout, "Americans' Increasing Belief in Life after Death: Religious Competition and Acculturation," *American Sociological Review* 64 (1999): 813–835.

28. Richard O'Connor, *The Spirit Soldiers: A Historical Narrative of the Boxer Rebellion* (New York: G. P. Putnam's Sons, 1973).

29. William Sims Bainbridge, "New Religions, Science and Secularization," in *The Handbook of Cults and Sects in America*, a volume of *Religion and the Social Order*, ed. David G. Bromley and Jeffrey K. Hadden (Greenwich, Ct.: JAI, 1993), 277–292.

30. Anson MacDonald, *My First Life* (Timonium, Md.: Institute for Spiritual Exploration, 2020), an unwritten and perhaps fictitious book.

31. Paul French, *Young Man MacDonald* (New York: Norton, 2026), Paul French was the pseudonym of science fiction writer Isaac Asimov who presented psychohistory in his *Foundation* series, and the book title alludes to an influential psychoanalytic psychohistory: Erik H. Erikson, *Young Man Luther* (New York, Norton, 1958).

32. John D. Barrow and Frank J. Tipler, *The Anthropic Cosmological Principle* (New York: Oxford University Press, 1986).

33. William Sims Bainbridge, 1997 "The Omicron Point: Sociological Application of the Anthropic Theory," in *Chaos and Complexity in Sociology: Myths, Models and Theory* ed. Raymond A. Eve, Sara Horsfall, and Mary E. Lee (Thousand Oaks, Ca.: Sage Publications, 1997), 91–101.

34. Anson MacDonald, *Prospectus for Immortality* (Timonium, Md.: Institute for Spiritual Exploration, 2002), a fictitious publication; in science fiction, Don A. Stuart was the pseudonym of editor John W. Campbell, Jr., and Anson MacDonald was the pseudonym of his friend Robert A. Heinlein.

35. Anson MacDonald, *Techniques and Technologies* (Timonium, Md.: Institute for Spiritual Exploration, 2011), a fictitious book, unless somebody writes it soon.

36. FM-2030, *Are You a Transhuman?* (New York: Warner, 1989).

37. David van Biema, "God vs. Science," *Time* 168 (13 November 2006): 48–55; Gary Wolf, "The New Atheism: The Church of the Non-believing," *Wired* (November 2006): 182–193.

38. William Sims Bainbridge, "The Coming Conflict Between Religion and Cognitive Science," in *Foresight, Innovation, and Strategy: Toward a Wiser Future*, ed. Cynthia G. Wagner (Bethesda, Maryland: World Future Society, 2005), 75–87.

39. William Sims Bainbridge, "Challenge and Response," Speech to the 2003 Haldane award banquet of the World Transhumanist Association, Yale University, June 28, 2003, http://www.transhumanism.org/index.php/th/more/363/

40. Herbert Blumer, "Social Movements," in *Studies in Social Movements*, ed. Barry McLaughlin (New York: Free Press, 1969), 8–29.

Bibliography

Adler, Alfred. *Understanding Human Nature*. Greenwich, Ct.: Fawcett, 1954.

Adler, Margot. *Drawing down the Moon: Witches, Pagans, Druids, Goddess-worshippers and Other Pagans in America Today*. Boston: Beacon Press, 1979.

Armstrong, Karen. *A History of God*. New York: Knopf, 1994.

Asahara, Shoko. *The Day of Destruction*. Tokyo: Aum Publishing Company, 1989

Atran, Scott. *In Gods We Trust: The Evolutionary Landscape of Religion*. Oxford, England: Oxford University Press, 2002.

Axelrod, Robert. *The Evolution of Cooperation*. New York: Basic Books, 1984.

Bainbridge, John Seaman. *The Study and Teaching of Law in Africa*. South Hackensack, N.J.: F. B. Rothman, 1972.

Bainbridge, Lucy Seaman. *Round the World Letters*. Boston: Lothrop, 1882.

———. *Helping the Helpless in Lower New York*. New York: Fleming H. Revell, 1917.

———. *Jewels From the Orient*. New York: Fleming H. Revell, 1920.

———. *Yesterdays*. New York: Fleming H. Revell, 1924.

Bainbridge, William Folwell. *Along the Lines at the Front: A General Survey of Baptist Home and Foreign Missions*. Philadelphia: American Baptist Publication Society, 1882.

———. *Around the World Tour of Christian Missions*. New York: Blackall, 1882.

Bainbridge, William Seaman. *The Cancer Problem*. New York: Macmillan, 1914.

Bainbridge, William Sims. *The Spaceflight Revolution*. New York: Wiley-Interscience, 1976.

———. *Satan's Power*. Berkeley, Ca.: University of California Press, 1978.

———. *Dimensions of Science Fiction*. Cambridge, Ma.: Harvard University Press, 1986.

———. *Experiments in Psychology*. Belmont, Ca.: Wadsworth, 1986.

———. *Sociology Laboratory*. Belmont, Ca.: Wadsworth, 1987.

———. *Survey Research: A Computer-Assisted Introduction*. Belmont, Ca.: Wadsworth, 1989.

———. *Goals in Space: American Values and the Future of Technology*. Albany, New York: State University of New York Press, 1991.

———. *Social Research Methods and Statistics*. Belmont, Ca.: Wadsworth, 1992.

———. *The Sociology of Religious Movements*. New York: Routledge, 1997.

————. *The Endtime Family: Children of God.* Albany, N.Y.: State University of New York Press, 2002.

————, ed. *Encyclopedia of Human-Computer Interaction.* Great Barrington, Ma.: Berkshire, 2004.

————. *God from the Machine.* Lanham, Md.: AltaMira, 2006.

Bainbridge, William Sims, and Mihail C. Roco, eds. *Managing Nano-Bio-Info-Cogno Innovations: Converging Technologies in Society.* Berlin: Springer, 2006.

————, eds. *Progress in Convergence.* New York: New York Academy of Sciences, 2007.

Barrett, Justin L. *Why Would Anyone Believe in God?* Walnut Creek, Ca.: AltaMira, 2004.

Barrow, John D., and Frank J. Tipler. *The Anthropic Cosmological Principle.* New York: Oxford University Press, 1986.

Barrows, John Henry. *The World's Parliament of Religions.* Chicago: Parliament Publishing Company, 1893.

Beck, Lois, and Nikki Keddie, eds. *Women in the Muslim World.* Cambridge, Ma.: Harvard University Press, 1978.

Becker, Howard S. *Outsiders.* Glencoe, Ill.: Free Press, 1963.

Beloff, John, ed. *New Directions in Parapsychology.* Metuchen, N.J.: Scarecrow Press, 1974.

Ben-David, Joseph *The Scientist's Role in Society.* Englewood Cliffs, N.J.: Prentice-Hall, 1971.

Berger, Peter L. *A Rumor of Angels: Modern Society and the Rediscovery of the Supernatural.* Garden City, N.Y.: Doubleday, 1969.

Berger, Peter L., and Thomas Luckmann. *The Social Construction of Reality: A Treatise in the Sociology of Knowledge.* Garden City, N.Y.: Doubleday, 1966.

Bhushan, Bharat, ed. Handbook of Nanotechnology. Berlin, Springer, 2006.

Bloom, Paul. *Descartes' Baby: How the Science of Child Development Explains what Makes Us Human.* New York: Basic Books, 2004.

Blumer, Herbert. *Symbolic Interactionism: Perspective and Method.* Englewood Cliffs, N.J.: Prentice-Hall, 1969.

Boak, Arthur Edward Romilly. *A History of Rome to 565 A. D..* New York: Macmillan, 1955, 515.

Boyer, Pascal. *Religion Explained: The Evolutionary Origins of Religious Thought.* New York: Basic Books, 2001.

Bransford, John D., Ann L. Brown, and Rodney R. Cocking, eds.. *How People Learn: Brain, Mind, Experience, and School.* Washington, D.C.: National Academy Press, 1999.

Braude, Ann. *Radical Spirits.* Boston: Beacon Press, 1989.

Bromley, David G., and Jeffrey K. Hadden, eds. *The Handbook of Cults and Sects in America.* Greenwich, Ct.: JAI, 1993.

Bromley, David G., and Phillip E. Hammond, eds. *The Future of New Religious Movements*. Macon, Ga.: Mercer University Press, 1987, 59-79.

Bromley, David, and Larry Greil, ed. *Defining Religion*. Amsterdam: JAI Elsevier, 2003.

Burton, O. Vernon, ed. *Computing in the Social Sciences and Humanities*. Urbana, Ill.: University of Illinois Press, 2002, 51-66.

Cameron, A. G. W., ed.. *Interstellar Communication*. New York: Benjamin, 1963.

Campbell, Colin. *Toward a Sociology of Irreligion*. New York: Herder and Herder, 1972.

Carden, Maren Lockwood. *Oneida: Utopian Community to Modern Corporation*. Baltimore: Johns Hopkins Press, 1969.

Chan, Lois Mai. *Cataloging and Classification*. New York: McGraw-Hill, 1994.

Charles Y. Glock and Rodney Stark, *Religion and Society in Tension*. Chicago: Rand McNally, 1965.

Cherlin, Andrew. *Marriage, Divorce and Remarriage*. Cambridge, Ma.: Harvard University Press, 1981.

Childe, V. Gordon. *Man Makes Himself*. New York: New American Library, 1951.

Clark, Terry N. *Prophets and Patrons: The French University and the Emergence of the Social Sciences*. Cambridge, Ma.: Harvard University Press, 1973.

Cloward, Richard A., and Lloyd E. Ohlin. *Delinquency and Opportunity*. New York: Free Press, 1960.

Cooley, Charles Horton. *Human Nature and the Social Order*. New York: Scribner's, 1922.

Cornish, Edward, ed. *Exploring Your Future*. Bethesda, Md.: World Future Society, 2000.

Curry, Melvin D. *Jehovah's Witnesses: The Millenarian World of the Watch Tower*. New York: Garland, 1992.

Darnton, Robert. *Mesmerism and the End of the enlightenment in France*. New York: Schocken, 1970.

Davis, Kingsley Mikhail S. Bernstam, and Rita Ricardo-Campbell, eds. *Below-Replacement Fertility in Industrial Societies: Causes, Consequences, Policies*. New York: Population Council, 1987.

de Chardin, Pierre Teilhard. *The Future of Man*. New York: Harper and Row, 1964.

de Forest, Louis Effingham. *Ancestry of William Seaman Bainbridge*. Oxford: Scrivener, 1950.

de Garis, Hugo. *The Artilect War*. Selden, N.Y.: Marilyn June Janson Literary Services, 1999.

Dennett, Daniel C. *Darwin's Dangerous Idea*. New York: Simon and Schuster, 1995.

―――. *Breaking the Spell: Religion as a Natural Phenomenon*. New York: Viking, 2006.

Dentan, Robert Knox. *The Semai*. New York: Holt, Rinehart, and Winston, 1968.

Dick, Steven J. *Plurality of Worlds: The Origins of the Extraterrestrial Life Debate from Democritus to Kant*. Cambridge, England: Cambridge University Press, 1982.

Dohrman, H. T. *California Cult*. Boston: Beacon, 1958.

Durkheim, Emile. *The Elementary Forms of the Religious Life*. London: Allen and Unwin, 1915.

―――. *The Rules of Sociological Method*. Chicago: University of Chicago Press, 1938.

―――. *Suicide*. New York: Free Press, 1951 [1897].

―――. *The Division of Labor in Society*. New York: Free Press 1964 [1893].

Edelstein, Alan. *An Unacknowledged Harmony: Philo-Semitism and the Survival of European Jewry*. Westport, Ct.: Greenwood, 1982.

Edge, Hoyt L., Robert L. Morris, Joseph H. Rush, and John Palmer. *Foundations of Parapsychology*. Boston: Routledge and Kegan Paul, 1986.

Ehrlich, Paul R. *The Population Bomb*. New York: Ballantine, 1968.

Elgin, Duane. *Awakening Earth*. New York: William Morrow, 1993.

Erikson, Erik H. *Young Man Luther*. New York, Norton, 1958.

Ettinger, Robert C. W. *The Prospect of Immortality*. Garden City, N.Y.: Doubleday, 1964.

―――. *Man into Superman: The Startling Potential of Human Evolution — and how to Be Part of It*. New York: St. Martin's Press, 1972.

Eve, Raymond A., Sara Horsfall, and Mary E. Lee. *Chaos and Complexity in Sociology: Myths, Models and Theory*. Thousand Oaks, Ca.: Sage Publications, 1997.

Faris, Robert E. L.. and H. Warren Dunham. *Mental Disorders in Urban Areas*. Chicago: University of Chicago Press, 1939.

Festinger, Leon. *Theory of Cognitive Dissonance*. Evanston, Ill.: Row, Peterson, 1957.

Finke, Roger, and Rodney Stark. *The Churching of America, 1776-1990*. New Brunswick, N.J.: Rutgers University Press, 1992.

FM-2030. *Are You a Transhuman?*. New York: Warner, 1989.

Fortune, Reo F. *Sorcerers of Dobu*. New York: E. P. Dutton, 1932.

Frankl, Viktor. *Man's Search for Meaning: An Introduction to Logotherapy*. Boston: Beacon Press, 1962.

Frazier, Kendrick, ed. *Paranormal Borderlands of Science*. Buffalo, N.Y.: Prometheus, 1981.

Freud, Sigmund. *The Future of an Illusion*. Garden City, N.Y.: Doubleday, 1927 [1961].

Fukuyama, Francis. *Our Posthuman Future: Consequences of the Biotechnology Revolution*. New York: Farrar, Straus, and Giroux, 2002.

Fuller, R. Buckminster. *Operating Manual for Spaceship Earth*. New York: Pocket Books, 1970.

Gans, Herbert J. *The Urban Villagers*. New York: Free Press, 1962.

Garber, Stephen J., ed. *Looking Backward, Looking Forward*. Washington, D.C.: National Aeronautics and Space Administration, 2002.

Gazzaniga, Michael S., ed., *Cognitive Neuroscience: A Reader*. Malden, Ma.: Blackwell, 2000.

Glock, Charles Y., and Rodney Stark. *Christian Beliefs and Anti-Semitism*. New York: Harper and Row, 1966.

Goulart, Ron. *An Informal History of the Pulp Magazines*. New York: Ace, 1972.

Gould, Stephen Jay. *Rocks of Ages: Science and Religion in the Fullness of Life*. New York: Ballantine, 1999.

Gouldner, Alvin W. *The Coming Crisis of Western Sociology*. New York: Basic Books, 1970.

Grob, Gerald N. *Edward Jarvis and the Medical World of Nineteenth-century America*. Knoxville, Tenn: University of Tennessee Press, 1978.

Gusfield, Joseph R. *Symbolic Crusade*. Urbana, Ill: University of Illinois Press, 1963.

Guttentag, Marcia, and Paul F. Secord, *Too Many Women?: The Sex Ratio Question*. Beverly Hills, Ca.: Sage, 1983.

Hadden, Jeffrey K., and Douglas E. Cowan. Religion on the Internet. New York: Elsevier, 2000.

Halbwachs, Maurice. *Le Causes de Suicide*. Paris: Felix Alcan, 1930.

Halliday, Michael Alexander Kirkwood, Angus McIntosh, and Peter Strevens. *The Linguistic Sciences and Language Teaching*. London: Longmans, 1964.

Hansel, C. E. M. *ESP — A Scientific Evaluation*. New York: Scribner's, 1966.

Hartshorne, Hugh, and Mark A. May, *Studies in Deceit*. New York: Macmillan, 1928.

Heider, Fritz. *The Psychology of Interpersonal Relations*. New York: Wiley, 1958.

Henry, Andrew F., and James F. Short, *Suicide and Homicide*. Glencoe, Ill.: Free Press, 1954.

Henry, Jules. *Jungle People*. New York: J. J. Augustin, 1941.

Herberg, Will. *Protestant, Catholic, Jew: An Essay in American Religious Sociology*. Garden City, N.Y.: Doubleday, 1955.

Herman, David, ed. Narrative Theory and the Cognitive Sciences. Stanford, Ca.: Center for the Study of Language and Information, 2003.

Hirschi, Travis, and Michael Gottfredson, eds. *Understanding Crime*. Beverly Hills, Ca.: Sage, 1980.

Hirschi, Travis. *Causes of Delinquency*. Berkeley, Ca.: University of California Press, 1969.

Hollingshead, August B., and Fredrick C. Redlich. *Social Class and Mental Illness*. New York: Wiley, 1958.

Homans, George Caspar. *Social Behavior: Its Elementary Forms*. New York: Harcourt, Brace Jovanovich, 1974.

———. *Coming to My Senses: The Autobiography of a Sociologist*. New Brunswick, N.J.: Transaction, 1984.

Houghton, Walter R. *Neely's History of the Parliament of Religions and Religious Congresses at the World's Columbian Exposition*. Chicago: Neely, 1893.

Howard, Philip N., and Steve Jones, eds. *Society Online*. Thousand Oaks, Ca.: Sage, 2003.

Hughes, James. *Citizen Cyborg*. Cambridge, Ma.: Westview, 2004.

James, William. *Essays in Psychical Research*. Cambridge, Ma.: Harvard University Press, 1986.

Jarvis, Edward. *Report on Insanity and Idiocy in Massachusetts*. Boston: White, 1855.

———. *The Autobiography of Edward Jarvis*. London: Wellcome Institute for the History of Medicine, 1992.

Jelen, Ted G., ed. *Sacred Markets, Sacred Canopies*. Lanham, Md.: Rowman and Littlefield, 2002.

Jenkins, Philip. *Mystics and Messiahs: Cults and New Religions in American History*. New York: Oxford University Press, 2000.

Jones, H. Spencer. *Life on Other Worlds*. New York: Mentor, 1951.

Kahn, Herman, and Anthony J. Wiener. *The Year 2000*. New York: Macmillan, 1967.

Kanter, Rosabeth Moss *Commitment and Community*. Cambridge, Ma.: Harvard University Press, 1972.

Katz, Elihu, and Paul Lazarsfeld, *Personal Influence*. Glencoe, Ill.: Free Press, 1955.

Kaufmann, Walter A. *Nietzsche: Philosopher, Psychologist, Antichrist*. Princeton, New Jersey: Princeton University Press, 1974.

Kelley, Dean. *Why Conservative Churches are Growing*. New York: Harper and Row, 1972.

Klein, Bruce J., and Sebastian Sethe, eds. *The Scientific Conquest of Death: Essays on Infinite Lifetimes*. Birmingham, Alabama: Immortality Institute, 2004.

Kurzweil, Ray. *The Age of Spiritual Machines: When Computers Exceed Human Intelligence*. New York: Viking, 1999.

Larner, Christina *Witchcraft and Religion: The Politics of Popular Belief*. New York: Blackwell, 1984.

Laslett, Peter *The World We have Lost*. London: Methuen, 1965.

Letkemann, Peter. *Crime as Work*. Englewood Cliffs, N.J.: Prentice-Hall, 1973.

Lévi-Strauss, Claude. *Structural Anthropology*. New York: Basic Books, 1963.

———. *The Raw and the Cooked*. New York: Harper & Row, 1969.

Lewis, Ioan M. *Ecstatic Religion*. Baltimore: Penguin, 1971.

Liebman, Robert C., and Robert Wuthnow, eds. *The New Religious Right*. New York: Aldine, 1983.

Luhrmann, T. M. *Persuasions of the Witch's Craft*. Cambridge, Ma.: Harvard University Press, 1989.

Malthus, Thomas. *An Essay on the Principle of Population*. London: J. Johnson, 1798.

Marks, David. *The Psychology of the Psychic*. Amherst, N.Y.: Prometheus, 2000.

Masaryk, Thomas G. *Suicide and the Meaning of Civilization*. Chicago: University of Chicago Press, 1970 [1881].

Maslow, Abraham. *Religions, Values, and Peak-Experiences*. New York: Viking, 1970.

McIntosh, Angus, M.L. Samuels, and Michael Benskin. *A Linguistic Atlas of Late Mediaeval English*. New York: Aberdeen University Press, 1986.

McIntosh, Christopher. *The Astrologers and their Creed*. New York: Praeger, 1969.

———. *Eliphas Lévi and the French Occult Revival*. London: Rider, 1972.

———. *The Rose Cross and the Age of Reason: Eighteenth-century Rosicrucianism in Central Europe and its Relationship to the Enlightenment*. New York: E.J. Brill, 1992.

———. *Ludwig II of Bavaria, the Swan King*. London: I. B. Tauris, 1997.

———. *The Rosicrucians: the History, Mythology, and Rituals of an Esoteric Order*. York Beach, Me.: S. Weiser, 1997.

———. *Gardens of the Gods: Myth, Magic and Meaning*. London: I. B. Tauris, 2005.

McKinney, A. H. *Triumphant Christianity: The Life and Work of Lucy Seaman Bainbridge*. New York: Fleming H. Revell, 1932.

McLaughlin, Barry, ed. *Studies in Social Movements*. New York: Free Press, 1969.

Merton, Robert K. *Social Theory and Social Structure*. New York: Free Press, 1968.

———. *Science, Technology and Society in Seventeenth-century England*. New York: Harper and Row, 1970.

Mooney, Chris, *The Republican War on Science*. New York: Basic Books, 2005.

Moravec, Hans P. *Mind Children: The Future of Robot and Human Intelligence*. Cambridge, Ma.: Harvard University Press, 1988.

Morselli, Henry. *Suicide: An Essay on Comparative Moral Statistics*. New York: Appleton, 1882 [1879].

Nevius, Helen S. Coan. *Our Life in China*. New York: Robert Carter, 1869.

———. *The Life of John Livingston Nevius*. New York: Fleming H. Revell, 1895.

Nevius, John L. *Demon Possession and Allied Themes, Being an Inductive Study of Phenomena of Our Own Times*. New York: Fleming H. Revell, 1896.

Newell, Allen. *Unified Theories of Cognition*. Cambridge, Ma.: Harvard University Press, 1990.

Nordhoff, Charles. *The Communistic Societies of the United States*. London: John Murray, 1875.

Norris, Pippa, and Ronald Inglehart. *Sacred and Secular: Religion and Politics Worldwide*. Cambridge, England: University of Cambridge Press, 2004.

Noyes, John Humphrey. *History of American Socialisms*. Philadelphia: Lippincott, 1870.

Numbers, Ronald L. *Prophetess of Health: Ellen G. White and the Origins of Seventh-day Adventist Health Reform*. Knoxville, Tenn.: University of Tennessee Press, 1992.

O'Connor, Richard. *The Spirit Soldiers: A Historical Narrative of the Boxer Rebellion*. New York: G. P. Putnam's Sons, 1973.

Ogburn, William Fielding. *Social Change with Respect to Culture and Original Nature*. New York: B. W. Huebsch, 1922.

Orwell, George. *1984*. New York: Harcourt Brace Jovanovich, 1949.

Parsons, Talcott. *The Social System*. New York: Free Press, 1951.

Picard, Rosalind W. *Affective Computing*. Cambridge, Ma.: MIT Press, 1997.

Pickering, W. S. F. *Durkheim's Sociology of Religion*. London: Routledge and Kegan Paul, 1984.

Pope, Liston. *Millhands and Preachers*. New Haven, Ct.: Yale University Press, 1942.

Pope, Whitney. *Durkheim's "Suicide" — A Classic Analyzed*. Chicago: University of Chicago Press, 1976.

Randi, James. *The Magic of Uri Geller*. New York: Ballantine, 1975.

Redfield, James, and Carol Adrienne. *The Celestine Prophecy: An Experiential Guide*. New York: Warner, 1994.

Redfield, James. *The Celestine Prophecy*. New York: Time Warner, 1993.

Rhine, J. B. *New Frontiers of the Mind*. New York: Farrar and Rinehart, 1937.

———. *Extra-Sensory Perception*. Boston: Bruce Humphries, 1964 [1934].

———, ed. *Progress in Parapsychology*. Durham, N.C.: Parapsychology Press, 1971.

Richardson, James T., ed.. *Regulating Religion: Case Studies from Around the Globe*. New York, Kluwer, 2004.

Richardson, James T., Joel Best, and David G. Bromley, eds. *The Satanism Scare*. New York: Aldine de Gruyter, 1991.

Roco, Mihail C., and Carlo D. Montemagno, eds. *The Coevolution of Human Potential and Converging Technologies*. New York: New York Academy of Sciences, 2004.

Roco, Mihail C., and William Sims Bainbridge, eds. *Societal Implications of Nanoscience and Nanotechnology*. Dordrecht, Netherlands: Kluwer, 2001.

———, eds. *Converging Technologies for Improving Human Performance*. Dordrecht, Netherlands: Kluwer, 2003.

————, eds. *Nanotechnology: Societal Implications*, 2 volumes. Berlin: Springer, 2006.

Rogerson, Alan *Millions Now Living Will Never Die: A Study of Jehovah's Witnesses*. London: Constable, 1969.

Saler, Benson, Charles A. Ziegler, and Charles B. Moore. *UFO Crash at Roswell: The Genesis of a Modern Myth*. Washington, D.C.: Smithsonian Institution Press, 1997.

Saliba, John A.. *Understanding New Religious Movements*. Walnut Creek, Ca.: AltaMira, 2003.

Schumaker, John F., ed. *Religion and Mental Health*. New York: Oxford University Press, 1992.

Schur, Edwin M. *Crimes without Victims*. Englewood Cliffs, N.J.: Prentice-Hall, 1965.

Scott, John Finley. *Internalization of Norms*. Englewood Cliffs, N.J.: Prentice-Hall, 1971.

Seager, Richard Hughes. *The World's Parliament of Religions*. Bloomington, In.: University of Indiana Press, 1995.

Seaman, Louis Livingston. *From Tokio through Manchuria with the Japanese*. New York: Appleton, 1905.

————. *The Real Triumph of Japan: The Conquest of the Silent Foe*. New York: Appleton, 1906.

Seoane, Consuelo Andrew. *Beyond the Ranges*. New York: R. Speller, 1960.

Seoane, Rhoda Low. *The Whole Armor*. New York: R. Speller, 1965.

————. *Uttermost East and the Longest War*. New York, Vantage Press, 1968.

Shaw, Clifford, and Henry D. McKay. *Delinquency Areas*. Chicago: University of Chicago Press, 1929.

Shklovski, I. S., and Carl Sagan. *Intelligent Life in the Universe*. New York: Dell, 1966

Simon, Herbert A. *The Sciences of the Artificial*. Cambridge, Ma.: MIT Press, 1996.

Smith, Christian. *American Evangelicalism*. Chicago: University of Chicago Press, 1998.

Smith, George H. *Atheism: The Case Against God*. Buffalo, N.Y.: Prometheus, 1979.

Sorokin, Pitirim A. *Social and Cultural Dynamics*. New York: American Book Company, 1937.

Spady, Richard J., and Richard S. Kirby. *The Leadership of Civilization Building*. Seattle, Wa.: Forum Foundation, 2002.

Spradley, James P. *You Owe yourself a Drunk*. Boston: Little, Brown, 1970.

Stark, Rodney. *The Rise of Christianity*. Princeton, N.J.: Princeton University Press, 1996.

Stark, Rodney, and Charles Y. Glock. *American Piety: The Nature of Religious Commitment*. Berkeley, Ca.: University of California Press, 1968.

Stark, Rodney, and Roger Finke. *Acts of Faith*. Berkeley, Ca.: University of California Press, 2000.

Stark, Rodney, and William Sims Bainbridge. *The Future of Religion*. Berkeley, Ca.: University of California Press, 1985.

————. *A Theory of Religion*. New York: Toronto/Lang, 1987.

————. *Religion, Deviance and Social Control*. New York: Routledge, 1996.

Stark, Rodney, Bruce D. Foster, Charles Y. Glock, and Harold E. Quinley. *Wayward Shepherds*. New York: Harper and Row, 1971.

Stark, Rodney, ed. *Religious Movements*. New York: Paragon House, 1985.

Sutherland, Edwin H. *Principles of Criminology*. Philadelphia: Lippincott, 1947.

Thomas, W. I. *The Unadjusted Girl*. Boston: Little, Brown, and Company, 1923.

Thrasher, Frederic M. *The Gang*. Chicago: University of Chicago Press, 1927.

Tipton, Steven M. *Getting Saved from the Sixties: Moral Meaning in Conversion and Cultural Change*. Berkeley, Ca.: University of California Press, 1982.

Tönnies, Ferdinand. *Community and Society*. East Lansing, Mi.: Michigan State University Press, 1957.

Toulmin, Stephen Edelston, and June Goodfield, *The Fabric of the Heavens*. New York: Harper, 1961.

Turner, James. *Without God, Without Creed: The Origins of Unbelief in America*. Baltimore, Md.: Johns Hopkins University Press, 1985.

Ulansey, David. *The Origins of the Mithraic Mysteries: Cosmology and Salvation in the Ancient World*. New York: Oxford University Press, 1989.

Wagner, Adolph Heinrich Gotthilf. *Die Gesetzmässigkeit in den Scheinbar Willkürlichen Menschlichen Handlungen vom Standpunkte der Statistik*. Hamburg: Boyes und Geisler, 1864.

Wagner, Cynthia G., ed. *Foresight, Innovation, and Strategy: Toward a Wiser Future*. Bethesda, Md.: World Future Society, 2005.

Wallace, Anthony F. C. *Religion: An Anthropological View*. New York: Random House, 1966.

Wattenberg, Ben J. *The Birth Dearth*. New York: Ballantine, 1987.

Wescott, Roger W. *The Divine Animal*. New York: Funk and Wagnalls, 1969.

Westfall, Richard S. *Science and Religion in Seventeenth-century England*. New Haven, Ct.: Yale University Press, 1958.

White, A. D. *A History of the Warfare of Science with Theology in Christendom*. Gloucester, Ma.: Peter Smith, 1978 [1896].

Whitehouse, Harvey, and James Laidlaw, eds.. *Ritual and Memory: Toward a Comparative Anthropology of Religions*. Walnut Creek, Ca.: Altamira, 2002.

Whitehouse, Harvey, and Luther H. Martin, eds.. *Theorizing Religions Past: Archaeology, History, and Cognition*. Walnut Creek, Ca.: Altamira, 2004.

Whitehouse, Harvey. *Modes of Religiosity: A Cognitive Theory of Religious Transmission*. Walnut Creek, Ca.: Altamira, 2004.

Whyte, William Foote *Street Corner Society*. Chicago: University of Chicago Press, 1943.

Wilson, Bryan, ed. *The Social Impact of New Religious Movements*. New York: Rose of Sharon Press, 1981.

Wilson, Clifford. *Crash Go the Chariots*. New York: Lancer, 1970.

Wilson, Edward O. *The Insect Societies*. Cambridge, Ma.: Harvard University Press, 1971.

———. *Sociobiology: The New Synthesis*. Cambridge, Ma.: Harvard University Press, 1975.

———. *Consilience: The Unity of Knowledge*. New York: Knopf, 1998.

Wrong, Dennis H. *Population and Society*. New York: Random House, 1977.

Wuthnow, Robert *Experimentation in American Religion*. Berkeley, Ca.: University of California Press, 1978.

Young, Michael, and Peter Willmott. *Family and Kinship in East London*. Glencoe, Ill.: Free Press, 1957.

———. *The Symmetrical Family*. New York: Pantheon Books, 1973.

Zweig, Stefan *Mental Healers*. New York: Viking, 1932.

Index